Women and Religious Traditions

Third Edition

Women and Religious Traditions

Leona M. Anderson & Pamela Dickey Young

OXFORD
UNIVERSITY PRESS

OXFORD
UNIVERSITY PRESS

Oxford University Press is a department of the University of Oxford.
It furthers the University's objective of excellence in research, scholarship,
and education by publishing worldwide. Oxford is a registered trade mark
of Oxford University Press in the UK and in certain other countries.

Published in Canada by
Oxford University Press
8 Sampson Mews, Suite 204,
Don Mills, Ontario M3C 0H5 Canada

www.oupcanada.com

Library and Archives Canada Cataloguing in Publication
Women and religious traditions / Leona M. Anderson
& Pamela Dickey Young. — Third edition.

Includes bibliographical references and index.
ISBN 978-0-19-900619-9 (pbk.)

1. Women and religion. 2. Women—Religious aspects.
l. Anderson, Leona, 1951–, editor ll. Young, Pamela Dickey, 1955–, editor

BL458.W64 2014   200.82   C2014-903785-6

Cover image: Jeremy Woodhouse/Photographer's Choice RF/Getty Images

Oxford University Press is committed to our environment.
Wherever possible, our books are printed on paper which
comes from responsible sources.

Printed and bound in Canada

8 9 10 — 21 20 19

Contents

Contributors

Leona M. Anderson is Professor Emerita in the Department of Religious Studies at the University of Regina. Her research interests include Sanskrit literature, classical and popular Hinduism, Hindu ritual, and iconography. Her publications include the *Vasantotsava: Indian Spring Festival, Text and Contexts* (1993/4); *The Ganesh Festival* (colour video [VHS] documentary, 1999 and 2009), and *The Orishas of Cuba* (DVD, 2008). Her current research focuses on Santería traditions in Cuba and the Ashtavinayakas in India. She received her PhD in Religious Studies from McMaster University and studied Sanskrit at the Deccan College, Pune.

Stephanie Balkwill is a doctoral candidate in the Department of Religious Studies at McMaster University, with a specialization in Buddhism and East Asian Religions, and is also undertaking a PhD Diploma in Gender Studies and Feminist Research at the same institution. She is committed to bringing the stories of women to the popular narrative of Chinese Buddhist history that is often told in textbooks about the tradition, and her doctoral dissertation investigates the lives, activities, and faith of Buddhist women in the Northern Wei dynasty (386–534 CE).

L. Clarke is Associate Professor of Islam and Chair of the Department of Religion at Concordia University, Montreal. Among her recent publications are "Hijáb According to the Hadíth: Text and Interpretation," in *The Muslim Veil in North America: Issues and Debates* (2003); "Women as Prophets," in *Encyclopedia of Women and Islamic Cultures* (2004); "Muslim & Canadian Family Law," with P. Cross, 2006; and "Iddah [Wife's dower in Muslim law]," in *Oxford Encyclopedia of the Islamic World* (2009).

Monique Dumais, a retired professor in theology and ethics at the Université du Québec à Rimouski, is the author of *Les droits des femmes* (1992), *Femmes et pauvreté* (1998), *Choisir la confiance* (2001), and *Femmes et mondialisation* (2009), and co-editor with Pierrette Chassé of *Au vent du large: Les Ursulines de Rimouski* (1970–2005) (2005). In 1976, she was a co-founder of the Quebec collective L'autre Parole for feminist and Christian women.

Michelle L. Folk received her doctorate in the Philosophy of Religion from Concordia University in Montreal. Her past research has focused on medieval South Indian women saints from Hinduism's bhakti tradition who rejected the brahmin-prescribed role of wife and mother, and on how identity was constructed by male and female Tamil bhakti saints through narrative. Her current interests include Tamil inscriptional materials and monasticism.

Doris R. Jakobsh is Associate Professor in the Department of Religious Studies at the University of Waterloo. She has degrees from the University of British Columbia (PhD), Harvard University (MTS) and University of Waterloo (BA). She is the author of *Relocating Gender in Sikh History: Transformation, Meaning and Identity* (2003, 2005) and *Sikhism* (2011), along with numerous chapters and journal articles, and editor of *Women in Sikhism: An Exploration* (2010), as well as the two-volume *World Religions: Canadian Perspectives* (2013). In 2010 she led a group of students on a three-month tour to experience the religions and cultures of India.

Jacoba Kuikman is Associate Professor of Religious Studies at Campion College, University of Regina. Her research interests include, in addition to women in Judaism, the politics of Jewish identity, especially with respect to Indian Jews (the Bene Israel), and the politics of memory in relation to the Holocaust/Shoah.

Dawn Martin-Hill is Mohawk, Wolf Clan, from the Six Nations of the Grand River. A mother of four children and grandmother of two, she holds a PhD in cultural anthropology and is one of the founders of McMaster University's Indigenous Studies Program, of which she is currently Academic Director. She has published in the areas of Indigenous knowledge and Indigenous women, decolonization of women, and Indigenous medicine in contemporary practices. Central to her research interests is the establishment of Indigenous knowledge as an intellectual discipline for Aboriginal scholars. She is a co-principal investigator for the Indigenous Health Research Development Program and is the recipient of many awards and grants. She has also directed and produced three films focused on traditional knowledge as a means of healing from historical trauma: *Let's Become Again*, *Mothers of Our Nations*, and *The Dish with One Spoon*. Her book *The Lubicon Lake Nation: Indigenous Knowledge and Power* (2007) outlines the struggle for land, culture, and survival.

Eva Neumaier studied anthropology and Indian and Tibetan Studies at the University of Munich (dissertation 1966, "Habilitation" 1976). After fieldwork in India and Ladakh, she taught as Professor of Religious Studies at the University of Calgary (Canada), the University of Chapel Hill, North Carolina, and the University of Alberta, Edmonton (Canada). Her main interests are the intersection of literary religion and local traditions, contemplative strands of Buddhism, and the roles of women in Buddhism. She has published several books and numerous articles in academic journals.

Lee D. Rainey teaches Chinese studies at Memorial University of Newfoundland. Her research focuses on classical Chinese philosophy, and she has written articles on the concept of *qi*, the Confucian philosophy of music, and the hidden language of the women of Hunan. She is the author of *Confucius and Confucianism: The Essentials* (2009) and *Decoding Dao: Reading the Dao De Jing and the Zhuangzi* (2014).

Carmen Webb has taught at Mount Royal University and the University of Calgary. Her current research focuses on contemporary women who attend all-women Buddhist retreats in the United States and how such events engage contemporary discourses and factor into identity construction. She is also currently developing a course that uses multidisciplinary methods to engage concepts related to Mary, mother of Jesus, and Mary Magdalene from a feminist, materialist standpoint.

Pamela Dickey Young is Professor of Religious Studies at Queen's University in Kingston, Ontario. She is author of many books and articles on feminist theology, women and religion, and religion and sexuality. Her current research focuses on Religion, Gender and Sexuality Among Youth in Canada (www .queensu.ca/religion/Faculty/research/dickeyyoung.html). Her most recent book is *Religion, Sex and Politics: Christian Churches and Same-Sex Marriage in Canada* (2012).

Preface

Oxford University Press is pleased to present this third edition of *Women and Religious Traditions*.

Why study women and religion? The disciplines of Religious Studies and Women's Studies are both central to understanding society and individuals, but the overlap between them is particularly important. Editors Leona M. Anderson and Pamela Dickey Young note that years ago, when feminist scholars first discovered how underrepresented women were in religious scholarship, they decided to fill the gap by developing courses about women and religion. To understand why women have been so neglected, it is necessary to examine the multiple layers—social, biological, and psychological—that make up a particular religion. At the same time, examining the roles that women *do* play in religion sheds light on how women conceive of and contextualize both their public and private worlds.

In recent years, scholarship in this field has flourished. The third edition of *Women and Religious Traditions* builds on the in-depth analysis of the first two editions while maintaining its reader-friendly appeal and straightforward organization. Additions include an expanded introduction to the study of women and religion, new discussions of lived religion in each chapter, a new case study on women in Chinese traditions, and new end-of-chapter glossaries. The end product is a comprehensive text that provides a balanced introduction to the field for students new to the discipline while offering advanced students a deeper understanding of the relationship between feminist inquiry and religious studies.

Oxford University Press is grateful to the following reviewers for their insightful comments, which helped to shape this new edition:

Nicole Libin, Mount Royal University
Susan Medd, Brandon University
Michele Murray, Bishop's University
Ariana Patey, Memorial University
Anne M. Pearson, McMaster University
Veronique Tomaszewski, York University

Introduction

Leona M. Anderson and Pamela Dickey Young

Many years ago we discovered that women were underrepresented in texts for the study of religious traditions. *Women and Religious Traditions* seeks to remedy that deficiency. It has grown out of our experience in teaching, and is intended for courses in both World Religions and Women and Religion.

Each of the following chapters explores the situation of women in an important religious tradition. In addition, this third edition includes five thought-provoking case studies designed to encourage discussion of specific situations. We hope that it will provide readers with enough background and direction to encourage further work on women in religious traditions.

Having said that, we must emphasize that it is not self-evident how "religion" ought to be defined. Even the scholarly construction of specific religious traditions is a particularly Western idea. It grows out of a Christian-informed imperialistic view that tends to classify religious phenomena in categories that best fit Christianity and that only more tenuously fit other traditions. Nevertheless, there is much value in examining how women are perceived and treated in different traditions. Thus instead of trying to define religion, in this book we simply take traditions that Western scholars generally define as religious and look at women in them.

Religious traditions are not monolithic and univocal. We make no attempt to identify the most "authentic" or "correct" version of any particular religious tradition, myth, or symbol. Rather, we are interested in the way different religious traditions, myths, and symbols have privileged male experience in the past and how they are being rewritten today to include female experience.

Although some first-wave feminists, beginning in the late nineteenth century, did write about religion, the focused study of women in religious traditions is a product of second-wave feminism, which began in the 1960s. Second-wave feminism examined the privileging of maleness and the second-class status often accorded to women. Feminist scholars in North America and Europe wondered what roles religion had played in imposing second-class status on women. Religious texts were analyzed for their patriarchal content and assumptions, for whether and in what ways they accorded power and privilege to men. Religious histories were searched for histories of women, and religious symbols were interrogated to determine how they might have influenced perceptions of women. This research was initially limited to Judaism and Christianity and conducted by insiders to those traditions who wanted to determine whether it was possible to be feminist and religious at the same time. Soon, however, other women were exploring less patriarchal alternatives such as neopaganism and Wicca (see Chapter 9).

In the 1980s feminist scholars of religion began examining other traditions and feminists within those traditions started to write their own critiques. At the same time questions began to be raised about issues of race, ethnicity, class, and geography—issues to which the early second-wave feminists had given scant attention. Scholars of colour, people from outside the first world, and others asked *which* women the feminist scholars were talking about, and who was entitled to speak for various religious traditions.

By the 1990s the study of women and religion was vast and diverse, and there was general agreement that no single perspective was capable of encompassing all aspects of the subject. Furthermore, there were women in all religious traditions who did not accept feminist critiques (if they had encountered them at all) and whose own religious lives followed more traditional patterns.

There is no single way to capture the religious lives of women because those lives are so diverse. For example, being a Hindu woman in India could mean vastly different experiences, rituals, and practices, depending on a wide variety of life circumstances, including where in India she lives, what caste she is from, what rituals her family traditionally follows, and whether she is married or a widow, as well as her own choices with regard to Hinduism. The life circumstances of a Hindu woman living in North America will include factors that could make her practice of Hinduism very different from that of her Indian sister. If she is a convert, there might be many variants again. Although religious traditions (and localized forms of religions) may try, through their authority structures, to impose a certain way of being religious on adherents, that imposition is always partial and incomplete.

As will be made clear below, we know that the category "woman" is fluid rather than fixed. Nonetheless, we still think it is important to study women and religious traditions for a number of reasons. In most religious traditions, scholarship by and about women is relatively recent. Too often, the subject of women is still an afterthought in the study of religion, even though at least half the practitioners of every religion are female. Women's religious roles often go unnoticed and unanalyzed, and women's specific contributions to religious life are neglected.

One reason to study women and religion is to provide context for the marginalized place to which women have often been relegated in both the practice and the study of religion. Not only do women have many religious roles that are not recognized in the scholarly literature, but those roles that are recognized are often devalued, with the result that they are not seen as crucial or central to the traditions. No religion can be reduced to the "official" version presented by (usually male) spokespersons.

The category "women" is not itself an uncontested one. Feminist work has historically distinguished between biological sex (male or female) and "gender," which is understood to reflect social constructions of ways to act properly based on one's given maleness or femaleness. For many years now, feminist theory has maintained that the gender roles assigned to men and women are in reality socially constructed and therefore can be reconstructed in other ways. Recently, some scholars have begun to argue that not only gender but also sex itself is socially constructed. Our tendency to sort individuals into separate male and female categories, and on that basis build whole societies, is itself a construction, not a necessity (Delphy, 2001). Of course there are different reproductive roles, but why has so much rested on the differences (even opposition) between those roles, rather than on other biological categories such as eye colour and age? For feminist theorists, the bifurcation of humanity into male and female is the product of a hierarchized world view that upholds both patriarchy and heterosexism.

In many—perhaps most—religious traditions, one is ascribed a certain gender role on the basis of an essentialized view of one's biological sex. Thus, one's biological sex becomes the marker for assigning particular gendered religious and moral roles and expectations. Gender in this case is synonymous with sex: your sex prescribes your gender. Today many religious traditions have made some movement towards reconstruction of gender roles; the ordination of women in most Protestant Christian churches and in liberal Judaism is one example. In such cases, gender is separated from sex and understood to refer to those socialized (hence changeable) roles and attributes that are stereotypically associated with each sex. Even so, there has been virtually no recognition of the degree to which religious doctrine, practice, and belief are based on categories and concepts grounded in the supposed bedrock of biological sex. The notion of "sex" as a sharply bifurcated category continues to be treated as given, whether imposed by a deity or simply as a general presupposition about the universe. This essentialized stance is reflected in religious symbolism: the "maleness" of the god of Western monotheistic traditions, for example, or the interactions of the gods and goddesses of Hinduism. This leaves unexamined how "sex" itself is socially constructed and imbued with meaning and cultural import.

In recent years, many of the university departments that were once called "Women's Studies" have been renamed "Gender Studies." This renaming points to a number of changes in the way scholars view both women and gender. If gender and sex are both socially constructed, then the category of "woman" is not a stable one and is not one opposed to a singular other category "man." Rather, both must be understood as fluid. The notion of gender studies reflects that fluidity. We have moved away from the notion that there are only two sexes/genders and towards the idea that genders are multiply constructed, albeit with strong pressure from hegemonic forces that influence outcomes while masking their own power. Gender studies seeks to take into account transgender and transsexuality as well as to allow for a wide range of queer sexualities.

In this book we do not assume that the category "women" is necessarily constructed on a bedrock of biological essentialism. Rather, we use that category to pinpoint certain issues in the study of religion that are often neglected. We focus on certain ways of seeing "women" as a category and explore the implications of religious systems that treat men and women differently. We note that men have generally been ranked above women in a variety of ways. We read various religious traditions through the category "women" to shed light on features of these religions that have often been ignored. At the same time, we acknowledge that the term *women* is multivalent and context-dependent, and that no one can speak to or for all women.

We assume that patriarchy has existed in many historical times and places, and that religious traditions have generally been interwoven with social systems that not only exalt maleness over femaleness but also distribute wealth and power (societal and religious) on the basis of male privilege. Patriarchal social systems elevate males, and roles associated with maleness, over females and, to a greater or lesser degree, render women's voices and experiences inconsequential if not invisible. Patriarchy is not the only form of privilege, however, and it is often intertwined with other forms of privilege that exalt some people and diminish others on the basis of race, class, and sexual orientation.

Rosemary Radford Ruether's (1972) astute analysis of "dualisms" within Christianity led feminist critics of religion to note how the male–female dualism that underlies the privileging of male over female informed the dualism that privileges mind/soul over body/nature in many religious traditions. Thus early feminist analysis of sex and gender in religious traditions focused on the dualisms that connected men to god (or the Ultimate), mind, and spirit, and women to body and nature. Looking at religious traditions from a feminist perspective, one is often struck by the tendency of religions to view men as closer to whatever is considered most important, and women as closer to that which is of lesser value. In Hinduism, for example, men are sometimes considered better equipped for the religious quest, while women are seen as best suited for worldly tasks such as producing children and maintaining the household. In religions such as Christianity and Judaism, men have generally been considered closer to God by reason of their masculinity, while women have been seen as somewhat removed from God by reason of their femininity. Indeed, many religious traditions view women, and issues associated with women, as problematic. Women are presented as weak or ignorant, temptresses, deceivers, or simply distractions. As such, they are to be controlled, secluded, and sometimes shunned.

We do not think that there is any single convincing explanation for patri-archal privilege. A number of scholarly works have addressed this question, and the jury is still out. In this book we will not attend to the "why." Rather, we will look at the "how" of patriarchy—how it has functioned in various religious traditions.

We have asked our contributors to take a feminist approach to their material, exploring whether and how a particular tradition (or set of traditions) has sorted people into gender and sex categories and what that has meant for women in terms of status, roles, power, and so on. Within each tradition there are women who themselves question its treatment of women, but there are also women who are content as they are and have no interest in questioning their status and roles. Our contributors have tried to portray the full spectrum, taking seriously the integrity of the tradition under discussion and exploring its inner diversities. In this book we use the term *feminist* broadly to include women in a wide variety of positions that seek to change the systemic portrayal of women as inferior to men.

It is important to recognize that feminist theories and methodologies are multiple. Though all feminists share a concern for the position and status of women, they do not necessarily agree on where that concern should be focused. Although feminist theories and methodologies tend to focus on issues of power and the ways it manifests itself in a given social context, privileging some mem-bers and disenfranchising others, they are also attentive to difference—gender, racial, economic, or otherwise—and the way it is constructed. We would advise students interested in feminist theory and methodology to consult Klassen, *Women and Religion: Critical Concepts in Religious Studies* (2009) and Juschka, *Feminism in the Study of Religion: A Reader* (2001). There are also several jour-nals that publish current research in the field, including the *Journal of Feminist Studies in Religion*.

The selection of religious traditions explored in this book is not exhaustive by any means: the traditions included are simply the ones that are most often explored in religion courses in North American universities and colleges. The decision to arrange them in roughly chronological order reflects the structure of many courses on women and religion. Each chapter addresses several specific topics that we think are central to understanding how women live, experience and negotiate their religious lives. The author of each chapter addresses each of these topics in her own way.

1.   History and status of women: Here contributors make some general observations about the history of the tradition and the status and roles of women within it.
2.   Texts, rituals, and interpretations: Each chapter contains some discussion of texts and rituals as they reflect and affect the status of women, though these discussions are more detailed in the case of text-based traditions, in which

questions of interpretation are particularly important. For example: How are women depicted in the texts and the interpretive tradition? Whose interpretations are considered authoritative? How do these interpretations affect women in the tradition? Do women accept them? Do women interpret their roles differently from the way men interpret them?

3. Symbols and gender: Each chapter looks at the way the tradition's symbols are gendered or interpreted in relation to gender. Several comment on the roles of goddesses and other important female figures. They also comment on the ways in which these figures function as symbols and describe various strategies used by women in these traditions to retrieve and reimagine these figures so that they can empower women.

4. Individual and family structures and traditions: Each chapter examines how the tradition influences and is influenced by ideals regarding the family. But ideals are often far from the lived reality of women's lives; therefore that lived reality is also discussed.

5. Sexuality: Each chapter explores how the tradition configures sexuality and the implications of that configuration. Some chapters look at rituals related to women's sexuality, such as those celebrating the birth of a daughter, first menstruation, and so on. Others examine the way women's sexual relationships (heterosexual and same-sex) are configured.

6. Social change: Contributors were asked to explore how the tradition in question might promote social change in the status of women.

7. Official and unofficial roles of women: Questions here include whether women play roles that are not necessarily privileged as "central" but that allow for interesting reinterpretations. Are there lifestyle alternatives for women? In this context, several chapters explore the opposition between "domestic" and "public" spaces and the impact this distinction has on the religious lives of women. Other chapters look at the propensity of the traditions in question to elevate women who support their men and serve as guardians of family piety.

8. Backlash: In most traditions, advances in women's rights have been met with backlash of one kind or another. Backlash has been particularly common in Judaism, Christianity, and Islam, but it has also been evident in some of the other traditions examined in this text.

9. Unique features: Our assumption throughout this volume is that every religious tradition is unique; therefore we invited contributors to comment on particular features of their traditions that affect women.

References

Delphy, Christine. 2001. "Rethinking Sex and Gender". Pp. 411–23 in Juschka (2001).

Juschka, Darlene, ed. 2001. *Feminism in the Study of Religion: A Reader.* New York: Continuum.

Klassen, Pamela, with Shari Goldberg and Danielle Lefebvre, eds. 2009. *Women and Religion: Critical Concepts in Religious Studies.* 4 vols. New York: Routledge.

Ruether, Rosemary Radford. 1972. *Liberation Theology: Human Hope Confronts Christian History and American Power.* New York: Paulist Press.

Russell, Letty M., and J. Shannon Clarkson, eds. 1996. *Dictionary of Feminist Theologies.* Louisville, KY: Westminster John Knox.

CHAPTER 1

Women in Hindu Traditions

Leona M. Anderson

Bathing in the river Ganga at Varanasi.

Shutterstock © Pal Teravagimov

Anandamayi Ma (1896–1982)

Anandamayi Ma was a Hindu saint whose devotees believed her to possess divine powers, including the power to heal by touch alone and to foresee the future. Born to a poor brahmin family in what is now Bangladesh, she did not have any formal religious training, but began showing signs of extraordinary religious sentiment in childhood. The sound of religious chanting could send her into a trance during which her body might appear to lengthen or shrink, and she is said to have taken on the appearance of various goddesses Although she was married by the age of 13, she did not go to live with her husband for several years, and when he finally did touch her, he received an electric shock that threw him across the room. He became her devotee and lived a celibate life thereafter. Anandamayi travelled widely and established a network of ashrams throughout India. Her religiosity is exemplified in her poetry. For example:

> I am what you consider me to be, not more, not less . . .
> This body is like a musical instrument; what you hear depends
> upon how you play it (in Lipski, 1969: 69).

Introduction and Overview

As almost every textbook on Hinduism will tell you, "Hindu" is a modern Western term derived from an older term used to identify the people living along the Indus River, in the northwestern part of the Indian subcontinent. Because the term originated as a geographic designation, there is a lot of confusion as to what exactly it means to be a Hindu. One characteristic of Hinduism is clear, however, and that is its diversity—a diversity that extends to the status of women within the Hindu fold.

Hinduism is often presented as a total way of life that encompasses a multitude of images, ideas, rituals, and traditions. There is no founder and no single authoritative book, although there are many sacred texts. Hinduism is the most ancient of the living religions, having reached a high state of development by 1500 BCE, and it has survived the missionary efforts of other religions. The many gods and goddesses who populate Hindu traditions have made Hinduism unusually tolerant and accepting of non-Hindu beliefs.

Women's roles in Hinduism differ depending on many factors, including region, caste, occupation, and education, so that it is virtually impossible to point to a single coherent image of "woman." One must, therefore, speak to the question of women in India in a pluralistic fashion, recognizing that there are a number of relevant concerns and clusters of concerns. This chapter will look at several of those concerns, but it is by no means exhaustive.

Basic Concepts

Hinduism envisions the world in terms of an endless cycle of birth and death known as **samsara**, which repeats itself over long periods of time. The present age, characterized by political strife, war, poverty, and so on, is part of the last stage of this cycle, which will come to an end several eons from now, when the world will have become so degenerate that it will be destroyed; then the cycle will begin again. Humans undergo a sequence of births and deaths that parallels that of the world. *Samsara* refers to the cyclical pattern of birth and death undergone by individuals as well as that undergone by the world.

Samsara is not haphazard but governed by the law of action and reaction, cause and effect, known as the law of **karma** (literally, "action"). The doctrine of karma is a doctrine of consequences. As a moral law, it means that every action, every thought, has a result. There are no shortcuts. Individuals are responsible for their actions not just in one lifetime but over many lifetimes. Our position in this life is determined by our past actions, and our current actions will determine our subsequent births. The primary goal in each lifetime is to attain a better birth by performing morally good actions, so that eventually one may attain *moksha*: liberation from the cycle of birth and death.

There are three paths that serve as general guidelines for the attainment of *moksha*: the path of knowledge, the path of action, and the path of devotion. These paths are not exclusive; many Hindus practise all three. Nor are they the only means available to reach the final goal.

The path of knowledge emerges out of the earliest of Hindu texts, the **Vedas**, and especially the texts known as the Upanishads. The basic idea is that knowledge—not just ordinary, discursive knowledge, but intuitive knowledge of truth—will lead to *moksha*. An important concept here is that of **Brahman**, which is equated with *prana* (breath, life) and is said to permeate the world as salt permeates water (*Chandogya Upanishad* 6.13; in Hume, 1966: 248). A second important concept is that of atman: the individual's innermost self or soul, or the universal self. The religious quest in the Upanishads is to grasp the fundamental identity of Brahman and atman—to recognize that one's essential self transcends individuality, limitation, decay, and death. Ascetic discipline assists in the process of disengagement from worldly attachments, including attachment to one's individual existence. Although the Vedas did acknowledge a few women as authorities, and there is some evidence that women were even permitted to discourse on sacred texts (Young and Sharma, 1999: 62), in general the path of knowledge restricted women by associating them with the physical world of multiplicity and appearance (*maya*) and thus opposed to the spiritual realm of unity. The goal of the path of knowledge is to transcend *maya*.

The second path is the path of action. The emphasis in this path is on **dharma**, which is often understood as action in accordance with certain social and ritual standards. The details of these standards have been gradually worked out from the texts known as the Brahmanas (c. 500 BCE) through later texts, including the **Dharmashastras** (law books).

The rules of dharma encompass rules of caste behaviour. Caste is a complicated system of social stratification that could be described as a set of occupational categories, although in modern India each caste encompasses a large range of occupations and social statuses. A typical formulation is that there are four basic castes, the highest of which is identified with religion. The duties of the **brahmin** caste, which is mandated to study and teach the sacred Vedas, are purely religious. The primary duty of the second caste, the kshatriyas (rulers or warriors), is to protect their subjects; at the head of this caste stands the king. The third caste, the vaishyas, includes merchants, bankers, and landowners. They have the moral responsibility of wealth. Finally there are the shudras (labourers), whose duty is to serve the other three castes. Within this system there are seemingly infinite subdivisions. Outside it there are large numbers of people who typically perform menial tasks and are referred to as outcastes or, as Mahatma Gandhi called them, Harijans (people of god).

A second system of classification identifies four stages of life (*ashramas*): student, householder (devoted to marriage and the production of children), forest-dweller (gradually withdrawing from worldly responsibilities), and, ultimately, renouncer. In this last stage, the individual abandons all possessions and attachments and becomes a wandering ascetic, living on alms and seeking only union with the divine.

The impact of the caste and *ashrama* systems on the position and status of women is significant. Both situate women within clear structural boundaries and assign them clear roles. As Biernacki (2007: 36) notes, caste divisions appear to be just as fundamental to Indian society as the gender divide. Chakravarty (1998) has described the caste system as *brahmanic patriarchy*, a term that emphasizes that both **brahmanism** and patriarchy are key features that must be taken into consideration when analyzing the position of women in India.

As Omvedt explains in a review of Chakravarty's work, women's dharma was to be chaste and subservient, especially to their husbands, but their essential nature was understood to be one of undisciplined sexuality, which needed to be controlled by their male protectors and guardians; thus women were secluded in the household and taught that their only hope for liberation lay in devoting themselves to their husbands as if they were gods (Omvedt, 2000: 187). In effect there was a kind of caste-patriarchal bargain: high-caste women accepted a life of subordination and seclusion in exchange for a share in the status and wealth of their husbands (Omvedt, 2000: 187).

Some scholars argue that women belong to the lowest of the four castes, the shudras (see Bandyopadhyay, 2008: 105); others, that women in effect form a distinct fifth caste (see Bagwe 1995). Given that caste is associated with social function, understanding women as a distinct caste might allow for a shift in the social value of women. At the very least, positioning women as a separate group among several diffuses the intensity of opposition inherent in the gender binary.

The *ashrama* system assigned a high value to the second stage of life, especially for women. Women fulfilled their spiritual destiny through marriage and were mandated to treat their husbands as gods. Women came to be identified with the domestic sphere, and widows, because they no longer contributed to that sphere, were treated with contempt. Excluded from the public realm, women were also generally excluded from the renunciation stage of the *ashrama* system, because they were not permitted to travel alone, and perhaps also because the strong social prohibition against nakedness for women made it impossible for them to adopt a way of life usually symbolized by nudity. More often than not, they were also excluded from ascetic religious orders.

The final path is that of **bhakti** (devotion), which emphasizes personal attachment to one specific deity among a pantheon of gods and goddesses. The multiplicity of goddesses who are worshipped in this context provides us with insight into the conception of the feminine in Hindu culture. The goddess is identified with the physical world, nature, orderliness, and intensity. The earth, for example, is depicted as a goddess, as is the Indian subcontinent. From the seventh to the twelfth centuries CE, a variety of devotional movements developed and more religious options became open to women, who began to frequent temples, lead devotional groups, and compose songs. A significant number of female devotees came to be acknowledged as saints.

During the colonial period, the Vedic tradition was reinterpreted in response to European critiques of Hinduism. Customs such as child marriage and **sati** (immolation of widows on their husbands' funeral pyres) came under attack as Hindu reformers sought to rid the tradition of elements they believed did not represent its core. As this core was further defined, however, it became clear that less extreme expressions of brahmanic patriarchy were still to play major roles. The sanctity of marriage, the ban on widow remarriage, and the authority of husbands in the home all came to be seen as central to Hinduism. As Omvedt argues, "A new brahmanism was being constructed, which saw brahmans as the elite representatives of a broader 'Hindu community' whose characteristics included the extension of the devoted wife, the **pativrata**, to all castes" (Omvedt, 2000: 189).

Women emerged as freedom fighters and supporters of Indian independence from Britain, which was achieved in 1947. Article 15 of the Indian constitution prohibits discrimination against any citizen on the grounds of religion, race, caste, sex, or place of birth. Nevertheless, even today, women in India are far from equal to men. One could well argue that nationalism, alongside colonialism, reified the idea of the Hindu woman, especially the upper-caste Hindu woman, who guards the inner sanctum of Hindu culture. Both the nationalist and the colonialist agendas resonate with traditional patriarchal control of women. The popularity of Hindu fundamentalist movements has resulted in even more rigid interpretations of male and female roles.

The experience of Hindu women cannot easily be homologized to the Western experience, especially with respect to feminism. As Chitnis argues, whereas feminist anger in the West is in part a response to the hypocrisy of a culture that stresses equality and individual freedom yet denies social and legislative equality to women, that concept of equality is not really relevant in the highly stratified society of India (cited in Humes, 2000: 145). Nevertheless, Hindu women are active in their efforts to modernize. Among the numerous institutions that focus on women's issues is the Centre for Women's Development Studies in New Delhi, a research centre that works toward the realization of women's equality and development in all spheres of life. The feminist press Kali for Women is also important in this regard. Yet though efforts on this front are ongoing, the status of most women in India remains well below that of men.

Texts and Interpretations

We have already noted that Hinduism has no single authoritative text. Rather, in addition to the Vedas, there are numerous books, composed over millennia, that are considered sacred to one degree or another. These texts are excellent sources of information on the status of women in Hindu traditions at particular times and in particular places, as viewed through the eyes of their male authors.

The Vedas and the Vedic Age

The Vedas are said to have been composed by the **Aryans**, an Indo-European-speaking people who appeared on the subcontinent about 1500 BCE. *Veda* means "knowledge", and these texts are considered to be repositories of all knowledge. The Vedas are often divided into three categories: the hymn books, the earliest of which is the *Rig Veda*; the Brahmanas or priestly manuals; and the Upanishads and Aranyakas, which are more philosophical.

Vedic religion was life-affirming, and its sacrificial rituals focused on achieving the basic goals of life: progeny, good crops, prosperity, longevity, and so on. Women obviously played a crucial role in the production of children, but they were also necessary partners in the sacrificial rituals that their husbands were required to perform (Young 1987: 60ff).[1] The *Shatapatha* and *Taittiriya Brahmanas* make it clear that the participation of both spouses was required: "a ritual without a wife is not a ritual" (*TB* 2.2.2.6; see also *SB* 1.3.1.12). Even in the Vedic era, however, it is clear that the role of husband and father was paramount.

The sacrificer's wife played an important cooperative role in the rituals. According to the *Aitareya Brahmana*, "A wife is a comrade, a daughter a misery, and a son a light in the highest heaven." The same text states that a man should look on his wife as his mother, as through her he would be reborn in the form of his son (vii.13). Commenting on the role of the sacrificer's wife, Jamison writes that "One of the wife's most important roles is that of injecting sexuality into the perfect, ordered world of the ritual" (1996: 53).

Female imagery plays a minor role in the Vedic texts. There are goddesses, to be sure, but they tend to be minor figures compared to the great goddesses who would eventually develop: the Vedic goddesses are often likened to cows that provide milk for the benefit of the world. The four corners of the fire pan used in sacrificial rituals are said to be shaped like nipples (*SB* VI.5.2.16–19). Symbolism relating to female fertility can also be seen in references to plowing and the planting of seeds. Womb imagery is common in early Vedic references to initiation and coming of age ceremonies. As Kaelber notes, it is usually found in association with rites of passage and passage symbolism (1989: 133).

A primary aim of the sacrifice was to restore or reinvigorate Prajapati, the deity who exhausts himself in creating the world. Later on, the goddesses **Durga** and **Kali** would be said to require blood offerings to restore the vital creative power that they expend when they create the world.

Another important myth is the eternal struggle between the gods (*devas*) and the demons (*asuras*). In this context, the goddess **Vac** (intelligible speech) plays a significant role. In the *Shatapatha Brahmana* the gods give Vac to the demons in exchange for Soma (an intoxicating beverage personified as a god) (3:2:4:3ff). In this same text, Vac is equated with the earth and tries to escape the gods by hiding in the sap of the plants and the trees (IV.6.9.16). There are hints also that it is through Vac, or sexual union with her, that Prajapati creates. Speech is the intermediary between humans and gods, and this intermediary function is especially evident when the gods offer Vac up in sacrifice. It is also clear that Vac's actions have eternally paradigmatic effects when it comes to women: that is, women are the way they are because in the beginning Vac did this or that. Here is one myth of Vac's creation:

> Both the gods and asuras were born of Prajapati. The gods inherited mind, sacrifice and heaven and the asuras inherited speech (Vac) and the earth. The sacrifice, thinking that he could lure Vac into the camp of the gods because she was a woman, beckoned to her but she disdained him. So it is, we are told, that a woman, when beckoned, at first disdains man. He tried again and Vac just nodded "no." When he tried a third time, Vac said "come to me." Thereupon the gods warned him that women are alluring, and advised him to make her come to him. Finally Vac approached him and when she did, the gods enveloped her completely in fire, making her into an offering of the gods. So it was that the asuras were deprived of speech (*SB* lll.2.1.19f; trans. Eggeling, 1885).

The Upanishads

The Upanishads (c. 500 BCE–500 CE) are basically philosophical texts that emphasize the relationship between student and teacher. Although most of the teachers were men, a few women are presented as authoritative, among them a female philosopher named Gargi who challenges an eminent sage. The Upanishads privilege the idea of renouncing the world and tend to place a lower priority on worldly concerns such as long life and progeny.

Because women were generally unable to practise renunciation, their status appears to have declined from the earlier period when they played a role in the sacrifice. And because they were associated with the world of impermanence, they came to be identified as obstacles to the attainment of *moksha*. Although there are Upanishads that glorify the goddess, such as the *Devi Upanishad*, they are later (ninth century) and less well known.

If women were central to the family-oriented religion of the early Vedas, in time they became silent and invisible in all rituals except those involving pregnancy. Meanwhile, their roles in the domestic realm came to be increasingly rigidly controlled as institutions such as child marriage, purdah (the veiling and seclusion of women), and the prohibition of widow remarriage crept into the tradition, and the study of the Veda fell almost exclusively to males.

The Laws of Manu

Regulations governing morality in Hinduism tend to vary with caste, stage of life, region, and local custom. However, the legal tradition as represented in the Dharmashastras had a profound influence on the status of women. One dharmashastra in particular, known as *The Laws of Manu*, has played a pivotal role in the subordination and mistreatment of Indian women since the colonial period, when the British entrenched its prescriptions in law, giving it a general authority that it had never had in the past (see Kishwar 2000).

It is difficult to know the degree to which *The Laws of Manu* reflects actual practice at the time of its composition (probably between 200 BCE and 200 CE). Though it more likely reflects an ideal, many of its prescriptions regarding women are found elsewhere in the literary tradition. According to *Manu*, women are subordinate to their fathers, brothers, and husbands: "Her father protects [her] in childhood, her husband protects [her] in youth, and her sons protect [her] in old age; a woman is never fit for independence" (ix.3). It is *Manu* that commands women to worship their husbands as if they were gods and declares marriage to be the supreme mode of female religious fulfillment. *Manu* also reflects the seemingly universal notion that women are dangerous (ix.13, 17), and warns women that disloyalty will bring them all sorts of harm, including rebirth into the womb of a jackal (ix.29–30). Though *Manu*'s authority is contested today, the social conditions it describes still exist: for example, women's position in society still depends to a great extent on that of their husbands and sons.

The Epics

There are two major epic narratives in the Hindu tradition, the *Mahabarata* and the *Ramayana*, the first composed between 400 and 200 BCE and the second between 300 BCE and 300 CE. Though neither features a great goddess, and the goddesses that do appear are subject to male authority, both **Draupadi**, from the *Mahabarata*, and **Sita**, from the *Ramayana*, are of interest for our study. Draupadi is a dramatic, rebellious personality, while Sita never rebels.

Draupadi

The frame story of the *Mahabarata* revolves around a conflict between two branches of one family: the endearing Pandava brothers and their followers, and their not-so-endearing cousins, the Kauravas. Draupadi is the beautiful and intelligent wife of the five Pandava brothers, with each of whom she is said to have spent one year.

Draupadi takes issue with the forces of patriarchy and male power. When Yudishthira, the eldest of the Pandavas, gambles her away in a game of dice,

Duryodhana, the winner of the bet, insists that she be publically disrobed. She prays to Krishna (an avatar of the god Vishnu) for help, and he preserves her honour by ensuring that the fabric of her sari continues to lengthen as it is pulled away. When the attempt to disrobe her is finally abandoned, Draupadi lets down her coiffed hair and vows that she will not knot it again until she has washed it in Duryodhana's blood. Accordingly, when another of the Pandavas later kills Duryodhana, he collects blood from the corpse and takes it to Draupadi so that she can fulfill her vow. In a modern version of this story, by Mahasveta Devi, the Draupadi figure is depicted as a tribal rebel named Dopdi who is raped by the authorities. Dopdi turns her assault against her attackers, confronting them with their own brutality. In this way Mahasveta's Dopdi highlights female resistance to hegemonic powers.

A word should be added here on the *Bhagavad Gita* ("Song of the Lord"), which is part of the *Mahabarata* but is also extracted from it as a separate text of great importance to Hinduism. Focusing on issues of war and power, it is almost entirely lacking a female voice.

Sita

One of the most pervasive role models for Hindu women is Sita, the heroine of the *Ramayana* and the personification of wifely fidelity and purity. Hindu women strive to live up to her example, and brides are commonly blessed with the words "be like Sita." Yet Sita has no particular identity of her own; she is so completely submissive to her husband, Rama, that she gives up her life to protect his honour. Indeed, Sita refuses independence—refuses to accept life on any terms other than those prescribed by her position as the wife of Rama, to whom she owes blind obedience. The first part of the story has been summarized by H.P. Shastri as follows:

> Rama, the eldest son of the king of Ayodhya Dasartha, wins Sita in an archery contest. Rama is forced into exile in the forest, accompanied by Sita and his brother Lakshmana. While in the forest, Rama is lured away by a demon in the form of a golden deer. At Sita's request, Rama chases after the deer, and while he is away, the demon Ravana abducts her. Aided by the monkey king Sugriva, his minister Hanuman, and the monkey army, Rama besieges Lanka, defeats Ravana's armies, kills Ravana, and brings Sita back. Upon her rescue, Rama makes the following surprising statement:
>
> > Lovely One, the ten regions are at thy disposal; I can have nothing more to do with thee! What man of honour would give reign to his

passion so far as to permit himself to take back a woman who has dwelt in the house of another? Thou hast been taken into Ravana's lap and he has cast lustful glances on thee; how can I reclaim thee, I who boast of belonging to an illustrious House? (1952: 335–6).

Sita is shocked, but she recovers quickly, orders that a funeral pyre be built, and throws herself into the flames. The gods rescue her and she emerges unscathed. Rama is crowned king but continues to be plagued by jealousy, and the people of Ayodhya doubt Sita's purity because she has lived in the house of another man. Sita becomes pregnant and is banished to the forest, where she gives birth to two sons, Lava and Kusa.

When Sita returns to the kingdom with her sons, some 15 years later, she declares her chastity before the assembly, which requests the earth to swallow her up as proof of her purity. Rama admits that she is virtuous and begs to be forgiven for abandoning her. The earth breaks open and swallows Sita up.

Throughout all these ordeals, Sita retains her composure and character. Her love for Rama does not waver, even after he has rejected her. She says, "So I, thus well-equipped and of the top rank, well versed in all the aspects of dharma, O revered one, can I ever be expected to disrespect my lord when [a] husband is the god for all . . . women[?]" (Shastri, 1952: 338–9).

For some, it is difficult to imagine why Sita is so beloved in India, given what Hess, in "Rejecting Sita," describes as " the relentless reminders of the husband's superiority, the horrifying abuse inherent in the model of the hus-band-lord and the worshipful wife who lives only to guard her purity and sur-render to his will, [and] the sacralizing of the whole arrangement by making the perpetrator an incarnation of God"—all themes that typify the Sita char-acter (1999: 8). Clearly, the patriarchal brahmanic system constructed Sita to send the message that a good Hindu woman should obey her husband without question, even when he abuses her. Response to this construction has been mixed. Some reject it entirely, while others, such as the feminist economist Bina Agarwal, try subvert it. In a 1985 poem, for example, Agarwal calls on Sita to "speak your side of the story, / We know the other side too well" (quoted in Richman, 2001: 239).

At the same time, the Sita myth is dear to many women precisely because it expresses their experience and concerns. As the Bengali writer Nabaneeta Dev Sen notes (1998: 18), village women's retellings of Sita's story in the form of songs portray her as the typical suffering wife, patiently bearing loneliness, insecurity, and injustice. Songs on themes such as Sita's birth, wedding, abduc-tion, pregnancy, abandonment, and childbearing allow women to complain about the physical risks, neglect, and disenfranchisement they experience in their own lives.

Symbols

One of Hinduism's most appealing characteristics is its rich female symbolism. There are probably as many goddesses in Hinduism as there are gods, and they are not entirely dominated by their male counterparts. The goddesses are intriguing for a number of reasons. First, their sheer number is staggering; even Buddhism pales in comparison. No other living religious tradition displays such an ancient, continuous diverse history of goddess worship. Second, the goddesses of Hinduism offer an interesting counterpoint to goddess-challenged traditions. Because much of the work on goddesses in the Western world focuses on the past as a central source of meaning, the goddesses of Hinduism are important as contemporary examples of "living" goddess traditions. Finally, the goddesses are noticeably diverse and complex, and each is unique; this tends to put to rest the myth of the one-dimensional mother goddess. As the example of Sita, above, suggests, there is no necessary parallel between the status of female divinities and that of women in Hinduism, though many would like this to be so. Hindu goddesses in even the earliest texts were conceptualized from a male vantage point in a patriarchal effort to describe the qualities and behaviour desired of women in various capacities.

One recurring paradigm presents two types of goddesses, or one goddess with two sides: one nourishing and protective, the other fearsome and destructive. In her study of local goddesses in Orissa, Foulston found that "The goddess is considered to have an inherently dual nature; although she is generally peaceful and benevolent, she might be capable of acts of violence" (2002: 118). O'Flaherty (1980) characterizes these two types as goddesses of the breast and goddesses of the tooth. In the first category we find goddesses whose primary function is to create and nurture life, responding to prayers for safe childbirth, sons, and prosperity. Almost always associated with male gods who control or shelter them (for example, in marriage), they are auspicious, safe, and domesticated, and their powers are determined by social and cultural norms.

High-ranking goddesses provide sustenance. For example, Sri-Lakshmi, the consort of Vishnu, is associated with riches and abundance at the level of both the family and the state. She is a goddess of fertility and purity, a model wife and obedient servant of her husband, often depicted as devoutly massaging Vishnu's feet while he sleeps at the end of the cosmic cycle of creation.

By contrast, goddesses of the second type are ambivalent, dangerous, and often erotic. Often depicted as sexually threatening, they devour the male's essence; play non-feminine, martial roles; and are called on in times of crisis such as epidemics, warfare, and famine. Goddesses of this type are generally unmarried, and if they are married they tend to dominate their male consorts, though according to Kinsley, they may also be tamed by marriage (1986: 115). Chinnamasta is another goddess of this type. She is depicted as headless, feeding herself and others with her lifeblood as she stands on top of a copulating couple. In fulfilling her role as sustainer and maintainer of life, she exhausts and destroys herself.

Wendy O'Flaherty, the prolific professor of the History of Religions at the University of Chicago, argues that the Hindu female cannot be simultaneously erotic and maternal (1973: 102, 111). Madhu Kishwar notes that Indian men are trained to revere consort goddesses and to hold non-consort goddess figures in "fear and awe"; she goes on to argue that "a woman who rises above being sexually accessible, consort of none, nor in search of a consort, tends to command tremendous awe and reverence" (Kishwar, 1997: 25).

To the extent that the goddess embodies symbiosis, the interconnections that sustain life, she is a powerful force that permeates all things. In Hinduism, the goddess is sometimes envisioned as the entire cosmos, an all-encompassing being that is present everywhere, in every god and each blade of grass. At the end of each cycle of time she is said to draw the world into her womb and then to exist as the seed of the universe—until the next creation, when she grows and blossoms forth. As a spider weaves its web, the goddess creates the universe out of her own body. The mountains are her bones, rivers her veins, trees her body hair, the sun and moon her eyes. Thus the goddess connects all spheres of reality. She is a mediator, and devotion to her focuses on the improvement of life in this world. She is a great healer with the cooling effect of healing waters. She is nourishment, the food of the earth, and no one is denied her blessings. The immanence of the goddess is rooted in everyday subsistence—and this is one basis for the feminist position that women are equal to men.

Early Goddesses

Compared to later Hindu traditions, the early Vedas contain surprisingly few goddesses, and those who do appear play relatively minor roles. Early Vedic religion is dominated by male deities such as the warrior god Indra, and the god of fire, Agni. The goddesses of the Vedas are often associated with the human and natural worlds: Prithvi, the goddess of the earth; Usas, the dawn; Ratri, the night; Nirrti, decay and corruption; Sarasvati, the river; Vac, speech; and Sri, prosperity.

The *Saundaryalahari*

The *Saundaryalahari*, a text composed about 1000 CE, conceives of the universe as animated and controlled by feminine power. In it, we find an example of the notion that the male deity Shiva can act only when he is united with the female **Shakti**; on his own, he is unable to stir (verse 1). The goddess is supreme, and the text describes her in detail, starting with her diadem and continuing down through the separate parts of her body, ending with her feet and a prayer that the poet may drink the water in which they are bathed. Here, too, the universe is said to be created by her from a speck of dust, but Shiva shatters it and uses it to dust himself as with ashes (vol. 2). Through the closing and opening of her eyes the earth is dissolved and created (vol. 24).

Yoni

A pervasive feminine symbol in Hindu ritual and mythology is the **yoni**, the female genital organ. Shiva's penis, the *linga*, and the goddess's vagina are common motifs in Hindu temples and iconography. The *yoni* symbolizes female creativity, the power of life-giving force. Typically the *yoni* is depicted as smallish against the backdrop of the usually huge *linga*.

One of the most important goddess temples is at Kamarupa in northeastern India, which is revered as the most potent of all Shakti sites. It enshrines no image of the goddess. Instead, in a corner of a cave within the temple, there is a block of stone with a *yoni* imprinted on it. The *yoni* is moistened by water dripping from a spring within the cave, and devotees leave offerings of flowers and leaves on it. Once a year, during the goddess's menses, the temple is closed for three days; on the fourth day, the doors are opened and pilgrims are allowed in. It is said that during those three days, the spring water that keeps the *yoni* moist turns a pale red colour. Priests wipe the *yoni* clean, and the cloths they use are prized by pilgrims who believe them to have great powers.

Family Structures and Traditions

Vrats

Austerities known as **vrats** (vows) play an important role in the religious lives of many Hindu women. While a married woman (as a pativrata) will observe a vrat for the welfare and good fortune of her husband and family, and a widowed woman for the continued protection of her family and departed husband, a single woman might take a vow in hope of finding a good husband. In addition, vrats are sometimes taken when an obstacle arises.

In practice, most vrats involve fasting, and they often include the narration of a legend tracing the origin of the vrat. The observance of vrats has been linked to ideals of wifeliness; vrat rituals tend to demarcate domestic space as women's space and give this space a religious orientation in the promotion of prosperity and fertility within the household. Thus vrats represent attempts to realize in their day-to-day lives what patriarchy requires of women (Bannerji,

2001: 199). At the same time, vrats are highly individualistic and function in the lives of Hindu women in more than one way. Women observe vrats as social events that have religious elements but they also give women an opportunity to interact with one another in the preparation of food, in art, and in discourse (Pearson 1996: 200ff.).

A popular vow among women in North India is to Santoshi Ma, a goddess popularized in Vijay Sharma's 1975 film *Jai Santoshi Ma* (*Hail Santoshi Ma*), about the efficacy of making a vow to her. After the film's release, this vrat became immensely popular across North India.

Women's Devotional Songs

Women's folk songs illustrate the perpetual articulation and reinterpretation of women's social and religious roles in oral traditions (Gold, 1996: 13). Women sing devotional folk songs about the gods (Shiva, Krishna Sita) and about their own experiences with their husbands, their children, and so on. Some of these songs have women complaining about the habits, behaviour, and character of their husbands. According to Gold, many of these songs depict husband-and-wife exchanges and construct a fictional intimacy that strongly contradicts anything visible or permissible in public; or they reflect on the culturally enforced distance between spouses and attempt in various ways to bridge this distance (1996: 16). These songs give voice to women's grievances and subvert the image of women as compliant participants in their oppression. They seem to illustrate Bannerji's point that "women make their idea of god their criticism of man's world" (2001: 202).

Sexuality

The variety of Hindu views on sexuality can be understood only in the cultural context of India, especially in the case of kinship and marriage structures. The control of women's sexuality in Hinduism, as in other traditions, is intimately linked to notions of purity and sexual loyalty: "Women are not to have any independent sexuality outside of the context of marriage" (Bannerji, 2001: 197). The practice of child marriage underscores women's lack of control over their own sexuality. The chaste wife, on the other hand, should be attractive and always ready for her husband's pleasure (Bannerji, 2001: 198).

Notions of sexual liberation that originated in the West cannot be easily transplanted onto Indian soil, where community takes precedence over individuality. Nevertheless, there are certain features of Hinduism that might be understood to challenge traditional gender roles.

Tantra

The term "Tantra" generally refers to a group of traditions and practices so complex and variable that it almost defies definition. However, central to Tantric traditions is ritual practice that often involves the sexual act, whether metaphorically or literally, as part of a highly controlled ritual event. Tantric practice seeks to harness "desire" for the attainment of enlightenment. André Padoux argues that tantric practice attempts to "place kama, desire, in every sense of the word, in the service of liberation . . . not to sacrifice this world for liberation's sake, but to reinstate it, in varying ways, within the perspective of salvation" (cited in Urban, 2003: 8). It is this emphasis on desire that has stimulated the fascination with Tantra in popular culture, in which, according to Urban, it is "usually . . . defined as 'sacred sex'" (2003: 2).

As Urban notes, some scholars argue that Tantra accords women a more important role than traditions that depict them as the lesser part of the male–female binary (2003: 6). Others, however, argue that traditionally there have been two schools of Tantra: a more conservative "right-handed" school in which the feminine is primarily a metaphor and women themselves are usually absent, and a more transgressive "left-handed" school in which women are present, but only as bodies that are used to serve male interests. As Biernacki explains:

> Textually, we commonly see women represented in transgressive, "left-handed" Tantras as preeminently suppliers of potent fluids, menstrual blood, and conduits for male ecstatic (and enstatic) experience. . . . in the "right-handed" traditions, . . . usually woman is displaced by the metaphor of feminine imagery. She is an inner principle, the goddess within the (male) practitioner (Biernacki, 2007: 30).

While Biernacki agrees that this view is generally descriptive of early Tantric texts, she argues that later texts offer greater possibilities for women as agents and even speak of women as gurus (Biernacki, 2007: 11).

Androgynes

Androgyny is not unusual in Hindu mythology and iconography. The most common androgyne is Ardhanarishvara, the lord whose right half is male and left half female. Usually understood in terms of Shiva and Shakti, the image is an ancient one, dating from the middle of the first century CE, if not earlier (Goldberg, 2002: 26). Like other androgynous figures, Ardhanarishvara is a male construction that expresses male attitudes towards the female. Although Shakti is the active energy behind Shiva, the male side is dominant: for example, when he chants the Vedas, she smiles (Goldberg, 2002: 99).

How women perceive this figure is unclear (Goldberg, 2002: 133). However, androgynes are sometimes seen as symbols of equality and balance. Philosophically, Ardhanarishvara can be understood as representing the eternal unity of male and female principles, the non-duality of Shiva and Shakti. The image functions as a devotional device to aid worshippers (Goldberg, 2002: 11) who seek self-realization of their inner male and female principles. At the same time, we should remember that these are male-defined images and as such are often associated with male fears of loss of power and virility (O'Flaherty, 1973: 284, 308).

Gender Ambiguity

In the Tantric tradition in particular, individuals are understood to be composed of both male and female principles. The primary deity in Tantra is envisioned as both male (Shiva) and female (Shakti), and most of Hinduism's male gods are conceptualized as incomplete without their feminine counterparts. In Hindu mythology, it is not unusual for male deities to transform into females. For example, Vishnu transforms himself into a beautiful woman in order to win back the nectar of immortality from the demons who have stolen it, and Krishna takes on a female form to destroy a demon. In some Hindu myths a male deity takes on a female form specifically to experience sexual relations with another man, and at the Jagannatha temple in Orissa, Balabhadra, the ascetic elder brother of the deity Jagannatha, is homosexually seduced by a transvestite (Nanda, 1999: 22). Male transvestitism seems to be the norm among the worshippers of Vishnu known as *sakhibhava*, and devotees of Krishna sometimes imitate his beloved Radha, to the point of simulating menstruation, engaging in sexual acts with men as acts of devotion, and even undergoing castration (Bullough, 1976: 267–8, Kakar, 1981, and Spratt, 1966: 315, all in Nanda, 1999: 21).

The *Hijra*

An interesting example of gender ambiguity can be seen in the *hijras*, whose cultural identity is shaped by their renunciation of male sexuality. Defined in Hindu culture as neither men nor women, *hijras* may also be seen as combined men/women or as an institutionalized third gender (Nanda, 1999: 20). Generally, *hijras* dress as women and use female terms to refer to themselves. They live together in households throughout India, and traditionally support themselves by performing at weddings, after the birth of children, and at temple festivals (Nanda 1999: ix).

Although they often identify themselves with the sexually ambiguous figure of Shiva, *hijras* will also identify themselves as wives of Krishna, and the experienced gender identity of many is female (Nanda, 1999: xix). Some are born hermaphrodites and some undergo an emasculation operation, although it is not clear how many fall into each category.

Hijras' main object of worship is the mother goddess Bahuchara Mata, in whose name they pronounce blessings on newborns and newlyweds. The origin of her worship is as follows:

> Bahuchara was a pretty, young maiden in a party of travellers passing through the forest in Gujarat. The party was attacked by thieves, and, fearing that they would outrage her modesty, Bahuchara . . . cut off her breast, offering it to the outlaws in place of her virtue. This act, and her ensuing death, led to Bahuchara's deification and the practice of self-mutilation and sexual abstinence by her devotees to secure her favour. Bahuchara is also specifically worshipped by childless women in the hope of bearing a child, particularly a son (Nanda, 1999: 25).

Linking the *hijras* to both Shiva and the mother goddess, emasculation is the source of their ritual power (Nanda, 1999: 24).

"As human beings who are neither men nor women," writes Nanda, *hijras*

> call into question the basic social categories of gender on which Indian society is built. This makes them objects of fear, abuse, ridicule, and sometimes pity. . . . [But] they are also conceptualized as special, sacred beings who have achieved their status through ritual transformation. . . . Thus, where Western culture strenuously attempts to resolve sexual contradictions and ambiguities, by denial or segregation, Hinduism appears content to allow opposites to confront each other without resolution. . . . It is this characteristically Indian ability to tolerate, even embrace, contradictions and variation at the social, cultural, and personality levels that provides the context in which the hijras can not only be accommodated, but even granted a measure of power (Nanda, 1999: 23).

Fire

A word about the Canadian director Deepa Mehta's 1996 film *Fire* seems in order here. This film depicts the relationship between two middle-class women, Radha and Sita, married to two brothers in an extended family. The title of the film itself is evocative in the Hindu context. While it is true that Sita (the name was changed to Nita in the Hindi version of the film) is not the only role model for Hindu women, she is a powerful one. The film is about the rejection of the traditional mould of marriage for women and about the sexual relationship that develops between Radha and Sita. The film sparked a controversy in India and was interpreted by some as an all-out attack upon Hindu values. It was banned in Delhi and Mumbai after violent demonstrations (Naim, 1999: 955). Critics argued that it presented India as homophobic; that it reflected Western perceptions of the plight of Indian women; and that it demeaned and caricatured Hindu family life. The film's defenders argued that lesbian love is not uncommon in Indian literature and tradition, but its critics maintained that the film suggests that lesbian relationships are most likely to arise when women are treated badly by men (Kishwar, 1998: 7) or that female homoeroticism is "caused" by denial of women's natural heterosexual desires—that is, a sexually denied heterosexual female becomes a lesbian.

Other Gay, Lesbian, Bisexual, and Transsexual (GLBT) Issues

Hindu views of sexuality are diverse, and there is much debate regarding the legitimacy of various sexual orientations. Texts are not explicit in forbidding non-heterosexual relationships. Indeed, *kama*—pleasure, love, and enjoyment—is one of the four pursuits in which humans may legitimately engage; the others are dharma (duty), *artha* (wealth), and *moksha* (liberation). The emphasis on love as an eternal force that binds the lover to the beloved is an important theme in the Hindu devotional tradition. *Kama* also refers to erotic and sexual pleasure of all types, as described in the ancient Sanskrit guide to erotic pleasure called the Kama Sutra.

The Gay and Lesbian Vaishnava Association provides information and support for GLBT members of the Vaishnava sect (dedicated to Vishnu as the supreme god) and examines third-gender issues in the context of the devotional tradition. Amara Das Wilhelm, a devout Vaishnava, tells us that "[t]hroughout Vedic literature, the sex or gender of the human being is clearly divided into three separate categories according to *prakriti* or nature. These are *pums-prakriti* or male, *stri-prakriti* or female, and *tritiya-prakriti* or the third sex" (2008: 4).

At the same time, Hindus tend to be conservative about matters relating to sex and family. Although there are numerous websites and blogs offering support for GLBT Hindus, and same-sex weddings are sometimes conducted with family support and in accordance with traditional Hindu ritual practice, many GLBT Hindus have left their religious communities, and reports of same-sex partners who commit joint suicide point to the social stigma that is still attached to alternative sexualities (see Ruth Vanita, activist and co-founder of *Manushi*, 2005).

That GLBT issues and personalities are becoming more visible is evidenced by the popularity of transgendered Rose Venkatesan's TV and radio talk shows (2008–12), which challenged gender inequality on a regular basis. Venkatesan was one of the first prominent Indians to undergo sex reassignment surgery. Her latest venture, a film entitled *Cricket Scandal*, examines the match fixing, but includes a love story between a cricket captain and a transsexual. Gay pride celebrations and parades in Mumbai, Delhi, Bangalore, and Kolkata, although relatively recent, have drawn large numbers of participants. Early Pride celebrations tended to focus on the injustice of Section 377 of the Indian penal code, which until its repeal in 2009 criminalized GLBT sexual relations and was commonly used to intimidate members of the GLBT community, although violations were rarely prosecuted. Adele Tulli's documentary *365 without 377* tells the personal stories of three members of the GLBT community celebrating the first anniversary of the section's repeal. The decriminalization of GLBT relations was an important landmark, but much of Indian society remains deeply conservative and homophobic.

There have also been numerous attempts to create a global South Asian GLBT identity by organizations such as Trikone (since 1986), which also publishes a magazine of the same name. Trikone's mission is to offer "a supportive, empowering and non-judgmental environment, where GLBT South Asians can meet, make connections and proudly promote awareness and acceptance of their sexuality in society" (www.trikone.org). Organizations like Trikone presume an audience that shares a distinctive yet global identity (Shah 1998: 150).

Social Change

The forces of change are as diverse as the roles of women on the Indian subcontinent. Among them are the following.

Bhakti

The bhakti tradition swept the subcontinent from the seventh to the twelfth centuries CE, emphasizing individual and personal spirituality. At its best, bhakti cut across caste, class, and gender lines and removed many of the barriers of ritual and religious practice established previously. Women in the bhakti tradition came to be recognized as spiritual leaders and models of devotion. Though it is true that this movement was rooted in brahmanic patriarchy, there is evidence that among certain groups women's religiosity did, in fact, challenge existing norms. The bhakti path is not woman-centred, but many women have been recognized as great devotees, including Andal in the ninth century and Mirabai in the sixteenth (see the following boxes).

ANDAL

Michelle L. Folk

The leading female saint of the Vaishnava movement is a ninth-century Tamil poet named Andal. Her poems, the *Tiruppavai* ("Sacred Vow of Pavai") and *"Nacciyar Tirumoli"* ("Sacred Song of the Lady") are included in the *Four Thousand Verses of the Alvars*, a collection often referred to as the Tamil Veda.

The Alvars ("those who dive deep into the divine") were a group of Vaishnava poet-saints who lived in South India between the seventh and tenth centuries and were believed to be incarnations of the attributes and/or companions of Vishnu. The only female Alvar, Andal was believed to be the incarnation of Vishnu's second consort, the Earth goddess Bhudevi, and is worshipped as such at the temple in her hometown of Srivilliputtar. The Alvar temple there, built in the thirteenth century, houses a manifestation of Vishnu flanked by Andal as his consort and the eagle Garuda.

Andal expresses her longing for union with Krishna (see Dehejia, 1990: 4) by imagining herself as one of the *gopis* (cowherding girls) who were said to have dallied with him, using sexual imagery as the metaphor for ultimate realization.

MIRABAI (1498–1546)

Leona M. Anderson

Mirabai was born at the height of the bhakti movement and is often credited with breaking down gender barriers. She was the only daughter of a Rajput chieftain in what is today Rajasthan. Her mother died when she was a child, and she was largely raised by her grandfather. On his death, an uncle arranged a marriage for her, but Mirabai took no interest in her earthly spouse, believing herself to be married to Lord Krishna. When her husband died, Mirabai is said to have been abused by her conservative male relatives, who locked her in her room and tried to poison her. During this time, she began to frequent the temple and converse with the *sadhus* (wandering ascetics), and eventually settled in Vrindavan (a town closely associated with Krishna).

Claiming the freedom to worship Krishna as her husband, Mirabai compared the longing of the individual to merge with the universal to the wife's longing to merge with her husband. She passionately describes the madness of her love and the pain of separation, using the traditional clichés of Indian love poetry to express deep religious emotion. The following extract comes from her poem "The Wild Woman of the Forests":

> The wild woman of the forests
> Discovered the sweet plums by tasting,
> And brought them to her Lord—
> She who was neither cultured nor lovely,
> She who was filthy in disarrayed clothes,
> She of the lowest castes.
> But the Lord, seeing her heart,
> Took the ruined plums from her hand.
> She saw no difference between low and high,
> Wanting only the milk of his presence.
> Illiterate, she never studied the Teachings—
> A single turn of the chariot's wheel
> Brought her to Knowledge.
> Now she is bound to the Storm Bodied One.
> By gold cords of Love, and wanders his woods.
> Servant Mira says:
> Whoever can love like this will be saved.
> My Master lifts all that is fallen,
> And from the beginning I have been the handmaiden
> Herding cows by his side
>
> *(Hirshfield, 1995: 135)*

Women Priests

The strengthening of brahmanic and patriarchal structures that typified the colonial period meant that women were largely excluded from the religious sphere. Today, however, many women are accepted as spiritual leaders (Omvedt, 2000: 190).

Hindu priesthood is traditionally a male domain and resistant to change. Yet there are no scriptures that prohibit women from performing priestly duties, and challenges to the male monopoly on priesthood have been underway since at least 1976. Today, schools throughout India teach women to perform rites of worship and marriage, read religious texts, and conduct various sacrifices (Manjul, 1997: 38); by 1999 more than 7,000 women of all castes had graduated ("Women Priests for the Jet Age", *Times of India*, 23 June 2002). Women now train other women, and the city of Pune has two schools that train female priests. There has been resistance, especially from male priests who resent the competition and argue that Hinduism did not confer upon women the right to perform rituals. Female priests receive a fee, though sometimes not as much as their male counterparts, and they use the income to supplement their family incomes (Manjul, 1997: 39). Though the numbers of women priests in India are still small, they are growing, and women priests are gaining steadily in popularity. As one client reasons, "Women priests do not take shortcuts while performing rituals" ("Women Priests"). Women priests are also gaining a foothold in other locations, including Australia, the Caribbean, and North America, where increasing numbers of women are officiating at ceremonies and rituals (Ramirez, 2008). For an insightful description and analysis of the ways women's roles in the temple context are being expanded and transformed in North America, see Dempsey, *The Goddess Lives in Upstate New York* (2006).

The training of women priests is not restricted to Brahmin women. Dalit women priests officiate at some temples, although this practice is controversial in these communities (Dorairaj, 2008). While women priests typically officiate at domestic rituals and sometimes at family shrines, the temple's inner sanctum is still generally regarded as the domain of male priests, but this too is slowly changing. For example, women priests perform rituals at temples administered by the Mata Amritananamayi Ashram in Kerala.

Women's Official and Unofficial Roles

The dichotomy between the public sphere as male space and the private, domestic sphere as the space of women is reflected in the dichotomy of the spiritual and the material. Women's roles tend to fall into the latter category and are often constructed with reference to the dharma, duty, specific to women. A woman's dharma is to devote herself to the well-being of her husband, family, and community. This is not to say that Hindu women in India do seek *moksha* as a religious goal. However, the path to *moksha* for women is still generally considered to lie in the faithful performance of religiously sanctioned domestic duties.

The role of women has been further complicated since the colonial era. Victorian gender ideology, based on the "natural" division of society into male and female spheres, was imposed on Indian society (Chatterjee, 1993: 35–157). Male and female categories became racialized, and private and public domains were altered. In public life, adaptation to Western norms was a necessity; but in the private sphere such adaptation would have been tantamount to annihilation of Indian identity (Chatterjee, 1993: 121). Thus the sacred duty of preserving the national culture fell to women. Partha Chatterjee writes: "In demarcating a political position in opposition to colonial rule, Indian nationalists took up the woman's question as a problem of Indian tradition" (1993: 119); and Mrnalini Sinha adds "[t]he Anglo-Indian strategy of using women's subordination in India as a handy stick with which to beat back Indian demands for political equality had converted the "woman-question" into a battleground over the political rights of Indians" (1995: 45). The result was a convenient explanation both for continuing to see women as guardians of conservative traditional Hinduism and for excluding women from public institutions.

Wives and Mothers

The duties of women centre on service to others, especially their husbands and children. In a very immediate way, a Hindu woman is defined by her relationships and in particular by the male on whom she is dependent at any particular moment in her life: father, husband, son.

Puberty rituals mark a significant moment in the lives of Hindu women. This is particularly true in South India, where the celebration of female fertility, marked by the first menstruation, is widely ritualized. Although in North India "the onset of menstruation is a rather quiet affair" (Alex, 2010: 317), puberty rituals for women in South India are noted for their elaborate ceremonies and festive sentiment (see, for example, Pintchman, 2007).

The role of wife is primary, and marriage is arguably the single most important life-cycle ritual for women. The ideal wife, the **pativrata** (literally, one who has taken a vow to her husband), vows to serve her husband as a god and to provide him with children (especially sons). Though there are many variations on this theme, generally women's primary roles are to produce sons and to facilitate their husbands' salvation by freeing them from mundane domestic responsibilities so that they can devote themselves to earning religious merit. By surrendering to her husband, by obliterating her own wishes, the ideal wife (especially the upper-caste wife) enhances the qualities of her husband and gains salvation for herself as well as for him (Omvedt, 2000: 188). The *Laws of Manu*, for example, states that a "virtuous wife should constantly serve her husband like a god, even if he behaves badly, freely indulges his lust, and is devoid of any good qualities. Apart [from their husbands], women cannot sacrifice or undertake a vow or fast; it is because a wife obeys her husband that she is exalted in heaven" (115).

It is uncommon for a woman to remain unmarried in Hindu India. Unmarried women are considered unfortunate, and failure to marry reflects badly on the woman's family as well as herself. An unmarried woman belongs to no recognized social category (Phillimore, 1991: 331), and women who do not follow the conventions that mandate marriage are often deemed dangerous.

Indian women's strategies for building a stable family life are varied, but their foremost concern is their children. Women can demand obedience, love, and service from their children in a way that they cannot from their husbands. As mothers, women are culturally revered. The popularity and power of mother figures such as Anandamayi Ma and Ma Nirmala Devi, who command huge

Women of Kamakhya, in northeastern India, perform rituals connected with a marriage celebration.

followings among men, demonstrate this cultural reverence (Kishwar, 1997: 25). As Bannerji remarks,

> It is not surprising that women frequently try to use the ideology of motherhood to their own advantage. As she is only sexual "for," rather than "in" herself, motherhood becomes a woman's preferred vocation in which a physicality of a direct but different sort with young children gives her some satisfaction and keeps the husband at bay within socially approved sanctions (2001: 198–9).

Woman as mother represents the nation or motherland, while man as father represents the state. Patriarchal control is exercised by the paternalistic male rulers of the state who offer protection to its women and children on the assumption that they cannot protect themselves. For women, the price of accepting this protection is relinquishing control over their sexuality (Basu and Menon, 1998, cited in Goldberg, 2002: 169, n. 2).

Widows

There are roughly 30 to 50 million widows in India today. Many now are able to remain in their homes and are treated with respect. But others face a bleak future, especially those who are uneducated and unprovided for by their husbands or relatives. Traditionally, especially in the higher castes, widows were not permitted to remarry, wear jewellery, or dress in any colour but white, and until independence in 1947 it was the norm for widows to shave their heads. They were often considered to be a burden to the family, and although there is no authoritative religious scripture to support this treatment, they were often shunned in the belief that their wifely devotion had not been strong enough to keep their husbands alive. In some cases a widow could escape such censure by performing sati, which represented the final and most perfect act of self-effacement and fulfillment of her religious duty. Through sati a woman could achieve her greatest honour in orthodox Hinduism.

Many widows have gone to live in pilgrimage centres, especially Vrindavan, which is sometimes referred to as the City of Widows. This custom was the subject of Canadian director Deepa Mehta's third film in the trilogy that began with *Fire* (see above) and *Earth*. Set in the late 1930s, *Water* (2005) revolves around a child widow who is taken to a widows' ashram in Varanasi. Despite protests that forced Mehta to shoot the movie outside India, the film was released in India in 2007 and received relatively good reviews.

Although such characterizations tend to represent widows as uniformly powerless and in need of an external saviour, Mastey (2009) found widows' responses to their condition to be highly individualized: a significant number of those she interviewed actually seemed to prefer widowhood to marriage.

Today remarriage is no longer forbidden; however, many widows are not willing to remarry because of the risk that would pose to their relations with their children (Kishwar, 1997: 24). The Indian government provides a small pension for less fortunate widows, although most women report that it is difficult to collect. There are also a number of training centres for widows, including Aamar Bari ("My Home") in Vrindavan, which opened in 1998 (Coulter, 2002). Organizations such as the Self-Employed Women's Organization in Ahmedabad have recently introduced a scheme whereby a woman can purchase insurance against her husband's death. Yet Mahatma Gandhi believed that a real Hindu widow was a treasure, a gift to humanity (Kishwar, 1997: 25). He further described her as one who had learned to find happiness in suffering and who had accepted suffering as sacred humanity.

Sati

The term "sati" means "good woman"—specifically one who serves her husband in every way. However, as we have seen, it may also refer to a widow who immolates herself on her husband's funeral pyre. The practice of sati is sometimes understood with reference to Sati, the consort of Shiva (see p. 36 below), and sometimes to Sita's fire ordeal. (In modern times the term has also been mistakenly applied to so-called dowry deaths, in which wives are set ablaze by husbands or in-laws who are not satisfied with the women's dowries; when their saris "accidentally" catch fire from contact with a kerosene stove; see Oldenburg, 2002: 200–8).

The British banned sati in 1829, and they were supported in this move by reformers such as Raja Ram Mohan Roy, who argued that the practice was not intrinsic to Hinduism. Modern Indian laws on the subject include the Commission of Sati (Prevention) Act, 1987, which problematically equates sati with suicide and treats it as a voluntary act.

Two famous and controversial satis of recent times were 18-year-old Roop Kanwar, who died in Rajasthan in 1987 (Oldenberg, 1993) and 65-year-old Kuttu Bai, who died in 2002 in Madhya Pradesh. In both cases, it was suspected that the act was not voluntary, but forced by family members or neighbours, perhaps in the hope of profiting from the erection of a shrine to the woman's memory. Such shrines are very popular: in 2005, a Rajasthan Tourism guide even advertised the state as "famous for its sati matas." (As a result of the criticism that this publication received, the references to sati temples were subsequently removed; see "Rajasthan Tourist Guidebook Encourages Visits to Sati Temples").

In the context of the religious life, Courtright (1995) has observed that wifely and ascetic duties are sometimes combined in the *jivit satimata* (living sati): a woman who intended to commit sati on her husband's death at their husband's pyre but was prevented and remains alive even though she no longer eats, drinks, or sleeps, sustained in life by the heat of her "pativrata dharma." According to Harlan, "the living satimata remains in this world but is no longer of it" (1992: 173).

Whatever the case, the practice of sati is deeply troubling, especially from a feminist perspective. Hawley (1993: 176) comments that feminists are reluctant to reduce sati "to its lowest common denominator—misogyny—and dismiss it. In part this is because the subject is difficult, and women themselves have differed on how to evaluate it." He notes further that "[b]y thinking about this common, complex object, feminists speak not only to the world but to each other. While they push back the boundaries of external ignorance, they also establish boundaries that divide and clarify their own group" (1993: 176). In this way, sati "points to both the crudeness and the subtlety with which patriarchal mystification can operate" (Hawley, 1993: 176).

Sisters

One of the most popular festivals in North India is Raksha Bandhan, observed in July or August. *Raksha* means protection, and *bandhan* means tie or bond. Together, they refer to a bond that unites male and female, usually brothers and sisters. The ritual is simple: the sister places a dot of kumkum (turmeric or saffron powder) on her brother's forehead and then ties a thread around his wrist. The thread symbolizes the bond between them: the sister seeks prosperity and good fortune for her brother, and, in accepting the thread, the brother promises to protect her and usually offers a gift in return. The myth behind this festival tells us that when the gods suffered a terrible defeat at the hands of the demons and Indra lost his kingdom, his consort Indrani prepared a charm and tied a thread around his wrist. Indra then easily defeated the demons and won back his kingdom.

Asceticism

Sexual abstinence in India is commonly believed to bestow extraordinary power on human beings; it is also one of the paths to liberation. Indian mythology tells of sages who practise such extreme asceticism that Indra's throne in the heavens starts shaking. In these cases, the gods usually send some exceedingly attractive nymph to distract the ascetic from his meditation. The message is clear: women impede asceticism (*Shiva Samhita* 5.3 in Bahadur, 1981; cited in Goldberg, 2002: 137).

Asceticism in India is mainly a male pursuit (Sethi, 2000: 13). Women who renounce the world are treated with ambiguity at best and antagonism at worst. The only specific prohibitions on female asceticism are found in the Dharmashastras, which forbid orthodox Brahmanical fourth-stage-of-life renunciation (Teskey-Denton and Collins, 2004: 23). Nevertheless, the female renouncer was widely considered dangerous because she was not bound to a male:

> By being wedded to a heavenly consort, the renouncer is like a pros-
> titute, the eternal bride . . . who lives her religious life outside male
> control. In seeking union with God, she is also similar to the widow
> who displays loyalty to her marital ties even beyond the life of her hus-
> band. Her self-denying and ascetic lifestyle is similar to the widow. . . .
> However such autonomy and agency was available only in relation to
> God. It is highly improbable that this had any significant impact on
> transforming gender relations among the laity (Sethi, 2000: 6, 14).

Nevertheless, there have always been female sadhus (*sadhvis*), and they have been treated with a great deal of respect. The epics also speak with respect of several *sadhvis*. Examples include Madhavi and Sulabha in the *Mahabharata* (Van Buitenen, 1978: vol. 3, 404–5, 410–11; Sørensen, 1904: 657; Badrinath, 2008); Vedavati in the *Ramayana* (Shastri, 1952: vol. 3, 420–2); and older female renouncers such as Sabari and Svayam Prabha in the *Ramayana* (vol. 2, 154–8; vol. 2, 295–7). Many of Hinduism's most revered female poets and mystics opted out of sexual relations, including Andal, Mirabai, Akka Mahadevi (who walked naked in twelfth-century Karnataka), and Lal Ded (also known as Lalla or Lalleshwari; fourteenth-century Kashmir), all of whom came to be treated as virtual goddesses.

Today, women account for a small percentage of India's renouncer popula-tion. Some sects refuse admission to women, fearing their corrupting influ-ence on male celibates; others, such as the Juna Akhara, are mixed, and a few are all-female. Teskey-Denton identifies three distinct modes of female asceti-cism: renunciation, whereby the woman symbolically dies to her former life and takes up a new one; celibate studentship, which involves service to a guru, meditation, and study; and tantric asceticism, which may entail a wide variety of practices (Teskey-Denton and Collins, 2004: 218–38).

To live the life of the *sadhvi* has been one of the few ways that a woman could escape the oppressive life of a widow, and so it is not surprising that a significant proportion of female renouncers have taken up this life after their husbands' death. Because widows and female ascetics both forgo jewelry and wear plain white saris, the two categories are sometimes indistinguishable (see Clementin-Ojha, 2000: 147).

Backlash

An obvious example of backlash can be seen in the movement that is sometimes called Hindu fundamentalism. However, it is important to note that this fundamentalism differs significantly from Christian and Islamic fundamentalisms in at least two respects. First, it is less a religious movement than a political one, represented by three parties— the BJP (Bharatiya Janata Party), the RSS (Rashtriya Swayamsevak Sangh), and the VHP (Vishwa Hindu Parishad)— and supported by a range of organizations, institutions, and temple networks that embrace the Hindu nationalist ideology known as **Hindutva** and seek to transform India into a Hindu state. Second, to the extent that it is a religious movement, Hindu fundamentalism reflects the diversity of Hinduism, with its multitudes of sacred texts, personalities, deities, and paths to liberation; some sects do not even require belief in a particular god. Hindu fundamentalism is not based on the claim of one true god, one true path to salvation, or a literal reading of sacred text. Indeed, one might argue that Hinduism is one of the most disorganized of religious traditions, and this characteristic makes religious and political solidarity difficult to attain.

An important feature of Hindu fundamentalism is its rejection of the West. Hindus of this persuasion see themselves as defending their tradition against the onslaught of Western colonialism and Western imperialism, against those Western traditions that claim an exclusive belief system and impose that belief system on others. Hindu fundamentalists are not missionaries and do not seek to convert others to their beliefs. Nor do they seek the creation of a Hindu state that prohibits the practice of other religions; although the charge of intolerance is often used to discredit them, their intolerance is not comparable to that exhibited periodically by Western religions. What Hindu fundamentalists do seek is to restore what they see as essential to the grandeur of the Hindu tradition, understood in their particular way.

The impact of Hindutva ideology on women is significant, because it calls for women to return to their traditional roles within the family (Robinson, 1999: 188). RSS and BJP literature is full of images of Hindu mother and consort goddesses such as Sita, who represent the traditional ideal of the chaste, devout Hindu woman who is subservient to the needs of her family. The fundamentalist position seems to be that though women and men are equal, there are essential differences between them (Robinson, 1999: 188). As Ratna Kapur and Brenda Crossman note,

> The BJP has stated that "men and women are equal but they are not the same." Since women are not the same as men, they are not to be treated the same as men. Accordingly, the BJP's policies emphasize the ways in

which women are different from men, and in so doing reinforce sexist stereotypes that have contributed to women's inequality. For example, the BJP support policies that emphasize women's roles as mothers and wives (maternal health care), while rejecting policies that go too far beyond these traditional roles for women (compensation for house-work) (1994: 42–3).

In her 2012 documentary "The World Before Her," Indian/Canadian film-maker Nisha Pahuja documents the tension between the contemporary world and the traditional/fundamentalist world on two fronts: that of the contest-ants in the Miss India pageant, which fundamentalists label immoral, and that of an annual fundamentalist camp that seeks to train young girls in what it means to be a good Hindu woman, including the duty to fight Western influ-ences by any means necessary. Hindu women are attracted to fundamentalism partly because it affirms their roles as mothers, wives, and daughters and partly because it does not reject popular Hindu traditions (Robinson, 1999: 196).

There are numerous organizations and roles for women within the vari-ous fundamentalist parties. The female wing of the RSS, for example, provides physical, intellectual, and spiritual training designed to promote "virtues" such as physical courage and strength as well as devotion to the ideals of Hindu womanhood. Both the BJP and the VHP also have women's organizations that affirm women's social importance, though decision-making is predominantly male. Much attention is paid to female members of parliament such as Uma Bharati of the VHP, who was elected in 2014 and appointed to the cabinet of BJP Prime Minister Nandra Modi, and Sushma Swaraj, also elected and named to the cabinet in 2014. Female renouncers such as Rithambara have also helped to promote the fundamentalist agenda. In keeping with the notion that holy women are embodiments of Shakti, they are referred to as *matajis* ("respected mothers"; Erndl, 2000: 94).

On the devotional front, a primary image is Durga, the eight-armed female warrior. Also important is the female image of Mother India, which portrays the country itself as a great goddess. This image was important during the campaign for independence and continues to provide inspiration, focusing attention on the importance of mothering and reproduction. The image of the motherland is also that of the reified woman (Sarkar, 2001: 51), and it is not without violent overtones. According to Sarkar, "the woman in this vision of Hindutva conceives and nurtures her sons as instruments of revenge; she gives birth to masculine violence; the space for this violence is reserved for men." (2001: 284).

Hindu fundamentalism presents a challenge to women's rights as well as to their individuality. Masculine images that glorify strength and moral fortitude,

such as the soldier and the warrior monk, are paradigmatic for male fundamentalists, while females adopt the roles of heroic mothers, chaste wives, or
celibate warriors (Banerjee, 2006). Because women in these movements uphold
women's traditional roles in family and home (Robinson, 1999: 189), they reject
the Indian women's movement as contrary, selfish, and Western (non-Hindu).

Unique Features

Several features of Hinduism are unique. The following sections focus on two
of these: the worship of Durga and Kali, both of whom represent a living tradition of goddess worship; and the way, according to tradition, different parts
of the Indian subcontinent have been sacralized by the dismembered body of
the goddess.

Durga

One of the most popular deities of the Hindu pantheon is Durga, the warrior
queen who rides a lion into battle and uses her beauty to seduce her victims into
a fatal confrontation. She is unmarried and possesses dangerous power. In her
most important role, she slays the buffalo demon Mahisha.

The story of Durga first appeared in the sixth century and can be summarized as follows (based on Kinsley, 1986: 96–7). The demon Mahisha is granted
a boon that he will be invincible to all opponents except a woman. Intoxicated
with pride, he challenges Indra and, having defeated him, takes over heaven and
begins harassing the devotees of the gods. Angry and frustrated, the gods gather
and emit their collective energies, out of which emerges a beautiful woman,
riding a lion, who possesses their characteristics and wields eight different
weapons, each representing one of the gods. Because Durga is unprotected by
a male deity, Mahisha assumes that she is helpless, but she challenges him to
battle. Ultimately, he transmutes into a buffalo and Durga decapitates him.

As Kinsley notes, "Durga is created because the situation calls for a
woman, . . . a peculiar power possessed by the goddess" (1986: 97). Furthermore,
"[a]lthough she is created by the male gods and does their bidding . . . [she] fights
without direct male support." Instead, she

> creates female helpers from herself. The most famous of these are the
> goddess Kali and a group of ferocious deities known as the Matrikas
> (mothers), who usually number seven. These goddesses seem to
> embody Durga's fury and are wild, bloodthirsty, and particularly fierce
> (Kinsley, 1986: 97).

As a female warrior, Durga turns the model of the submissive, subordinate Hindu woman upside down. "Unlike the normal female, Durga does not lend her shakti to a male consort but rather *takes* power from the male gods in order to perform her own heroic exploits" (1986: 97). By creating Durga from their own energies, the gods surrender any power they might have had to control her.

Once the demon has been slain and world order has been restored, Durga says that she is "quick to hearken to the pleas of her devotees and that she may be petitioned in times of distress to help those who worship her" (Kandiah, 1990: 23). Thus she becomes a personal saviour as well as a cosmic one.

One of the most important festivals in the Hindu calendar is the autumn festival of Durga Puja, during which the story of her victory over Mahisha is recited. The central image of the festival shows Durga with multiple arms, each bearing a weapon, standing on her lion and plunging her trident into the demon's chest. Clearly, this image highlights Durga's role as ferocious warrior and maintainer of the cosmic order (Tewari, 1988).

Yet Durga is also worshipped in her domestic capacity as the wife of Shiva and the mother of several divine children, and during her festival she even takes on the role of a returning daughter. The devotional songs sung to welcome her home and bid her farewell make no mention of her roles as warrior or cosmic saviour. Instead, she is identified with Parvati, the wife of Shiva, and as the daughter of Himalaya and Mena (Coburn, 1991). During Durga Puja, it is customary for daughters to return to their home villages, and their arrival is the cause of much celebration. At the end of the festival, the image of the goddess is removed and carried away for immersion in a local river. Many women gather around the image to bid it farewell, and it is not uncommon to see them weeping as the goddess, their "daughter," leaves to return to her husband's home (Coburn, 1991: 153).

The various roles of Durga do not readily blend into each other. Her ability to slay the forces of evil does not seem to give her any authority over her husband, Shiva; in fact, her position as consort does not seem to differ significantly from that of her female devotees. Still, Durga's power does serve as a reminder of the potential energy and ability in the female deities, and, as Pintchman argues, Hindu women can draw strength from her. Nevertheless, in Pintchman's view, there is "no inherent, invariable relationship between powerful goddesses and the advocacy of women's empowerment" (2000: 191).

Kali

Kali is one of the most popular goddesses in Hinduism. Strong, independent, ruthlessly violent, a threat to men and women alike, she embodies raw power, and for many Western women she represents the strength that lies unrealized in women generally. A Google search shows that her constructed capacity for empowering women is a major theme in internet culture. This is not necessarily the way she is viewed in India, however, and it is important not to lose sight of the fact that Kali herself is a product of patriarchal thought.

Kali makes her first appearance in the textual tradition in the story of Durga's battle with Mahisha, in which she emerges from Durga's forehead. Her appearance is simultaneously horrifying and mesmerizing: black in colour, with red eyes and a lolling red tongue, she wears a necklace of human heads, a girdle of human arms, and two dead bodies as earrings. She has three eyes and her hair hangs loose. In two of her four arms she wields a sword and the head of the demon she has just slain. With the other two, she motions her followers to fear not and confers boons. Sometimes she wears a tiger skin, but generally she is naked except for her girdle of human arms. She stands on the body of a figure, sometimes identified as Shiva. Her Shakti—her female power—energizes the entire world, but she prefers to dwell in the cremation grounds, where dissolution is the order of the day.

Interpretations of Kali's image often see her dark colour as representing depth and infinity (as in the void of space), the unknown and unknowable. Her blackness is understood to transcend all colours, as it is the absence of colour— "Just as all colours disappear in black, so all names and forms disappear in her" (*Mahanirvana Tantra* 13.5, in Avalon, 1972: 295)—and at the same time evokes our fear of the dark. Her nakedness represents a pure, untouched state, a state of innocence. But she is a naked killer, strong and hot, unafraid of her body and uninhibited by ordinary rules of human society. Without the illusion of clothes to cover her up and protect her, she shows us exactly what and who she is. She challenges us, provokes us to confront ourselves directly.

Her dishevelled hair forms a curtain of illusion. Her red, lolling tongue dramatically depicts the fact that she consumes all creatures. She tastes the flavours of the world, so to speak, and finds them intoxicating. She is all-devouring Time, the one who swallows the living and keeps their skulls around her neck, symbolic of her action, as trophies of battle or of the ultimate victory of death over life. Her sword cuts through ignorance, ego, and illusion; the severed head indicates the sum total of conscious knowledge, marking the separation of intellect, reason, and ordinary thought from true wisdom; the waistband of human arms represents work that hands and arms perform in the world and reminds us that all deeds produce karma and that the binding effects of this karma can be overcome—severed, as it were, by Kali. She blesses her worshippers by cutting them free from karmic bondage (Kinsley, 1997: 87–9).

In contrast to Shiva's sweet expression, plump body, and ash-white complexion, Kali's emaciated limbs, angular gestures, and fierce grimace convey a wild intensity. Her loose hair, skull garland, and tiger wrap whip around her body as she stomps and claps to the rhythm of the dance. She teaches us to confront suffering, pain, our own inevitable decay and death. Kali laughs mockingly at us when we ignore, deny, or try to explain away these facts of our existence. (See, for example, Kinsley, 1986.)

There are numerous Kali temples throughout the subcontinent, but she is most popular in Bengal. Animal sacrifice is an indispensable part of Kali worship: goats, sheep, and buffalo are commonly sacrificed at her temples (Banerji, 1992: 175). One of the most famous Bengali saints, Ramakrishna (1836–86), devoted his life to the worship of Kali, composing numerous poems in her praise. Kali is revered as the mother of the universe and all of its creatures. All of humanity is her offspring and she is fiercely and sweetly protective. She comforts and offers solace to those who seek her and her devotees tend to form intimate and loving bonds with her.

Kali's human and maternal qualities continue to define the goddess for most of her devotees to this day, but they never forget her demonic, frightening nature and the truths she reveals. The eighteenth-century Bengali poet and Kali devotee Ramprasad Sen mentions these characteristics repeatedly in his songs but is never put off or repelled by them. Kali may be frightening, mad, and a forgetful mistress of a world spinning out of control, but she is still the Mother and as such must be accepted by her children. In the following poem, Sen has to beg and cajole her to get what he wants. He often insults her, calling her stony-hearted and more. The relationship between deity and devotee here is very personal and passionate:

> Can there be compassion in the heart of one who is the daughter
>   of a mountain?
> If she is not unkind, can She kick her husband in the chest?
> Thou art called "compassionate" in the world; but there is no trace
>   of compassion in Thee, O Mother!
> Thou wearest a necklace of heads cutting them off from mothers' sons
> The more I cry "Mother, Mother", the more Thou turnest deaf ears
>   to my cries (in Sinha, 1966: 141).

In Bengal, where she is most popular, some female saints are regarded as embodiments of Kali. Among them is the blissful mother Sri Anandamayi Ma (see box, page 2).

The Shakti Peethas

The Shakti Peethas ("places") are sites that are believed to have been sacralized by the goddess. One myth of the origin of these holy sites is as follows (adapted from Kinsley, 1986: 37–8).

Sati was the daughter of Daksha Prajapati and the consort of Shiva. Daksha decided to perform a great sacrifice, and he invited all the gods except Shiva. Insulted by this slight to her husband, Sati attended the sacrifice, rebuked her father, and threw herself into the sacrificial fire. When Shiva discovered what had happened, he rushed to the sacrifice, hoisted Sati's corpse over his shoulder and began to dance the Tandava dance, signalling the end of the world. Fearing the worst, Vishnu hacked Sati's corpse from Shiva's shoulder and the pieces of her body fell to earth, scattering all over India (paraphrased from Kinsley, 1986: 37–8).

Each place where a piece of Sati's body fell to earth is considered sacred. The number of such sites varies, depending on the source, from 18 to 51. At many of these locations, temples have been erected to honour the part of the goddess's body that fell there: her breasts, hair, tongue, arms, eyes, feet, brains, nose, lips, chin, vagina, and so on. These sites are among the oldest and most important pilgrimage centres in India (see Singh 2010).

Note

1. There is some evidence that women were even permitted to perform sacrifices (Altekar, 1983: 198ff.).

Glossary

Aryans Indo-European-speaking people who appeared on the Indian subcontinent about 1500 BCE.

atman The individual's innermost self or soul or the universal self.

bhakti Devotion.

Brahman The absolute or supreme spirit.

brahmanism A social formation dominated by members of the brahmin (priestly) caste.

brahmin A member of the priestly caste.

dharma Duty, virtue.

Dharmashastras Law books.

Draupadi Heroine in the *Mahabarata* epic, and wife to its five heroes, the Pandava brothers.

Durga A goddess sometimes equated with the Great Goddess in Wicca.

Hindutva Literally, "Hinduness"; in modern parlance, the ideology of Hindu nationalism.

Kali A bloodthirsty but benevolent goddess.

kama Love, pleasure (including physical pleasure).

karma In Hinduism, literally "act" or "deed"; to be distinguished from Buddhist karma (the consequences of acts, words, and thoughts).

Laws of Manu   One of the **Dharmashastras**; a pivotal text for the subordination and mistreatment of women.

moksha   Freedom, liberation.

pativrata   Literally, one who has taken a vow of loyalty to her husband; a term for a married woman.

sadhvi   A female renouncer.

samsara   The cycle of birth and death.

Sanskrit   The language of many ancient Hindu sacred texts.

Shakti   Female power.

sati   Literally, "good woman"; a woman who immolates herself on the funeral pyre of her husband; the practice of immolation.

Sita   The wife of Rama and heroine of the *Rāmāyāna*.

Vac   The goddess of speech.

Veda   "Knowledge"; the Vedas are the oldest and most sacred texts in Hinduism.

vrat   Vow, religious observance commonly taken by women in Hinduism.

yoni   The female genital organ; often found in conjunction with the male *linga*.

Further Reading

Bacchetta, Paola. 2002. "Hindu Nationalist Women: On the Use of the Feminine Symbolic to (Temporarily) Displace Male Authority". Pp. 51–68 in Laurie L. Patton, ed. *Jewels of Authority: Women and Textual Tradition in Hindu India*. New York: Oxford University Press.

Biardeau, Madeleine. 2004. *Stories about Posts: Vedic Variations around the Hindu Goddess*. Chicago: University of Chicago Press.

Hiltebeitle, Alf, and Kathleen M. Erndl, eds. 2000 *Is the Goddess a Feminist? The Politics of South Asian Goddesses*. New York: New York University Press.

Jeffery, Patricia, and Amrita Basu, eds. 1997. *Appropriating Gender: Women's Activism and Politicized Religion in South Asia*. New York: Routledge.

Kinsley, David. *Hindu Goddesses: Visions of the Divine Feminine in the Hindu Religious Tradition*. 1986. Berkeley: University of California Press

McDaniel, June. *Offering Flowers, Feeding Skulls: Popular Goddess Worship in West Bengal*. 2004. New York: Oxford University Press.

McDermott, Rachel Fell, and Jeffrey J. Kripal, eds. 2003. *Encountering Kali: In the Margins, at the Center, in the West*. Berkeley: University of California Press.

Pintchman, Tracy, ed. *Women's Lives, Women's Rituals in the Hindu Tradition*. 2007. New York: Oxford University Press.

Robinson, Catherine A. *Tradition and Liberation: The Hindu Tradition in the Indian Women's Movement*. 1999. New York: St Martin's Press.

Uberoi, Patricia. *Freedom and Destiny: Gender, Family, and Popular Culture in India*. 2009. New Delhi: Oxford University Press.

Vanita, Ruth, and Saleem Kidwai, eds. 2000. *Queering India: Same-Sex Love and Eroticism in Indian Culture and Society*. New York: Routledge.

Films and Online Resources

365 Without 377. 2022. 53 mins. Directed by Adele Tulli. Follows three characters in Mumbai celebrating the first anniversary of the repeal of Section 377 of the Indian Penal Code.

Arranged Marriages. 2001. 52 mins. Directed by Carol Equer-Hamy. Explores issues of arranged marriages in India. Further information online at www.filmakers.com/index.php?a=filmDetail&filmID=1129.

Bearing the Heat: Mother Goddess Worship in South India. 1994. 45 mins. Directed by Kristin Oldham. University of Wisconsin–Madison, Center for South Asia. Various ways of worshipping the Mother Goddess in South India.

Dadi's Family. 1981. 58 mins. Directed by James MacDonald, Rina Gill, and Michael Camerini. Odyssey Series, PBS. The lives of women in rural India and their struggle over different interpretations of an ideal family.

Given to Dance: India's Odissi Tradition. 1985. 57 mins. University of Wisconsin–Madison, Center for South Asia. The film details traditions of temple dancers at the Jagganath temple in Puri, India.

The Never Ending Path. 2006. 35 mins. Directed by Annette Danto. Karite Pictures. The lives of women in rural Tamil Nadu.

Serpent Mother. 2000. 30 mins. Directed by Allen Moore. Mystic Fire Video Inc. Worship of the snake goddess Manasha in Vishnupur, Bengal, India.

Wedding of the Goddess. 1987. 76 mins. Film Distribution Office, Center for South Asian Studies, Madison, Wisconsin. A documentary on the Chitterai Festival in Madurai, India, with historical background on the festival and the re-enactment of the marriage of the god Sundareshvara and the goddess Minakshi.

The World Before Her. 2012. 90 mins. Telefilm Canada and The Rogers Group of Funds through the Theatrical Documentary Program. The film follows two young women: one wants to become Miss India, the other a fierce Hindu Nationalist who is prepared to kill and die for her beliefs (see www.worldbeforeher.com/#!credits, accessed May 2013).

See "Women Make Movies", www.wmm.com, for a growing list of films about women in various religious traditions.

References

Agarwal, Bina. 2001. "Two Poems on Sita". Pp. 239–43 in Paula Richman, ed. *Questioning Ramayanas: A South Asian Tradition.* Berkeley: University of California Press.

Alex, Gabriele. 2010. "Rituals of First Menstruation in South India: A Comparison." Pp. 317–30 in Peter Berger, Roland Hardenberg, Ellen Kattner, Michael Prager, eds. *The Anthropology of Values: Essays in Honour of Georg Pfeffer.* Noida: Dorling Kinderley (India) Pvt. Ltd.

Altekar, Anant Sadashir. 1983. *The Position of Women in Hindu Civilization from Prehistoric Times to the Present Day.* Delhi: Motilal Banarsidass.

Avalon, Arthur, trans. 1972. *Tantra of the Great Liberation* (Mahanirvana Tantra). New York: Dover Publications.

Badrinath, Chaturvedi. 2008. *Women of the Mahabharata: The Question of Truth.* New Delhi: Orient Longman.

Bagwe, Anjali. 1995. *Of Woman Caste: The Experience of Gender in Rural India.* Calcutta: STREE.

Bahadur Srisa Chandra Vasu, Rai, trans. 1981. *Śiva Samhitā.* Delhi: Satguru Publications.

Bandyopadhyay, Sekhar. 2008. "Caste, Widow-Remarriage, and the Reform of Popular Culture in Colonial Bengal". Pp. 100–18 in Sumit Sarkar and Tanika Sarkar, eds. *Women and Social Reform in Modern India: A Reader.* Bloomington, Indiana: Indiana University Press.

Banerjee, Sikata. 2005. *Make Me a Man: Masculinity, Hinduism, and Nationalism in India.* Albany: SUNY Press.

———. 2006. "Armed Masculinity, Hindu Nationalism and Female Political Participation in India: Heroic Mothers, Chaste Wives and Celibate Warriors." *International Feminist Journal of Politics* 8, 1: 62–83.

Banerji, Sures Chandra. 1992. *Tantra in Bengal: A Study of Its Origin, Development and Influence.* New Delhi: Manohar Publications.

Bannerji, Himani. 2001. *Inventing Subjects: Studies in Hegemony, Patriarchy and Colonialism.* London: Anthem Press.

Biernacki, Loriliai. 2007. *Renowned Goddess of Desire: Women, Sex, and Speech in Tantra.* Oxford, New York: Oxford University Press.

Bullough, Vern L. 1976. *Sexual Variance in Society and History.* New York: Wiley Interscience.

Chakravarty, Uma. 1998. *Rewriting History: The Life and Times of Pandita Ramabai.* New Delhi: Kali for Women Press.

———. 2003. *Gendering Caste: Through a Feminist Lens.* Calcutta: Stree.

Chatterjee, Partha. 1993. *The Nation and Its Fragments: Colonial and Postcolonial Histories.* Princeton, NJ: Princeton University Press.

Clementin-Ojha, Catherine. 2000. "Outside the Norm: Women Ascetics in Hindu Society". Pp. 145–158 in Alice Thorner and Maithreyi Krishnaraj, eds. *Ideals, Images and Real Lives: Women in Literature and History.* Hyderabad: Orient Longman.

Coburn, Thomas B. 1991. *Encountering the Goddess: A Translation of the Devi-Mahatmya and a Study of Its Interpretation.* Albany: State University of New York Press.

Coulter, Diana. 2002. "In India's Town of Widows, a Home for the Forgotten". *Christian Science Monitor*, 10 July: 8.

Courtright, Paul B. 1994. "Iconographies of Satī". Pp. 27–53 in John Stratton Hawley, ed. *Satī: The Blessing and the Curse: The Burning of Wives in India.* New York: Oxford University Press.

———. 1995. "Sati, Sacrifice and Marriage: The Modernity of Tradition". Pp. 184–203 in Lindsey Harlan and Paul B. Courtright, eds. *From the Margins of Hindu Marriage: Essays on Gender, Religion, and Culture.* New York: Oxford University Press.

Dehejia, Vidya. 1990. *Āṇṭāḷ and Her Path of Love: Poems of a Woman Saint from South India.* Albany, NY: SUNY Press.

Dempsey, Corinne, G. 2006. *The Goddess Lives in Upstate New York: Breaking Convention and Making Home a North American Hindu Temple.* New York: OUP.

Devī, Mahāsveti. 1987. "Draupadi". Translated by Gayatri Spivak. In Gayatri Chakravorti Spivak, *In Other Worlds, Essays in Cultural Politics.* New York: Methuen.

Dorairaj, S. 2008. "Priest and Prejudice" *Frontline* 25, 23, 8–21 November. www.hindu.com/thehindu/thscrip/print.pl?file=20081121252309800.htm&date=fl2523/&prd=fline&.

Eggeling, Julius. 1885. *Satapatha-Brahmana,* Sacred Books of the East, vol. 26. Online at www.sacred-texts.com/hin/sbr/sbe26/index.htm.

Erndl, Kathleen M. 2000. "Is *Shakti* Empowering for Women? Reflections on Feminism and the Hindu Goddess". Pp. 91–103 in Alf Hiltebeitle and Kathleen M. Erndl, eds. *Is the Goddess a Feminist? The Politics of South Asian Goddesses.* New York: New York University Press.

Foulston, Lynn. 2002. *At the Feet of the Goddess: The Divine Feminine in Local Hindu Religion.* Brighton and Portland Oregon: Sussex Academic Press.

Gold, Anne Grodzins. 1996. "Khyal: Changing Yearnings in Rajasthani Women's Songs". *Manushi* 95: 13–21.

Goldberg, Ellen. 2002. *The Lord Who Is Half Woman: Ardhanārīśvara in Indian and Feminist Perspective.* Albany, NY: SUNY Press.

Harlan, Lindsey. 1992. *Religion and Rajput Women: The Ethic of Protection in Contemporary Narratives.* Berkeley: University of California Press.

Hawley, John Stratton. 1993. "Afterword: The Mysteries and Communities of Satī". Pp. 175–86 in John Stratton Hawley, ed. *Satī: The Blessing and the Curse: The Burning of Wives in India.* New York: Oxford University Press.

Hess, Linda. 1999. "Rejecting Sita: Indian Responses to the Ideal Man's Cruel Treatment of his Ideal Wife". *Journal of the American Academy of Religion* 67: 1–32.

Hirshfield, Jane, ed. 1995. *Women in Praise of the Sacred: 43 Centuries of Spiritual Poetry by Women.* New York: HarperPerennial.

Hume, Robert Ernest, trans. 1966. *The Thirteen Principal Upanishads.* 2nd edn. New York: Oxford University Press.

Humes, Cynthia Ann. 2000. "Is the *Devi Mahatmya* a Feminist Scripture?" Pp. 123–50 in Alf Hiltebeitle and Kathleen M. Erndl, eds. *Is the Goddess a Feminist? The Politics of South Asian Goddesses.* New York: New York University Press.

Jamison, Stephanie W. 1996. *Sacrificed Wife/Sacrificer's Wife: Women, Ritual, and Hospitality in Ancient India.* New York: Oxford University Press.

Kaelber, Walter O. 1989. *Tapta-Marga: Asceticism and Initiation in Vedic India.* Albany: State University of New York Press.

Kakar, Sundir. 1981. *A Psychoanalytic Study of Childhood and Society in India.* 2nd edn. Delhi: Oxford University Press.

Kandiah, M. 1990. *Śri Durga Devī Temple of Tellippalai.* Delhi: Sri Satguru Publications.

Kapur, Ratna, and Brenda Crossman. 1994. "Women and Hindutva". *Women against Fundamentalisms* 5: 42–3.

Kinsley, David R. 1986. *Hindu Goddesses: Visions of the Divine Feminine in the Hindu Religious Tradition.* Berkeley: University of California Press.

——. 1997. *Tantric Visions of the Divine Feminine: The Ten Mahāvidyās.* Berkeley: University of California Press.

Kishwar, Madhu. 1997. "Women, Sex and Marriage: Restraint as a Feminine Strategy". *Manushi* 99: 23–6.

——. 1998. "Naive Outpourings of a Self-Hating Indian: Deepa Mehta's *Fire*". *Manushi* 109: 3–14.

——. 2000. "From Manusmriti to Madhusmriti". *Manushi* 117: 3–8.

The Laws of Manu. 1975. Translated by G. Buhler. Delhi: Motilal Banarsidass.

Lipski, Alexander. 1969. "Some Aspects of the Life and Teachings of the East Bengal Saint Anandamayi Ma". *History of Religions* 9, 1: 59–77.

Manjul, V.L. 1997. "The Hitherto Forbidden Realm". *Manushi* 99: 38–9.

Mastey, Nimi. 2009. "Examining Empowerment among Indian Widows: A Qualitative Study of the Narratives of Hindu Widows in North Indian Ashrams." *Journal of International Women's Studies* 11, 2: 191–8.

Menon, Rita, and Kamla Bhasin. 1998. *Borders and Boundaries: How Women Experienced the Partition of India.* New Brunswick, NJ: Rutgers University Press.

Naim, C.M. 1999. "A Dissent on Fire". *Economic and Political Weekly*, 17–30 April: 955–7.

Nanda, Serena. 1999. *Neither Man nor Woman: The Hijras of India.* 2nd edn. Belmont, CA: Wadsworth. Excerpts © 1999 Wadsworth, a part of Cengage Learning, Inc. Reproduced by permission. www.cengage.com/permissions.

O'Flaherty, Wendy Doniger. 1973. *Asceticism and Eroticism in the Mythology of Śiva.* London: Oxford University Press.

——. 1980. *Women, Androgynes and Other Mythical Beasts.* Chicago: University of Chicago Press.

Oldenburg, Veena Talwar. 1993. "The Roop Kanwar Case: Feminist Response". Pp. 101–30 in John Stratton Hawley, ed. *Sati: The Blessing and the Curse: The Burning of Wives in India.* New York: Oxford University Press.

——. 2002. *Dowry Murder: The Imperial Origins of a Cultural Crime.* New York: Oxford University Press.

Omvedt, Gail. 2000. "Towards a Theory of Brahmanic Patriarchy". *Economic and Political Weekly* 35, 4: 187–91.

Pearson, Anne Mackenzie. 1996. *Because It Gives Me Peace of Mind: Ritual Fasts in the Religious Lives of Hindu Women*. McGill Studies in the History of Religions. Albany, NY: SUNY Press.

Phillimore, Peter. 1991. "Unmarried Women of the Dhaulu Dhar: Celibacy and Social Control in Northwest India". *Journal of Anthropological Research* 47, 3: 331–50.

Pintchman, Tracy. 2000. "Is the Hindu Goddess Tradition a Good Resource for Western Feminism?" Pp. 187–202 in Alf Hiltebeitle and Kathleen M. Erndl, eds. *Is the Goddess a Feminist? The Politics of South Asian Goddesses*. New York: New York University Press.

——, ed. 2007. *Women's Lives, Women's Rituals in the Hindu Tradition*. New York: Oxford University Press.

"Rajasthan Tourist Guidebook Encourages Visits to Sati Temples." 2005. *Indian Express*. www.infochangeindia.org/women/news/rajasthan-tourist-guidebook-encourages-visits-to-sati-temples.html. Accessed May 2013.

"Rajasthan should withdraw controversial guide." 2005. *Times of India*. http://articles.timesofindia.indiatimes.com/2005-06-03/edit-page/27857035_1_sati-roop-kanwar-usha-punia. Accessed May 2013.

Ramaswamy, Vijaya. 1997. *Walking Naked: Women, Society and Spirituality in South India*. Shimla, India: Indian Institute of Advanced Study.

Ramirez, Margaret. 2008. "Shashi Tandon: Fulfilling Hindu Priestly Duties and Starting a Quiet Revolution". *Chicago Tribune*, 10 July. www.chicagotribune.com/news/nationworld/chi-hindujul11,0,6607845.story.

Robinson, Catherine A. 1999. *Tradition and Liberation: The Hindu Tradition in the Indian Women's Movement*. New York: St. Martin's Press.

Sarkar, Tanika. 2001. *Hindu Wife, Hindu Nation: Community, Religion and Cultural Nationalism*. New Delhi: Permanent Black.

Sen, Nabaneeta Dev. 1998. "Lady Sings the Blues: When Women Retell the *Ramayana*". *Manushi* 108: 18–27.

Sethi, Manisha. 2000. "Caught in the Wheel: Women and Salvation in Indian Religions". *Manushi* 119: 13–17.

Shah, Nayan. 1998. "Sexuality, Identity, and the Uses of History". Pp. 141–56 in Alvin Eng and Alice Y. Hom, eds. *Queer and Asian: Queer and Asian in America*. Philadelphia: Temple University Press.

Shastri, H.P., trans. 1952. *The Ramayana of Valmiki*. London: Shanti Sadan.

Singh, Rana P.B., ed. 2010. *Sacred Geography of Goddesses in South Asia: Essays in Honour of David Kinsley*. Newcastle upon Tyne: Cambridge Scholars Publishing,

Sinha, Jadunath, trans. 1966. *Rama Prasada's Devotional Songs: The Cult of Shakti*. Calcutta: Calcutta Sinha.

Sinha, Mrnalini. 1995. *Colonial Masculinity: The "Manly Englishman" and the "Effeminate Bengali" in the Late Nineteenth Century*. Manchester: Manchester University Press.

Sorensen, Søren. 1906. *An index to the names in the Mahabharata; with short explanations and a concordance to the Bombay and Calcutta editions and P. C. Roy's translation*. London: Williams & Norgate.

Spratt, Philip. 1966. *Hindu Culture and Personality: A Psycho-analytic Study*. Bombay: Manaktalas.

Teskey-Denton, Lynn, and Steven Collins. 2004. *Female Ascetics in Hinduism*. Albany: SUNY Press.

Tewari, Naren. 1998. *The Mother Goddess Vaishno Devi*. New Delhi: Lancer International.

Urban, Hugh B. 2003. *Tantra: Sex, Secrecy, Politics and Power in the Study of Religion*. Berkeley and Los Angeles: University of California Press.

Van Buitenen, J.A.B., trans. 1978. *The Mahabarata*. Chicago: University of Chicago Press.

Vanita, Ruth. 2005. *Love's Rite: Same-Sex Marriage in India and the West*. New York: Palgrave Macmillan.

Wilhelm, Amara Das. 2008. *Tritiya-Prakriti: People of the Third Sex*. Philadelphia: Xlibris Corporation.

Young, Katherine. 1987. "Hinduism". Pp. 59–105 in Arvind Sharma and Katherine Young, eds. *Women in World Religions*. Albany: State University of New York Press.

Young, Katherine, and Arvind Sharma, eds. 1999. *Feminism and World Religions*. Albany: State University of New York Press.

CHAPTER 2

Women in Judaism

Jacoba Kuikman

Women praying at the Western Wall, Jerusalem.

Jo Milgrom

Wife and mother, grandmother and great-grandmother—Jo Milgrom has fused these rich traditional Jewish roles with a vibrant and creative career as an artist. Tapping the deep resources of the Jewish tradition as well as her own varied life experiences, Jo creates art from junk, infusing new life into everyday items that others have cast off. Jo is an assemblage sculptor and poet who mediates between biblical texts and personal experience through verbal and visual commentary. Rooted in the ancient Jewish tradition of textual **Midrash**, Jo's art is a playful reading between the lines of an often laconic text, in response to the invitation to "Turn it [the Torah] over, Turn it over, Everything is in it" (Mishnah, *Pirkei Avot* 5:22). With delicious wit and humour, Jo has rescued discarded objects of all kinds, including ritual objects, from oblivion. One of her favourite ritual objects is the mezuzah, the tiny enclosed parchment placed on the upper third of the doorpost of a Jewish home to symbolize an *axis mundi*, a vertical connection with the Divine. Her creative interpretation of this, one of the "most under-stated" and "unappreciated" of ritual objects, invites us to contemplate this threshold passage as the intersection of time and space, the arche-typal sacred moment.

Jo's creations use biblical motifs such as Eve in the Garden of Eden, the Burning Bush, and the binding of Isaac, one of the most terrifying stories in the bible. Incorporating feminist and political themes, she often overturns existing conventional and mainstream Jewish customs and assumptions. Jo challenges the view of tradi-tional Judaism that has regarded any visual image as promoting a form of idolatry.

Jo's book *Handmade Midrash: Workshops in Visual Theology* is a valuable resource for holistic learning. In the practice of handmade Midrash or interpretation, discarded materials are used to create something completely new and fresh—a visual and sometimes visceral response to certain, often difficult, biblical texts.

Jo has held several exhibitions of her extraordinary work both in the United States and Israel. She has taught at the Graduate Theological Union in Berkeley, California, and is currently teaching at the Schechter Institute for Jewish Studies in Jerusalem. She finds Israel to be controversial territory for relating ancient Jewish texts through visual arts.

Introduction and Overview

Judaism is one of the oldest civilizations originating in the ancient East. The earliest history of the Jewish people, from their beginnings until perhaps 400 BCE, is told in a collection of narratives in the Hebrew Bible.

The Second Temple period spans a time frame from about 515 BCE, when the Temple, destroyed by the Babylonians in 586 BCE, was rebuilt, until 70 CE, when the Romans destroyed it again. This event heralded the beginning of the rabbinic period, during which the rabbis would collect the vast number of interpretations of biblical texts that for centuries had been circulating orally and put them into writing as the Mishnah, which together with the Gemara (commentaries) would become the text known as the Talmud. Thereafter, normative Judaism would revolve around the study of that text—study that for almost 2,000 years would remain an exclusively male endeavour.

Expelled from their homeland in the first century CE, Jews in Christian Europe were subject to ongoing persecution, murder, ghettoization, **pogroms**, and expulsion. Those who survived did so in part through strict sex-role differentiation, with women raising children in the private sphere of the home and men active in the synagogue and study hall. The Enlightenment of the seventeenth and eighteenth centuries allowed Jews entrance to the modern world as citizens, and many Jews assimilated into European society. However, the liberal German Reform movement sought to restructure religious practice and worship to resemble the dominant Christian milieu. This marked the beginning of the modern period, which saw the slaughter of some six million Jews by Nazi Germany between 1938 and 1945 and the birth of the State of Israel in 1948.

History and the Status of Women

A brief overview of some of the pivotal biblical events will provide a framework for discussion of the foundational elements of Judaism and the place of women within it. Whether or not those "events" actually occurred is a question open for debate; however, Orthodox Jews take biblical texts to be literally God-given truth.

The Biblical Period

Genesis 12–17 tells us that the patriarch Abraham made a covenant with God. In return for Abraham's promise to obey God's laws concerning the individual and the community, God promised Abraham and his descendants the land of Canaan. In their old age, Abraham and his wife Sarah had a son named Isaac. In what is usually interpreted as a "test" of Abraham's faith, God commanded Abraham to sacrifice Isaac but at the last moment stayed Abraham's hand, thus fulfilling the promise that Abraham would have descendants: Isaac's son Jacob, later named Israel, would have 12 sons, whose descendants would come to be known as the 12 tribes of Israel. Although Jacob also had a daughter, Dinah, she is identified only as the victim of a rape that her brothers then avenge. (Virtually nothing else is said of Dinah herself, except for the suggestion that the rape was a consequence of her inappropriately independent attempt to visit some other women.) While Abraham, Isaac, and Jacob are the patriarchs of Judaism, their wives—Sarah (Abraham), Rebekah (Isaac), Leah, and Rachel (both wives of Jacob)—are the matriarchs, who continue to function as role models for Jewish women.

A famine drove Jacob and his family to Egypt, where for many years thereafter their descendants, the Israelites, lived in slavery. Finally, according to the Bible, a leader named Moses emerged—with the help of his older sister, Miriam, who saved his life when he was an infant (the dramatic story is told in Exodus 2). Moses led the Israelites out of Egypt, liberating them from slavery, and took them to Mount Sinai, where God gave them the Ten Commandments. This event, the so-called Exodus, occurred around the year 1280 BCE and was followed by a long period of wandering in the desert, which ended when they arrived at the "promised land" of Canaan.

Living among the Canaanites, the Israelites found themselves powerfully distracted and challenged by the Canaanites' culture and their religion of many deities. Military leaders who earned the title of judge, one of whom was a woman named Deborah, were chosen to fuse together a struggling and often divided people. Around 1020 BCE Saul was chosen as the first king of Israel. His successor David, a poet and author of many of the Psalms, is considered to be Israel's greatest king, a messiah and model for the future messiah. Establishing Jerusalem as the capital city, he built a sanctuary to God/El there. David's son, Solomon, then built the first Temple through heavy taxation and forced labour, which led to the secession of 10 of the 12 tribes. The 10 northern tribes came to be known collectively as the Kingdom of Israel, while the tribes of Judah and Benjamin, which remained in Jerusalem, were known as the Kingdom of Judah. The conquest of Israel by the Assyrians in 722 BCE resulted in the dispersal of the 10 tribes, and today they are known as the 10 lost tribes of Israel. A people called the Samaritans, extant in small numbers in Israel and Palestine, are thought to be descendants of Israelites who intermarried with Assyrians.

This period roughly marks the beginning of the Prophets, who inveighed against idolatry and social injustice but who also comforted God's "suffering servant," the people of Israel, especially following the destruction of the Temple in 586 BCE by the Babylonians and the exile into Babylon of most of Judah. The Jews exiled in Babylon nevertheless flourished, and, in the absence of the Temple, developed other forms of prayer and worship. Permitted to return to Jerusalem in 538 BCE after Cyrus conquered Babylonia, the Jews rebuilt the Temple, completing it by 515 BCE. About 100 years later, two leaders of the Jewish community that had remained in Babylonia, Ezra and Nehemiah, urged the Jews in Jerusalem to adopt an uncompromising loyalty to the one God and his laws. Conversion to Judaism was now discouraged, since converts were likely to bring their foreign gods with them—this despite the fact that, much earlier, an ancestor of the great King David, a Moabite woman named Ruth, had been a convert to Judaism.

The women of the Hebrew Bible are not uniformly represented. Although not mentioned as frequently as men, and often not named, they are presented as subjects of historical events in both the private and public domains. While the Hebrew Bible is an androcentric text, it is not difficult to find role models for contemporary Jewish women: Lot's unnamed wife, Yael, Dinah, Tamar, Ruth and Naomi, and Judith (from the apocryphal literature), all challenged the male status quo, whether through their curiosity, their compassion, or their sense of human justice. For the most part, however, when women are held up as models, the purpose is to support an androcentric model or structure.

The Second Temple Period

Following the conquests of Alexander the Great in the fourth century BCE, the Jews in Jerusalem found themselves once again living under foreign rule. Some Jews embraced elements of Greek culture, and the Bible was translated from Hebrew into Greek. In 164 BCE, however, when King Antiochus IV Epiphanes tried to force Greek religion on them, the Jews revolted and reclaimed the Temple (an event that modern Zionists have often used to show how "tough" Jews once were). Until the Roman conquest in 63 BCE, Israel was an independent kingdom centering on the Temple cult in Jerusalem under the leadership of the Hasmonean kings.

The next 100 years saw the rise of several distinct groups of Jews, including the wealthy and elitist Sadducees; the Pharisees, or sages, who sought to apply the Torah (the first five books of the Hebrew Bible, also known as the five books of Moses or Pentateuch) to everyday life and created the body of material known as the Oral Torah (later the Mishnah and Talmud); and the Essenes, an ascetic and apocalyptic group often associated with the Dead Sea Scrolls (the first of which were not discovered until 1947). The synagogue, which may go back as far as Ezra (c. 500 BCE), was promoted by the Pharisees as an additional institution of worship, alongside the Temple. Although Jewish textual sources say little or nothing about women's roles in the synagogue, some Greek and Latin inscriptions include references to women bearing titles such "head," "leader," "elder," and "mother of the synagogue" as well as "priestess." This material suggests that some Jewish women did assume leadership positions in the ancient synagogue (Brooten, 1982). Following the destruction of the Temple in 70 CE, the pharisaic tradition developed into rabbinic Judaism, which has defined Jewish practice in every sphere of life for the past 2,000 years. The rabbis—all men—re-read, reinterpreted, and recreated Jewish texts, practices, and ideas (see Satlow, 2006: 135).

The Middle Ages

The Middle Ages in Jewish history span the period from the completion of the Babylonian Talmud, somewhere between 500 to 600 CE, to the sixteenth century, when Jews were restricted to ghettos in Western Europe. While there were large, thriving populations of Jews in regions dominated by Muslims, Jewish communities in Europe were less secure and often persecuted by Christians who regarded Jews as Christ-killing spawn of the Devil, and their religion as obsolete since the coming of Christ. Despite this diversity, all were governed by the laws of the Talmud, which relegated women primarily to the domestic sphere. The main sources of information about women in the Middle Ages are the letters written to eminent rabbis seeking solutions to legal problems. Although written exclusively by men, this *responsa* literature suggests the discontent and frustration that women must have experienced in connection with issues such as marriage, divorce, and the inheritance of property. The first improvement in the status of Jewish women in Europe came in the tenth century, when Rabbi Gershon banned polygamy among Ashkenazi (European, especially German) Jews.

Writing by women themselves from this time is either nonexistent or unrecoverable. In the seventeenth century, however, a mother of 12 children known as Glückel of Hameln in Germany did write a memoir that offers important information about Jewish women of her time and place. Relatively well educated for her time, Glückel (1645-1724) is upheld as a model of piety and loving-kindness in traditional Judaism.

Jewish women in Western Europe enjoyed a higher standard of living and were more active in family economic affairs than Jewish women living in the

Islamic world (Baskin, 1991: 102). Even so, few had any religious education, and those who did remained on the periphery of male-centred Judaism. Jewish women in England seem to have enjoyed greater freedom, particularly in the economic life of their communities. But on the whole, the expectations of Jewish women in medieval Europe can be summarized by the prayer recorded by one set of parents on the occasion of their daughter's birth: "May she sew, spin, weave and be brought up to a life of good deeds" (cited in Baskin, 1991: 94).

In the eighteenth century, the Enlightenment and the French Revolution (1789) opened the way for the emancipation for European Jews, especially those in France and Germany, if they were willing to give up their traditional religious practices and beliefs and their sense of constituting a "nation." In the early 1800s, efforts by liberal-minded German Jews seeking civic equality to harmonize Jewish tradition with full participation in society led to the establishment of Reform Judaism. Although the Reform movement took various forms, it generally embraced modern ethics and a more liberal approach to the Bible, seeing it not as the literal word of God but as the human product of a long and conflicted Jewish history. It was an attempt to keep modern Jews within Judaism.

More traditional rabbis in Germany, fearing too great a compromise with modernity, founded the Conservative movement in the mid-nineteenth century. Although they sought to retain **Halacha** (Jewish law), as well as the traditional texts, they did not regard them as immutable, and were willing to adapt their interpretations to the modern context. By contrast, what might be called neo-Orthodox Judaism insisted on full retention of the Halachic core of Judaism, and embraced Western culture only to the extent that it did not interfere with religious practices such as eating only kosher food and keeping the Sabbath day holy. Eastern European Jewry remained largely Orthodox in the traditional (pre-Enlightenment) rabbinic sense. Finally, Zionism was a largely modern and secular movement that emerged in the later nineteenth century in response to the anti-Semitism that persisted in Europe despite the formal emancipation of Jews by that time.

Jewish immigrants to North America took their different denominational movements with them. Although developments in North American Judaism are beyond the scope of this chapter, it is important to mention the emergence of Reconstructionism in the 1930s. A purely American phenomenon, this movement began as a kind of philosophy focusing on Judaism as an evolving religious civilization; it was not based on any notion of revelation, but rather on perceived human needs.

Various forms of Jewish feminism during the 1960s in the United States agitated for full inclusion in the Jewish religious community, specifically equal participation in synagogue services. Although the pioneering feminist theologian Judith Plaskow (1983) argued that the basic problem is not legal or cultural but theological—specifically, the traditionally male concepts of God—other Jewish feminists called for changes in Jewish law to end both segregated worship and discrimination in divorce (Ozick, 1983). These demands eventually led to changes in most branches of Judaism. The first woman rabbi was ordained in 1972 by the seminary of the Reform movement in Cincinnati. The Conservative movement elected to include women in the *minyan* (the quorum of 10 men traditionally required for public prayer) and in 1985 ordained its first female rabbi through the Jewish Theological Seminary in New York City. The Reconstructionist movement ordained its first female rabbi in 1974 in Wycote, Pennsylvania, and gave women equality in all its rituals. The American **Havurah** movement, which in the past couple of decades has gained in popularity in major centres in Canada, is a traditional and egalitarian movement that has included women in every aspect of ritual and has experimented with inclusive language.

As Susannah Heschel, a leading feminist scholar, notes, however, women seeking positions as rabbis even in liberal congregations have often encountered prejudice and discrimination (1983: xvii). And much of the liturgy is still riddled with sexist language that is exclusive of women. For Orthodox women who want to practise their faith within a traditional framework, the gains of feminism are even slower. One of the major issues for them is the height of the partition (*mechitzah*) that separates women from men in the synagogue.

Vince Talotta/Toronto Star via Getty Images

The first female rabbis in three traditions: Sandy Sasso (Reconstructionist), Amy Eilberg (Conservative), and Sally Priesand (Reform).

Texts and Interpretations

The number of texts compiled throughout Jewish history is astounding. The major texts are the Hebrew Bible or Torah (although, strictly speaking, the Torah comprises only the five books of Moses, the "Pentateuch"), and the Jerusalem and Babylonian Talmuds, the latter of which is the better known. In addition there are vast bodies of *Midrashim* (stories that interpret the Torah), commentaries on the Torah, various mystical texts (the best known of which is the *Zohar*), *responsa* literature from the Middle Ages, the *Shulchan Aruch* (a compilation of Jewish law), the *Siddur* (prayer book), and the Passover **Haggadah**.

The foundation of the *Halacha* (Jewish law) is the Torah. According to traditional Judaism, the laws codified in the Bible are authoritative and, by and large, the basis for the later rabbinic development of law. Because rabbinic decrees are related to biblical laws, they are also considered authoritative. Traditional Jews understand Torah to be the revelation through which God, creator of the universe, made himself known in history, and they believe its laws to be valid for all Jews in all times and places.

Yet women know that the Hebrew Scriptures are deeply patriarchal (see Elior, 2004). Modern Jewish historians and biblical scholars argue that some of the biblical texts concerning women (and later interpretations of those texts) are products of societies in which women's perspectives were inconsequential and invisible. Notwithstanding the abiding importance of Torah in traditional Jewish religious life, therefore, Jewish feminists question the authority of these texts. The Bible is a product of a creative, dynamic tension between biblical traditions and the experience of the scholars who interpreted them in order to make them relevant in new contexts. That is, the biblical texts and subsequent interpretations reflect particular times, places, and world views that were deeply androcentric. Critical biblical scholarship, however, has recently drawn upon other tools, such as social-scientific analysis, to understand gender in the biblical period. Understanding ancient Israel as a social entity makes it possible to see religion as only one expression of the Israelite experience. When other resources, such as archaeological evidence, are considered, our knowledge of the people of the time extends beyond the content of the biblical text (Meyers, 1988: 6–23).

From a historical critical perspective, the Hebrew Bible presents a diversity of images of women, reflecting the viewpoints of different authors and different socio-cultural contexts writing in a variety of forms—legal, didactic, historical, and prophetic—over almost a millennium. Yet with the rare exception (such as the judge Deborah), these images represent woman only as wife and mother. Perhaps the epitomic biblical text exemplifying the good wife and mother is *Eishet Chayil*: "What a rare find is a capable wife" (Proverbs 31:10–31).

Although a few women, such as Sarah (the ideal wife and mother) and Deborah are held up as role models for women today, many others, such as Jacob's daughter Dinah, are almost completely forgotten, proving the androcentric nature of the biblical texts. Jephtha's daughter, who (like Lot's wife) is not even named, is sacrificed for male ideals, and her life, unlike Isaac's, is not saved. And when God gives the Torah to Moses at Mount Sinai, one of the central events moulding Jewish identity, Moses warns the people, "Be ready on the third day; do not go near a woman" (Exodus 19:15). The issue is ritual impurity: according to Leviticus 15:16–18, an emission of semen makes the male as well as his female partner unfit to approach the sacred. As Plaskow (1990) points out, however, Moses does not say, "Men and women do not go near each other" (25). At a key moment in Jewish history, women are invisible in the text even though, as part of the people of Israel, they must have been present. Many women experience themselves as excluded and invisible during the annual reading of this text at the festival of Shavuot, which celebrates the giving of the Torah. Jewish feminists must reclaim these stories by representing as "visible the presence, experience, and deeds of women erased in traditional sources" (28). Otherwise the Torah will continue to be a partial record of Jewish experience. As Plaskow points out, "Modern historiography assumes . . . that the original 'revelation' . . . is not sufficient, that there are enormous gaps both in tradition and in the scriptural record" (35).

Feminist historiography, therefore, involves reaching behind the text to discover how women actually lived during the biblical period. This involves retrieving women's experiences in texts, events, and processes that were suppressed, neglected, or erased by both the sources and the redactors and that never became part of Jewish group memory or collective identity. We are left with the task of adding them to the records. This approach "challenges and relativizes those memories that have survived" (Plaskow, 1990: 35). Feminist historiography incorporates "women's history as part of the living memory of the Jewish people" (36). The recovery of women's history is not transformative for Judaism, however, "until it becomes part of the community's collective memory" (36). Accepting the "Torah behind the Torah" would affirm that Judaism has always been "richer, more complex, and more diverse than either 'normative' sources or most branches of modern Judaism would admit" (51). Many, if not most, of the Halachic rulings concerning women are rooted in the rabbinic literature, especially the Talmud. Jewish tradition accords the same status and authority to this literature as it does to Torah, perpetuating the idea (promoted by the rabbis) that it too was given to Moses at Mount Sinai and was passed on orally until the rabbinic period, when it was written down.

The foundation of the Talmud is the **Mishnah**: a six-volume code of law that includes all legal developments since the time of the Torah and was circulated orally for perhaps hundreds of years before it was put into writing around the year 200 CE. In the generations that followed, the rabbis studied and debated these laws, seeking to understand their underlying legal rationales and to apply the laws to new contexts. Debates were recorded in the form of questions and answers and included all opposing positions and opinions. The fact that some of these oppositional narratives suggest rabbinic resistance to male domination of Jewish women makes it easier to recover a "usable past" for Jewish women today (Boyarin, 1996: 118). Called the Gemara, this literature, together with the Mishnah, came to be known as the Talmud, which means, literally, "the teachings" (Hauptman, 1974: 184–5). Academies in Babylonia and Jerusalem appended material unique to their own contexts; hence there are in fact two Gemaras and two Talmuds, although the Babylonian version is the better known, and it is the text usually referred to as "the Talmud." The Talmuds are the texts most frequently cited with respect to the laws pertaining to women, especially in regard to menstruation, adultery, and divorce—all of which involve the control of female sexuality.

Some stories in the Talmud describe women's extraordinary religious knowledge. Perhaps the best known of these women is Bruriah, wife of Rabbi Meir, a sage known for his extensive contributions to the composition of the Mishnah. Her male contemporaries respected her, and her views are cited throughout the Talmud. Yet unlike her husband, who is cited hundreds of times, Bruriah is not mentioned once in the Mishnah. It has been suggested that Bruriah is a literary creation, designed by the rabbis to demonstrate that women should be excluded from study. Is she a token woman signifying that women *are* allowed to study Torah, or is her function to reinforce the rabbinic injunction that women should *not* study Torah? Whatever the rabbis' original intentions, by the Middle Ages Bruriah represented "the folly of permitting women access to sacred learning" (Romney Wegner, 1991: 76). The eleventh-century biblical commentator Rashi records that Bruriah's overconfidence led her to be seduced by a student and she subsequently committed suicide. The message here is that women who abandon their assigned roles in traditional religion and culture will experience tragedy. By contrast, Rachel, the wife of Rabbi Akiba, is an exemplary role model as a woman whose sole purpose in life is to support her husband's endeavours. According to the Talmud, Rachel lived alone and in poverty for 12 years, enabling the intellectually gifted Akiba to study.

While there are also several Talmudic accounts of individual saintly women and their great compassion for the poor, the Talmud does not hesitate to ascribe less than positive attributes to women in general. A dominant theme is that women are not only different from men but also inferior to them, especially in terms of their "physical attributes, their cognitive and affective faculties, and their standards of morality" (Romney Wegner, 1991: 77). There are myriad stories that describe women "as excessively talkative, sharp-tongued, arrogant and outspoken," prone to "cruelty, jealousy, vengefulness and . . . mean treatment" of each other (Hauptman, 1974: 205). "Women also appear to be superstitious, suspected of being witches, desirous of luxury, and quick to anger" (Hauptman, 1974: 205). With respect to these texts, it is necessary to point out that the view of an individual rabbi should not be projected onto the rabbis generally (Hauptman, 1974: 197). Nevertheless, it may be argued that these oppressive texts are indicative of general misogynistic rabbinic attitudes of the time. In summary, the Talmud presents a composite image of women with both desirable and negative characteristics. Positive rabbinic opinions of women, however, are dependent upon women's acceptance of their roles as restricted to the home and family, and this, in turn, reflects the social conditions of the time.

Just as important as the legal content of the Talmud is the haggadic material: sections "that record rabbis' opinions on a variety of subjects, legends about biblical characters, and stories about contemporary rabbis and their families," some more or less historically true but with "legendary elements" (Hauptman 1974: 197). These materials are included in the Talmud because of their ethical intent and because the rabbis sought to educate their readers through stories about characters with whom they "could identify" (197). When Dinah, for example, ventured outside of her home and was raped (Genesis 34:1), her family became embroiled in war and deception. For the rabbis this confirmed that a woman's place was in the home. Haggadah, stories, parables, and anecdotes in the Talmud, like the legal, Halachic materials, are not uniform in the view of women that they present, but on the whole, the rabbinic haggadic tradition views the role of woman as wife and mother. Not surprisingly, the worst possible disaster a woman could face, in Haggadah as well as the Bible, was failure to produce a child. The 1999 Israeli film *Kadosh*, directed by Amos Gitai, captures the tragedy of the "barren" woman in a profound and moving way.

Symbols and Gender

Symbols, perhaps even more than rituals and beliefs, are windows to understanding a religious tradition. Almost any object or even person can serve as a symbol: that is, serve to represent something else. Thus Eve—the first woman, according to Genesis—is synonymous with temptation and sin in the Western mind. Yet symbols are ambiguous, their meaning depending on who interprets them. Thus Eve can also be interpreted as consciously exercising her free will in the service of change.

Eve and the Garden of Eden

The traditional Jewish views of men and women, their status, roles, and sexuality, are derived from two Creation narratives in the book of Genesis:

> And God said, "Let us make man in our image, after our likeness. They shall rule the fish of the sea, the birds of the sky, the cattle, the whole earth, and all the creeping things that creep on the earth." And God created man in His image, in the image of God He created him; male and female He created them (Genesis 1:26–7).

> The Lord God said, "It is not good for man to be alone; I will make a fitting helper for him. . . . So the Lord God cast a deep sleep upon the man; and while he slept, He took one of his ribs and closed up the flesh at that spot. And the Lord God fashioned the rib that He had taken from the man into a woman; and He brought her to the man. Then the man said, "This one at last is bone of my bones and flesh of my flesh. This one shall be called Woman, for from man was she taken" (Genesis 2:18; 21–3).

These two accounts of the creation of Adam and Eve seem to contradict one another. While the first tells of the simultaneous creation of male and female, each in God's image, the second maintains that Adam gave birth to Eve via his rib. Rabbinic commentators, uncomfortable with two contradictory accounts of creation, fashioned a Midrash that made it possible to read the two stories as one continuous text. It describes the creation of a primordial, bisexual humanoid (Genesis 1) who was subsequently split into two separate male and female beings (Genesis 2):

> R. Jeremiah b. Leazar said: When the Holy One, blessed be He, created Adam, He created him a hermaphrodite, for it is said, *Male and female created He them and called their name Adam* (Gen. v, 2). R. Samuel b. Nahman said: When the Lord created Adam He created him double-faced, then He split him and made him of two backs, one back on this side and one back on the other side. To this it is objected: But it is written, *And He took one of his ribs*, etc. (Gen. ii, 21) (*Midrash Rabba Genesis* VIII: 1).

The text implies that a hermaphrodite is not merely an androgynous being but two bodies, male and female, joined together. In Genesis 2, the two sides of the androgyne are separated into two separate beings. The fact that the Hebrew word for "rib," *tzela*, can also mean "side" adds support to this interpretation. But it is immediately countered in the Midrash with the rib account in Genesis 2. This objection led to the normative rabbinic view that woman was created second and therefore was subordinate to Adam, although rabbinic literature retained the notion of simultaneous and equal creation as a minority position.

Another attempt to explain the existence of two contradictory creation stories was made around the eleventh century in a Midrash entitled the "Alphabet of Ben Sira." Here Adam's wife in the first account of creation—his first wife—is not Eve but Lilith, who, because she was created equal, demands to be treated equally. When such treatment is denied her, she flies away to the Red Sea, where she joins a host of demons and gives birth to hundreds of other demons every day. The tradition of Lilith as demon is as old as the account in Isaiah 34:14, where she resides in a desolate wasteland in the company of owls, ravens, jackals, wildcats, hyenas, and goat-demons. But her demonic roots lie in ancient Sumerian mythology, in which she appears as one of the four vampire demons. A Babylonian terracotta relief (c. 2000 BCE) identified as Lilith shows a nude and beautiful goddess of the beasts, with wings and owl feet, who stands on two reclining lions and is flanked by owls (Patai 1990: 221–2, plate 31).

Medieval rabbis and mystics described Lilith as a seductress who returns to the Garden of Eden disguised as the Serpent who seduces Eve. She goes on to make a career of seducing men who sleep alone, causing them to have impure nocturnal emissions. The rabbinic message to women appears to have been a warning not to behave like Lilith lest they become demons like her. Simultaneously, the rabbis and the mystics demonized almost any kind of female behaviour that was independent and assertive. Today, however, Lilith has been reclaimed from the rabbis, and has a prominent feminist Jewish journal named after her—*Lilith: The Jewish Women's Magazine*.

Modern Jewish feminists, attracted to Lilith's rejection of male authority, have begun to reclaim her as a positive symbol and heroine for Jewish women. Rejecting the patriarchal nature of the Midrash, women are rewriting the story to include the powerful idea of sisterhood and friendship between Lilith and Eve (Plaskow, 1979: 206–7; see also Cantor, 1983: 40–50). Eve, too, needs reclamation by women. After all, she was the one who initiated change in the Garden of Eden. Perhaps the prohibition against eating from the tree of the knowledge of good and evil (Genesis 2:17) existed to be disobeyed. Eve, like Lilith, refused to submit to male authority and became a seeker of knowledge, a tester of limits. She is a conscious actor who decides to eat the fruit of knowledge without consulting Adam. Thus embedded in Jewish tradition are several possible interpretations of the Garden of Eden story. What is absent is a monolithic interpretation of Eve's action as constituting a fall from grace, similar to that found in Christianity. The accusation that Eve/woman is responsible for "original sin" is a later interpretation from authors with different theologies, such as St Augustine. In the text itself, man and woman share responsibility for the alteration of their status and roles (Meyers, 1988: 72ff.).

God and Goddess

Jewish tradition recognizes that equating the symbol of God as male with God is idolatrous. At the same time, the images of God that predominate in the scriptures and other Jewish texts are those of Father and King. Almost every action in Jewish life is preceded by a blessing of God as Lord and King of the earth. Major litanies on the holiest days of the Jewish calendar repeat the epithet "Our Father, our King." Traditional Jews use exclusively masculine pronouns for God even though most would contend that God transcends sexuality. The problem is that the concept of a monotheistic, personal God in a covenant relationship with the Jewish people is at the "living heart of the Jewish symbol system" (Gross, 1983: 236). It is impossible to engage a personal Ultimate without the use of masculine and/or feminine imagery. A turn to a non-personal Ultimate would require relinquishing the notion of the covenant relationship. (It is worth noting that the notion of a personal covenant with God is symbolized by the circumcision of Jewish males on the eighth day after their birth and is therefore limited to men.) At any rate, anthropomorphisms, as inaccurate as they are in speaking of God, are inevitable (Gross, 1983: 237). It should be no less possible to pray to a God-She than to a God-He, though it would also be no less incomplete.

The obstinate refusal to accept this argument is located in the nature of those who have created God language, especially those religious Jews who have shaped the contours of normative, traditional religious Judaism. Because of the Jewish tradition's androcentric nature, women have felt alienated from it, excluded as they are from its meaningful elements. A first step towards the transformation of this tradition might simply be to address God as "She." The pronouns, masculine or feminine or both, might then develop into richer images of God, whether gleaned from within the Jewish tradition itself or from other religious sources. Some feminist scholars, however, regard movement in this direction as feminizing a male model, and they argue that it would ultimately be ineffectual in addressing the theological problem of the deeply imbedded belief in the maleness of God.

Female God imagery does exist in the Jewish tradition, although it occurs in patriarchal contexts. For example, the rabbis usually speak of God and his *Shekhinah*, the feminine indwelling presence of God. In the Exodus story (3:14), God reveals God's self to Moses in gender-neutral terms as *Ehyeh-Asher-Ehyeh* ("I am who I am," or, literally, "I am who I will be"). However, God is celebrated as the Lord of War in Exodus 15, and his power is regarded as the privilege of maleness. The few images of God as Mother—for example, in Isaiah 42:14 and 66:13—or elsewhere in the Bible as wet nurse and midwife are overshadowed by the predominance of male imagery.

Plaskow points out that the making of the one male God was a long process in the course of ancient Israel's dissociation from the polytheistic Near East, where gender was not an issue, and argues that "the rise of the one male God was correlated with a deep concern for gender as a central determinant of appropriate behavior in both cult and society and the exclusion of women from public religious life" (1990: 125). The gradual development of male God language in Israel coincided with the gradual marginalization of women in the religious realm. Symbols here "are not simply *models of* a community's sense of ultimate reality. They also shape the world in which we live, functioning as *models for* human behavior and the social order" (126). Male images of God serve both to describe the divine nature and to support a social system that allocates power and authority to men:

> When God is pictured as male in a community that understands "man" to have been created in God's image, it only makes sense that maleness functions as the norm of Jewish humanity. When maleness becomes normative, women are necessarily Other, excluded from Torah and subordinated in the community of Israel. And when women are Other, it seems only fitting and appropriate to speak of God in language drawn from the male norm (Plaskow, 1990: 127).

Together, male God imagery and normative maleness constitute a powerful circular argument. Another problem with the male image of God is that it has ceased to function as a symbol and has become an idol instead. As a consequence, what is worshipped is maleness instead of God.

Plaskow's analysis goes further. Although images of divine authority are diverse, they abound in images of power and dominance. God, holy king of his chosen Israel, is represented as a holy warrior who approves of both the slaughter of foreign peoples and the treatment of women as booty and spoils of war (Numbers 31:17–18, 32–5). Images of God as holy king and warrior deny human power and authority and encourage passivity. They "fail to acknowledge or evoke from us the energy and empowerment" required to struggle against the very oppression and evil that such images generate (Plaskow, 1990: 132–4).

Nature provides a host of images for God that not only resonate with our experience but also nurture responsibility for our wounded environment. In Alice Walker's *The Color Purple*, for example, Celie, a poor, abused black woman, discovers a different face of God in conversation with her lover Shug—a face other than the "trifling" and "lowdown" one familiar to her. Shug knows all too well the white, male God found in church. Celie learns from Shug that God is also found in nature, in the colour purple, and not over or outside it. As Shug puts it, God would be "pissed off" if we did not notice the colour of flowers. Celie writes in her diary:

> My first step from the old white man was trees. Then air. Then birds. Then other people. But one day when I was sitting quiet and feeling like a motherless child, which I was, it come to me: that feeling of being part of everything, not separate at all. I knew that if I cut a tree my arm would bleed (Walker, 1982: 178).

The white, male God is displaced first by trees, then by air, and only then by other people. Symbols for God drawn from nature cross religious boundaries, nurturing friendships and solidarity with other women in a time when the world is in crisis.

Traditional Judaism is ambivalent about nature, however. Anything that looks like the veneration of nature was (and continues to be) associated with goddess worship, a tradition that was carefully erased by the biblical writers. Yet archaeological evidence indicates that the ancient Israelites worshipped three Canaanite goddesses: El's consort Asherah (represented as either a tree or a nude woman), Astarte, and the Queen of Heaven, also known as Anath (Patai, 1990: 34–53). Saul Olyan contends that Asherah also came to be regarded as the consort of the biblical YHWH (commonly mispronounced as "Yahweh") on the grounds that Asherah was El's main consort in Canaanite religion and that the biblical writers identify YHWH with El (1988: xiv). Her statue was introduced to Solomon's Temple by King Rehoboam, his son, in or about 928 BCE, and remained there for 236 of the 370 years that the Temple stood in Jerusalem. Worship of Asherah was opposed only by a few prophetic voices (Patai, 1990: 50, 52). It is significant that the Hebrew people clung to Asherah as the loving mother-consort of YHWH-El for six centuries. Perhaps the nature-oriented worship of her tree cult was an expression of resistance to the abstract monotheism to which she eventually fell victim.

Proverbs 8:30 tells us that Wisdom (that is, Torah) was active in creation together with God. In Proverbs 3:18, Wisdom is depicted as *etz chaim*, the Tree of Life to those who hold fast to her. Asherah may be the model for the portrayal of Wisdom as a tree in this passage. The tree metaphor found with reference to the majesty of Wisdom in Sirach 24:12–21 would support this possibility. Here Wisdom is patterned in luscious, rich images of fertility and fecundity. She is the all-nourishing Tree-Mother who invites us to "[c]ome to me, you who desire me, and eat your fill of my fruits" (see Kuikman, 2000; Wolfson, 1995: 123, n. 1).

Female images of Torah or Wisdom in rabbinic literature are more metaphorical in nature and include images of Torah as daughter of God or of the King; as bride of Israel, God, or Moses; and as the mother where the father is God (Wolfson,1995: 125, n. 12).

The strong prophetic condemnation of goddess worship in ancient Israel attests to its tenacity in the tradition. Yet the fact that the prophets condemned it does not mean that Israel was responsible for the death of the goddess, as some Christian feminists have claimed. The accusation that Jews killed the goddess is an echo of the long-standing charge that Jews killed Christ. Assertions that Judaism introduced patriarchy into the world (Heschel, 1990; von Kellenbach, 1994) overlook the evidence of patriarchy in other parts of the world. Moreover, the notion that early matriarchal goddess cultures were characterized by peace and harmony is probably wishful thinking, given that goddess-oriented societies today, such as India, do not necessarily promote equality and justice for women. Also overlooked or neglected is the history of the ancient nascent nation of Israel as small and struggling in the context of much larger Canaanite patriarchal cultures. What is disturbing here is the (perhaps unwitting) resurfacing in some Christian feminist writings of the old idea that Christianity is superior to Judaism. The Jewish feminist critique of the patriarchal nature of traditional Judaism is an internal matter, and Jewish feminists resent being placed in a position of defending what they believe needs to be challenged in traditional Judaism.

Feminist Jews who are not comfortable with goddess imagery have a host of non-gendered names for God on which to draw from biblical and other sources: God as lover or friend; companion or co-creator; fountain, source, wellspring, or ground of all being (Plaskow, 1990: 161–5). The Psalms furnish us with rock and refuge. The Jewish mystical tradition has provided the image of God as *Makom*, literally "place," a sacred place. To imagine God solely as male is simply not necessary, even in traditional Judaism.

Sexuality, Family Structures, and Traditions

The traditional Orthodox view of sexuality is rooted in rabbinic concerns for family unity, including the production of children and future generations. Sexuality is regarded positively, as the God-given means by which the human race propagates itself. Sexuality must be controlled and mastered, however, in order to render it holy. In the context of marriage, sexuality is "an expression of the noblest human creative impulse" (Kaufman, 1993: 124). Unlike many other religious cultures, Judaism has shown some sensitivity to female sexuality. For example, even though women's own voices and experiences are not represented in the Talmud, one tractate (*Baba Metzi'a*: 84a) teaches that women have a greater sex drive than men (Biale, 1984: 122). At the same time, however, because the female genital anatomy is internal while the male is external, the rabbis believed that women are passive. Thus they tell us that despite her strong sexual drive, a woman is "temperamentally inhibited in initiating sex" and therefore it is the man's responsibility to initiate sex when he knows that his wife desires it (125–6). By contrast, the rabbis saw male sexuality as active, in danger of "running wild," and in need of restraint through the restrictions of marriage, such as the obligation to procreate (122).

The tension that women supposedly experience between sexual desire and passivity was interpreted by the rabbis as part of the curse of Eve, which all women have supposedly inherited. While the first part of the curse according to Genesis 3:16 is the pain of childbirth, the second reads, "Your desire shall be for your husband, and he shall rule over you." Precisely what this passage means is not clear. Generally, though, women are seen as caught in a bind between sexual desire and servility: "Whether because she cannot initiate sex, or because she 'pays' for her sexual desire with total obedience, the woman's curse is bound up with her sexuality" (Biale, 1984: 125).

Traditional scholars sometimes contrast Judaism's attitude towards sexuality with the more negative attitude of classical Christianity, in which sexuality and original sin are seen as products of Eve's sin (see, for example, Kaufman, 1993: 123). But in fact the Talmudic literature is ambiguous. The rabbis say, "Let us be thankful to our forefathers, for if they had not sinned we would not have come into this world" (*Avodah Zarah*: 5a, cited in Biale, 1984: 121). Yet it appears that some of their views on sexuality do not differ all that much from those in other Western religious traditions. The rabbis saw sexuality as potentially dangerous and therefore in need of regulation (121). In addition to restricting sexual expression to marriage, they strictly forbade sexual contact during menstruation. The laws of *niddah* (a Hebrew term referring to a woman who is ostracized or excluded) are based on Leviticus 15:19: "When a woman has a flow of blood where blood flows from her body, she shall be a *niddah* for seven days; whoever touches her shall be unclean until evening." Two additional texts, Leviticus 18:19 and 20:18, explicitly forbid sexual relations during menstruation. During the biblical period, a woman would be prohibited from engaging in sexual relations with her husband for seven days, and she would remain unclean until she immersed herself in a mikvah (ritual bath).

The laws of *tumah* (ritual impurity) were complex and forbade several additional kinds of contamination, such as contact with leprosy and seminal discharge; the ultimate source of *tumah* was the corpse. The purpose of those laws was to prevent impure persons from entering the Temple, where the divine Presence resided (see Leviticus 11–15). After the destruction of the Second

Temple in 70 CE, most of them became inoperative, but the laws of *niddah* were retained when religious observance shifted from the public, cultic sphere of the Temple to the private sphere of family life (Biale, 1984: 147–8).

Contemporary justifications for the laws of family purity include the idea that mutual love and devotion can be expressed in ways other than physical. The separation, we are told, can be a time for "intimacy of the spirit," a break from mechanical, monotonous sex. Monthly separation, furthermore, is said to increase desire for sexual expression. There is a kind of revival in the practice of family purity laws among some Jewish women in that it affirms their independence and discourages the treatment of women as sex objects (Kaufman, 1993: 145–51). Some Jewish feminists adhere to family purity laws because of their symbolic value. For them, *tumah* signifies an end of a cycle, a dying, when the rich, potentially life-giving menstrual blood leaves the body. *Taharah* (ritual purity) represents the return to potential life in the womb. Menstruation is thus a nexus point, symbolizing both an end of life and the beginning of something new (Adler, 1976: 66).

Other feminist scholars, however, have raised several issues regarding the laws of *niddah*. A recurring question is why menstruation was the only form of impurity that remained after the destruction of the Second Temple. Recognition of ritual impurity (*tumah*) only in the context of menstruation suggests a stigma or taboo based on male fear of women's sexuality and menstrual blood (Cantor, 1995: 138; Koltun, 1976: 69). That the rabbis extended the period of women's impurity from 7 days to 14 would seem to cast doubt on protestations that *tumah* is not regarded as pollution, as it was in other ancient religious societies.

Scholars generally agree that the Talmudic tractate *Niddah* expresses the rabbis' disgust at female bodily functions. It also suggests fear, especially the fear of being overwhelmed by female sexual power. Thus it may have been in men's interest to create a system in which men did not have to deal with women's sexuality for half of each month (Cantor, 1995: 138). However, as one scholar observes, the *tumah/taharah* symbolic system is at least inclusive of women. Rachel Adler asks why one should reject it just because the later generations of rabbis "projected their repugnance for women upon it" (1976: 71).

Social Change

In a world full of injustices such as sexism, classism, capitalism, and racism, Judaism has embedded within it the seeds of social action. Yet the job of transforming unjust social structures has generally been left to the "often dirty" realm of politics, which has been unhelpfully severed from the realm of spirituality (Plaskow, 1990: 213). Unlike traditional Christianity, Judaism has always been infused with the notion that fidelity to Halacha and rootedness in the world go hand in hand, although the latter has not usually been translated into political terms (214). It is here that Jewish tradition and concrete feminist concerns for social justice converge most strongly.

The idea of working for peace and justice is rooted in the writings of the prophets, who criticized worship without the practice of social justice for those most in need, the orphan and the widow, and the poor:

> Is not this the fast that I choose: to loose the bonds of injustice, to undo the thongs of the yoke, to let the oppressed go free, and to break every yoke? Is it not to share your bread with the hungry, and bring the homeless poor into your house; when you see the naked, to cover them, and not to hide yourself from your own kin? (Isaiah 58:6–7)

The prophetic critique of religion devoid of social justice undermines observance of Jewish law for its own sake. Yet it is the intention of the law to infuse the world with justice. For example, even before the prophets, there is the command of God, through Moses, to "love the stranger, for you were once strangers in the land of Egypt" (Exodus 22:21). The Jewish tradition of *t'shuvah*— repentance (literally, turning around in a different direction)—contains the possibility of change at both the individual and the social or communal levels.

The mystical concept of Tikkun Olam (literally, "mending the world") has many layers of meaning and has not always been applied politically. But it has its roots in the mystical experiences and visions of the Prophets. Though never fully endorsed by the rabbis because of its intense speculation on the nature of God, mysticism has nevertheless persisted in Judaism; the idea of Tikkun Olam has ensured that Jewish mysticism has remained profoundly connected to the world and its problems. Isaac Luria (1534–72) sought to explain the demise of the great Jewish community in Spain in 1492 through the concept of Tikkun as well as two other concepts: *tzimtzum* and *shevirat ha kelim*. The mystical concept of creation, as Luria envisioned it, required *tzimtzum*, or the withdrawal of God from the universe, in order to make room for the creation. Miscalculation of God's own power resulted in *shevirat ha kelim*, or breaking of the vessels intended to hold the divine light. As a result, evil was released in the world, and the *Shekhinah*, God's feminine indwelling presence in the world, was exiled. The sparks of God were scattered and God's internal unity was disrupted. Tikkun Olam, in Lurianic understanding, meant "gathering the sparks" and returning them to the *Shekhinah*, the channel to God, and thus restoring God as well as the world. Originally, restoration required intense devotion to God and adherence to the commandments, but later transformations of Jewish mysticism (through Hasidism and the activism of the nineteenth century) added a more political dimension to the notion of Tikkun, as is evident today in the progressive magazine *Tikkun*.

Tikkun Olam, or "mending the world," can take different forms, but for Jewish women, Tikkun must begin with reform of the hierarchical leadership structures in most synagogues and in Jewish social institutions, as well as the various religious structures that exclude women. But it must also extend to the larger process of transforming political and economic structures of domination. Concern for Halachic change and fuller inclusion for women in the religious realm have been extended to include justice concerns for all women, everywhere, linking the spiritual and the political.

Women in Black, for example, is a network of women committed to peace and justice around the world. Its members dress in black and hold non-violent vigils wherever a certain context of injustice demands opposition. The movement began in Israel in 1988 with Israeli and Palestinian women and their supporters protesting the Israeli occupation of the West Bank and Gaza. Similarly, Bat Shalom is a feminist organization of Israeli women working together with Palestinian women's groups toward peaceful cooperation between Israelis and Palestinians.

Jewish dietary laws (*kashrut*) have traditionally reflected a concern for the welfare of animals and a sense of the sanctity of the basic necessity of eating. Feminist Jews and others concerned about the growing poverty in the world suggest that eating "low on the food chain" and a vegetarian diet would preserve more grain for world consumption. The inhumane raising of animals for food and the diseases linked with beef production would support this. *Kashrut* might be extended to prohibiting foods produced with pesticides and herbicides as well as foods containing hormones (Plaskow, 1990: 236). Many foods are produced for Western consumption using exploitative labour practices in poorer parts of the world. Placing these products on the list of forbidden (that is, non-kosher) foods might help to create a greater awareness of the economic and social conditions faced by people in developing countries and how the West is implicated in them.

The minor holiday of Tu Bishvat, the new year of trees, might be made into a major environmental holiday by emphasizing the interconnectedness and relational character of all life in the world (Plaskow, 1990: 237). Observance of such a day would help to undercut the dualism that pits nature and inferior matter against the superior realm of spirit and the divine. Recognition of the divine within, rather than outside, nature might nurture respect for the trees to which we, as physical beings dependent on oxygen, owe our existence. Besides providing us with that oxygen, trees remove carbon dioxide from the environment. The continued buildup of carbon dioxide in the ecosphere over the past few decades through increasing carbon emissions and rapidly diminishing forests around the globe has led to growing concerns about global warming. Recognizing the tree as sacred would not rule out an "I–Thou relationship"—to quote Martin Buber—with trees. In the 1994 Israeli film *Under the Domim Tree*, which tells the story of teenaged Holocaust survivors attending a youth camp/boarding school in Israel in the early 1950s, the most sought-after place for solitude and healing is under the domim tree, and it is almost always "occupied." The survivors' experience of sacred place is consistent with mystical Judaism, in which a non-gendered name for God is *Makom*—literally, "Place."

Celebration of Tu Bishvat as a sacred day for trees could connect with a larger esoteric philosophy common to many cultures and mythologies, that of the "Tree of Life," or Cosmic Tree. Often regarded as an all-nourishing Mother, the Cosmic Tree occurs in many myths as active in the creation of the world. She is *axis mundi*: she stands in the centre of the world, continuing to nourish it. She embodies the Divine in the cycles of rebirth, continual creation, and never-ending life. As we have seen, the ancient Hebrew goddess Asherah was often lovingly depicted in the form of a tree, and in Proverbs 3:18 Torah (Wisdom) appears as the Tree of Life.

Ritualizing concerns for the environment is another way of bringing together the spiritual and the political. In the case of Tu Bishvat, the spiritual realm might well be a means to sustain us through the long political struggle to establish a sustainable way of life.

Women's Official and Unofficial Roles

The complementary positions that women and men were assigned in the private and public spheres of traditional Jewish life are rooted in the ancient texts, particularly the Hebrew Bible. The survival of the ancient Israelites depended on childbearing. The four matriarchs of the Bible—Sarah, Rebekah, Rachel, and Leah—are regarded as models to be emulated, especially in the realm of motherhood. To be fertile was a blessing, while to be barren was a misfortune at best and a disaster at worst. When Ruth, the convert to Israel, is betrothed to Boaz, she is blessed with the wish that she will be "like Rachel and Leah, who together built up the house of Israel" (Ruth 4:11), and the wish comes true: her son, Obed, becomes the grandfather of King David, forerunner of the future messiah.

Sarah is exemplary in that she embodies the Jewish ideal of modesty. Her spirituality is evidenced by her fervent devotion to all her household tasks, including hospitality (Kaufman, 1993: 48–9). Sarah is one of the first women in the Bible to work quietly and subtly behind the scenes to help bring about redemption of the world—to bring the world to a state intended by God. One traditional interpretation of Sarah's banishment of Ishmael, the son of Hagar, her husband Abraham's concubine (Genesis 21), is that she is more spiritually astute than he, and therefore is able to see that Isaac, not Ishmael, is Israel's hope for the future (Aiken, 1992: 47). The traditional ideal of modesty and the notion that women live on a higher spiritual plane than men are recurrent themes that justify placing restrictions on women and limiting their roles to the private sphere. Indeed, in traditional Judaism Sarah is to be protected as one would an "invaluable pearl" (Ghatan, 1986: 65).

Some traditional Jewish women regard motherhood as an opening to the world of the spirit. "The fact that the tradition attributes prophecy, the ability to see the future, to several other biblical women besides Sarah, including Rebecca, Rachel and Leah, attests to the importance of these women as role models" (Frankiel, 1990: 6). Their exercise of power in the realm of the household reinforces the notion that men and women have different but complementary roles, although there are exceptions to this general rule, including the judge Deborah (Judges 3–16), and Huldah the prophetess (2 Chronicles 35:22–8).

Aside from the few female heroes already mentioned (such as Deborah the judge), who are exceptions to the male-centred biblical tradition, there are female figures in the tradition that might be referred to as negative role models. Yael, for example, who is mentioned in connection with Deborah, kills Sisera, a general of the Canaanite army at war with Israel, by hammering a tent peg through his skull when he seeks refuge in her tent (Niditch, 1989: 46).

The roles of women in Judaism vary depending on culture and location. The lives of Sephardi[2] women in Muslim-controlled medieval Spain, for example, were for the most part limited to the home. Then, in the late fifteenth century, under Christian pressure to either convert to Christianity or leave the country, many Jews converted but kept their Jewish traditions alive in secret, at great risk to their lives, always under threat from the Inquisition. Jewish women played an important role in maintaining certain observances—especially those related to the dietary laws and the Sabbath—in secret.

Peculiar to Central and Eastern European Jewish women was the recitation of *tkhines*, prayers in the colloquial Yiddish[3] rather than Hebrew, the language of public ritual and scholarship from which women were excluded. Though largely written by men, these prayers suggest that ordinary uneducated Jewish women could have rich religious lives around biological events such as menstruation, pregnancy, and childbirth, as well as various domestic duties. Although excluded from communal worship, women could develop individual spirituality in the context of the home (Weissler, 1991: 159–81).

A study of elderly, pious Kurdish and other Middle Eastern Jewish women living in Jerusalem in the 1980s reveals how they have sacralized the female domestic domain. This is a shift away from the study of female symbols and the official roles of women as described by men, in which women are treated as objects, to the study of women's lives as they are actually lived (Starr Sered, 1992: 7). Functioning within the male-oriented normative and religious system, they have developed "an alternative scale of measuring value and worth"; in the female domains of family and kitchen, caring for neighbours, giving to charity, and tending to tombs of family and saints, these women have "a great deal of power and autonomy" (4, 139). By creating their own traditions, these women have established a rich religious world of meaning and control.

The twentieth-century experience of North American Jewish women (and men) confirms that scholarly study and communal worship are not the "essence" of Judaism (Umansky, 1991: 284).[4] Indeed, religious studies scholar Jonathan Z. Smith affirms that there is no one, essential, pure Judaism to which all groups must conform (1982: 18). Rather, there are many Judaisms, not all of which regard rabbinic/Halachic Judaism as central or normative. Rejecting the normative exclusions of rabbinic Judaism, this non-essentialist approach privileges anthropological and sociological perspectives over theology, making it possible "to map the variety of Judaisms, each of which appears as a shifting cluster of characteristics over time" (Smith, 1982: 18). For example, many of the women who immigrated to the United States and Canada in the nineteenth century had been strongly influenced by the German Reform movement, where ethics were considered more important than study and prayer (Umansky, 1991: 284). Early in the twentieth century, these women began to form volunteer social, educational, and philanthropic organizations in both non-sectarian and Jewish contexts.

As society opened up to women in most spheres of life, some women sought rabbinic ordination. In 1972 the Reform movement ordained, for the first time, a woman, Sally Priesand. One of the first female rabbis hired by a Canadian congregation was Elyse Goldstein, at Holy Blossom Temple in Toronto, in 1983. The Reconstructionist Rabbinical College in Philadelphia began to accept openly gay and lesbian candidates for ordination in 1984. Today, Rebecca Alpert, one of the first women to be ordained there, works openly as a lesbian rabbi to Jews who have been relegated to or who have chosen to live on the margins of the Jewish religious establishment. She finds the margins a particularly advantageous vantage point from which to view the larger world in general and the Jewish and Reconstructionist world in particular, joining others at the margins—women of colour, other lesbians, Muslim women, the working classes (Alpert, 2001: 174–7). The freedom of the margins allows her to promote abortion rights, oppose the death penalty, and work with interfaith groups for peace and justice around the world (178–9). Furthermore, she has been welcomed by the unaffiliated—the approximately one-half of the American Jewish community that does not officially belong to the community through membership in a synagogue. Many of these unaffiliated Jews are themselves marginalized—as single, gay or lesbian, or poor—by Jewish communities that are, more often than not, middle-class and strongly family-oriented (179). Perhaps, over time, groups that currently feel marginalized will create their own centres, deposing rabbinic hegemony over women's personal lives, especially in the state of Israel.

Jewish women who feel themselves to be on the margins have created many new rituals, including ceremonies to celebrate "coming out" and gay marriage. Most Jewish rituals, such as birth, puberty, and mourning rituals, are male-created, and many of them are reserved for males. New rituals celebrating female persons include baby-naming ceremonies for girls, rituals connected with menstruation, and Bat Mitzvah (puberty or coming of age) ceremonies (Adelman, 1990). Jewish women have reclaimed ritual immersion (mikvah), traditionally prescribed for ritual impurity after menstruation or childbirth. Mikvah ceremonies are now performed for healing, especially for victims of rape or other traumas (Broner, 1999: 133–48). The Rosh Chodesh celebration that marks each month's new moon has evolved into a woman's holiday (Broner, 1999: 170–80). The Haggadah ("Telling," about the Exodus from Egypt) at the annual Passover Seder meal has been reimagined through Jewish feminist lenses (Broner, 1993; Broner, 1999: 76–104). The Exodus, the Festival of Freedom, becomes an example of "crossing borders" when women such as Moses' sister Miriam are named and written back into the Haggadah (Broner, 1982: 234–44). Following Homi Bhaba, it is at the overlap of boundaries or "domains of difference" that Jewish identities are negotiated (Bhaba, 1994: 2, 5). The border areas constitute a kind of interstitial space in which Jewish women can operate without rabbinic permission or sanction.

Unique Features

Jewish women are able to function as Jews in many ways, inside or outside the religious tradition. Perhaps the best-known Jewish women are those in public life, such as newswomen Barbara Walters and the late Barbara Frum or performers like Shelley Winters, Barbra Streisand, and Bette Midler. Other famous Jewish women include the great literary figure Emma Lazarus, who wrote the well-known verse at the base of the Statue of Liberty: "Give me your tired, your poor, / Your huddled masses yearning to breathe free"—words that were not heeded in the 1930s, when Jews fleeing Nazi Germany were denied entry. Rosa Luxemburg was a European revolutionary whose concern for the poor and persecuted extended well beyond Jewish suffering. And Emma Goldman— "Red Emma," as she became known—was dubbed the most dangerous female anarchist in the world.

A Jewish woman wishing to participate in her religion has a broad range of options, from Orthodox Judaism to Conservative or Reform to the Renewal movement, which combines elements of Orthodoxy with New Age insights. She may be a committed, passionate Jew and also an atheist. There is no body of theology in Judaism to which one must adhere to be a Jew. Judaism is not only a religion, but also a civilization. A Jew is anyone born of a Jewish mother; thus there is an ethnic (but not racial) dimension to Jewish identity. Conversion to Judaism is possible but difficult, and until recently in the state of Israel a Jew by choice was considered to be fully Jewish only if he or she converted through Orthodox channels. This ruling was recently overturned by Israel's High Court of Justice, which now recognizes conversions conducted outside Orthodox channels. However, the Israeli Chief Rabbinate, (which consists of two Orthodox rabbis, one Ashkenazi and one Sephardi), does not recognize these converts as Jews and will not permit them to be married or buried in Israel. (The Israeli newspaper *Haaretz* regularly addresses this issue.)

In the state of Israel, rabbinic or Halachic Judaism governs every aspect of life from birth to death, even among secular Jews. It demands gender segregation at all levels of Haredi (ultra-Orthodox) society. One example of this segregation that affects secular as well as religious women is the *Mehadrin* (meaning stringently kosher) bus system, which connects various Haredi populations in and around Jerusalem. Even though these buses travel through less Orthodox and secular communities, all women who use them are required to board and sit at the back of the bus. For even though the Israeli High Court of Justice has ruled that segregated seating is illegal on publicly funded buses, women who challenge or resist the practice risk inviting harassment (Bush, 2013).

Though still a minority in Israel, the Haredim have enormous influence. A much publicized example can be seen at the Western or "wailing" wall (*Kotel* in Hebrew) in Jerusalem, located at the site of the Temple that was destroyed in 70 CE. Since the 1980s, American and Israeli women have met to pray at the wall carrying a Torah scroll and wearing prayer shawls and tefillin (accessories traditionally worn only by men). Until recently, the women who gather to pray every month at the time of the new moon have been threatened by men from the male side of the partition, detained or arrested by the police, and forced to pray at a location out of sight of the public. Anat Hoffman, the Chair of Women at the Wall, heads up the women's rebellion against obstructionist and violent Haredi Jews.

On 11 May 2013, Israeli police for the first time arrested some ultra-Orthodox men who were harassing the roughly 100 women at the wall (Rudoren, 2013). The larger context of this social struggle is the ultra-Orthodox community's gradual loss of privileges such as government funding for segregated schools and exemption from compulsory army service for full-time students of Torah. The 2013 election saw the exclusion of Haredi presence in the new Likud coalition.

Journalist, peace activist, and former Knesset member Uri Avnery (2013) provides an interesting perspective on the supposed holiness and significance of the Kotel, arguing that it was not actually part of King Herod's Temple at all and thus has no intrinsic significance or holiness. Rather, the issue is female sexuality: since they arouse debilitating lust in men, women must be confined or hidden away. Jewish women in Israel are under the jurisdiction of the Chief Rabbinate, which continues to warn them against praying at the wall. Today the Women at the Wall are allowed to pray only at a location out of sight of the Haredi public, at an archaeological site known as Robinson's Arch.

Women who live within the Halachic framework may not see themselves as oppressed. Believing that their world is structured and ordered by God's will, they may appreciate their freedom from the male obligation to pray three times a day, and be satisfied to fulfill their three positive *mitzvot*, or commandments: lighting the Sabbath candles, ritual immersion, and separation of the challah (Sabbath bread) dough.

Women committed to the Jewish religious tradition but dissatisfied with the exclusively male language of the liturgy have created new blessings that reflect their experience. The "heart and soul and bones of Hebrew prayer" (Falk, 1996: xv) is the *berakha* (blessing), which encompasses every aspect of Jewish life. Substituting inclusive images of divinity for the traditional patriarchal formula—"Blessed are You, Lord, King of the Universe"—Marcia Falk has reached a whole range of Jews from the liberal denominations (Conservative, Reform, and Reconstructionist) to Havurah communities and unaffiliated Jews. Her *Book of Blessings* "is for those immersed in Judaism, and for those standing at its gates, looking for ways in" (Falk 1996: xxi). Recognizing that no personification of God can be all-inclusive, she proposed "a process of ongoing naming" that would reflect diversity of experience (Falk, 1996: xvii). For example, her rewriting of the traditional blessing before a meal ("Blessed are You, Lord, Our God, King of the Universe who brings forth bread from the earth") reads as follows: "Let us bless the source of life that brings forth bread from the earth" (Falk, 1996: 18). It is a communal formula that acknowledges diversity.

Women's rituals such as Rosh Chodesh, honouring the new moon that marks the beginning of the Jewish month, are proliferating. Other women's rituals, however, have been lost. An example is the ancient Israelite custom whereby "for four days every year the daughters of Israel would go out to lament the daughter of Jephthah the Gileadite" (Judges 11: 29–40). The story behind this custom centres on the warrior Jephthah, who made a vow to God that if he won a particular battle, he would offer up as a burnt sacrifice the first person to emerge from his house on his return home. That first person turned out to be his daughter. Norma Baumel Joseph refers to the Judges text in the Canadian documentary *Half the Kingdom* (1989): "here's our biblical authority . . . here's our legitimacy. It was lost to us; let's bring it back. . . . There's a time once a year . . . this is women's day . . . women celebrating women, mourning women." Judith Plaskow agrees, "that the Bible can be made to speak to the present day" (1990: 54), especially through the interpretative process called Midrash. Midrashim reflecting women's experiences of marginalization, exclusion, and Otherness are authoritative texts in a modern context, based on the rabbinic principle that texts require interpretation based on contemporary experience.

Produced by the National Film Board of Canada and directed by Francine Zuckerman with Roushell Goldstein, *Half the Kingdom* captures the diversity of Jewish women's lived experience. Although dated now, it reflects the ethos of the 1980s, which saw Jewish (and Christian) women agitating for their rightful place in their religious communities and is still relevant today. It begins with an old legend about a man, retold about a woman—"an old, arthritic [woman] gnarled and planting a tree":

> People walk by her and ask, "Why are you planting this tree, old woman? You'll never eat from its fruit." She answers: "There were trees planted by others when I came into this world. My job is to plant this tree for those who come after me. Our lot in life is not to finish everything but merely to begin."

In the film, Norma Joseph's partner concludes that it is no longer appropriate for him to say the infamous prayer recited by males in the synagogue every morning: "Thank God for not making me a woman." An Orthodox Jew and a professor at Concordia University in Montreal, Joseph herself concludes, "If there were things I couldn't accomplish, the next generation might."

Naomi Goldenberg, professor of Religious Studies at the University of Ottawa, also speaks in the film:

> I am a Jew, I'm an atheist, I'm a feminist: I would love to find a group of people with whom I could be all those things. . . . For me, Judaism is about freedom and dignity and human independence of thought in the face of lots of hardships and lots of sadness. I want my daughter to have a sense of that Jewish rebelliousness of spirit, a sense of that connection with vitality that Judaism has. I want her to have Judaism as a chisel to work on this monolithic Christian identity that's being handed out so much in Western culture and I'd like Judaism to be something or to have a place where my daughter could be comfortable.

In the state of Israel, Alice Shalvi—women's rights activist, professor, and principal of Pelach, one of the country's first schools for girls—tries to fuse a love of Judaism with general, secular studies. She seeks to integrate drama and theatre (regarded by some Jewish traditions as forms of lying and deception) into everyday Jewish life. In North America, Michele Landsberg, political activist and columnist for the *Toronto Star*, says, "Politics is my halacha: it's my law of being . . . how to live. Our political belief in democratic socialism and a fairer, more just world . . . guides us in our daily life in the way that Jewish law guides the Orthodox" (*Half the Kingdom*). On the future, Landsberg concludes: "If Judaism is too rigid and too formalized to accept this new stream of thought and experience that is coming from the women, then, I think, it will be simply amputating its living parts—and it will become a relic, a relic that can't go on being a creative and living force." The film ends with a story by the fifteenth-century Italian biblical commentator Sforno, narrated by Elyse Goldstein:

> There are two kinds of trees: there is a tree that stands up straight against the wind and when a big gust of wind comes it refuses to bend— it's going to be straight. What is going to happen to that tree: eventually a gust of wind strong enough is going to knock it over. But then there is a reed in the water and the reed bends with the wind. When the wind comes the reed doesn't fight the wind—it goes with the wind. . . .
>
> That is what Jewish feminists really are. . . . Many people would wish we were just a little breeze—oh, it's just a few crazy fringe Jewish women out there who want to change everything. No, we are that gust of wind and Judaism is either going to be that tree that's going to stand against us until it falls or it's going to be a reed in the water and bend with the changes and ultimately grow a great deal and become more beautiful and more blossoming as a result.

The last word on this documentary goes to Norma Joseph, who articulates this sentiment at the film's beginning:

> I love being a Jew: I want the community to survive; I want the tradition of Judaism to continue into the future and I want to have a part in being that future and I won't be silent.

Notes

1. When "El" or "Elohim" appears in the biblical text, it is translated as "God." When "YHWH" appears in the text it is translated as "Adonai" or "Lord." Eventually El and YHWH were conflated into a single deity.

2. Spanish Jews and their descendants are called Sephardim or Sephardi Jews, from "Sepharad" (an ancient name for Spain).

3. The Yiddish language is a combination of Hebrew and German written in Hebrew characters and spoken by Ashkenazi Jews. The Yiddish word *tkhines* is based on the Hebrew term *tkhinna*, which means "supplication."

4. Both Umansky and Sered, above, appeal to Carol Gilligan's study on gender and moral development, *In a Different Voice*.

Glossary

Haggadah   Literally, "The Telling"; non-legal material in the Talmud. It refers also to the booklet used at the annual Passover Seder (ceremonial meal) that tells the story of the Exodus from Egypt.

Halacha   Literally, the "way to walk"; the body of legal material in the Mishnah and Talmud followed by traditional or Orthodox Jews.

Havurah   Based on the Hebrew word *haver*, "friend"; small, egalitarian, home-based Jewish communities who worship together on Shabbat, the Sabbath.

mechitzah   The separation between men and women in segregated worship in Judaism.

Midrash   Jewish biblical interpretation that reads between the lines of a text to wrest meaning from it. *Midrash Rabbah* is a five-volume rabbinic commentary on the Torah.

minyan   The quorum of 10 men required for public prayer in Judaism.

Mishnah   The "oral Torah"; a six-volume body of material transmitted orally for some 200–300 years and put into writing in 220 CE. It is the basis for the later volumes of interpretation known as the Babylonian Talmud and the Jerusalem Talmud.

pogroms   Mob attacks on Jews, involving destruction of Jewish homes and synagogues as well as murder.

Further Reading

Adler, Rachel. *Engendering Judaism: An Inclusive Theology and Ethics*. Philadelphia: The Jewish Publication Society, 1998.

Hyman, Paula E. *Gender and Assimilation in Modern Jewish History: The Roles and Representation of Women*. Seattle: University of Washington Press, 1995.

"Jewish Women's Archive." *New Encyclopedia of Jewish Women*. http://jwa.org.

Peskowitz, Miriam, and Laura Levitt, eds. *Judaism since Gender*. New York: Routledge, 1997.

Rudavsky, T.M., ed. *Gender and Judaism: The Transformation of Tradition*. New York: New York University Press, 1995.

Films and Online Resources

Kadosh. 117 mins. Directed by Amos Gitai. Israel: Globus United, 1999. Hebrew with English subtitles. How Jewish women are sometimes victims of a religious lifestyle.

Making Trouble. 85 mins. Directed by Rachel Talbot. Brookline, MA: Jewish Women's Archive, 2006. Tells the stories of six of the greatest Jewish female performers of the last century.

Religions of the Book: Women Serving Religion. 29 mins. Produced by Michael J. Doyle. Princeton, NJ: Films for the Humanities and Sciences, 2003. Jewish, Christian, and Muslim women discuss the position of women in their religious traditions.

The Summer of Aviya. 96 mins. Directed by Eli Cohen. Israel: Shapira Films, 1988. Hebrew with English subtitles. The story of two Holocaust survivors—a mother and her daughter. Set in 1951.

See "Women Make Movies," www.wmm.com, for a growing list of films about women in various religious traditions.

References

Adelman, Penina V. 1990. *Miriam's Well: Rituals for Jewish Women around the Year*. 2nd edn. New York: Biblio Press.

Adler, Rachel. 1976. "Tumah and Taharah: Ends and Beginnings." Pp. 63–71 in Elizabeth Koltun, ed. *The Jewish Woman: New Perspectives*. New York: Schocken Books.

Aiken, Lisa. 1992. *To Be a Jewish Woman*. Northvale, NJ: Jason Aronson.

Alpert, Rebecca. 1997. *Like Bread on the Seder Plate: Jewish Lesbians and the Transformation of Tradition*. New York: Columbia University Press.

———. 2001. "On Being a Rabbi at the Margins." Pp. 173–80 in Rebecca T. Alpert, Sue Levi Elwell, and Shirley Idelson, eds. *Lesbian Rabbis: The First Generation*. New Brunswick, NJ: Rutgers University Press.

Avnery, Uri. 2013. *Women of the Wall*. www.counterpunch.org/2013/05/17/women-of-the-wall/.

Baskin, Judith R. 1991. "Jewish Women in the Middle Ages." Pp. 94–114 in Judith R. Baskin, ed. *Jewish Women in Historical Perspective*. Detroit, MI: Wayne State University Press.

Bhaba, Homi. 1994. *The Location of Culture*. London: Routledge.

Biale, Rachel. 1984. *Women and Jewish Law: An Exploration of Women's Issues in Halakhic Sources*. New York: Schocken Books.

Boyarin, Daniel. 1996. "Rabbinic Resistance to Male Domination: A Case Study in Talmudic Cultural Poetics." Pp. 118–41 in Steven Kepnes, ed. *Interpreting Judaism in a Post-Modern Age*. New York: New York University Press.

Broner, E.M. 1982. "Honor and Ceremony in Women's Rituals." Pp. 234–44 in Charlene Spretnak, ed. *The Politics of Women's Spirituality: Essays on the Rise of Spiritual Power within the Feminist Movement*. Garden City, NY: Anchor Press/Doubleday.

———. 1993. *The Telling*. San Francisco: HarperSanFrancisco.

———. 1999. *Bringing Home the Light: A Jewish Woman's Handbook of Rituals*. San Francisco: Council Oak Books.

Brooten, Bernadette J. 1982. *Women Leaders in the Ancient Synagogue: Inscriptional Evidence and Background Issues*. Brown Judaic Studies 36. Chico, CA: Scholars Press.

Bush, Lawrence. 2013. "Back of the Bus" in *Jewish Currents*. http://jewishcurrents.org/january-6-the-back-of-the-bus-13695.

Cantor, Aviva. 1983. "The Lilith Question." Pp. 40–50 in Susannah Heschel, ed. *On*

Being a Jewish Feminist: A Reader. New York: Schocken Books.

———. 1995. *Jewish Women/Jewish Men: The Legacy of Patriarchy in Jewish Life.* New York: HarperCollins.

Elior, Rachel. 2004. "Blessed Art Thou, Lord Our God, Who Hast Not Made Me a Woman." In Rachel Elior, ed. *Men and Women: Gender, Judaism and Democracy.* Jerusalem: Urim Publications, The Van Leer Jerusalem Institute.

Falk, Marcia. 1996. *The Book of Blessings: New Jewish Prayers for Daily Life, the Shabbat and the New Moon Festival.* New York: HarperCollins.

Frankiel, Tamar. 1990. *The Voice of Sarah: Feminine Spirituality and Traditional Judaism.* New York: HarperCollins.

Ghatan, H.E. Yedidiah. 1986. *The Invaluable Pearl: The Unique Status of Women in Judaism.* New York: Bloch.

Gross, Rita M. 1983. "Steps toward Feminine Imagery of Deity in Jewish Theology." Pp. 234–47 in Susannah Heschel, ed. *On Being a Jewish Feminist: A Reader.* New York: Schocken Books.

Half the Kingdom. 1989. Directed by Francine Zuckerman with Roushell Goldstein. Documentary. National Film Board of Canada, Studio D.

Hauptman, Judith. 1974. "Images of Women in the Talmud." Pp. 184–212 in Rosemary Radford Ruether, ed. *Religion and Sexism: Images of Woman in the Jewish and Christian Traditions.* New York: Simon and Schuster.

Heschel, Susannah. 1983. "Introduction." Pp. xiii–xxxvi in Susannah Heschel, ed. *On Being a Jewish Feminist: A Reader.* New York: Schocken Books.

———. 1990. "Anti-Judaism and Christian Feminist Theology." *Tikkun,* May/June: 25–8, 95–7.

Kaufman, Michael. 1993. *The Woman in Jewish Law and Tradition.* Northvale, NJ: Jason Aronson.

Koltun, Elizabeth. 1976. *The Jewish Woman: New Perspectives.* New York: Schocken Books.

Kuikman, Jacoba. 2000. "Christ as Cosmic Tree." *Toronto Journal of Theology* 16, 1: 141–54.

Meyers, Carol. 1988. *Discovering Eve: Ancient Israelite Women in Context.* New York: Oxford University Press.

Midrash Rabbah, Genesis. Vol. 1. 1939. Translated by Rabbi Dr. H. Freedman. Edited by Rabbi Dr. H. Freedman and Maurice Simon. London: The Soncino Press.

Milgrom, Jo. 1992. *Handmade Midrash.* Philadelphia: The Jewish Publication Society.

The New Revised Standard Version of the Bible. 1991. New York: Oxford University Press.

Niditch, Susan. 1989. "Eroticism and Death in the Tale of Jael." Pp. 43–57 in Peggy L. Day, ed. *Gender and Difference in Ancient Israel.* Minneapolis, MN: Fortress Press.

Olyan, Saul. 1988. *Asherah and the Cult of Yahweh in Israel.* Atlanta, GA: Scholars Press.

Ozick, Cynthia. 1983. "Notes toward Finding the Right Question." Pp. 120–51 in Susannah Heschel, ed. *On Being a Jewish Feminist: A Reader.* New York: Schocken Books.

Patai, Raphael. 1990. *The Hebrew Goddess.* Detroit, MI: Wayne State University Press.

Plaskow, Judith. 1979. "The Coming of Lilith: Toward a Feminist Theology." Pp. 198–209 in Carol P. Christ and Judith Plaskow, eds. *Womanspirit Rising: A Feminist Reader in Religion.* San Francisco: Harper and Row.

———. 1983. "The Right Question Is Theological." Pp. 223–33 in Susannah Heschel, ed. *On Being a Jewish Feminist: A Reader.* New York: Schocken Books.

———. 1990. *Standing Again at Sinai: Judaism from a Feminist Perspective.* New York: HarperCollins.

Romney Wegner, Judith. 1991. "The Image and Status of Women in Classical Rabbinic Judaism." Pp. 68–114 in Judith R. Baskin, ed. *Jewish Women in Historical Perspective.* Detroit, MI: Wayne State University Press.

Rudoren, Jodi. 2013. "Israeli Police Protect Women Praying at Western Wall." *Globe and Mail.* May 11, 2013.

Satlow, Michael L. 2006. *Creating Judaism: History, Tradition, Practice.* New York: Columbia University Press.

Smith, Jonathan Z. 1982. *Imagining Religion: From Babylon to Jonestown.* Chicago: University of Chicago Press.

Starr Sered, Susan. 1992. *Women as Ritual Experts: The Religious Lives of Elderly Jewish*

Women in Jerusalem. New York: Oxford University Press.

Tanakh. 1985. A New Translation of the Holy Scriptures according to the Traditional Hebrew Text. Philadelphia: The Jewish Publication Society.

Umansky, Ellen M. 1991. "Spiritual Expressions: Jewish Women's Religious Lives in the Twentieth-Century United States." Pp. 265–88 in Judith R. Baskin, ed. *Jewish Women in Historical Perspective.* Detroit, MI: Wayne State University Press.

Under the Domim Tree. 1994. Directed by Eli Cohen. From the novel by Gila Almagor. Hebrew with English subtitles. VHS. Wellspring.

von Kellenbach, Katherina. 1994. *Anti-Judaism in Feminist Religious Writings.* Atlanta, GA: Scholars Press (The American Academy of Religion).

Walker, Alice. 1982. *The Color Purple.* New York: Washington Square Press.

Weissler, Chava. 1991. "Prayers in Yiddish and the Religious World of Ashkenazi Women." Pp. 159–81 in Judith R. Baskin, ed. *Jewish Women in Historical Perspective.* Detroit, MI: Wayne State University Press.

Wolfson, Elliot R. 1995. *Circle in the Square: Studies in the Use of Gender in Kabbalistic Symbolism.* Albany: State University of New York Press.

CHAPTER 3

◇◇◇

Women in
Buddhist Traditions

Eva K. Neumaier

A woman prays outside a Buddhist temple in Bangkok, Thailand.

Voramai Kabilsingh

Born before the First World War into a middle-class Thai family, Voramai Kabilsingh (1908–2003) pursued from early on a life thought unfitting for a girl at that time, not only in Thailand but also in the West. Attending a Catholic school, she chose physical education as her major and graduated as the first woman ever with that major. As a young woman in 1926 she joined a group of Boy Scouts on a bicycle tour from Bangkok to Singapore. She started a career as a journalist and editor of a local newspaper, and in the 1940s she married a member of the Thai parliament and gave birth to a daughter, Chatsumarn Kabilsingh, who earned a PhD and was later ordained as Bhikkhuni Dhammananda, following in her mother's footsteps pioneering women's place in the Buddhist monastic communities.

Later in life, in 1956, Voramai Kabilsingh took the Eight Precepts suitable for a lay Buddhist from Pra Prommuni, vice-abbot of Wat Bavornnives, the royal residence since Rama IV. Whereas Thai novice nuns (*mae ji*), who also take the Eight Precepts, wear white robes, Voramai Kabilsingh designed her own light yellow robes, tailored according to the monks' style. This was a revolutionary act, signalling to Thai society that she claimed equal status with a **bhikkhu**, a fully ordained monk. It provoked a strong reaction from the monks' **sangha**, or community. They pointed out that in 1928 the then leader of the bhikkhu sangha (*sangharaja*), Jinavornsirivatna, issued an order forbidding future ordination of women. Even since the country adopted a constitution in 1932, this order from the *sangharaja* has remained valid and is a major stumbling block toward the reintroduction of ordination for **bhikkhunis** (nuns) in Thailand. Moreover, senior monks pointed out that for a woman to wear monks' robes would desecrate the sacred garments. They went to court with this issue but lost the case, as Voramai Kabilsingh pointed out that her robes were a different shade of yellow than the monks'.

Although this was a formal victory for her cause, Voramai still had to endure many forms of discrimination. In 1957 she bought a piece of land for the first Thai temple built exclusively for women. Realizing that poor education was an issue for Thai women, she also founded a school and an orphanage on these grounds. Her request to obtain full ordination as a **Theravada** ("Teaching of the Elder") bhikkhuni was rejected by the monks with the argument that the women's order was extinct and could not be revived because of the previous *sangharaja's* order. However, in 1971 she received full ordination in Taiwan under the Chinese tradition (Dharmaguptaka), an ordination that neither the Thai sangha nor the secular authorities recognized. While still carrying out the traditional duties of a Thai laywoman, Voramai taught the **Dharma** (Buddhist teachings; "Dhamma" in **Pali**), which until then was unheard of for a woman in Thai society. With her courageous life she had opened a door for Thai women to participate fully in Buddhist practice, and this door cannot be shut again.

Introduction and Overview

The Mahaparinibbana Sutta, the account of the **Buddha's** last months, has him make the following declaration shortly after realizing enlightenment:

> I will not pass away . . . until I have bhikkhu disciples . . . bhikkhuni . . . laymen disciples . . . laywomen disciples who are accomplished, skilled, learned, expert in the Dhamma, practised in accord with the Dhamma, properly practised, living in accord with Dhamma, who, having learnt from their own teacher, expound, teach, declare, set out, explain, analyze it and make it clear; who are able to refute in accord with Dhamma other teachings that appear, and then teach the wonderful Dhamma (Sujato, 2007).

Thus we might expect Buddhism to be the only religion that fully respects gender equality. But then we need to consider the following statement made by Bernard Faure: "Like most clerical discourses, Buddhism is indeed relentlessly misogynist, but as far as misogynist discourses go, it is one of the most flexible and open to multiplicity and contradiction" (Faure, 2003: 3). The Buddha's statement dates from roughly 500 or 450 BCE and Faure's from our time—a difference of 2500 years. In the following I will sketch the main developments from the early period of Buddhism to the rapid changes in our time, to let us appreciate these contradictory statements.

Buddhism is a religion with a 2500-year history; its sacred texts number in the tens of thousands and are preserved in numerous classical languages of Asia. Since the end of the nineteenth century, non-Asian people in Europe, the Americas, and Australia and to a lesser degree in Africa have gradually adopted Buddhism, and in many of these countries, it is the fastest growing of all religions. In absolute numbers, however, it is still a minority religion in the Western world. Yet Buddhism has played a significant part in a vast array of societies, cultures, and historical periods, from Iron Age India to the modern world. During the colonial period Buddhism waned in many Asian countries, only to regain momentum in the post-colonial times. By the end of the twentieth century, Buddhist meditation techniques were finding broad application outside the religious context.

What follows is a modest attempt to establish the historical background by examining relevant textual sources, trace the historical developments in some of the core Buddhist countries, and then examine the groundbreaking changes that are affecting Buddhist women in our own times. We shall first examine how women are depicted in the Buddha's life stories before turning to the most important facts and documents pertinent to the status and roles of women during the early period of Buddhism in India (c. 400–200 BCE). The situation of nuns in the Buddhist monastic order (sangha) requires detailed analysis, as the campaign to implement nuns' full ordination is (along with the rise of the lay meditation teacher) the most prominent feature of Buddhism in our time. But we shall also briefly explore the major feminine symbols common in some Buddhist traditions.

The Origins of Buddhism

The religious tradition that the modern world knows as Buddhism, and that calls itself "Dharma," originated in India around the middle of the millennium before the inception of the Common Era. The Buddhist community began as an ascetic movement of members of the social elite calling into question the hitherto common religious ideas of the Vedas and Upanishads. Its founder, a prince named Siddhartha Gautama, who later became known as the Buddha, the Enlightened One, was born into a noble family that ruled over a small principality in an area that is now on the Indian–Nepalese border.

Although he was brought up in the luxury common to his class, Siddhartha nevertheless experienced a yearning for a state of mind beyond suffering and beyond death. At age 29 he left his family and noble surroundings in order to pursue the life of an ascetic wanderer in search of enlightenment. After several years of arduous striving under the guidance of teachers of various systems of yoga, Siddhartha faced a personal crisis. With great vigour he had followed the time-honoured rules of asceticism, but to no avail. Close to death by starvation, he made one final attempt to seek the coveted spiritual breakthrough.

The following night, meditating under a fig tree, he gained insight into the law of karma (that is, he realized that all thoughts and activities have moral consequences that come to fruition either in this life or a later one, and that this life is only one in an endless chain of re-embodiments). Furthermore, he realized the so-called fourfold noble truth: that life is inevitably saturated with suffering (birth, sickness, old age, and death); that desire or yearning is the cause of suffering; that the end of yearning implies the end of suffering, which is **nirvana**; and that there is a path towards realization of nirvana, consisting of wisdom, morality, and contemplation. Only through moral and mental discipline, and ruthless inquiry into the true nature of things, could one gain nirvana; no gods or spirits, no magic could be of any help in this endeavour. This simplified rendering of the core ideas of Buddhism will help to explain why life-cycle rituals (e.g., baptism, coming of age, marriage) were absent in early Buddhism and are still of minor importance in contemporary Buddhism, where they exist at all.

When the morning dawned, Siddhartha had reached the inner assurance that his suffering had come to an end and that nirvana, a state beyond any description or words, had been achieved. He had become an Enlightened One, a Buddha. After several weeks of silence, assuming that no one would understand the insight he had gained, he decided to go to Benares, the holy city of India. For more than 40 years he wandered over the dusty roads of the eastern Ganges Valley. He shared his experience and his insight with those who were eager to hear it. The teaching of the fourfold noble truth was complemented with the teaching of interdependent origination, illuminating how all phases of life are interconnected and depend on each other. He also taught an elaborate system of meditation that would lead to the realization of nirvana. In the ascetic-spiritual view of the Buddha, there is no room for an omniscient and almighty god, male or female, or for concepts similar to the Christian concepts of sin or hell. One's present deeds determine one's future according to the rule of karma, which in general cannot be altered, not even by a god or a Buddha.

Soon after the Buddha had realized enlightenment, fellow ascetics and yogis were drawn to him. Although he never encouraged anyone to follow him, or to abandon their families, a following of men and women began to form. Among them were aristocrats, wealthy guild masters, artisans, tradespeople, courtesans, and ordinary folk, as well as beggars and even criminals. They were drawn to the Buddha in the expectation that they too would be able to attain a state of being beyond suffering, where they could see "things as they are," a state described as **"arhantship"** as long as the person was alive, and as "nirvana" once the person passed away. They would then be cleansed of distorted visions of reality, all forms of yearning and desire, and all forms of rejection and hatred.

Judging from extant literary sources, it seems that at first the Buddha's followers lived by simply imitating their master's way of life, a life of utmost simplicity. But when society took issue with some of the habits of this new community—such as former spouses wandering together through the countryside as fellow ascetics—the need for rules emerged. Each of the monastic rules ascribed to the Buddha (and there are several hundred) is introduced by a story that recounts the circumstances that necessitated its proclamation. A number of these rules deal with how women should behave within this newly founded ascetic community and how they should interact with laypeople, male and female. Monks and nuns were organized in two separate orders (sanghas), and the nuns' order is subordinate to the monks'—an issue that is contested today in some communities. The members of both orders are subject to a strict rule of chastity. From the very beginning of Buddhism, it was the monastic woman, the nun, who had abandoned family life and refrained from marriage and procreation, who was depicted in Buddhist literature and art, not the married woman and mother. Laywomen, including wealthy patrons of Buddhist institutions, occupied at best a supportive role.

The place of women in Buddhism has to be seen against the background of general social organization in India at that time. Many Buddhist doctrines and customs contested views and beliefs held in high esteem by Indians at that time. The status and roles of women in early Buddhist communities are defined and circumscribed by the mainly non-Buddhist society of early India. The *Laws of Manu* clearly prescribed that a woman must always be under the control of a man—her father, husband, or brother—and could never be master of her own life. The Buddhist nun challenged this view, in the past as today. Not long before the rise of Buddhism, Indian society changed from a mainly pastoral and semi-agricultural village-based society to an urban one typified by labour diversification, a rise in mercantilism, and artistic accomplishments. This urban climate provided women of the upper classes with opportunities to unfold their intellectual and artistic talents. Thus, I.B. Horner wrote,

> The birth of girl-children was no longer met with open-eyed and loud-voiced despair, for girls had ceased to be despised and looked upon as encumbrances. They were now allowed a good deal of liberty. Matrimony was not held before them as the end and aim of their existence, and they were not regarded as shameful if they did not marry; but if they did, they were neither hastened off to an early child-marriage, nor bound to accept the man of their parents' selection. Princesses and ladies of high degree seem to have had some voice in the matter of choosing their husband. As wife a woman was no mere household drudge, but she had considerable authority in the home, ranked

as her husband's helpmate, companion and guardian, and in matters both temporal and spiritual were regarded as his equal and worthy of respect. . . . Under Buddhism, more than ever before, she was an individual in command of her own life until the dissolution of the body, and less of a chattel to be only respected if she lived through and on a man (1930: 3).

Despite a general improvement in women's status, the early Buddhist community certainly challenged the social mores of Indian society when it began to accept women as wandering ascetics side by side with men. This novelty must have stirred some emotions among the general Indian populace. Many of the rules specific to the nuns' order were obviously designed to minimize society's discomfort with independent women, exempt from the reproductive routine and male supervision and outside the range of domestic duties, roaming the country. While women of the elite certainly enjoyed not only the privileges of their class but also a modest participation in such male-dominated fields as philosophical debating and governance (though only in the absence of a male heir), it was unheard of that they would join migratory ascetic groups in pursuit of mystical experiences. Given the circumstances of its beginning, the Buddhist traditions had the opportunity to include women more than did any other religious group emerging at that time.

Women's Official and Unofficial Roles

Women in Early Buddhist India

Throughout history, Buddhist women have participated in the practice of their faith. However, when reflecting on past periods, we can judge women's roles only on the basis of historical evidence—either inscriptions on stone or copper tablets or textual evidence. Over the millennia, the overwhelming majority of Buddhist texts were produced by monks writing for other men, whether monks or noblemen. Buddhist women, if they figured in these texts at all, did so only in subservient roles. Very few texts were written either by or about nuns. Thus the picture we gain is necessarily incomplete and biased.

Women in the Buddha's Life Story

The historical accuracy of the portrayal of women in the early Buddhist accounts from India remains in most cases questionable. A major problem is that the word of the Buddha, which makes up the core of the Buddhist scriptures, was not put into writing before the last or second last century BCE, several centuries after the founder's death. First, let us examine how women were represented in stories of the Buddha's own life. In a text from the first century CE, the Buddha's conception and birth are praised in the flowery language of court poetry (Johnston, 1936: 2–3). The verses hardly render a historical account, but speak articulately of the devotion that faithful Buddhists must have felt regarding his birth. Maya, his mother, is praised for her purity, and the conception happens "without defilement." The birth itself is miraculous, as the future Buddha enters the world through an opening in his mother's waist. Needless to say, the child is precocious. Idyllic as these accounts are, they nevertheless cannot conceal the impression that the woman here is seen only as a means to the end—that is, to glorify the founder's miraculous birth as a unique event. The Buddha's mother dies soon after his birth, and he is raised by her sister, Prajapati. We shall meet Prajapati again in several significant roles.

In accord with the custom of his time and class, while still at home Siddhartha marries and lives a life of luxury and splendour, surrounded by numerous concubines and female entertainers. His wife, Yashodhara, a maiden "of widespread renown, virtuous and endowed with beauty, modesty and gentle bearing" (Johnston, 1936: 25), is introduced as the mother of his only son, whom he calls, aptly, Rahula, which means "fetter." Seeing the women around him, including his wife, as abject, Prince Siddhartha leaves his palace in search of enlightenment. Later monk authors would use this episode to indulge in rhetoric that vilifies women as seductresses and as beings of low morality, disinclined to philosophical inquiries. Even today, some monks and laymen adhere to these views. But there is also a text (discussed in the "Marginal Voices" section below) that speaks with a very different voice and that tries to affirm Yashodhara's role in his achieving enlightenment.

During the years in which Siddhartha travels with groups of male ascetics and yogis, no encounter with a woman is recorded. However, when he is near death from extreme fasting, he meets a woman who offers him a savoury rice dish. Desperate to experience a breakthrough in his spiritual search, he accepts the dish and regains his strength. And in fact Siddhartha experiences a cataclysmic mystical ecstasy, his enlightenment, the following night. In this episode, the woman who offers him food is an embodiment of female compassion and exhibits the traditional virtue of generosity to mendicant yogis. Once Siddhartha is recognized as the Buddha, and a following has gathered around him, he again encounters women eager to become his followers, some as laypeople, others as ascetics or nuns (**bhikshunis**). The Buddha addresses women affected by typical "female" worries and sufferings, such as the premature death of a beloved husband or child, with empathy and compassion, but his interaction with them is not noticeably different from his interaction with men regarding the men's worries and sufferings. The texts telling the Buddha's life story were authored by later generations of monks who expressed in them their own view of women as subservient and ancillary to the aims of men. This is in contrast to some of what are presumably the Buddha's own words affirming women's spiritual potential as equal to that of men.

Whereas women are depicted as playing rather inferior roles in the Buddha's life story, numerous men are mentioned as exercising a decisive influence on the prince's life: his father, his teachers of yoga and Upanishadic philosophy, his fellow ascetics, and finally his fellow monks. Among the nuns, Prajapati, Siddhartha's aunt and stepmother, occupies a special position. As a leader of a group of noble women of his own extended family, she adopts the ascetic life style and subsequently asks the Buddha to formally acknowledge this step, which leads to the foundation of the nuns' order. Later, in China, she becomes the first female "patriarch" in the female Chan (Japanese Zen) lineage. Among the laywomen, Ambapali, a wealthy courtesan, is mentioned as the Buddha's devoted lay patron.

Nuns in the Early Sangha

Some of the Buddha's female disciples left us personal testimonies in the form of a collection of 73 poems in which they articulate their spiritual calling and their own enlightenment. This collection is known as **Therigatha**, the "Songs of the Elder [Nuns]" (Norman, 1983: 75–7). Some of the nuns refer to themselves as "daughter(s) of the Buddha, born from his mouth" (Horner, 1930: 171). An equivalent phrase—"son of the Buddha, born from his mouth"—is used by the early monks (contemporary with the nuns discussed here) who also left behind a collection of poems expressing their religious experiences. This phrase means that its author sees him- or herself as having been reborn from the Buddha's teaching (that is, through his mouth) and therefore rightly his son or daughter. The first international association of Buddhist women, founded in 1987, echoed this sentiment by adopting the name Sakyadhita, meaning "Daughters of Shakya (i.e., the Buddha)." The gender difference is erased here in the light of the spiritual experience, a fact that nun Soma expressed in the following lines:

> What should the woman's nature signify
> When consciousness is tense and firmly set,
> When knowledge rolleth ever on, when she
> By insight rightly comprehends the Norm? (Samyutta Nikaya V, para. 2)

Reading the "Songs of the Elder Nuns," one cannot help but have the impression that, at the beginning of the Buddhist traditions, Buddhist nuns saw themselves as equal to the monks. We shall see that in China nuns of the Chan tradition enjoyed this equality during various historical periods. While the biological difference in sex could not be erased, in the "Songs of the Elder Nuns" the culturally determined gender difference becomes negligible in the light of the nuns' firm ascetic commitment and their spiritual achievements. What mattered for the early Buddhists was obviously the individual's progress on the path toward enlightenment, and not the individual's gender. Enlightenment was available to both genders. In their poems, the nuns state as their reason for entering the monastic life the desire for freedom from the burdens of lay life, but also the yearning to transcend the endless cycle of rebirth and attain arhantship. A few tried to find ways to cope with what seemed arbitrary torment inflicted on them, such as the loss of a child.

The Buddhist monastic order was open to people from all walks of life. However, the majority of nuns mentioned in the "Songs" belonged to the upper castes (royalty and nobility, wealthy merchants, prominent Brahmins). Only two nuns were reported to have come from poor Brahmin castes, and four were courtesans. In the "Songs," some nuns are identified by their outstanding talents or achievements, including great wisdom (Khema, former consort of King Bimbisara), articulation in preaching the Buddhist religion (Dhammadinna, from a wealthy merchant family), expertise in the monastic rules and regulations (Patacara, also from a wealthy merchant family), paranormal insight (Bhadda Kunaleksha, a convert from Jainism), memories of her former lives (Bhadda, from the Kapila Brahmin caste), and so on. Bhadda was also known as very articulate in religious discourses, while others were renowned speakers and excelled in religious debates with followers of other religious traditions (Horner, 1930: 168–72). The early nuns were full members of the monastic order and were recognized for their extraordinary intellectual and spiritual talents and accomplishments. Even a few centuries later, we read in some donative inscriptions—stone or copper tablets attached to ancient Buddhist buildings, recording the donor's name and often the purpose of the donation—of nuns who carried the title "master of the **Tripitaka**" (the three collections of early Buddhist scriptures). However, soon after that period this title became the exclusive domain of monks (Schopen, 1997: 31). In our time, Buddhist nuns of various traditions are striving to gain access to the higher education so far reserved for monks, which will enable nuns to be known again as "masters of the Tripitaka."

Married as well as unmarried women entered the order, but among the authors of the "Songs," the unmarried nuns outnumber those who had been married or widowed. This fact permits the conclusion that, at the time of the Buddha, marriage was not mandatory for women as it had been in earlier and again in later times. As was the case for the monks, women who wanted to enter the order had to obtain their parents' consent and be free of debt and social bondage. In a few cases, women wanting to join the order asked their husbands for approval, which in most cases was given without hesitation. Thus, one may conclude that at the time it was seen as within the boundaries of normalcy for a woman to leave family and household life to join the mendicant order of the Buddha. On occasion, husband and wife decided to join the order together.

To enter the order, the Buddhist woman did not have to be a virgin, nor did she have to denounce the experiences of her previous life in the world. To the contrary, nuns often maintained some contact with their families. Although contact with men was restricted, the rules permitted nuns to care for their own male children up to the time of puberty (Hüsken, 1997: 470). Donative inscriptions dating from the first centuries of Buddhist history substantiate the claim that on occasion nuns maintained close contact with their families. Some nuns are recorded as having made significant donations to existing monasteries and temples (for instance, an elaborate masonry gate or wall) for the benefit of their deceased parents. Such inscriptions document, first, that these nuns maintained emotional and economic ties with their families; second, that they had control over substantial material wealth; and, third, that there was a belief that making donations would positively affect the fate of deceased parents (Schopen, 1997: 30–43, 56–67).

The Monastic Order and its Rules

The Buddhist monastic order, or sangha, is a self-governing body based on consensual decisions of the local monastic community. It is governed by two sets of rules (**Vinaya**), one for the monks and another for the nuns; the monks' rules predate the nuns' and served as a template for them. Men and women form independent communities and monasteries. Each local community that has its base in a monastery elects its own leader from among the eldest monks or nuns (in **Pali**, *thera*; in Sanskrit, *sthavira*—both meaning "elder") for a certain period of time, although in different periods and countries an emperor or king could appoint the leaders of important monasteries. Textual and epigraphic evidence suggests that during the first 200 years of Buddhism, the differences between the nuns' and monks' orders were insignificant. Local communities were independent, as there was no hierarchy, local or global, overseeing them, which made the branching out of numerous traditions possible.

These egalitarian and democratically organized communities of monks and nuns were later subject to changes that altered the situation of the nuns until recent times. Contrary to the original rule that required members of the sangha to keep distant from the ruler and the court system, centuries after the Buddha's death (usually dated 480 BCE), political functionaries began to exert some degree of control over the monastic system, and often used it to their own advantage.

Thus the independent and egalitarian nature of the Buddhist monastic system was undermined as kings and emperors meddled in monastic affairs, trying to prevent dissent among its members, or calling certain monks to serve as advisors and court officials. For instance, when the Indian Emperor Ashoka (ruled 269–232 BCE), a devout Buddhist monarch who transformed the local Buddhist movement into a world religion, convened a council to resolve a schism in the Buddhist sangha, he called only monks to attend it. In China, some T'ang emperors appointed Buddhist monks as advisors and bestowed positions on them, including that of court official. In Tibet, King Ral-pa-can (ruled 815–36 CE) not only appointed a monk as minister of religious affairs but also put the monks' sangha in charge of overseeing the Lower Assembly (Dargyay, 1991: 124ff.). In these and many more cases, only monks were called to the court, and as a result Buddhist nuns were pushed more and more into the background. While some of the monks' monasteries gained political influence, status, and significant wealth, nuns' monasteries remained dependent on the laity's voluntary contributions. Thus the nuns' status decreased in comparison with the monks' growing prestige.

But there were also exceptions. Recent research shows that the nuns' order flourished in Korea from the time Buddhism was introduced to the country (fourth century) until the Choson Dynasty (1392–1910) suppressed its practice. The status and influence that Korean nuns enjoyed in that period were exceptional, as they had access to education in Buddhist theory and control of economic resources (Cho, ed., 2011: 16–22). Chinese and Korean literary sources suggest that the Chan tradition and its Korean equivalent (son) were more accommodating to women than, for instance, the Pure Land tradition, which insisted that enlightenment can happen only in a male body. Educated women of the social elite in China and Korea often entered the Buddhist order once their husbands had died. In such cases they brought with them not only their social prestige and material wealth, but also their assertiveness and education.

The reasons for the dramatic change in the position of Buddhist nuns vis-à-vis Buddhist monks in South and Southeast Asian countries can be found in the gender preferences and restrictions governing the court culture as well as the general structure of society of the time. Court protocol often left no room for independent and celibate women—that is, nuns. They were left out of the political process and were excluded from those monastic institutions that garnered the most economic support and enjoyed the most significant political power. However, court cultures varied from country to country. Throughout most of China's history, Buddhism found support among the political and cultural elite, the literati, and was therefore to a certain degree part of the court system. Some nuns' monasteries were incorporated in the inner courtyards of the imperial palace where the nuns, mostly women of the elite, administered to the spiritual needs of the emperor's spouses and courtesans (Grant, 2009:

13–36). A few highly educated nuns who were members of the country's first families rose to the rank of advisor to the emperor.

When monks became advisors to emperors and kings, the construction of monasteries on palace lands and under the jurisdiction of the court was a frequent result (for example, the Tendai temple in Japan; rNam-rgyal monastery and Sera, Drepung, and Ganden monasteries in Tibet). The senior monks of these monasteries often enjoyed royal privileges and luxury as well as significant political influence. Being part of the power structure, these monastic institutions and their members became in practice defenders of the status quo and obstructors of change and innovation. Two examples may suffice. The first illustrates the general resistance to modernization put up by politically entrenched monastic institutions; the second exemplifies the resistance mounted by influential monks of some traditions to improving the nuns' status.

First, in the aftermath of the British invasion of Tibet in 1904, some secular cabinet ministers urged a general modernization of the Tibetan socio-political system. The Three Monastic Seats of the large state-funded monasteries—Sera, Ganden, and Drepung, all with enormous political influence—objected vigorously to any plans that would alter their privileged status. Melvyn Goldstein summarizes the situation:

> [The] Three monastic Seats . . . believed that they represented the fundamental interests of Buddhism and were obligated to preserve the religious values of the state. Thus, monasteries worked in the government to prevent modernization, which they believed to be detrimental to both the economic base of monasticism and the "value" monopoly of Tibetan Buddhism (1989: 816).

Second, since the late 1980s nuns from several Buddhist traditions (especially the Theravada and Tibetan traditions) have pushed for the reinstatement of full ordination for nuns (Tsomo, 1988: 236–57), an enterprise that gained momentum through the First International Congress on Buddhist Women's Role in the Sangha—Bhikshuni Vinaya and Ordination Lineages (held at the University of Hamburg, Germany, in 2007). But some powerful monks of these traditions tried with varying success to obstruct this effort by insisting on a strict literal interpretation of the pertinent monastic rules. The issue of full ordination for Buddhist nuns and its absence in some traditions will be discussed in more detail later in this chapter, under the heading "Buddhist Women in the Twentieth and Twenty-First Centuries."

The vast majority of the hundreds of monastic rules are the same for monks and nuns. Theirs is a life of simplicity and renunciation whose sole objective is to cultivate the conditions leading toward enlightenment; or such is the ideal.

Monks and nuns have their heads shaved and in most cases wear similar robes, with minor differences. Thus, outwardly, there are almost no differences. However, tradition has it that the Buddha was reluctant to create a nuns' order parallel to the monks' order. He agreed to do so only if the nuns were willing to accept the eight chief rules (Hüsken, 2010: 143–8):

1. Every nun, regardless of her seniority, is junior to even the youngest monk;
2. Nuns cannot spend the rainy season in a place where no monk is available (to instruct them in the monastic discipline);
3. Nuns must ask the monks to set the day of the confession ceremony and provide exhortations to them;
4. After the rainy season, a nun has to inquire before the monks' and the nuns' sanghas whether any fault can be laid to her charge;
5. A nun found guilty of a serious offence has to undergo discipline before both sanghas;
6. A woman who has completed the two years' novitiate must ask the monks' sangha for full initiation;
7. A nun must never revile or abuse a monk; and
8. Nuns cannot reprimand monks for violation of monastic rules and proper conduct, but monks can reprimand nuns.

Every nun, even the most senior and respected one, had to consider every monk as senior regardless of how junior a rank in the sangha he held. This rule can be observed today in every Buddhist country, where in the streets nuns bow to passing monks and make room for them while the monks do not return these gestures of courtesy and reverence. Another aspect of the eight chief rules affecting nuns' lives is the fact that the nuns' sangha is under the jurisdiction of the local monks' sangha. This implies that the ordination of nuns depends on the monks' cooperation and participation. Needless to say, in our time some fully ordained nuns object to some or all of these rules, pointing out that they were a later addition. But we have also records of the Chan monk Guanxi who had to work as a gardener for the nun Moshan Liaoran when he could not answer her probing questions (Grant, 2009: 30). This was clearly a case where a nun reprimanded a monk.

Despite some rhetoric to the opposite effect, in reality Buddhist men quite often seem to be unaware of Buddhist nuns living in their neighbourhood, or of the existence of significant nunneries. For instance, the Tibetan monastery of Labrang Tashikyil, located in Gansu Province, China, which in 1995 housed about 1,600 monks, enjoys government patronage in that it is designated a national heritage site. It is the destination of large tour groups and receives significant public funds. Its spiritual leader has his residence in the provincial capital of Lanchou and enjoys the privileges of a high-ranking government official. However, three small nunneries next to the famous Labrang monastery exist in abhorrent poverty and deprivation. They receive no support from the government or from the rich monks' monastery. Another example is the blindness of modern scholars: an article describing and discussing the monastic communities in a remote valley of the Himalayas does not mention any of the six or seven nunneries also in that valley (Crook and Shakya, 1994: 559–600). This is all the more regrettable as one of the nunneries dates back to at least the twelfth century and houses significant artwork from that period.

While in general Buddhist nuns did not enjoy the appreciation and veneration so readily given to monks, some Chinese and Korean nuns in the past did gain fame and even political influence. Several collections recount their life stories and achievements (Tsai, 1994; Grant, 2003 and 2009; Cho, ed., 2011).

The subordinate and economically as well as politically deprived status of nuns resulted in the formation of alternative organizations in some countries, as will be discussed later under the heading "Social Change in the Wake of Colonialism." In the last few decades, the situation of Buddhist nuns and the status of women in the various Buddhist traditions have been subject to significant changes, which will be discussed in the section "Buddhist Women in the Twentieth and Twenty-First Centuries."

The Buddhist Laywoman

In traditional Asian societies, the Buddhist laywoman stands in the shadow of the renunciant male, the monk. She provides him with food when he comes begging for alms to her door. She is praised for her generosity, patience, and self-effacing attitude as mother and wife. If she displays piety and devotion for the faith, society heaps praise on her.

I.B. Horner, a pioneering British scholar of the early twentieth century, gave a detailed discussion of the literary sources pertinent to women during the early centuries of Buddhism in her book *Women under Primitive Buddhism: Laywomen and Almswomen*, first published in 1930 and reprinted many times since. It is still a valid and indispensable source of information. Horner arranged the material in two sections, "The Laywomen" and "The Almswomen." The part dealing with the sources pertinent to laywomen categorizes women according to their social positions as mother, daughter, wife, widow, and woman worker. In contrast to pre-Buddhist times, Horner points out, women in the early Buddhist communities gained acceptance and status in their own right, despite lingering tendencies to hold on to some pre-Buddhist ideas with regard to the proper place of women in society.

The improved status of women in Buddhist communities is apparent in inheritance practices. For instance, Bhadda Kapilani, although married, appears to have been the sole owner of her property: it is said that when she renounced the world, "she handed over her great wealth to her kinsfolk" (Horner, 1930: 54, quoting the Pali commentary on *Therigatha*: 37). In another case, also reported in the commentary on the *Therigatha*, a father, on entering the monastic order, bestowed all his property on his daughter (Horner, 1930: 54ff.). Epigraphic documents from about the same period substantiate the impression received from the textual sources that women owned property and could decide how to dispose of it. Inscriptions dating from 120 to 80 BCE at the ancient Buddhist site of Bharhut illustrate this point: 14 inscriptions identify nuns as major donors, while 24 identify monks (Schopen, 1997: 30). Moreover, Horner draws our attention to the fact that, with very few exceptions, it was the usage of the time to speak of one's parents as "mother and father" (in Pali, *matapitaro*; Horner, 1930: 5ff.). The idea that this widespread convention may reflect the social status of women at that time finds support in the contemporary custom whereby men identified themselves by their mother's clan name. For instance, the Buddha's own mother belonged to the clan of Gotama, and he was known accordingly as Siddhartha (his personal name) Gautama (the adjectival form of his mother's clan name). Interestingly, in later Buddhist texts (from roughly the beginning of the Common Era on) the Buddha is known as Shakyamuni, "the wise of the Shakya"—Shakya being his father's clan name—and the custom of referring to him by his mother's clan name became obsolete. Does this change in naming conventions signal a change in the social status of women? Possibly, if we consider, for instance, a passage found in the *Milindapanha*, a text composed possibly around the beginning of the Common Era. Here Nagasena, a senior Buddhist monk, advises King Milinda (Pali for the Greek Menandros) as follows:

> There are, O king, these ten sorts of individuals who are despised and contemned [*sic*] in the world, thought shameful, looked down upon, held blameworthy, treated with contumely, not loved. And what are the ten? A woman without a husband, O King, and a weak creature, and one without friends or relatives. . . . (Horner, 1930: 26)

This passage follows the same line of thinking as *The Laws of Manu*, where the possibility of a woman living in independence was strictly ruled out. Several centuries lie between the conception of the earliest Buddhist texts and the *Milindapanha*. Would socio-cultural changes during this period permit speculation about the causes that led to the change in women's social position? Or did later scribes insert this phrase into an already existing text? Because of the dearth of socio-historical sources from ancient India, we have no answers to these questions.

In pre-modern times, the monastic institutions of some Asian countries refused to recognize women, lay or monastic, as equal partners. This was in line with the structures of pre-modern societies. Laywomen were rarely mentioned in classical Buddhist texts, and then only if they quietly affirmed the main concepts of Buddhism (generosity, compassion, patience, humility), supported the monks with food donations, and created an atmosphere conducive to the practice of Buddhism among her family members. However, the dearth of historical sources should not lead to the conclusion that Buddhist women were left outside the living faith. As already indicated above, the situation of the Buddhist nun and laywoman was much better documented in East Asian than in South Asian countries. With the increasing influence of modernity, Buddhist women around the world have gained more visibility in their individual societies, a process that we shall explore towards the end of this chapter.

Unique Feature: The In/Visibility of Buddhist Women

Until recently it was widely assumed that the Buddhist woman had become invisible, as the literary sources of Buddhist India failed to mention them from about the beginning of the Common Era. Scholars have taken opposite views as to when and under what traditions of Buddhism women were more integrated into the monastic hierarchy, and when they came to be seen in a more positive light. Horner (1930) has provided evidence that in the early days of Buddhism, women were integrated into the monastic system and advanced—like their male counterparts—to arhantship or sainthood. She claims that Buddhism significantly improved the status of women: "Thus, amid many currents, intricate but potent, the tide turned; and in its flow the position of women, as manifested in secular affairs, became one which was no longer intolerable and degraded; women were acknowledged at last to be capable of working as a constructive force in the society of the day" (Horner, 1930: 2).

In contrast to Horner, Diana Paul (1985: 303) argues that the **Mahayana** movement provided women with a better chance to become recognized and valued as integral members of the Buddhist communities. She stresses that because of the Mahayana emphasis on generosity and compassion, this movement saw the Buddhist layperson as equal if not superior to the monk or nun. Furthermore, in the Mahayana tradition a plethora of female deities embody the major spiritual and ethical concepts of Buddhism, which, Paul insists, points toward a valorization of women in general. Miranda Shaw tried to establish evidence that **Vajrayana**, or tantric Buddhism, the "crowning cultural achievement of the Pala period" (1994: 20), propelled the female practitioner to the forefront. Both authors relied on texts whose primary concern is to elaborate Buddhist doctrine rather than to record the lives of actual Buddhist women. As voluminous as the Buddhist literature in Indian and Tibetan languages is, these texts either iconize woman as the embodiment of perfect wisdom (*prajnaparamita*) or portray her as a threat to morality. But they fail to give a realistic representation of how Buddhist nuns and laywomen lived in a given society. While it is undeniable that women continued to be Buddhist practitioners throughout the centuries, the question that needs to be asked is this: Did Buddhist women, monastic as well as laywomen, have status and power equal to Buddhist men? The general answer, applying to all Buddhist countries and periods of Buddhism's long history, is no. Further, it remains an enigma that within the vast Buddhist literature preserved in Indian and Tibetan languages, there is not one text (with the exception of some parts of the *Therigatha*) that can be attributed with certainty to a female author. If tantric women were so learned, as Shaw believes, why did they leave no texts behind while their male partners did? Why do almost all tantric lineages comprise men and have only male founders?

In the Tibetan literature, Ma-gcig Lab-sgron (b. 1055) is often mentioned as an example of women's presence in Buddhist traditions, particularly the tantric tradition. Jérôme Edou says of her, "She is woman and mother, but she is also *Dakini* and deity, legitimized as such by being an emanation of the 'Great Mother of Wisdom,' Yum Chenmo, as well as of Arya Tara, who transmitted to her teachings and initiations. In this way she becomes an equal of the greatest Tibetan masters of her time" (1996: 6). He also admits that the only source containing information about her life is her biography, which "is far from being a historical work in the modern sense. Like most Tibetan sacred biographies, Machig's life introduces us to the magico-spiritual universe where the marvelous occupies center stage and the historical facts often recede into the background" (Edou, 1996: 3). It says a lot about the self-definition of contemporary Buddhist women in Tibet that the modern reincarnation of Ma-gcig Lab-sgron, Rig-'dzin Chos-nyid bZang-mo (1852–1953), pledged to be reborn as a man. This was in line with a common Tibetan prayer, popular among laypeople in particular, that addresses Buddha Amitabha and asks for rebirth in his Buddha realm, **Sukhavati**. A key sentence says, "May I not be reborn as a woman."

In the Far East, the situation with respect to literary sources is different. In China not only the political and ritual activities of the emperor and his court but personal life experiences were put into writing in poetry and funerary inscriptions. We have numerous first-person accounts of Buddhist nuns in

China and Korea. These literary sources provide us with insight into their life experiences and worldview (Grant, 2003 and 2009; Cho ed., 2011). Accounts of the lives of 65 eminent nuns from the fourth century to the sixth (Tsai, 1994) show that a few of them served as advisors to the emperor. In the late Ming period (1368–1644) women emerged not only as educated readers but also as sophisticated authors. The writings of seven female Chan masters document the contributions that Chinese nuns made to Chinese Buddhism (Grant, 2009). Contemporary Chinese nuns build on the achievements of these prior generations. Chinese and Korean nuns, primarily of the Chan tradition, have authored numerous texts and gained reputations as "Masters of Meditation (Chan or Son)" in the past as well as in the present.

Because of the records kept in East Asia (mainly Korea and China), we know that women had access to advanced education as well as family fortunes. Thus we get the impression that nuns enjoyed a more equal position there than in South and Southeast Asia. Both the nuns' access to education and the economic basis of the monasteries were major factors in deciding the fate of the bhikshunis' monasteries. Where Buddhist monasteries were required to produce their own food, as was and is customary in East Asia, the monks and nuns' monasteries stood on largely equal footing. However, where the monasteries depended for their subsistence on donations from laity and government, the nuns' communities took second place. This was the case in the Theravada countries of South and Southeast Asia and in the Mahayana countries of Central Asia (Tibet and Mongolia). In these countries nuns were—as far as we know—excluded from higher education, another factor that worked to their disadvantage. With regard to each cultural and historical context, we must ask this: Who shaped the prominent strands of Buddhist philosophy, who occupied the decision-making ranks within the monastic institution, who controlled the economic resources of the Buddhist institutions, who had access to its educational offerings, who composed the most common texts, and, finally, for whom were those texts written? By pondering these questions, one comes to understand the varying degrees of gender imbalance across the enormous diversity of Buddhist institutions and organizations. In our own time, substantial changes can be seen in the status of women within the various Buddhist traditions.

To sum up, one can say that while Buddhist renunciant women were almost equal to their male peers during the first few centuries of Buddhist history, their status and influence, not to mention those of Buddhist laywomen, declined thereafter, albeit with significant local differences. The causes of this decline are only partially known and vary from country to country. Not until the collapse of the colonial powers in Asia did the issue of the status and power of Buddhist renunciant women surface again.

Feminine Symbolization in Later Buddhist Thought

The symbolization of woman, apparent in various goddesses and symbols of feminine nature and values, occurs within a broader framework of religious and philosophical theorizing. The status of women and the symbolization of the feminine were significantly influenced by two major developments within Buddhism—that is, the rise first of Mahayana, the Great Vehicle, and then of Vajrayana, tantric Buddhism.

Mahayana Philosophy

Around the beginning of the Common Era, a new way of thinking took hold of the Buddhist communities in India. It became known as Mahayana, the Great Vehicle, because it was more inclusive in nature than the preceding Vehicles (*Yana*), which came to be derogatorily named **Hinayana**, Lower Vehicles. The main ideas propagated by Mahayana can be summarized as follows.

First, the spiritual goal was redefined from arhantship to buddhahood. While the pre-Mahayana traditions emphasized that enlightenment consisted of the elimination of desire, aversion, and ignorance, the Mahayana claimed

© 100nights/iStockphoto

Young nuns studying at the Kalaywa monastery in Yangon, Myanmar.

that enlightenment means buddhahood, that is, omniscience and limitless compassion, in addition to the elimination of desire, aversion, and ignorance.

Second, the Mahayana path towards enlightenment was not so much the eightfold noble path, but the 10 stages that a Buddha-to-be, or **bodhisattva**, had to master in the course of numerous lifetimes. The key elements were to develop consummate wisdom, which entailed a pledge not to realize nirvana until all sentient beings in the entire universe were also able to do so, and to cultivate an empathy that would embrace every living creature in love and respect, "like one's own mother."

Third, the ideal of the solitary monk entranced in meditation while sitting under a tree was often mocked: the new ideal was the Bodhisattva who lived in the world and put his or her compassion and love into action within it. The Bodhisattva was in some cases a layperson, and in a few cases female. Several Mahayana texts develop an image of the feminine and paint a picture of Buddhist women. Diana Paul extracts two conflicting ideas of the feminine from these texts:

> The first is the notion that the feminine is mysterious, sensual, destructive, elusive, and closer to nature. Association with this nether world may be polluting and deadly for the male and therefore must be suppressed, controlled, and conquered by the male in the name of culture, society and religion. Female sexuality as a threat to culture and society provides religion with a rationale for relegating women to a marginal existence (1985: xxiv).

A good example of this attitude is provided in the origin myths of the Tibetan people as it is told in Buddhist texts: A female Rock Demon was infatuated with a male monkey, who in reality was a Bodhisattva. When she tried to seduce him, the monkey referred to his religious vows of chastity and declined her invitations. In response the Rock Demon indicated that she was consumed by passion and lust and that if he was not willing to comply, a male Rock Demon would certainly do so, and this would result in populating the world with many little demons, creating havoc. In the end, the male Bodhisattva monkey gives in "for the benefit of all sentient beings." In this narrative, the female is wild, cannibalistic, and destructive, while the male is tame, celibate, pious, and compassionate (Stein, 1972: 37–9). Paul presents the second ideal as follows: "The second theme is the notion that the feminine is wise, maternal, creative, gentle, and compassionate. Association with this affective, emotional, transcendent realm is necessary for the male's fulfillment of his religious goals and for his release from suffering. Sexuality may be either controlled or denied in the feminine as sacred" (1985: xxv). This second aspect, the feminine as sacred, finds its most salient manifestation in the ideal of the Perfection of Wisdom, symbolized as a female and called "the mother of all Buddhas." While this phrase received wide circulation and approval among Buddhist traditions in China, Japan, Vietnam, Tibet, and Mongolia, it is questionable whether it had any positive effect on the status and roles of women as members of society. Ursula King (1995: 16) observes that the "symbolic ascendancy of the feminine often goes with a social denigration and low status of women in everyday life," and that one must distinguish "between the place given to women in the world of religious imagination and that accorded to them in the actual world of religious life."[1] King expresses here a fact that can be observed in various cultures and periods, from Confucian China, with its cult of the Queen of Heaven, to medieval Europe, with its cult of Mary, mother of Jesus. The female who is feared as a threat to the male, to culture, and to religion is transformed into a symbol of sanctity and thereby neutralized. Thus worship of the sacred feminine (as defined by males) permits control and subjugation of women as social beings. It would be a gross mistake, therefore, to assume that women enjoyed status and prestige similar to those accorded to men in traditions that extolled the feminine as a supreme symbol of sanctity.

A few Mahayana texts, however, suggest that gender differences are as empty as all other distinctions. Some of these texts, such as the *Teachings of Vimalakirti*, are humorous in that they make fun of the self-righteousness of monks and ordinary people (Paul, 1985: 220–32). Did such texts influence Buddhist societies' thinking about the position and status of women? No substantive evidence is available to support this.

Vajrayana

After Mahayana, another wave of new ideas spilled over the Buddhist communities of India around the middle of the first millennium. This new tradition became known as Vajrayana, the Diamond Vehicle, often referred to as "tantric Buddhism." It adopted common Mahayana ideas but infused them with a plethora of colourful rituals and imagery. Unlike the preceding Buddhist traditions, Vajrayana Buddhism viewed sexuality as an instrument to realize the enlightened state. However, the use of sexuality was highly circumscribed and regulated. Intercourse had to be carried out without seeking or experiencing desire or pleasure; the male had to prevent ejaculation by absorbing the semen into the spinal pathway. Women became essential participants in these sexual rites. David Snellgrove argues that these female partners, as well as the female tantric deities, were never more than handmaidens of the male masters and male deities (1987: 150). However, Shaw argues that

The presence of women and women's teachings, as well as affirma-
tions of female energy and spiritual capacities, are distinct features
of tantric religiosity. When one considers the historical position of
Tantra, an influx of feminine elements and insights is consistent with
the social inclusiveness of the movement and its receptivity to symbols, practices, and insights from new quarters (1994: 205).

Buddhist tantric texts rarely distinguish between earthly human beings
and symbolizations of them. For instance, the concept of *dakini* oscillates
between real women (most of low-caste or tribal backgrounds) and various
degrees of abstract symbolization. The Buddhist *dakini* shares this grey space
between reality and religious fantasy with witches and fairies and similar nocturnal creatures. Whether tantric Buddhism had any social impact remains
unverifiable, as pre-modern India did not keep historical and social records.
Tantric practice was always considered a secret activity that sought to avoid the
daylight and public scrutiny. Its social influence, therefore, remains unknown.
Tibetan tradition is the sole living Buddhist tradition that has embraced tantric
Buddhism without reservations. Tibetan monks of the Gelug order who have
become experts in tantric practice emphatically insist that all texts describing
sexual practices have to be understood as allegories and that they should never
be enacted literally. Other Tibetan monastic orders tend to understand these
texts in a more literal way.

Marginal Voices: Texts and Interpretations

Buddhism, like many other religions, was founded by a man; its main dignitar-
ies are men; men occupy the decision-making ranks and form the hierarchy;
men have written the normative texts, the master narrative; and men speak
publicly for the religion. In ancient times, only selected texts and narratives
that were considered fundamental had a chance of being put in writing. In
South Asia—where texts had to be hand-copied onto prepared palm leaves
until the nineteenth century, when European colonial powers introduced
the printing press—personal life experiences were hardly considered worthy
of reproduction. In China, block printing allowed mass reproduction of texts
on paper from the ninth century on. The custom of engraving on tombstones
the most remarkable aspects of a person's life became a way of highlighting an
individual's accomplishments. In this way, we learn about the lives of eminent
nuns in China.

The marginal texts fall into two categories: texts that render a feminine
perspective on the master narrative and texts that were composed by Buddhist

women, expressing their life experience. The first category is represented in an ancient Sanskrit text found in the mountainous area of Gilgit (in present-day Pakistan). It describes the two key events of the Buddha's life—his leaving home and family, and his enlightenment—in a way that strays significantly from the master narrative (Strong, 1995: 9–18). The master narrative says that the Buddha's father tried to prevent the fulfillment of the prophecy that his son might become a Buddha by surrounding him with beautiful women and grand luxury and by confining him to the palace grounds. During an outing, the future Buddha became aware of the suffering inherent in sickness, old age, death, and birth. He reacted with disgust to the seductiveness and youthful beauty of the palace women. Seeing his wife and his newborn son as nothing but fetters that would chain him to this life of suffering, he secretly left his wife, parents, and palace to become a mendicant ascetic. This master narrative does not indicate that the future Buddha felt any remorse for leaving his wife and newborn son or that he had any concern for their future life. Feminist scholars have pointed out that there is a systemic misogyny represented here.

However, the Sanskrit text found in Gilgit renders a different account, although it retains some elements of the common narrative, such as the father's intent to ensure that his son would not become an ascetic by immersing him in sensual pleasures. The night before his departure, the future Buddha reminds himself of his filial duties to ensure the continuation of his lineage, and he has intercourse with Yashodhara, his main wife, who becomes pregnant with their first and only son. But the future Buddha has dreams announcing his impending enlightenment, while Yashodhara has dreams foreshadowing her husband's departure. When the future Buddha realizes the sadness his wife feels, he attempts to convince her that these dreams are "nothing but dreams." When she begs him to take her along, he responds, "So be it; where I am going, I will take you." His quest for enlightenment by fasting finds a parallel in Yashodhara's health. When he becomes emaciated, she loses weight, and when finally the Buddha realizes enlightenment, her son is born. The text constructs this parallel by insisting that Yashodhara's pregnancy lasts for six years because she fasts while the future Buddha immerses himself in ascetic practices for six years. While the common story interprets the son's name, Rahula, as "fetter," this alternative story treats the name as deriving from Rahu, the divinity of the lunar eclipse, thus pointing to the lunar eclipse that happened at the moment of the son's birth while, at the same moment, his father, the Buddha, eclipsed the sun as the Enlightened One. This narrative seems to present the son as the fruit of enlightenment, who could be born into this world only when his father realized enlightenment. It is a rare text portraying the future Buddha as a loving and tender husband.

Another text in this category is the *Teachings of Vimalakirti* (Thurman, 1976), where we find a humorous discourse about gender. Here the highly respected monk Shariputra meets a fairy in Vimalakirti's house who engages him in a philosophical yet witty debate. In the context of exploring the ineffable nature of reality, Shariputra asks the fairy why she would not change her female sex—endorsing the common opinion that the female sex is less suitable for realizing enlightenment than the male. The fairy retorts as follows: "I have been here 12 years and have looked for the innate characteristics of the female sex and haven't been able to find them. How can I change them? Just as a magician creates an illusion of a woman, if someone asks why don't you change your female sex, what is he asking?" (Paul, 1985: 230). When the monk continues to pressure the fairy on the issue of innate characteristics, she transforms him into her own female body, and transforms her own body into that of the monk. Shariputra is confounded by this transformation, while the fairy declares, "if you can change into a female form, then all women [in mental state] can also change. Just as you are not really a woman but appear to be female in form, all women also only appear to be female in form but are not really women. Therefore, the Buddha said all are not really men or women" (Paul, 1985: 230). This text argues that sex and gender distinctions are as "void of inherent existence" as all other phenomena. This argument that gender is irrelevant finds popularity among Chan nuns in China. Classical Indian literature preserved hardly any factual information about peoples' lives and activities. It focused almost exclusively on philosophical, spiritual, and mythic discourse. In contrast, East Asian societies took a keen interest in recording the aspirations and activities not only of rulers but also of people that the society considered influential. For this reason we have a substantial body of Chinese and Korean texts reporting the lives and activities of Buddhist nuns belonging to different Buddhist traditions.

Kathryn Ann Tsai (1994) has translated a collection of lives of 65 eminent Chinese nuns. She notes rightly that the nuns' convents were subject to interference not only from the state, the emperor, and the aristocracy, but also from the monks' sangha. Unlike monks, nuns were prevented from setting up convents outside the boundaries of cities and other settlements, which would have made them less susceptible to interference. Some of these nuns were renowned for their profound learning and wisdom. A few served as advisors to the emperor. A more recent collection of biographies of nuns from the sixth to the twentieth century lists 200 names, but these accounts are not yet translated into a Western language.

In the literary heritage of the Chan tradition (Japanese, Zen), we find rich testimonies of women's striving for enlightenment and most importantly their recognition as women Chan masters forming their own lineages. The Chan practice, with its unrelenting focus on realizing emptiness—that is, the universal lack of any inherent identity or existence—found it difficult to adhere to the general gender discrimination found in other Buddhist traditions. In contrast, the popular Pure Land tradition held that the female body is unsuitable for realizing enlightenment: thus a woman had first to be reborn as a man in the Pure Land. By the time of the Song Dynasty (960–1279) a kind of transgender terminology came in use. Eminent Chan nuns known for their determination were praised as *da zhangfu*, or "great gentleman," while Chan monks aspired to cultivate a *laopo xin*, or "grandmotherly spirit." Linji (d. 867), the originator of the Chan practice known in Japanese as *Rinzai*, called out "It is all because of your grandmotherly kindness" when he returned to his teacher Huangbo (Grant, 2009: 32). A seventeenth-century Chan monk admonishes the audience at the occasion of the ordination of a nun: "Having discarded the white [clothes of a layperson] and donned the black [clothes of a monastic], she has distanced herself from worldly dust. Although a woman, she [now can be regarded] as having the body of a man" (Grant, 2009: 30). In seventeenth-century China, some learned Buddhist nuns were recognized as Chan Masters and, like their male peers, left behind "discourse records" (*yu lu*) together with sermons, spiritual exchanges, letters, and poems as well as biographical excerpts. Funerary eulogies composed by their monastic peers provide details of their spiritual striving, culminating in poems like this:

> Before my mother and father were born:
> Emptiness congealed silent and complete
> Originally there has been nothing lacking;
> The clouds disperse, revealing the blue sky (Grant, 2009: 47).

The Chan tradition relies not only on the primary ideas of emptiness, as found in the *Perfection of Wisdom Sutras* (*Prajnaparamita*), but also on the teachings of the universality of Buddha nature (*tathagata-garbha*) present in every existing thing. In advanced Chan practice this may be put into symbols and wordings reflecting pregnancy and birth, as was the case with Qiyuan Xinggang (1597–1654). Grant calls her "the matriarch of seventeenth-century women Chan masters, not only because she was the one of the first to set foot on the stage in that century but also because she left seven women Dharma successors, one of whom wrote a relatively detailed biographical account of her teacher's life" (2009: 37). This Dharma heiress, Yikui Chaochen, records the following encounter between Qiyuan Xinggang and her male master:

> He asked her: "The divine nature is not illusory. What was it like when you were [nourishing] the [spiritual] embryo?" Our Master replied: "It [felt] congealed, deep and solitary." Master Shiche said: "When you gave birth to the embryo, what was it like?" Our Master replied: "It was

like being completely stripped bare." Shiche said: "When you met with the founder, what was it like?" Our Master said: "I availed myself of the opportunity to see him face-to-face." Shiche said: "Good! Good! You will be a model for those who come after" (Grant, 2009: 47f).

Finally her teacher Shiche affirmed her as a rightful Chan master in the lineage of Dharma transmission. Qiyuan Xinggang condensed this experience in these lines:

> Now with scepter in hand, the lineage continues;
> No present, no past, it soars into the vast emptiness.
> If you still want to know what the true scepter is,
> The immovable Tathagata is in my hand (Grant, 2009: 48).

Qiyuan Xinggang became a renowned Dharma teacher and a role model for women Chan practitioners. She left behind letters directed not only to her monastic disciples but also to laypeople, men and women, providing them with spiritual guidance. Soon a large community of nuns gathered around her who had now become the abbess of the Lion-subduing Chan Cloister. Her main disciple, the nun Yikui Chaochen describes the vibrancy of this place:

> To this day, [the fact that we] have respectfully kept the pure regulations and do not depend on almsgivers is all due to the quality of the Master's arrangements. In time, [the monastery] became a hub of activity for Chan followers. Because the meditation halls were cramped and small and it was difficult to accommodate the assembly, the Master added two rooms to the West Dharma Hall, as well as a section of monk's living quarters. They were all completed within a couple of days, and the Master simply entrusted the matter to fate and did not anguish and worry over it (Grant, 2009: 68).

Shortly before her death Qiyuan Xinggang composed a death poem that crystallizes her enlightenment:

> Like the moon shining on a thousand rivers,
> The disk of luminosity is pure and unsullied.
> Now I will teach by sitting in the lotus position;
> Sentient beings will look and see through it all.
> If you ask what the last phrase is,
> Clapping my hands, I will say it is this (Grant, 2009: 74).

These precious testimonies detailing the lives and achievements of women Chan masters are available to us because they were collected and "included in a privately printed edition of the (expanded) Buddhist canon known as the *Jiang dazing jing*. The carving of the blocks for this collection began in 1579 on Mount Wutai . . .and it was not until 1677 that the first complete edition was printed" (Grant, 2009: 12).

Throughout Chinese history, some nuns expressed their own experiences through poetry. These poems "are to be found scattered in various different sources: a very, very few in collections of their own, somewhat more in anthologies of women's poetry, and many others embedded in biographical and other sorts of anecdotal and historical accounts" (Grant, 2003: ix). The ones Grant has translated in her book *Daughters of Emptiness* span a period from the third to the twentieth century. Miaozong (1095–1170) was granddaughter of a prime minister and highly educated; later she became a disciple and subsequent Dharma heir to the famous Chan master Dahui Zonggao. Her poem:

> Suddenly I have made contact with the tip of the nose,
> And my cleverness melts like ice and shatters like tiles.
> What need for Bodhidharma to have come from the West?
> What a waste for the Second patriarch to have paid his respects!
> To ask any further about what is this and what is that
> Would signal defeat by a regiment of straw bandits! (Grant, 2003: 33)

Buddhism was transmitted to Korea about 1600 years ago and the monks' and nuns' sanghas became established at the same time. The History of the Three Kingdoms (*Samguk yusa*), compiled in 1145, contains records of Buddhist nuns and female lay practitioners. Women of the nobility dedicated part of their fortunes to establish Buddhist temples and monasteries. Several of these women became nuns in their later lives. In the sixth century a Korean nun travelled together with some monks as one of the first Buddhist missionaries to Japan (Cho, ed., 2011: 16ff.). By the eighteenth century Buddhism was held in contempt, as Confucianism had been the state religion since the late fourteenth century. It is all the more uncommon that the country's prime minister, an ardent Confucian scholar, composed a eulogy for Master Chongyu, a nun, preserved in the Collected Works of Ponam (*Ponamjip*):

> The Master's lay surname was Kang. She was the daughter of a common family of P'yongyang. Her character was calm and pure, and she had none of the desires of ordinary people. From a young age she placed her faith in the Buddhas and patriarchs. . . . From early in the morning until night she intoned the Buddhist scriptures, unaware of

the passing of time. She broke the night by worshipping the Big Dipper, then she would enter her room and quietly close her eyes and sit in meditation, but she would not go to sleep . . . [Years later] the Master came bringing her good clothes, saying, "I am going to Hwajang hermitage at Changdan to have my hair shaved and become a nun." When she said this, she was already over sixty years of age. I consoled her, saying, "Do you really need to do this?" politely trying to dissuade her. The Master said, "Death is not far off, and I wish to go and enter nirvana. If I do not take the tonsure, I fear I will not be able to achieve my desire." Then, tears streaming down, she said, "I am sad that I cannot promise to meet you again." . . . On the fifteenth of the eleventh month in 1782, the Master died at the age of sixty-six years. (Heo, 2011: 93–5).

This is a rare insight into the spiritual life of a Buddhist nun who lived centuries ago. We shall return to Korean nuns when discussing the historical developments leading up to our times.

The survival of texts that record the lives of Buddhist nuns largely depends on circumstances and the luck of discovery. While some texts, like the Gilgit manuscript and the Vimalakirti sutra, frame Buddhist theory from a perspective of gender equality or irrelevance, others, like the Chinese records of important nuns and female Chan Masters and the equivalent records of Korean nuns, give us insight into their own thoughts, meditation practice, and standing in society. Nevertheless, these literary testimonies are a minority in comparison to the large number of texts promoting a male-centred view of Buddhism and extolling the lives of famous and influential Buddhist monks.

Social Change in the Wake of Colonialism

In the past, the fate of the various Buddhist traditions and institutions in Asia was connected with the political and economic history of each country. As different as the histories and cultures of the various Buddhist countries were, the situations of the women were equally varied. In general, Buddhist monasticism was the sole voice for all followers of the faith. The role of the Buddhist laity was mainly to provide the monks, and to a much lesser degree the nuns, with subsistence (robes, food, medicine, and shelter). In the course of time, as monastic institutions received huge donations in the form of land and bonded labourers, they often formed states within the state. The interlocking of monarchy and Buddhist institutions came to an abrupt end with the incursion of European colonial powers. Buddhist institutions lost not only their most affluent donors and sources of income, but also the basis of their political influence and prestige.

In missionary schools, local youth of the upper classes were confronted with modern ideas and their parents were exposed to the political and economic power of the West. Some Asian students at these schools were inspired to reform their own religious traditions to bring them more in line with modern thinking. The most prominent of these students was Anagarika Dharmapala (1864–1933) from Sri Lanka, who laid the foundations for a reformed modern Buddhism. Efforts to revive the Buddhist tradition focused on strengthening the role of the laity and improving the education of monks and, later, nuns. Buddhist women who had received a modern education championed reform of their native faith and fought for public recognition of Buddhist nuns: Voramai Kabilsingh and her daughter Bhikkhuni Dhammananda b. 1944 in Thailand; Cheng Yen (b. 1937) in Taiwan; and Pophui (1887–1975) in Korea, to name only a few.

In Taiwan in the 1950s, Master Hsin Yun created Fo Guang Shan, a movement that complemented traditional Buddhist contemplative training with social work. The organization operates seniors' homes, mobile health-care facilities, schools, and orphanages as well as traditional monasteries. Monks and nuns live and practise together, and file into the main temple hall side by side for rituals and ceremonies. Nuns are the heads of many of the movement's North American temples. They teach and conduct meditation sessions and are the superiors of other ordained members of the movement. Despite strong patriarchal tendencies in Chinese culture, Buddhist nuns and nunneries in China seem to enjoy more respect and support than those in South and Southeast Asia. Today in Taiwan the public respects the bhikshunis for their spiritual and social leadership (Shih, 1999: 427–31).

In Korea, both laywomen and bhikshunis were a visible part of Buddhism until the late fourteenth or early fifteenth century, when the Choson Dynasty adopted Confucianism as the state religion. Buddhist institutions, including the nuns' sangha, remained without state support and recognition until the Japanese occupation of Korea (1910–45). The support provided by Korea's colonial masters became the foundation for a strong modern nuns' order.

In Tibet, which began to embrace Buddhism in the eighth century, no bhikshuni sangha was ever formally established. When the People's Republic of China took over Tibet in the 1950s, restrictions were imposed on religious groups and institutions, but they were eased after Mao's death, and contact with the PRC opened the door to modernity, including gender equality, for Tibet. Tibetan nuns overwhelmingly follow tantric Buddhism and are not fully ordained. Monks of the Kagyu and Nyingma order supported the foundation or renovation of nunneries, mainly in Eastern Tibet (Goldstein /Kapstein, 1998). Sertha in Sichuan Province has become a large religious centre attracting hundreds of Tibetan women as well as Buddhists from abroad. However, it is not known whether Tibetan nuns living in Tibet are striving to obtain ordination and access to the monastic education that has traditionally been the prerogative of monks. In recent years, some nuns have instigated or participated in anti-government demonstrations.

Buddhist Women in the Twentieth and Twenty-First Centuries

The transmission of full ordination for women seems to have vanished in different countries at different times, with the consequence that only the rank of novice (*shramaneri*) was open to women who sought the life of a Buddhist renunciant. Destitute women, rather than women seeking enlightenment, turned to becoming nuns, and this situation further undermined the nuns' status in the eye of the public. By the late nineteenth century, full ordination was unavailable to Buddhist nuns in all of South and Southeast Asia (with the partial exception of Vietnam) as well as Tibet, the Buddhist Himalayan kingdoms, and Mongolia. In the view of the general public, they were as novices inferior to the monks who had full ordination. But even in countries where Buddhist nuns did have access to full ordination (such as China, Korea, and Vietnam) they were traditionally barred from higher education and therefore denied access to the monastic ranks.

Two responses to this state of affairs can be distinguished: providing social services as part of the Buddhist ethic of compassion, and working to make full ordination available to nuns of all Buddhist traditions. In general, one can say that improving the nuns' education and status meets the strongest opposition in those traditions where monasticism and government are closely intertwined (such as Tibetan-speaking areas, Thailand, and Myanmar). Nevertheless, some open-minded monks in those traditions are working to give nuns access to all the levels of Buddhist learning from which they have been barred, that is, mainly the philosophical and theoretical study of Buddhism. The situation began to change in the late twentieth century and continues to do so.

In Sri Lanka, novice nuns providing social services formed the **Dasasila Mata**, Mothers of the Ten Precepts. This movement enjoys a better public reputation than the sangha of fully ordained monks because its members are not involved in politics and are not tainted by the largesse of government support (Barnes, 1996: 262–7). Chandra Khonnokyoong (1909–2000), a Thai nun and renowned meditation teacher, founded the Wat Phra Dhammakaya organization, which maintains meditation centres that are open to lay people. Cheng Yen (also Shi Ciji and Shengyan) founded the Buddhist Compassion Relief

Foundation in 1966, which became the largest charity in Taiwan and provides over US$20 million per year in charity projects around the world (Lopez, 2002: 227).

The second strategy was to work towards the reinstatement of full ordination for nuns. As was mentioned above, by the twentieth century bhikshuni ordination was available only in the Chinese, Vietnamese, and Korean sanghas. In other Buddhist countries, it had either disappeared over the centuries (e.g., Sri Lanka) or never been introduced (e.g., Tibet, Thailand). Some Buddhist traditions insist that the realization of enlightenment requires a life as a fully ordained monk or nun. If full ordination is not available to them, then nuns belonging to those traditions are barred from unfolding their full spiritual potential and reaching enlightenment. At the same time, the lack of full ordination prevents access to monastic ranks, higher education, and financial support. Thus striving to make bhikshuni ordination available in those traditions where it was absent became a prime goal for Buddhist nuns in the late twentieth and early twenty-first centuries. However, this has proved to be a thorny issue, entangled in often-contradictory interpretations of the textual sources regulating ordination.

To complicate the situation further, there are three different **Vinaya** lineages: Theravada, followed by the monastics in South Asia and Southeast Asia; Mulasarvastivada, followed by the Tibetan Buddhists; and Dharmaguptaka, followed by East Asian Buddhists. Most lineages require that those senior monks and nuns who bestow full ordination on the novice nun must have been ordained in the same lineage, although exceptions were made in the past when extraordinary circumstances required them. Buddhist as well as secular scholars debated the issue at "The International Congress on Women's Role in the Sangha" in Hamburg, Germany, in 2007. The papers presenting the different and sometimes conflicting views were published a few years later (Mohr and Tsedroen, ed., 2010). The movement to reinstate full bhikshuni ordination was spearheaded by a few highly educated nuns: Bhikkhuni Dhammananda, Ayya Khema, Thubten Chodron, and Jampa Tsedroen. Buddhist monks educated at Western universities supported the nuns' aspirations with acumen (Ajahn Brahm, Bhikkhu Sujato, Bhikkhu Analayo, Bhikkhu Bodhi). The Dalai Lama lent his support, and the conference yielded significant results.

In the Theravada tradition, senior monks from Sri Lanka, Thailand, and Myanmar have long been opposed to the reintroduction of bhikshuni ordination, but Western Theravada monks used modern research methods to explore the possibilities. Determined nuns from Sri Lanka and Thailand first sought full ordination from the Chinese sangha in Taiwan or Hong Kong. Relying on the findings of carefully researched Vinaya texts, they were able to convince those opposed to the reintroduction of full ordination and brought about an irrevocable change in the last decade. In Sri Lanka there are now many hundreds if not thousands of fully ordained nuns. Novice nuns from Thailand and Myanmar (Burma) now obtain full ordination in Sri Lanka. But when they return to their own countries they still face significant discrimination and in some cases even imprisonment. The political and judicial systems of Thailand and Myanmar do not (yet) recognize bhikshunis as part of the Buddhist sangha. Bhikkuni Dhammananda, supported by some influential lay people, is working towards changing these laws in Thailand, but progress is slow. The situation in Myanmar is still lagging behind.

Korean nuns always had access to full ordination but suffered setbacks from the fifteenth century onward. In our time "the Korean bhikshuni community made remarkable advancements in its social presence and internal strength" (Cho, ed., 2011: 33). The bhikshuni sangha is now recognized on the same level as that of the bhikshus and the nuns participate as equals in the governing committees. With advancements in education and general prosperity, the status and public recognition of Korean nuns has risen significantly. Cho (2011: 36–8) lists six factors accounting for the extraordinary success of the Korean bhikshuni sangha: cohesive collective power, economic improvement, emphasis on meditation as the main practice, embracing the changes in Korean society, a general rise in the status and role of women in modern Korean society, and the assistance that female clergy offer women as they make the transition from extended families to nuclear ones.

Buddhism in Tibet has evolved in four branches: Nyingma, Kagyu, Sakya, and Gelug. Because the first two traditions practise mainly tantric Buddhism, they do not emphasize strict observance of Vinaya rules. Some monks have supported the nuns' communities of their own traditions and helped them build monasteries housing hundreds if not thousands of nuns. The Gelug tradition developed a well-defined academic education leading to a degree (*geshe*) similar to a doctorate in Buddhist philosophy. To be fully ordained is a prerequisite for completing these lengthy academic studies; thus novice nuns are excluded from them. Nevertheless, in the late twentieth century, some novice nuns living in exile in India were admitted to these studies, and in 2012 the Office of the Dalai Lama granted them the new title *rimed geshe*. Kelsang Wangmo, a novice nun of German descent, was the first one to receive this title after 16 years of studying Tibetan Buddhist philosophy. However, despite all the well-documented research, numerous submissions to the most senior Gelug monks and meetings with representatives of the Tibetan Department of Religion and Culture, part of the exile administration, full ordination for nuns within the Tibetan Gelug tradition has still not been established (Tsedroen, 2008: 205 ff.).

Buddhism became known as a religion in the West beginning in the late nineteenth century, and soon people from Europe and North America began to practise it. At first, the revised or **"Protestant" Buddhism** propagated by the

English-educated elite from Sri Lanka gained much attention. After the end of the Second World War, however, all forms of Buddhism produced shoots in the West. Soon Buddhism in its ancient Asian form encountered the new intellectual movements of the West. In Europe, Buddhism became known mainly through scholarly translations of major texts. In North America, immigrants from Buddhist countries continued their own traditions as increasing numbers of people were introduced to Buddhism, whether through contact with their ethnic Buddhist neighbours, through deployment in Asia during the Korean and Vietnamese wars, or through cultural trends such as the Beat movement, which introduced Buddhism to American pop culture. Contemporary Buddhism is characterized by almost endless variety and diversity. Where once the various Buddhist traditions were segregated by cultural and language boundaries, globalization took Tibetan Buddhism to Taiwan and South Africa, Theravada to Australia, and Chinese Chan to North America, to give a few examples. The interaction between these various Buddhist communities and the main movements of our times—human rights, gender equality, and gay rights—furthered this diversity. Western women began to challenge the ingrained gender bias of many Buddhist traditions. They demanded to be trained as Zen priests in Japan, and eventually, after overcoming many obstacles, succeeded (Boucher, 1988: 133–44). Article 2 of the Universal Declaration of Human Rights (www. un.org/en/documents) enshrines equality between men and women. Based on the UN declaration, women in many religious traditions have challenged patriarchal structures. In Asia as well as the West, well-educated, fully ordained bhikshunis are striving to see women filling some of the administrative ranks alongside monks. Influential politicians and public figures, mostly men, are supporting the bhikshunis' aspirations. In the West, numerous laywomen have become meditation teachers, leaders of Buddhist centres, and outspoken critics of the patriarchal structures that remain. This is a new phenomenon, as laity traditionally did not function in these capacities. While some women teachers follow traditional teachings and practices, others devise new ways. For instance, Sylvia Wetzel, a well-known German meditation teacher, blends Theravada meditation with Tibetan Tara rituals. Women teachers are discovering hitherto forgotten female masters and including their names in recitations of individual lineages, which traditionally have consisted of male teachers only. Many retreat centres would not be functioning without the women who manage and support them. Over the last decades, several associations of Buddhist women have been formed in various places: Sakhyadhita is a global association with a strong component of Buddhist nuns, while the Network of Buddhist Women of Europe (www.buddhistwomen.eu) is affiliated with the European Buddhist Union. These and many other groups are organizing conferences and thus making global networking possible.

Buddhist lay practitioners adhere to five precepts: not to harm any living creature, not to steal, not to engage in harmful speech, not to consume alcohol or drugs, and not to engage in sexual misconduct. The canonical texts do not specify what constitutes sexual misconduct, but there is a general agreement that sexual activity should be guided by mutual respect. Monks and nuns have to abstain from any form of sexual activity. The Theravada Vinaya prohibits the ordination of individuals who do not clearly fall into one of two categories—men and women—or who are prostitutes. The gay rights movement confronted some Buddhist assumptions about the correct use of sexuality. In general, sexual orientation does not play a significant role in either lay or monastic Buddhist communities. Zen and Chan communities seem not to care about it. While male homosexual practice is documented in Tibetan monasteries, in June 1997, the Dalai Lama affirmed that from a Buddhist point of view, lesbian and gay sex is generally considered sexual misconduct. In fact, in his book *Beyond Dogma*, he has written that "homosexuality, whether it is between men or between women, is not improper in itself. What is improper is the use of organs already defined as inappropriate for sexual contact" (cited at www.religioustolerance.org/hom_budd.htm). As they have in other religions, gays and lesbians have formed their own groups within different Buddhist traditions. Gay and lesbian Buddhist communities now exist in most major cities. Chinese Buddhist gays and lesbians held a national conference in Hong Kong in 1996. In Germany lesbians have formed their own Buddhist community, which offers annual practice days and networking. Historically, male homosexuality was at least tolerated if not openly accepted in certain sanghas (for example, in Tibet), while some traditions, such as the **Shingon** school of Japanese Buddhism, have even considered male same-sex love a means toward realizing enlightenment.

Summary

Returning to the two quotations at the beginning of this chapter, we can see that both are accurate despite their apparent contradiction. We have encountered the Buddha's female disciples, masters of the *Tripitaka*, who rightly called themselves his daughters, born again from his teaching. We have met Chinese and Korean Chan nuns, some in the past and some in the present, who have rightfully taken their places as teachers and heads of their own lineages; built monasteries and managed them as abbesses; and left behind poems that try to articulate their ineffable enlightenment experience. We have also been confronted with a thundering silence when we looked for Buddhist women and nuns from later periods in India and Southeast and Central Asia, who had no opportunity to express their own worldview, or their experiences as women striving for enlightenment. For centuries, Buddhist women and nuns were invisible in many countries, but they are now racing to the foreground of social awareness and asking for their rightful places beside the monks and in society. In present-day Korea, the nuns' order has a very visible presence not only in monastic organizations but also among the general public. In Taiwan, nuns have built the largest charity in the country and provide essential social services. In the Western world, which has become acquainted with Buddhism in the last two centuries, women are taking up leadership positions. As meditation teachers they are exploring new ways of meaningful practice, while as scholars and nuns they are advocating the reintroduction of full ordination for nuns in all Buddhist traditions. As Buddhists in the West adopt many of the cultural and social concerns of the modern world (such as feminism, gender equality, gay rights, social concerns for the deprived, democracy, individualism, and concern for the environment), a new form of Buddhism is emerging that will eventually claim its own position on the wide spectrum of Buddhisms shaped by individual cultures and societies (Queen, 2000). Buddhism, like other major religions, faces the task of integrating general human rights, including gender equality, into its religious thinking and practice.

Note

1.   I owe this reference to Danielle Lefebvre, graduate student of Religious Studies at the University of Alberta.

Glossary

arhantship (*also* arhatship)   The state of being an arhant (also "arhat")—a person who has reached enlightenment while still alive; the ideal of the Theravada tradition.

bhikku (Pali), bhikshu (Sanskrit)   A Buddhist monk.

bhikkuni (Pali), bhikshuni (Sanskrit)   A fully ordained Buddhist nun.

bodhisattva   A person who is on the path to complete enlightenment, a Buddha-to-be; the ideal of the Mahayana tradition.

Buddha   "The Enlightened One"; the title adopted by Siddhartha Gautama, founder of Buddhism.

dakini   A female figure straddling the boundaries between woman (mostly young and seductive), sorceress, and fairy; important as the consort of the male practitioner in tantric traditions.

Dasasila Mata   "Mother of the Ten Precepts," name for a lay renunciant in Sri Lanka who has taken ten precepts but is not a fully ordained *bhikshuni*.

Dharma (Sanskrit), Dhamma (Pali)   The teachings of the Buddha.

Hinayana   "Lower Vehicle"; derogatory designation for those Buddhist schools that evolved prior to the Mahayana.

Mahayana   "Great Vehicle"; a development of Buddhism that originated around the beginning of the Common Era and branched into many schools; common mainly in China, Japan, Korea, Vietnam, Tibet, Nepal, Bhutan, and Mongolia; see also **bodhisattva**.

nirvana   The end of suffering; the goal of Buddhist spirituality.

Pali   The Middle Indian language in which the texts of the Pali canon are written. The Theravada tradition considers Pali a sacred language.

"Protestant" Buddhism   The Buddhism promoted by reformers such as Anagarika Dharmapala in Sri Lanka in the late nineteenth and early twentieth centuries: stripped of folk elements, rituals, and legends, and emphasizing ethics, reason, and humanism.

sangha   The community of Buddhists; in broad terms, the fourfold community consisting of monks, nuns, lay men, and lay women; in a more restricted sense, monks and nuns.

Shingon   Japanese school of tantric Buddhism.

Sukhavati   Buddha Amitabha's "pure land," where spiritually advanced followers enjoy his presence and teaching.

Tantra   A class of Buddhist texts presented as "Buddha word"; the Tantras form part of the Tibetan Buddhist canon and contain the teachings of Vajrayana.

Theravada   "Teaching of the Elder"; a Buddhist school originating before the Common Era; practised mainly in Sri Lanka, Myanmar, Thailand, Cambodia, and parts of Vietnam.

Therigatha   "The Songs of the Elder [Nuns]," a collection of poems attributed to early Buddhist nuns.

Tripitaka   "Three collections"; the name of the original Pali-language Buddhist canon.

Vajrayana   "The diamond vehicle," also known as tantric or Tibetan Buddhism, which emerged before the middle of the first millennium CE; common mainly in Tibet, Bhutan, Nepal, and Mongolia, and to a lesser degree in Japan and Vietnam.

Vinaya   The collection of Buddhist monastic rules and guidelines.

Further Reading

Allione, Tsultrim. 1984. *Women of Wisdom*. London: Routledge & Kegan Paul.

Cabezón, José Ignacio, ed. 1992. *Buddhism, Sexuality, and Gender*. Albany: State University of New York Press.

Cho, Eun-Su, ed. 2011. *Korean Buddhist Nuns and Laywomen*. Albany: State University of New York Press.

Grant, Beata. 2009. *Eminent Nuns: Women Chan Masters of Seventeenth-Century China*. Hawai'i: University of Hawai'i Press.

Horner, I.B. 1990. *Women under Primitive Buddhism: Laywomen and Almswomen*. 1930. Rpt Delhi: Motilal Banarsidass Publishers.

Joy, Morny. 2006. "Gender and Religion: A Volatile Mixture." *Temenos the Nordic Journal of Comparative Religion* 42, 1: 7–43.

Mohr, Thea, and Jampa Tsedroen, eds. 2010. *Dignity & Discipline: Reviving Full Ordination for Buddhist Nuns*. Boston: Wisdom Publications.

Paul, Diana. 1079. *Women in Buddhism: Images of the Feminine in Mahāyāna Tradition*. Berkeley: University of California Press.

Queen, Christopher S., and Sallie B. King, eds. 1996. *Engaged Buddhism: Buddhist Liberation Movements in Asia*. Albany: State University of New York Press.

Tsomo, Karma Lekshe, ed. 1988. *Sakyadhītā: Daughters of the Buddha*. Ithaca, NY: Snow Lion Publications.

Wurst, Rotraut. 2001. *Identitätim Exil: Tibetisch-Buddhistische Nonnen und das Netzwerk Sakyādhitā*. Marburger Studien zur Afrika und Asienkunde, Series C, vol. 6. Berlin: Dietrich Reimer Verlag.

Films and Online Sources

Bhikkhuni: Revival of the Women's Order. Forthcoming. Directed by Wiriya Sati. Budaya Productions.

Cave in the Snow. 2002. 52 mins. Directed by Liz Thompson. Firelight Productions. A documentary on Tenzin Palmo, one of the first Western women to become a Buddhist nun. Inspired by the biography by Vicki Mackenzie. Further information online at www.firelight.com.au/cave.html.

The Living Goddess. 1975. 30 mins. Directed by Frank Heimans and Josette Heimans. The life of Kumari Devi, a virgin girl-child installed as a deity in Nepal.

Network of Buddhist Women of Europe Website: www.buddhistwomen.eu.

To the Land of Bliss. 2002. 47 mins. Directed by Wen-jie Qin. Documentary on Pure Land Buddhism. Further information online at www.der.org/films/to-the-land-of-bliss.html.

See "Women Make Movies," www.wmm.com, for a growing list of films about women in various religious traditions.

References

Barnes, Nancy J. 1996. "Buddhist Women and the Nuns' Order in Asia." Pp. 259–94 in Christopher S. Queen and Sallie B. King, eds. *Engaged Buddhism: Buddhist Liberation Movements in Asia*. Albany: State University of New York Press.

Boucher, Sandy. 1988. *Turning the Wheel: American Women Creating the New Buddhism*. San Francisco: Harper & Row.

Cho, Eun-Su, ed. 2011. *Korean Buddhist Nuns and Laywomen*. Albany: State University of New York Press.

Crook, John, and Tsering Shakya. 1994. "Monastic Communities in Zangskar: Location, Function and Organisation." Pp. 559–600 in John Crook and Henry Osmaston, eds. *Himalayan Buddhist Villages: Environment, Resources, Society and Religious*

Life in Zangskar, Ladakh. Delhi: Motilal Banarsidass.

Dargyay, Eva K. 1991. "Sangha and State in Imperial Tibet." Pp. 111–27 in Ernst Steinkellner, ed. *Tibetan History and Language: Studies Dedicated to Uray Géza on His Seventieth Birthday.* Wiener Studien zur Tibetologie und Buddhismuskunde Heft 26. Wien: Arbeitskreis für Tibetische und Buddhistitische Studies, Universität Wien.

Edou, Jérôme. 1996. *Machig Labdrön and the Foundations of Chöd.* Ithaca, NY: Snow Lion Publications.

Faure, Bernard. 2003. *The Power of Denial: Buddhism, Purity and Gender.* Princeton: Princeton University Press.

Goldstein, Melvyn C. 1989. *A History of Modern Tibet, 1913–1951: The Demise of the Lamaist State.* Rpt 1993. New Delhi: Munshiram Manoharlal.

Goldstein, Melvyn C., and M. Kapstein. 1998. *Buddhism in Contemporary Tibet: Religious Revival and Cultural Identity.* Berkeley: University of California Press.

Grant, Beata. 2003. *Daughters of Emptiness. Poems of Chinese Buddhist Nuns.* Boston: Wisdom Publications.

Grant, Beata. 2009. *Eminent Nuns. Women Chan Masters of Seventeenth-Century China.* Hawai'i: University of Hawai'i Press.

Heo, Heung-sik. 2011. "Two Female Masters of Two Eras: Differences and Commonalities in Roles." Pp. 91–117 in Eun-Su Cho, ed. *Korean Buddhist Nuns and Laywomen.* Albany: State University of New York Press.

Horner, I.B. 1930. *Women under Primitive Buddhism: Laywomen and Almswomen.* Rpt 1990. Delhi: Motilal Banarsidass.

Hüsken, Ute. 1997. *Die Vorschriften für die Buddhistische Nonnengemeinde im Vinaya-Pitaka der Theravādin.* Monographien zur indischen Archeologie, Kunst und Philologie 11. Edited by Marianne Yaldiz. Berlin: Dietrich Reimer Verlag.

———. 2010. "The Eight Garudhammas." Pp. 143–8 in Thea Mohr and Jampa Tsedroen, eds. *Dignity & Discipline. Reviving Full Ordination for Buddhist Nuns.* Boston: Wisdom Publications.

Johnston, E.H., trans. 1936. *The Buddhacarita or Acts of the Buddha.* Rpt 1972. Delhi: Motilal Banarsidass.

King, Ursula, ed. 1995. *Religion and Gender.* Oxford: Blackwell.

Lopez, Donald S., ed. 2002. *A Modern Buddhist Bible. Essential Readings from East and West.* Boston: Beacon Press.

Mohr, Thea, and Jampa Tsedroen, eds. 2010. *Dignity & Discipline. Reviving Full Ordination for Buddhist Nuns.* Boston: Wisdom Publications.

Norman, K.R. 1983. *Pāli Literature Including the Canonical Literature in Prakrit and Sanskrit of all the Hinayāna Schools of Buddhism.* A History of Indian Literature 7, 2. Edited by Jan Gonda. Wiesbaden, Germany: Otto Harrassowitz.

Paul, Diana Y. 1985. *Women in Buddhism: Images of the Feminine in Mahāyāna Tradition.* 2nd edn. Berkeley: University of California Press.

Queen, Christopher S., ed. 2000. *Engaged Buddhism in the West.* Boston, MA: Wisdom Publications.

Queen, Christopher S., and Sallie B. King, eds. 1996. *Engaged Buddhism: Buddhist Liberation Movements in Asia.* Albany: State University of New York Press.

Schopen, Gregory. 1997. *Bones, Stones, and Buddhist Monks. Collected Papers on the Archeology, Epigraphy, and Texts of Monastic Buddhism in India.* Honolulu: University of Hawaii Press.

Shaw, Miranda. 1994. *Passionate Enlightenment: Women in Tantric Buddhism.* Princeton, NJ: Princeton University Press.

Shih, Heng-Ching. 1999. "Buddhist Spirituality in Modern Taiwan." Pp. 427–31 in Takeuchi Yoshinori Takeuchi, ed. *Buddhist Spirituality—Later China, Korea, Japan, and the Modern World.* New York: Crossroad Publishing.

Snellgrove, David. 1987. *Indo-Tibetan Buddhism: Indian Buddhists and Their Tibetan Successors.* Boston: Shambhala.

Stein, R.A. 1972. *Tibetan Civilization.* Translated by J.E. Stapleton Driver. London: Faber and Faber.

Strong, John S. 1995. *The Experience of Buddhism. Sources and Interpretations.* Belmont, CA: Wadsworth.

Sujato, Bhante. 2007. "Bhikshunis in Theravada." Accessed 28 Feb. 2014 at www.congress-on-buddhist-women.org/fileadmin/files/bhikkhuniforTibet2_01.pdf.

Thurman, Robert A.F. 1976. *The Holy Teaching of Vimalakīrti.* University Park: Pennsylvania State University Press.

Tsai, Kathryn Ann. 1994. *Lives of the Nuns: Biographies of Chinese Buddhist Nuns from the Fourth to Sixth Centuries.* Honolulu: University of Hawaii Press.

Tsedroen, Jampa (Carola Roloff). 2008. "Generation to Generation: Transmitting the Bhukshuni Lineage in Tibetan Tradition." Pp. 205 ff. in Karma Lekshe Tsomo ed., *Buddhist Women in a Global Multicultural Community.* 9th Sakyadhita Conference. Kuala Lumpur: Sukhi Hotu Publications.

Tsomo, Karma Lekshe. 1988. "Prospects for an International Bhiksunī Sangha." Pp. 236–57 in Karma Lekshe Tsomo, ed. *Sakyādhitā: Daughters of the Buddha.* Ithaca, NY: Snow Lion Publications.

Yoshinori Takeuchi, ed. 1999. *Buddhist Spirituality—Later China, Korea, Japan, and the Modern World.* New York: Crossroad Publishing Company.

CHAPTER 4

◇◇◇◇

Women in Chinese Traditions

Lee D. Rainey

Offering incense at a temple in Shanghai.

Yi Nianhua and Gao Yinxian

Nu shu is a special script used by women in the remote rural area of Jiang Yong County, Hunan Province, to write diaries, letters, histories, biographies, songs, and poems. The women most responsible for our knowledge of *nu shu* were Yi Nianhua and Gao Yinxian: two of seven "sworn sisters" who often met to read *nu shu* compositions together while they worked.

Orphaned at the age of four, Yi Nianhua was raised by her grandparents, and her grandfather taught her how to read Chinese characters; but she learned the **"hidden women's writing"** from her aunt. A talented writer, Yi was recognized for the literary quality of her work. The death of her husband when she was 29 was a great blow. Yet she continued writing, as well as collecting and memorizing other women's texts, and eventually taught the hidden script to her granddaughter.

Gao Yinxian learned the women's writing from her mother. After marriage, she moved to another village and wrote to her six "sworn sisters" who lived in other villages. Like Yi's, Gao's life was difficult, as we can see in this poems addressed to the goddess (*Niangniang*) Feng Gu:

> Feng Gu Niangniang please hear my words;
> My miseries are written down,
> O Niangniang who hears a thousand worries, receive my
>   true heart.
> Why have I again not borne a son,
> When I was fated to be born with a woman's name?
>
> There is happiness in other people's homes,
> Alone in my room, there is never a day of joy.
> From dawn to darkness,
> No day passes without sorrow and regrets.[1]

The tradition of reading and writing *nu shu* was passed down from generation to generation, but the texts themselves were not. As death approached, a woman would tell her family to burn her *nu shu* texts—her most precious possessions—as an offering to the dead, so that they would follow her to the next world. Thus when Hu Chizhu died in

1979, her sworn sisters, including Gao and Yi, burned dozens of books of women's writing at her funeral.

When researchers began to investigate the hidden women's writing, both Yi and Gao were in their eighties. Anxious to teach scholars how to read the script and to explain the tradition, they generously shared all their texts and helped to translate them into Chinese characters. Today the hidden women's writing is known around the world.

Introduction and Overview

Chinese culture has long been perceived in the West as exotic, and Chinese traditions as mystical. Early Western missionaries blamed **Confucianism** and Buddhism for what they saw as the oppression of Chinese women, and twentieth-century Chinese reformers emphasized the image of the downtrodden woman as part of their general critique of traditional China. Thus the stereotype of the meek, oppressed Confucian woman persists alongside the stereotype of the dragon lady—imperious, mysterious, and powerful.

It is clear that religious traditions have shaped the lives of women in China throughout history. Chinese women have found ways to work within their traditions, reshaping the thought of some and incorporating the strictures of others. Women in both traditional and modern China have not simply been the passive recipients of whatever the traditions have had to say about women.

History and Status of Women

Ancient China

The active role of women in Chinese religious traditions was never clearer than in very ancient times, when there was not only a Mother Goddess but a large number of other female deities: Nu Gwa (or Nu Wa; see Paper, 1999: 51) created human beings; Xi Wang Mu, the Queen Mother of the West, held the secrets of immortality; and Tou Mu, the North Star, controlled the books of life and death. In addition, most shamans or mediums (*wu*) were women: they served as intermediaries with the gods and the forces of nature, communicating with the dead, dancing and praying to promote fertility or to end a drought, calling back the souls of the sick, performing divinations, exorcizing building sites, serving as matchmakers, and forecasting the weather. The ancient texts that record these activities indicate that the shamans worked directly for the ruler, and that their role was not limited to the performance of religious rituals: they also offered political advice.

Over time, however, the goddesses, shamans, and women in general all lost ground. The Millet Queen—the earliest ancestor of the Zhou Dynasty (c. 1040–256 BCE)—was transformed into the "Lord of Millet," some states banned women from court entertainments, the matrilineal system of inheritance was abandoned, and texts began to appear that characterized women as dangerous, the source of moral and political decline (*Guo Yu*, "Chou Yu"; *Zuo Zhuan*, "Duke Zhuang," 692 BCE; *Zuo Zhuan*, "Duke Chao," 509 BCE; see Legge, 1960).

Confucianism

By the time Confucius (551–479 BCE) was seeking solutions to the continual social upheaval of the Warring States period (722–221 BCE), the status of women had declined. Confucius began by talking about ritual, which he understood to encompass not only religious ritual, but the moral and social actions that hold a society together. He believed that the social chaos of his time was the result of a breakdown in proper relationships between people, a loss of mutual respect, and erosion of the idea of mutual responsibility. Even in its simplest "please-and-thank you" form, ritual conveys mutual respect, establishes social trust, and delineates relationships. One example is the social ritual of exchanging greetings, which serves to acknowledge, show respect for, and define the status of both parties involved.

The essential requirement for the performance of these social-political-religious rituals is morality, which for Confucius consisted in the exercise of virtues such as loyalty, honesty, sincerity, filial piety (see below), and moral courage. A person with all these virtues would have the ideal attitude that he called *ren* (humanity). Confucius defined humanity as "not doing to others what you would not have done to yourself" (*Analects* 4.15). He encouraged his followers to look first to themselves and then, through ritual, to treat others as they would wish to be treated.

Ritual can be truly understood only by moral beings who have been trained to examine their own consciences and to follow the dictates of conscience in their public life. Confucius called such people **junzi**—"gentlemen." The foundation of the Confucian gentleman's morality was filial piety: respect for and service to one's parents. Government would be best served by gentlemen whose grounding in filial piety and education in the ancient classics would equip them to offer the ruler (ideally, a *junzi* himself) sage moral and political advice, while serving as examples to the people. Then, by internalizing the moral example set by the government, the people would become happy and prosperous.

Confucius rarely had anything to say about women, and it is clear that his philosophy was intended almost entirely for men. In a culture that was becoming increasingly patriarchal, the concept of filial piety applied to men in relation to their fathers and grandfathers. Confucius and his followers understood the political and social influence of upper-class women to be among the major impediments to the implementation of their program. In practical political terms, they abhorred the influence that wives, mistresses, and shamans had on rulers, and in theoretical terms, they believed that they—educated Confucian gentlemen—should be the ones to offer political advice and carry out the rituals of state. According to the classic Confucian texts, the downfall of states was often the consequence of women's meddling.

By the time of the great Confucian Mencius (371–289 BCE), about two generations after Confucius, we see ritual gradually developing in two directions. First, there was an increase in specific regulations (how one should eat, for example); second, there was a stronger set of rules dealing with the separation of men and women. Separation included separate living quarters in the home, separate spheres of activity, and detailed regulations concerning the interaction of men and women. This separation seems to have been widely discussed among Confucians at this time and was the subject of many debates. (The significance of Confucian debates on the separation of the sexes has been compared to that of the debates in first-century Judaism over keeping the Sabbath; Fehl, 1971: 96.) As they developed, Confucian views on ritual were applied not just to royal courts, but also to the home and the rituals and relations of people in the family.

Warring States Era Daoism

Confucianism was not the only tradition that began in Warring States China. Daoism also began at this time. This school was based on the **Dao**, the Way—the ultimate pattern of change in nature and the universe. Daoism is said to have begun with the shadowy figure of Laozi, roughly contemporary to Confucius.

Human beings find their proper place, Daoists argue, only when they act in harmony with the Dao, which Daoist texts, particularly the *Laozi* (also called the *Dao De Jing*), often describe as passive and weak—characteristics associated with women. This has led some scholars to see Daoism as a feminist tradition, in opposition to a masculine Confucianism (Chen, 1974: 51–64). Yet the Dao is not feminine, since it encompasses all things, and the female imagery used to evoke it represents the male point of view. The *Laozi* argues that aggressive, "macho" action will always fail because it is not in harmony with the Dao, which is never aggressive and performs all its actions without looking for praise or exalting itself. Women and the Dao resemble one another, the *Laozi* says, because both are passive, quiet, and meek. Its critique of attributes usually associated with masculinity set Daoism sharply apart from the mainstream in the Warring States period. Despite their preference for what they saw as feminine attributes, however, Daoists did not argue for the equality of men and women. And although Daoist texts do at least talk about women, what they say is not necessarily positive.

Buddhism

Buddhism, predominantly Mahayana, reached China in the first century CE, carrying with it a view of women that was already well established: women were dangerous temptations to celibate monks, and enlightenment was not possible in a female body. Women could become nuns, however. The concept of religious professionals living in celibate communities under strict rules was new to China. Nuns were described as women who had "left the family" (*qu jia*). The Vinaya sutras (texts regulating the behaviour of monks and nuns) set out the inferiority of nuns: monks always took precedence over nuns, no matter how senior, nuns were not allowed to teach monks, and so on. Still, however low the status of nuns, the existence of their order gave Chinese women an option other than marriage and motherhood—an option they had not had before.

Women became the primary devotees of Buddhism in China, and they remain so today. In traditional China, women prayed at temples, set up altars in their homes, and went on pilgrimages. Lay Buddhists—men and women alike—took the Three Refuges (the basic profession of Buddhist faith), followed the Five Precepts, practised vegetarianism, and joined societies that recited sutras. Women raised money for religious projects and organized festivals and pilgrimages. Devotion to Buddhism was seen as proof of virtue. As women's lives became more circumscribed, so that they were virtually confined to the home, nuns would visit their quarters and often provide a basic education that would otherwise have been out of reach.

Organized Daoism

More organized forms of Daoism began as a tradition of spiritual healing among ordinary people during the Han Dynasty (206 BCE–220 CE). Always eclectic, it also taught that immortality could be attained in this life, and over time it grew to encompass almost all the popular deities. Daoism thus covers a wide gamut of practices: from the search for immortality to healing, meditation, good works, and the performance of rituals for personal and social purposes. It continues to have temples and followers throughout China.

One of the earliest forms of Daoism, the Celestial Masters of the second century CE, had women priests, and women achieved high rank in the organization. Later, women also became *Daoshi* (Daoist Masters), and a few were said to have achieved immortality by following a path just as rigorous as the men's. Daoism includes the texts of Warring States Daoism, though it understands those texts as manuals in immortality. So, while the tradition uses early Daoist texts, such as the *Laozi*, that do privilege the female over the male, it did not argue for the equality of women. This may be because, with the growth of the organization, Daoism took in Confucian and Buddhist ideas as well. Early in its development, it began to talk about rituals, morality, and family harmony in the same way that Confucianism had. From Buddhism Daoism took the ideas of celibacy, **karma**, and *samsara* (the cycle of rebirth). Although Daoism, unlike Buddhism, has a formal head (the Celestial Master), its organization otherwise follows the Buddhist model. The Daoist order of nuns, like its Buddhist forerunner, offered women the possibility of a life in religion; and in Daoism, as in Buddhism, it was socially acceptable for women to practise their faith as they wished, to attend temples for healing or to devote themselves to particular deities. Daoism does not see itself as a radical alternative to Confucianism and Buddhism, but as a place where all these traditions meet.

Popular Religion

Popular religion is just as pervasive today in China as it was in the past. Expressions of popular religiosity take many forms, from the worship of local gods and the use of mediums to contact the dead to participation in traditional New Year's celebrations. Confucian, Buddhist, and Daoist ideas, deities, rituals, and practices are all incorporated into the great fabric of everyday practice. At a funeral, for example, no contradiction is seen if Daoist monks pray and Buddhist monks recite sutras for the dead during a service conducted according to the Confucian tradition. Today, as in the past, most people do not think in the sectarian terms typical of Western traditions. While a few might identify themselves as strictly Confucian or Buddhist, most practise all traditions. Thus at New Year's, a family may gather to perform a Confucian ancestral veneration ritual (see p. 126 below) and then enjoy a Buddhist vegetarian meal. In traditional China, people also visited Buddhist temples at New Year's to pray to **Guan Yin**, the bodhisattva of compassion, and local temples to pray to local deities. "All the Buddhas teach the same **dharma**," it is said. What this means is that people perceive little fundamental disagreement among the teachings of all the "great" traditions.

Mediums or shamans, many of whom were women, continued their work despite the disapproval of the rich, educated elite, which scorned many popular religious beliefs as superstition, and the eventual outlawing of mediumship in the thirteenth century.

Texts, Interpretations, and Rituals

The following sections will examine fundamental Confucian, Daoist, and Buddhist attitudes towards women as expressed in the traditions' texts and rituals.

Confucianism

The **Confucian classics** were traditionally thought to have been either written or edited by Confucius, although modern scholarship has disproved this. They cover a wide range of topics and genres, including poetry, history, ritual, and philosophy. Although they were not seen as the word of a god, and thus were not considered sacred, they were believed to contain the wisdom of the ancients.

In traditional China, men studied the classics in order to pass the civil service examinations and gain the power and prestige of a government job. It was this that gave the Confucian classics their enduring authority as the foundation of Chinese society. Because of their importance to the elite and their use in government, they gradually came to be considered authoritative by ordinary people as well.

One of the oldest classics, the *Shi Jing* (Book of Poetry), sets out the differences in status of sons and daughters this way: while sons sleep on a couch and play with sceptres, daughters sleep on the ground and play with tiles: "it will be theirs neither to do right or wrong / They will think only about the spirits and food / And how to cause no sorrow to their parents" (*Shi Jing*: 245). As in other Confucian classics, such as the Book of History, meddling women are blamed for the downfall of states:

> A clever man builds strong walls
> A clever woman overthrows them
> Beautiful is the clever wife
> But her heart is cruel as the owl
> Women with long tongues forecast evil
> Disasters are not sent down from heaven
> They originate in wives (Karlgren, 1950: 264)

Women, especially beautiful women, are dangerous: "Where there is extreme beauty, there will surely be extreme wickedness" (*Zuo Zhuan*; see Legge, 1960:

192). While women are not blamed for bringing evil into the world (as Eve was in the Judeo-Christian tradition), they are seen as problematic.

The *Li Ji* (Book of Rites) describes in detail how both state and private rituals, from funerals to marriages, were to be carried out. It also prescribes separation of the sexes: women were to live in the inner quarters of the house, men in the outer; men and women were not to sit on the same mat, and not to touch when handing one another something; and so on.

Marriage was understood as the union of two families. The chapter entitled "The Meaning of Marriage" in the Book of Rites begins by stating its purpose: "The ritual of marriage is meant for the love between families of two surnames. For those above, the ancestors, it is to maintain services in the ancestral temple; for those below, descendants, it is to secure children to carry on the family line" ("Hun Yi," *Li Ji*). The roles of husband and wife were seen as separate but complementary: women were to serve, obey, and maintain harmony within the household, while men were to fulfill their responsibilities outside the home.

The Book of Rites minutely describes funeral rituals as well. The manner in which such rituals were to be carried out depended on the social status of the deceased. The rituals of ancestral veneration required the participation of both husband and wife, but were performed for his ancestors only. Although "women's rituals" involving matters such as childbirth presumably existed, they are not mentioned in the ritual texts. The only specifically female ceremony described in the Book of Rites is a hair-pinning ritual performed to mark a woman's coming of age.

Women lost status at court as well, although they continued to carry out the women's "side" of the rituals. By the time of the Han Dynasty (206 BCE–220 CE), when Confucianism became the state orthodoxy, women's social and political roles had declined significantly from the heights of ancient times. This diminished view of women's status would percolate throughout Chinese society over the centuries that followed.

Daoism

In the second century CE, a man named Zhang Daoling received a series of revelations from Laozi, the reputed author of the *Laozi*, who by this time had become a god. The extensive revelations encompassed rituals for curing disease, praying to the gods, and reciting the *Laozi*, as well as for the organization of Daoism. These revelatory texts became the basis for the Daoist canon, which today comprises 1,426 volumes. As the tradition progressed, it added texts on outer and inner alchemy—instructions on how to become immortal either through meditation or through the ingestion of special elixirs.

The Daoist texts record women becoming immortals, though we are told that a woman's path to immortality is different from a man's because of the difference in yin and yang (see p. 127 below). Thus while the quest for immortality required that adepts of both sexes practise "inner alchemy" (*neidan*), along with diet, breathing, and sexual techniques, the female inner alchemy (*nudan*) takes into account female anatomy and sexuality. The Daoist priesthood, open to married people, gave the same status to husbands and wives who acted as priests. The Daoist organization depended on female followers, who to this day make up the majority of Daoists, and female local leaders.

Buddhism

Buddhist sutras were already formed by the time Buddhism came to China. The sutras were mostly written by men and from a male point of view, but there is such a wide variety of sutras that it is not surprising to find a variety of views of women. Mahayana Buddhism was, and is now, the dominant form of Buddhism in China. Some Buddhists, following the thinking of the Mahayana school, Madhyamika, argued that, given the insubstantial nature of the human body, gender does not matter in terms of enlightenment. The majority of sutras, however, held that gender does matter, because a woman, in a female body, is not capable of enlightenment—this despite early sutras clearly setting out the names and roles of women who had become enlightened. Other sutras, such as the Pure Land sutras, argue that women have such a terrible time in life that they should look forward to a rebirth as men in the Pure Land.

The majority of sutras assume that nuns, because they are chaste, are more holy than sexually active women. Yet, as we have seen, even nuns are ranked far below monks in terms of authority. Some texts, especially the meditation sutras, describe all women as tempters, without virtue, and intellectually weak. As a result, like Confucianism, Buddhism wanted to control female sexuality: in Buddhism, women were most virtuous when sexually inactive; in Confucianism, women were most virtuous when chaste, whether married, single, or widowed. Chinese cultural notions of the necessity of submission from women fit in with many Buddhist notions of the lower status of women.

Ancestral Veneration

If one were forced to choose one basic element that underlies all religious practice in China, it would be the belief that ancestors remain closely connected to their descendants by bonds of love and respect. Thus a fundamental practice in all Chinese religious traditions is the ancient ritual of **ancestral veneration**.

Predating Confucius perhaps by as much as a millennium, it centres on a set of wooden tablets (ancestral plaques), each inscribed with the name of a deceased ancestor, to which family members bow, offer food, drink, and incense, and report family events.

Women as well as men were venerated as ancestors. As Chinese society became patrilineal, however, the ancestors that a woman venerated were those of her father or her husband. When a woman became an ancestor, her plaque was linked to her husband's and she was venerated by their sons or by the male line of her husband's family.

Symbols and Gender

The basic gender symbol, which permeates all the traditions of China, is the **yin-yang** symbol. Most Westerners are familiar with the circle that is divided into black (yin) and white (yang) intertwining halves with a small circle of black in the white half and a matching circle of white in the black half. The implications of this symbol were articulated most clearly by the Confucian Dong Zhongshu (179?–104? BCE), and it is this understanding of the yin-yang theory that has lasted down to our time. Yang represents the heat of summer, the time of the most warmth and light, while yin represents winter, the time of deepest cold and dark. Yin wanes in the spring, as yang grows, then grows again the autumn, as yang declines. The cycle repeats itself each year. A similar alternating pattern is found in the smaller cycle of night and day.

As a result, winter/summer and autumn/spring are not simply opposites: they are bound together in a cycle that balances the movements of yin and yang. Dong Zhongshu and many other thinkers used the yin-yang theory as the basis for theorizing about how the universe worked. Assuming that all things would ideally play their part in the balance and harmony of yin and yang, they theorized that if the elements of human life, from physical health to government, could be brought into the proper balance, they too would share in the harmony of the universe. The yin-yang theory of balance is still the basis of traditional Chinese medicine.

Han Dynasty Confucians compiled long lists of what they saw as "opposites" and categorized their components in terms of yang and yin: heaven/earth, ruler/subject, father/son, active/passive, outer/inner, sun/moon, birth/death, giving/receiving, male/female, and so on. The Confucians claimed that in each case, the two components of the pair were essentially opposites, like yin and yang, and were thus complementary. Clearly, though, that was not true. Preference was always shown for the first (yang) component; these were the things that society rewarded or approved of (active, birth, ruler, and so on), while the yin elements (passive, death, subject, etc.) were seen in a more negative light. It is also clear that these pairs of "opposites" do not all relate to one another in the same way that yin and yang do: for example, fathers do not wax or wane in relation to their sons. Finally, the most problematic part of the yin-yang theory is the assignment of gender: men are yang and birth; women are yin and death. The odd correlation of women with death and men with birth reflects the preference for yang. The yin-yang theory, which is accepted throughout Chinese culture and remains as popular as ever, has always served as a metaphysical basis for male superiority: men and women are obviously different, it is argued, but complementary to one another just as yin and yang are. Men and women are different but equal, the tradition says: this is the way the universe works.

The yin-yang theory worked well with Confucian ideas of women's roles as wives, mothers, and daughters. It worked just as well with Buddhist ideas of the secondary and inferior status of women, even as nuns. Thus the patrilineal and patriarchal nature of traditional Chinese culture found its theoretical base in the yin-yang theory.

Family Structures and Traditions

As we have seen, Confucianism was the greatest influence on family life in traditional China. The concept of filial piety extended Confucian influence deep into family structures. Because a daughter would leave her birth family to live with her husband's people, she was worth less to her parents than a son who would carry on the family line and the veneration of its ancestors. Marriage was a union of two families, undertaken to produce sons to carry on the family line and the veneration of ancestors. Ancestral veneration followed the male family line, and on marrying into the family, a woman was expected to be filial towards her husband's parents. Women were to be modest and chaste, that is, sexually active only in marriage, and widows were to remain loyal to the memory of their husband.

Both Buddhism and Daoism offered women an alternative to marriage in the form of life as a nun. Although a woman who chose the monastic option would not be able to fulfill her filial duty to her parents, this was less of a problem for women than it was for men, because they were not part of the patrilineal family line and so less crucial to the family's future survival.

In modern times there have been some changes. Women can now divorce their husbands, although this is not encouraged by the courts, which offer marriage counselling, or by families, which may disown female relatives who divorce. While sexual activity is expected of men, women are still expected to be modest and chaste, and this double standard applies at all ages.

Nor is sex the only area where traditional values are still practised. There are few forms of social welfare in modern China, and few people receive a pension when they retire. This means that parents still prefer a son, because he (and his wife) can be expected to care for them in their old age, whereas a daughter will be expected to care for her husband's parents. Having a son became more important than ever after China imposed its one-child policy in 1979. The 2010 census reported 118 boys born for every 100 girls (the worldwide rate is 105 boys to 100 girls). It may be that, given the one-child policy, the birth of girls is not being reported. The Chinese government has outlawed the use of sonograms except when medically necessary, since parents who know that the fetus is female may decide to abort it. Nevertheless, sonograms are still being used. Should the current gender imbalance continue, we can expect to see more kidnappings of girls and young women for forced marriages (some have already been reported) and a rise in general social unrest.

The Chinese economic boom was created by millions and millions of workers moving from rural areas to work in urban factories—a phenomenon that has been described as the largest human migration in history. If both parents leave home to find work, their children must be cared for by grandparents or other family members, and although migrant workers are usually able to return home at Chinese New Year, for many this is the only time they can see their children. If it is only the husband who leaves for the city, he may become involved with other women and even begin another family. Meanwhile, his wife is left to care for both the children and the aging parents as well as to maintain the farm—responsibilities that are often overwhelming. Not only does China have one of the highest suicide rates in the world: it is also unlike any other country in that female suicides outnumber male suicides by three to one. And rural suicides outnumber urban suicides by the same ratio. There are many factors involved in these suicide rates, but traditional values are certainly a major component.

Sexuality

The yin-yang theory and Confucian, Buddhist, and Daoist thought came together in traditional China both to affirm existing sexist attitudes and to provide theoretical rationales for them. Although all traditions agreed that sexuality, particularly female sexuality, had to be controlled, none of them (with the possible exception of Buddhism) saw sex as evil. Buddhist and Daoist nuns and monks were expected to be celibate, but Buddhist and Daoist priests could, and did, marry. It was generally assumed that all adults who were not monks or nuns would engage in sexual activity—the issue for religious traditions was how to handle it. Chinese culture has typically believed that sex is a natural part of marriage, not only enjoyable but necessary to good health.

More than 1500 years after Confucius, the Neo-Confucian Zhu Xi (1130–1200 CE) wrote a handbook entitled *Family Rituals*, in which he explained not only how rituals should be performed, but the thinking behind them. In this way many people were exposed to the standard Confucian beliefs about women. Like the unknown authors of the Book of Rites, Zhu Xi claims that a complementary balance exists between male and female. Here, for example, he describes how ancestral veneration should be performed at the New Year, the solstice, and the full moon:

> The participants, in full attire, from the presiding man on down, all enter the gate and take up their places. The presiding man faces north at the base of the ceremonial staircase. The presiding woman faces north at the base of the western steps. When the presiding man's mother is alive, she assumes a special place in front of the presiding woman. The wives of the presiding man's younger brothers and his younger sisters are slightly behind the wife, to her left. The wives of sons and grandsons, daughters, and female attendants are to the rear of the presiding woman in rows with the most senior at the eastern end. When everyone is in place, the presiding man washes his hands, dries them, goes up the stairs, and inserts his official plaque. He opens the tablet case, takes the spirit tablets of his ancestors, and puts them in front of the case. The presiding woman washes, dries, goes up the stairs, and takes the spirit tablets of the ancestresses and sets them to the east of the men's tablets (Ebrey, 1991: 14).

Both the man who presides over the ritual and his wife, the presiding woman, handle the tablets. Yet the ancestors they venerate are his, not hers, since she has only married into the family. As well, only the man addresses the ancestors; the woman does not. The man initiates each step in the ritual, while the woman simply follows his lead. In other words, even though both have essential roles to play, they are not equivalent. Although some scholars argue that women's participation in such rituals points to a balanced and reciprocal relationship between the sexes (e.g., Paper, 1999: 58), the woman's role is clearly not equal to that of the man.

Women took part in ancestral veneration rituals, first as daughters in their father's home, venerating their paternal ancestors, then in their husband's home, venerating his ancestors. As a woman's status increased in her husband's home, as she produced sons and grew older, she would assist her husband at these rituals, providing the food and handling the female ancestral tablets.

Neo-Confucian ritual handbooks return to the idea of complementarity between men and women when discussing funeral rituals. The presiding male mourner was the eldest son of the deceased; the presiding female mourner was the wife of the deceased. However, the son was thought to have a much closer relationship than any woman, to his father (and other male ancestors) because he shared in the same *qi* (life energy) (Ebrey, 1991: 71, 105).

Ancestral tablets were created for women as well as men, provided that the woman was either the first wife of a male member of the clan or the mother of male heirs, although her tablet would not be displayed until after her husband's death (Ebrey, 1991: 52–3). Thus her status as an ancestor and the level of funeral ritual accorded to her depended on her relationship to her husband and his family. Before marriage, a woman would have been present at the ancestral rituals of her natal family as a junior member, standing behind her grandmother, mother, and aunts, but would not have been an active participant. After marriage, once her status in her husband's home had increased with the birth of sons, she would assist her husband at these rituals, handling the female ancestral tablets and offering food. If her husband was the eldest son, she might eventually become the senior wife in the clan. Thus her status in these rituals depended on her marriage.

The degrees of mourning—what clothes were worn, what food was eaten, what rituals carried out, and for how long—depended on the patrilineal line. Once married, a woman mourned her husband's parents more than her own, though both husband and wife owed some degree of mourning ritual to her parents. The ritual texts portray the roles of men and women as complementary. However, this complementarity did not apply to sexual behaviour. Confucians were deeply concerned with the chastity of women. A woman's virtue, they argued, consisted primarily of preserving her virginity before marriage, of modesty and sexual loyalty in marriage, and of continuing loyalty to the memory of her husband in widowhood. As we have seen, one of the primary ways of ensuring women's chastity, at least in large, well-to-do households, was through strict separation of the sexes. Women lived in separate quarters where they had no opportunity to meet men other than their husbands, and they were carefully chaperoned in mixed company.

Marriage was never understood as a romantic relationship between two individuals: it was the bringing together of two families, and its purpose was the production of children, particularly sons, to carry on both the husband's family name and the veneration of its ancestors. Marriages were arranged by the families, and ideally the couple would meet for the first time on their wedding day. Parents were responsible for maintaining their daughter's virginity and her reputation as modest and chaste. Once married, a woman lived with her husband's extended family, to whom she was expected to show obedience and filiality. Sexuality was considered a normal, indeed necessary, part of adult life. In some cases, before marriage, the couples were given "pillow books" by their families so that they might explore many areas of sexual enjoyment. Sex in marriage was not seen as evil; it was part of the order of nature and thus a duty for all men and women. Outside marriage, however, sexuality was dangerous, and the way to lessen that danger was to insist on women's chastity, not men's.

The separation of women and men extended from household to ritual. The Neo-Confucian Sima Guang said, "In managing a family . . . what is most important is ritual. And the separation of males and females is the chief element in ritual." In addition to repeating the Confucian prohibition on men and women sitting together, he insisted that they should not pass things directly to each other, and advised men to avoid their brothers' wives (Ebrey, 1984: 47–8).

Widowhood put women in an awkward position: widows were supported by their husband's family, with whom they had no direct blood relationship except through their children. Some families wanted to get rid of the widow but keep the dowry she had brought; she, on the other hand, might want to leave the family, either to remarry or to live alone, but want to take her bridal dowry with her. The complex economic, familial, and emotional issues that widowhood raised had to be addressed by the Neo-Confucians, who wanted to promote harmonious family relationships. Zhu Xi and his Neo-Confucian school insisted that widows should remain loyal to the memory of their husbands and never remarry. Yet a widow who remained loyal could well be starved by her husband's family, perhaps to force her to turn over her dowry. Widowers were encouraged to remarry in order to continue the family line.

A man might divorce his wife for any of seven "conditions": disobedience to her husband's parents, barrenness, adultery, jealousy, incurable disease, talkativeness, or theft. However, divorce was prohibited if the wife had mourned his parents, if he had become wealthy or received high honours during the marriage, or if her parents were dead. Although wealthy and upper-class men did take concubines, particularly if the first wife was infertile, she always retained her status as the first wife, and remained in charge of the household.

The practice of **foot-binding** was first mentioned in the Song Dynasty (970–1279 CE), but may be even older. Its origins are not clear, though speculation suggests that it began with the taping of the feet of dancers in the Imperial Palace and gradually filtered down through the rest of society. Bound feet were objects of sexual fantasy—much as breasts are in the West—and were thought to decrease the risk of infidelity because they made it difficult for a woman to walk without assistance. They were also a sign of conspicuous consumption: a family that bound its women's feet did not need to have them go out to work. Foot-binding soon became a sign of good breeding; girls with unbound feet would find it virtually impossible to marry. The proverb was, "If you love your son, don't go easy on his study; if you love your daughter, don't go easy on her feet." Thus when girls were about age four or five, their feet were wrapped with two metres of bandages, which were then tightened to prevent further growth. The toes were bent under and into the sole of the foot, breaking the bones and bringing the toe and heel close together. The 8- to 13-centimetre feet produced by this process—which could lead to gangrene, paralysis, and even death—were called "golden lotuses."

Foot-binding was not a religious practice: no tradition is linked to its development. Confucians were of two minds about it. Although some Confucian scholars argued that it deformed the body given to us by our parents and thus was not a filial practice, most accepted it as a way of maintaining chastity.

Chastity was discussed solely in terms of heterosexual intercourse. Same-sex relationships were not generally seen as interfering with the duty to marry and have children. This tolerance probably reflected the separation of men and women in traditional China. Men socialized outside the home, in restaurants and tea houses, while women stayed home or visited each other. Mixed gatherings were rare except at theatres or temples. It is not surprising, then, that men's significant emotional relationships were with other men and women's with other women. Often close friends would swear oaths of brother- or sister-hood, binding themselves to a lifelong friendship.

It is not always clear to what extent sexuality was part of these relationships. The extravagant and loving language used in letters between close friends may well indicate gay or lesbian relationships; but it's also possible that we read more into that language than we should. Traditional China, like many other cultures that have kept men and women in separate universes, clearly knew about same-sex relationships, but it seems to have been troubled by them only when they interfered with the functioning of the family.

In modern China, by contrast, Communist puritanism has made homosexuality illegal, and many Chinese people insist that only Westerners are gay or lesbian. The last decade has seen some loosening of attitudes, but in China and in overseas Chinese communities it is still generally believed that sexuality is reserved for heterosexual marriage.

Official and Unofficial Roles of Women

Much of what we have seen so far is what patriarchal religious traditions imposed on women. Yet Chinese women did not simply follow the rules that were given to them. As in other cultures, women thought about their religious traditions and wove them into their lives in many different ways.

Can a Confucian woman be a *junzi* (gentleman)? If so, in what ways? How does gender influence how we understand the term "gentleman"? Early Confucianism did not exclude women from the category, but it did not explicitly include them either. One of the first women to address this question was Ban Zhao (c. 45–120 CE), who had helped her brother to write an extensive history, the *Han Shu*, and then completed it after his death; she was a court historian and a well-known scholar, tutor to the empress, and, when the empress became regent, her advisor. However, she is best known for a treatise on moral behaviour entitled *Nu Jie* ("Women's Instructions"), which she claimed to have written as a guide for her daughters. Ban Zhao advocated education for women because of their important role in the inner world, which was an important foundation for the outer. Regarding women's qualities she wrote,

> Women have four qualities, that is, womanly attainments, womanly speech, womanly appearance, womanly skills. As to attainments, a woman does not have to be extraordinarily intelligent; in speech she does not need to be clever; in appearance, she does not need to be beautiful; in skill, she does not need to be more than average. Being gentle and composed, quiet, chaste and orderly, careful in what she does, and to follow the rules—this is the real womanly attainment (cited in Swann, 1932: 86).

The "rules" that Ban Zhao refers to are the rules of behaviour set out in the Confucian classics. Women were to be thoughtful in dealing with others and were admonished to do all their work carefully. Ban Zhao argued that women should follow the instructions first of their fathers, then of their husbands, and that they should not remarry if widowed. She did, however, also expect husbands to follow the rules and maintain a harmonious household. For a husband to strike his wife would break the harmony of the household and therefore be immoral, and Ban Zhao advised the wife who had been beaten to leave.

What we see in the *Nu Jie* is one of the first of many attempts by educated women not simply to obey the rules laid down for them, but to become active moral agents within the framework of their tradition. For example, there were countless stories of wives and widows who remained loyal to their husbands through many trials. When pushed to abandon their moral principles, some women committed suicide. Rather than reject the Confucian tradition, women often internalized it, seeing themselves as ethical actors working to become, in their own way, gentlemen.

This response to Confucianism was most often seen in upper-class women who felt a responsibility to set an example, but it filtered down to ordinary people as well. One of the most remarkable glimpses into the attitudes of ordinary women can be found in the "hidden writing" of women like Yi Nianhua, Gao Yinxian, and their "sworn sisters" in southern Hunan (p. 118).

The elite of traditional China always described peasant women as "superstitious" and "ignorant," but it's clear that the women of Hunan did know the teachings of the "great" traditions: they wrote about the Buddhist concepts of karma and *samsara*, and they boasted that they had "done their duty" to their husbands' families according to Confucian tradition. More important to them than Confucius and the Buddha, however, were their local, mostly female, deities, to whom they wrote prayers expressing their deepest wishes: for family reunion, a good husband, children (particularly sons), good fortune, divine assistance. One prayer describes how its author prepared to compose it:

> Seven days ago I fasted,
> Five days ago I burned incense,
> Three days ago I boiled fresh water,
> And washed my clothes and myself.
> Today I sit peacefully in an empty room,
> To write an offering to the goddess Gu Po.
> I offer it to ask Gu Po's blessing and protection,
> To bring my husband safely home soon (Rainey, 1995: 145).

Prayers were written on paper or fans and then placed before statues in various temples.

These women believed in an afterlife, and wrote poems to calm and reassure restless spirits. But their writings do not suggest "superstitious" fear: rather, the women who wrote the hidden texts seem to have wished to ensure that the spirits of the dead were content. Ancestral veneration rituals are rarely mentioned in the hidden writings (Rainey, 1995: 139).

Shamans or mediums, the inheritors of the office of *wu*, were extremely important for communicating with the dead. Official Confucianism rejected the idea that the living could be possessed by the spirits of the dead, and by the time of the Ming Dynasty (1368–1644 CE) mediumship was illegal. Yet mediums have continued to practise into modern times. The fact that the demand for their services has come mostly from women suggests that many women have been dissatisfied with the Confucian focus on veneration of male ancestors. Women turned to mediums to satisfy a need to deal directly with the dead of their families, both natal and marital.

One of the most common rituals undertaken by women in traditional China was the pilgrimage. While Buddhist pilgrims often sought to make merit by travelling to sites such as Putuo Island (sacred to Guan Yin), others went to venerate particular deities and perhaps pray for favours such as the birth of a son. A seventeenth-century text tells of a pilgrimage to Mount Tai that was organized entirely by women. The purpose of the pilgrimage, one of the leaders says, was "partly to build up good fortune, partly to enjoy the sites" (Dudbridge, 1992: 41, 46). The motives behind the ritual, then, were not only religious: a pilgrimage also gave women a rare socially acceptable opportunity to travel, to

Buddhist women praying at a traditional Daoist temple in Taipei, Taiwan.

© photoncatcher/iStockphoto

see new things, to enjoy one another's company, and, their critics claimed, to look for sexual adventures. In the novel, the women hold a three-day ceremony at a temple dedicated to the Three Agents—gods associated with heaven, earth, and water—and plan to celebrate the birthday of Guan Yin with a similar ceremony. The hidden writings indicate that these women often went on pilgrimages together to mountain temples.

The women who organized pilgrimages also celebrated festivals, particularly those of their local gods and *niangniangs*. Women generally took part in all the festivals of traditional China, including the New Year in the first month of the lunar calendar; Qing Ming, in the third lunar month, when the graves of the family were swept and cleaned; the Dragon Boat Festival on the fifth day of the fifth month; and Zhong Qiu, the mid-autumn or moon festival, on the fifteenth day of the eighth month. In addition to the standard rituals such as ancestral veneration, however, some of these festivals included family or home rituals that were conducted exclusively by women. One female ritual associated with the New Year, for example, was the veneration of the God of the Stove, or the Kitchen God, who reported the family's activities over the year to heaven; the family would smear honey on his lips to ensure a good report. The women's hidden writings also tell of a spring planting festival: the night before the rice seedlings were set out, many women (especially those who had just married and those who had no children) returned to their natal homes and stayed there until the rice had been planted. The hidden writings tell us of many festivals that involved women meeting together in each other's homes and others where they returned to their natal homes. For example, beginning on the fifteenth day of the new year there were women's gatherings at which women read the hidden texts together. Thus women organized and carried out a number of religious activities that were not acknowledged by the elite traditions.

Women all over China initiated their own pilgrimages, celebrated festivals, prayed to the gods, and fed the unhappy spirits of the dead. They wrote their own prayers and developed their own worship rituals. Popular religion seems to have allowed women more freedom than the officially recognized traditions did, though always within the strictures of the larger society.

Local deities did occasionally become more widely known, a phenomenon we see from about 800 to 1100 CE across China. One possible reason for the rise in popularity of certain deities may have been the invention of the printing press and dissemination of books and pamphlets (contrary to Western mythology, the first printed book was the *Diamond Sutra*, produced in China in 868 CE). Among the deities that became nationally popular in this period was Guan Yin: the bodhisattva of compassion and mercy who began in the Mahayana traditions of India as a male bodhisattva named Avalokiteshvara. When Guan Yin first appeared in China, he was still male (as he remains in Tibet), but beginning around the tenth century CE, he came to be depicted as female. Scholars have suggested that one reason for this transformation may have been the association of local female deities with the figure of Guan Yin. Stories about Guan Yin (all outside the Buddhist sutras) portray her variously as a filial daughter, a nun, a chaste woman, or a teacher. However the change happened, Guan Yin remains the most popular deity in China. Today images of Guan Yin can be found not just in Buddhist temples, but also in homes and even taxis.

Guan Yin was particularly important to women because, in addition to representing compassion, she brought children—a central concern for women whose status in their husbands' homes depended on producing heirs. Most women had a picture or statue of Guan Yin, or an altar for her, in their rooms. There are reports from sociologists that modern-day devotees both admire and envy Guan Yin's freedom as a woman who is not locked into the social structure. A pilgrim song says, "First, she does not suffer the ill-humour of in-laws; second, she does not eat food provided by a husband; third, she does not carry a son in her stomach or a grandson in her arms; fourth, she sits lightly on a lotus throne" (Levering, 1994: 221).

Another deity who grew past her local roots in southern China is Ma Zu, who saves people from danger, especially on the sea, and, like Guan Yin, also gives and protects children. One of her titles is Holy Mother of Heaven. Ma Zu is said to have been a shy, devout young woman who died young saving her father and all but one of her brothers from drowning. She is still particularly popular in southern China and in Taiwan.

In the Daoist tradition, three of the major deities are female. Xiwangmu gave birth to the world and rules all the immortals; she is a divine teacher, and in time came to be seen as offering salvation to the faithful who held her talismans. Mother of the Dao, or Mother Li, descended into this world and was a perfect filial daughter; after giving birth to Lord Lao (Laozi), she taught him all the secrets of the universe and then returned to the heavens as a watchful mother. Doumu, Dipper Mother, is the mother of the nine gods of the stars that make up the Big Dipper, a saviour and teacher.

In general, women were devoted to deities who specialized in problems such as childlessness, illness, or family strife. In the hidden women's writings, we see women gathering to pray to local deities, calling them names such as "honoured aunt" and "Niangniang," which means "queen" or "goddess" and is often added to the end of the deity's name. Women prayed to Niangniang in their homes and would also travel together to her temple to offer incense and gifts:

> I take up my pen to write these words
> To respectfully send them to Longyantang, Yuan township,
> Where the famous Gu Niangniang manifests her spiritual power.

Every year in the second month we look forward to all the excitement.
Households come with incense.
Facing the altar that keeps out wind and rain,
With the green mountains in the background, full of colours,
And in front, the scenery is so beautiful.
Gu Niangniang sends down blessings . . .
Famous Gu Niangniang, heed us well,
And never forget your concern.
We yearly bring you incense and count on your will.
Gu Niangniang is profoundly good,
And her good name is known everywhere
Famous Gu Niangniang send down blessings;
Receive this fragrant incense and bless us all (Rainey, 1995: 151).

The writers of the hidden texts offered gifts that included fans, embroidery, and books with prayers written in the women's script. A woman who had given birth to a son with the help of Zisun Niangniang would return to Zisun Niangniang's shrine and leave shoes and red eggs (the celebratory gift given when a boy is born). Women who had no sons would take these gifts home in hopes of sharing in the good luck associated with them (Rainey, 1995: 150). They would also hang pictures of tigers in order to encourage the birth of a son.

At home, as part of their responsibility for the spiritual welfare of the household, women made offerings of incense, food, drink, and prayers to the God of the Stove, the household gods in charge of the well or the doorway, hungry ghosts (the spirits of the dead who had no family and could cause trouble in the homes of others), and any other spirits who might cause mischief.

When a woman was pregnant, other women would pray for her at the local temple. During and just after childbirth, other prayers were offered to ensure the health and well-being of mother and child. During illness, women would exorcize the house to try to get rid of the evil spirits. This was done by sweeping the room, hanging charms, reciting mantras or sutras, and offering the spirits food. At funerals as well, women performed rituals not mentioned in the official ritual texts, so as to drive off evil spirits and preserve the health and luck of the family.

Some women played significant roles as Daoist nuns. Zu She was the founder of Qingwei (Pure Emptiness) school and there were other leaders and founders of convents and schools (Despeux and Kohn 2003: 149–50). All were involved in personal pursuit of perfection and in rituals and exorcisms for the benefit of the community. Among the Chinese Buddhist traditions, Chan (Zen) was the most open to women, and we have records of female Chan students and teachers.

In sum, women played active religious roles in traditional China: they were shamans, mediums, and nuns; they made pilgrimages to sacred sites and organized lay associations that performed good works, such as famine relief, in the name of a particular deity; and in the household setting they performed a variety of rituals for the well-being of their families. By contrast, although women were required to play some role in the patriarchal rituals of ancestral veneration, that role was always secondary and the ancestors venerated were never their own.

It was in the "great traditions" of Confucianism, Buddhism, and Daoism that women took second place. Although Buddhist and Daoist nuns were often praised for their holiness and advice, they could not shake the subordinate status that was predetermined by their traditions.

Social Change

The culture of traditional China was a closed system in which political, religious, and social mores supported and reinforced one another. There were some criticisms of the world view that this culture implied. Li Ru-chen (1763–1800) wrote a parody of traditional culture in his book *Ching Hua Yuan* ("Flowers in the Mirror"), in which men have their feet bound and their ears pierced and women sit for the Confucian civil service examinations. However, serious examination of traditional culture and the status of women really began only when the political foundations of the culture began to crack. By the nineteenth century it was becoming clear that the Qing Dynasty could not protect China against the encroachments of Western powers determined, as the German Kaiser Wilhelm put it, to "carve China like a melon."

Kang Youwei (1858–1927), one of the best-known Confucians of the time, was part of a political movement that wanted to reform the Qing Dynasty government and make it a constitutional monarchy. He also established a "natural foot" society in 1881 aimed at ending foot-binding. By then, Western missionaries had also begun to campaign against foot-binding, an effort in which they were joined by a number of the Chinese intelligentsia. Kang wrote about the Great Harmony, an ideal society in which men and women were equal. From the beginning, reform movements in China saw political and social reform as closely tied to the status of women. Critiques of traditional China throughout the twentieth century used the status of women as "proof" of the inequity and cruelty of traditional society.

This is most clearly seen in the **May Fourth movement**, a loose coalition of reformers, including novelists, poets, artists, journalists, and students, who came together in the 1920s in an intellectual and cultural crusade aimed at bringing modern science and democracy to China. Across the wide range of reformers, Confucianism was held responsible for the decadent political situation, the backwardness of China, and the oppression of women. The slogan of the May Fourth movement was "Down with Confucius and his shop." The most popular play of the time was Ibsen's *A Doll's House*: the slam of the door as Nora turns her back on tradition was seen as a call for freedom from a traditional culture that enslaved women. Young men and women who saw filial piety as blind loyalty and family responsibilities as suffocating were not interested in reforming traditional Chinese culture: they wanted to scrap the whole thing.

Buddhism and Daoism were summarily dismissed as "superstitious." Buddhism had contributed to the backwardness of China, the reformers argued, because it encouraged "otherworldliness" and excused social inequity as a result of karma. Daoism was seen as corrupt and representative of the worst kind of superstition and non-scientific thinking. However, neither of these traditions was criticized for its views of women to the degree that Confucianism was.

Christianity played some role in the reform movement. Missionaries had arrived in China beginning in the mid-nineteenth century with a mindset of cultural and racial superiority, and they were tarred with the brush of imperialism. They also insisted that anyone converting to Christianity give up all participation in the rituals of ancestral veneration—a condition that many people could not accept because it would have meant severing their family ties. Despite all their efforts, therefore, neither Roman Catholic nor Protestant missionaries were very successful at finding converts in China. Nevertheless, as we have seen, missionaries did object to what they saw as the subservient status of women in China, and they opened schools for girls as well as boys, in which they taught Western ideas about democracy and the roles of men and women. As a result, many twentieth-century reformers—including Sun Yatsen, considered the founder of modern China, and members of the May Fourth movement— came from missionary-school backgrounds. Whether Christian missions were a positive or negative influence in China is still a subject of debate, but in terms of reform, Christianity's influence cannot be ignored.

The attitudes of the May Fourth movement were echoed in the thinking of the Chinese Communist Party. More and more women, particularly young women, took on active political and social roles, organizing demonstrations and boycotts and, from the 1930s on, engaging in guerilla warfare against the Japanese. Eventually, some joined Sun's political party, the Guomindang, while others joined the Communist Party, which organized women's unions; enacted laws that let women initiate divorce; forbade foot-binding, forced marriages, and domestic violence; established schools, and promoted education for women.

After the Communists took power in 1949, gender equality was guaranteed in the 1950 constitution. The Marriage Law of 1950 not only gave women the right to divorce and choose their own husbands, but outlawed polygamy, attempted to abolish the dowry system, and raised the status of widows by making it legal for them to remarry. As in many communist countries, despite expectations that communism, together with the entry of women into the workforce, would bring equality, traditional attitudes persisted among both party cadres and the general population.

The communist view of religion as the opiate of the people, plus the government's suspicion of international ties, meant that all religions were persecuted and suppressed, although to protect its image, the state did set up some government-controlled religious bodies. Christian missionaries were expelled. Religious leaders of all kinds, and some of their followers, were imprisoned, tortured, or killed. Monks and nuns were defrocked. Religious buildings were closed and used for other purposes, and much of what was left of religious practice went underground. Nevertheless, during the Cultural Revolution (1966–76) religions would be viciously attacked once again as representatives of the traditional culture that had to be destroyed (see Levering, 1994).

By 1982, the government had realized that it could not prevent people from being religious. Accordingly, it adopted a new policy designed to control *how* they were religious. In addition to ending economic restrictions, it began to allow certain religious bodies more freedom, albeit within strict bounds. Only five religions are recognized by the Chinese government: Buddhism, Daoism, Islam, and Christianity (Roman Catholic and Protestant). Each religion has a "patriotic" central body (e.g., the National Daoist Association) that receives instructions from the government and is expected to enforce them internally. Each organization is limited in the amount of missionary work and fundraising it can do. Unapproved meetings and texts are forbidden, as are overseas financial support and contact with foreigners, including the Chinese of Hong Kong and Taiwan. All religious sites must be registered. No religion may preach to anyone under the age of 18, and no member of the Chinese Communist Party is allowed to join a religious organization. Texts and sermons must be approved by the Religious Affairs Bureau.

Despite these restrictions, there are now Buddhist temples in all provinces, as well as Buddhist publishers, seminaries, training centres, and lay groups. With the exception of Tibetan Buddhism, the Buddhist tradition in China seems to be making a comeback. Although Daoism has been slower to recover, temples are now being constructed and Daoist priests are reviving traditional rituals such as exorcism. A training program for nuns has also begun, and men and women recite scriptures in Daoist centres (Levering, 1994: 203). Even

Christianity has grown in modern China, with both Protestant and Roman Catholic churches, seminaries, and publishing companies.

If one of the main problems facing religions in China today is government control, another is friction with an unlikely source: the tourist industry. Chinese governments at every level—federal, provincial, and local—have poured millions into rebuilding and refurbishing important temples and religious sites damaged during the Cultural Revolution. They have not invested this money to support religion, but to encourage international tourists and the fast-growing domestic tourist market. This has led to friction with some local communities, whose members now have to pay a fee to enter their own temples, as if they were tourist attractions, and resent having their rituals, meditation sessions, and prayers treated as tourist photo ops. Other communities, however, have taken an active role in efforts to attract tourists: the most extreme example is the Shaolin temple complex, which has been criticized inside and outside China as a corrupt tourist trap.

A further difficulty is that, while we know that religions are growing again, hard information on numbers and infrastructure is not easy to come by. Given the government restrictions and surveillance that religion is subject to in China, it is not surprising that we do not see the same dynamic activity from nuns and laywomen there that we can see in Taiwan, for example. A visitor to any Buddhist or Daoist temple will see that the majority of devotees are female, but information on the actual numbers of followers and how they practise their religion are often not available.

The most amazing resurgence has been in popular religiosity. Traditional funeral rituals and ancestral veneration have been revived, and many texts on those subjects are now available across China. Yet religious practice is still not completely tolerated. The recent persecution of Falun Gong, a new popular religion combining traditional beliefs with the practice of meditation and *qigong* (a series of physical exercises), shows the government's fear of large and organized religious groups. Both male and female Falun Gong followers have been imprisoned, tortured, and killed.

Buddhism in Tibet is still severely repressed because it is closely tied to the people's political and cultural aims. Many Tibetan monasteries and convents have police guards outside and cameras and microphones inside. Dissent is not tolerated, and those who take part in demonstrations face imprisonment or death. As a result, more than 90 nuns, monks, laymen, and laywomen have turned to self-immolation as the only form of protest left, dousing themselves with gasoline and setting themselves on fire. The Chinese government's response has been to arm police and soldiers with fire extinguishers. Clearly Tibet is not to be permitted even the modest amount of religious liberalization allowed elsewhere in China.

There have been several major Daoist studies conferences since 2003. In 2011, the theme was women, women in Daoist history, practices associated with women traditionally, the social and religious roles of women today, as well as traditional women's internal alchemy and modern forms of *qigong*.

Steps have also been taken to re-evaluate various traditions and their attitudes toward women. For example, some scholars, especially in Hong Kong and Taiwan, have argued that Confucianism can indeed encourage science and democracy. They maintain that the Confucianism practised in traditional China, with its arbitrary use of power, authoritarianism, and subordination of women, was inconsistent with "real" Confucianism. The "New Confucians," led by scholars such as Tu Wei-ming, maintain that Confucianism provides the moral base for Chinese society and Chinese culture cannot function without it. Women have also begun to investigate the Confucian tradition, asking the perennial question: Can a woman be a Confucian gentleman? Some have argued that Confucianism can include women: that women can be equal partners in a family that values mutual deference, mutual authority, and mutual respect. They suggest that the classic Confucian notions of respect and mutual responsibility can be recovered and used to counter authoritarian interpretations. The senior partner in a relationship—a husband or father—is not permitted to act cruelly or immorally, and it is the right of junior partners to speak out about injustice. As one scholar puts it, "Confucianism cherishes at its heart, equality in education and the *li* [principle] of change. These two principles, an equal opportunity to learning and an attitude of openness and flexibility, do not contradict feminism" (Woo, 1999: 137).

Critiques of Confucianism continue, however. For example, the Taiwanese feminist Lu Xiulian argues that Confucianism speaks only to men, equates maleness with humanity, and sees women as second-class human beings (see Reed, 1994: 227). In mainland China, the 1988 television documentary *River Elegy* argued that Chinese civilization is dead and stifling, and that Confucianism is largely to blame. In practical terms, it can be argued that the vast majority of people agree. Family strictures, especially as they affect women, have begun to loosen, if slowly. Many people have abandoned ancestral veneration; others practise it only for form's sake. There is also growing anecdotal evidence that women are beginning to perform ancestral veneration rituals for their own parents, and to follow matrilineal descent lines when doing so. In Taiwan, I have seen women and their husbands venerating the ancestral plaques of the wives' parents. This was explained as a consequence of the social dislocation that followed the civil war and the move from China to Taiwan, but the fact that it happened at all is dramatic.

In Taiwan, Hong Kong, Singapore, Vancouver, and Toronto, wherever the Chinese community has spread, it has brought along the practices and views of traditional China. In Toronto and Vancouver there are dozens of Daoist temples and scores of Buddhist ones that have to some degree adapted to Western culture. The impact of the West has been especially strong among the young. Even in Taiwan, where traditional Chinese thought has remained dominant, changes can be seen. The practice of shamanism was legalized in 1989, and there is now an association of shamans, the vast majority of whom are women.

Chinese communities outside China have incorporated many new ideas from Western culture into their traditional practices. A small but telling example is the white bridal dress. White has always been the colour of mourning, worn at funerals. Yet in Canada, Taiwan, and Hong Kong, many brides now wear a white dress for the ceremony and then change to red, the traditional wedding colour, for the reception. Growing numbers of younger Chinese people do not practise ancestral veneration, or do so only to please their parents. Yet many people still pray to the gods; restaurants and homes still have traditional altars; and statues of Guan Yin still adorn dashboards.

As new social structures and ways of thinking transform traditional practice, Chinese women find themselves in an odd situation. Obviously the traditional Confucian mindset has to change. The problem is that Confucianism has no priesthood, no organization, no central body or head. Those who want to effect change in the Roman Catholic Church, for example, can work with priests, theologians, cardinals, even the pope. In the case of Confucianism, however, there is no organization to approach. The New Confucians may reread and reinterpret the Confucian classics, but their efforts are not likely to change traditional thinking. The only way to reform Confucian ritual is by changing everyday practice and uprooting the assumption that family is defined by the patrilineal line, and this would require a very strong initiative from a large number of people. Modern Chinese women, like their mothers and grandmothers, have taken one of three routes: go along with tradition, abandon the tradition altogether, or change the tradition in their own lives to suit themselves. It is important to note that simply ignoring Confucianism is not an option: it must be challenged, because Confucian notions continue to permeate Chinese thinking about gender, law, society, and religiosity.

Changing Buddhism is both easier and harder than changing Confucianism. Because there are early Buddhist sutras that show women as enlightened beings, as teachers, preachers, and missionaries, there are grounds for arguing against the later notion that women cannot become enlightened. But Buddhism too has no central authority. As a result, women must either change the thinking of their particular school or temple or lay out their own paths.

The foremost example of a woman taking her own path is Dharma Master Cheng Yen, a Buddhist nun in Taiwan who founded the Buddhist Compassion Relief Tzu Chi Foundation. In the early 1960s, she became convinced that women could take on the same religious responsibilities as men and sought out a like-minded Dharma Master who would ordain her. In 1966 she set up her own foundation, which now has four million members. They provide medical, financial, or spiritual aid to anyone in need; they were the first on the scene in the 1999 Taiwan earthquake, just as they were after an earthquake in Mexico. The foundation has offered medical services and distributed food from Haiti to Thailand. It runs free hospitals, seniors' homes, medical training colleges, and schools. Cheng Yen rejects many of the traditional rituals and beliefs of Buddhism and has, in essence, founded a new school that is socially active and sees itself as returning to the basics of Buddhism. She asks her followers to have the heart of a bodhisattva towards all and to build the Pure Land here on this earth. Her followers say that she is a reincarnation of the Buddha.

The three million members of the Fo Guang Shan order, based in Taiwan also operate a number of social and educational programs. Nuns outnumber monks four to one, and much of the international leadership is female. Because the lineages of nuns in Theravada and Tibetan Buddhism have been lost, Fo Guang Shan has been instrumental in ordaining nuns for those traditions.

Like Dharma Master Cheng Yen, some Buddhist and Daoist nuns and lay-people have struck out on their own. The Chinese traditions are unique in that, in most cases, they are not centrally organized, and this can allow women to forge their own path. But it can also work against women, because it means there is no central body to legislate the changes women want. Thus Buddhist monks may continue to reject Cheng Yen's views, and neighbours may continue to look askance at women who venerate their natal family's ancestors.

Western-style fundamentalism does not, strictly speaking, exist in Chinese culture. This fundamentalism, associated with the exclusivist belief in the literal truth of a text such as the Bible or Quran, is not found in traditions such as Confucianism or Buddhism, which do not hold their texts to be sacred. However, to the extent that fundamentalism means an unswerving belief in a tradition, a demand for purity of practice, and, often, nostalgia for the past, it does exist, especially in more conservative Chinese communities. In Taiwan, for example, all-male Confucian groups still understand Confucianism in traditional terms and blame the problems of modern society on those who seek to change or abandon the tradition. Similarly, there are Buddhists, both monks and laypeople, who reject any proposal for change. Even those whose only religious affiliation is with popular traditions may worry that radical changes will destroy the foundations of Chinese culture.

For 50 years, the Communist government in China attempted to stamp out religiosity, but it proved to be spectacularly unsuccessful. Since restrictions were lifted, popular practice, Buddhism, Daoism, and Christianity have sprung back to life. But the experience of the twentieth century has changed these traditions irrevocably. Exposure to other cultures, rethinking of the traditions, and reassessment of the roles of women has seeped through Chinese culture. The traditions are changing, however slowly and bit by bit.

Note

1. All uncredited translations are the author's.

Glossary

ancestral veneration   The ancient practice of offering food and drink to wooden plaques representing the family's ancestors.

Confucian classics   A set of texts that, over time, became the basis of Confucian teaching and the imperial civil service examinations.

Confucianism (Chinese: *Rujiao, Ruji*)   Ancient tradition best articulated by Confucius (Kongzi), 551–479 BCE.

Dao   "The Way"; though understood variously by different schools of thought, the Dao in Daoism refers to the source and activity of all things.

dharma (Buddhist)   The teachings of the Buddha.

foot-binding   A practice dating at least from the Song dynasty (970–1279 CE) whereby girls' feet were wrapped with bandages to keep them from growing.

Guan Yin (Avalokiteshvara)   The bodhisattva of compassion and mercy. A male figure in India, Tibet, and early in China, but considered female in China, Korea, and Japan.

junzi   The ideal Confucian gentleman, educated in the classics, who practises ritual and humanity. A gentleman should reform himself and the world around him.

karma   Literally, and in Hinduism, "act, deed"; in Buddhism and Daoism, the consequences of acts, words, and thoughts.

May Fourth movement   A broad movement of social reformers who, in the 1920s and 1930s, blamed Chinese tradition, especially Confucianism, for China's backwardness and particularly for the low status of women.

nu shu **(women's hidden writing)**   An alphabetical writing system used by women in rural southern Hunan.

yin-yang   The Chinese theory that everything in the world can be categorized as half of a pair whose two components works in the same complementary way as summer and winter.

Further Reading

Adler, Joseph A. 2006. "Daughter/Wife/Mother or Sage/Immortal Bodhisattva? Women in the Teaching of Chinese Religion." *ASIANetwork Exchange* 14, 2. www.asianetwork.org/exchange/2006-winter/anex2006-winter-adler.pdf

Andors, Phyllis. 1983. *The Unfinished Liberation of Chinese Women, 1949–1980*. Bloomington: Indiana University Press.

Donaldson, John A. 2007. "Tourism Development and Poverty Reduction in Guizhou and Yunnan." *The China Quarterly* 190 (June).

Ebrey, Patricia Buckley. 1993. *The Inner Quarters: Marriage and Lives of Chinese Women in the Sung Period*. Berkeley: University of California Press.

Gilmartin, Christina K., Gail Hershatter, Lisa Rofel, and Tyrene White, eds. 1994. *Engendering China: Women, Culture and the State*. Cambridge, MA: Harvard University Press.

Grant, Beata. 2008. *Eminent Nuns: Women Chan Masters of 17th Century China*. Honolulu: University of Hawai'i Press.

———. 2008. "Women, Gender, and Religion in Premodern China: A Selected Bibliography of Secondary Sources in Chinese and Western Languages." In *Nannu: Women and Gender in Early Imperial China* 10 (January): 152.

Jarschok, Maria, and Shui Jingyun. 2010. *Women, Religion, and Space in Chinese Islamic Mosques, Daoist Temples, and Catholic Convents*. London: Routledge.

Leung, Beatrice. 2005. "China's Religious Freedom Policy: the Art of Managing Religious Activity," *The China Quarterly* 184 (October).

Li Yu-ning, ed. 1981. *Chinese Women: Through Chinese Eyes*. New York: East Gate Books.

Ma Xisha et al. 2011. *Popular Religion and Shamanism*. Leiden: Brill.

Potter, Pitman. 2003. "Belief in Control: Regulation of Religion in China." In Daniel L. Overmyer, ed., *Religion in China Today*. Cambridge: Cambridge University Press.

Yao, Esther S. Lee. 1967. *Chinese Women Past and Present*. Berkeley: University of California Press.

Films and Online Resources

Nu Shu: A Hidden Language of Women in China. 59 mins. Directed by Yue-Qing Yang, 1999. A documentary on Huan-yi Yang of Hunan Province and the tradition of women's writing that she practises.

Sakyadhita ("Daughters of the Buddha") International Association of Buddhist Women: www.sakyadhita.org

Thosamling (Tibetan) Nunnery: www.thosamling.com

Women Active in Buddhism: lhamo.tripod.com

Women in Daoism: www.daoiststudies.org

Zen Women: Stories from the Case Records of Tang Dynasty China: www.zenwomen.com

See "Women Make Movies," www.wmm.com, for a growing list of films about women in various religious traditions.

References

Chen, Ellen M. 1974. "Tao as the Great Mother and the Influence of Motherly Love in the Shaping of Chinese Philosophy." *History of Religions* 14: 51–64.

Despeux, Catherine, and Livia Kohn. 2003. *Women in Daoism*. Cambridge, Mass.: Three Pines Press.

Dudbridge, Glen. 1992. "Women Pilgrims to T'ai Shan: Some Pages from a Seventeenth-Century Novel." Pp. 39–64 in Susan Naquin and Chun-fang Yu, eds. *Pilgrims and Sacred Sites in China*. Berkeley: University of California Press.

Ebrey, Patricia Buckley. 1984. *Family and Property in Sung China: Yuan Ts'ai's Precepts for Social Life*. Princeton, NJ: Princeton University Press.

———. 1991. *Chu Hsi's Family Rituals*. Princeton, NJ: Princeton University Press.

Fehl, Noah E. 1971. *Li, Rites and Propriety in Literature and Life: A Perspective for a Cultural History of Ancient China*. Hong Kong: Chinese University Press.

Karlgren, Bernhard. trans. 1950. *The Book of Odes. Bulletin of the Museum of Far Eastern Antiquities* 22.

Legge, James. 1960. *The Ch'un Ts'ew with the Tso Chuan*. Hong Kong: University of Hong Kong Press.

Levering, Miriam. 1994. "Women, the State, and Religion Today in the People's Republic of China." Pp. 171–225 in Arvind Sharma, ed. *Today's Woman in World Religions*. Albany, NY: SUNY Press.

Paper, Jordan. 1999. *Through the Earth Darkly: Female Spirituality in Comparative Perspective*. New York: Continuum.

Rainey, Lee. 1995. "The Secret Writing of Chinese Women: Religious Practice and Beliefs." Pp. 130–64 in Katherine Young and Arvind Sharma, eds. *The Annual Review of Women and World Religions*. Albany, NY: SUNY Press.

Reed, Barbara. 1994. "Women and Chinese Religion in Contemporary Taiwan." Pp. 225–45 in Arvind Sharma, ed. *Today's Woman in World Religions*. Albany, NY: SUNY Press.

Swann, Nancy L. 1932. *Pan Chao: Foremost Woman Scholar of China*. New York: Russell and Russell.

Woo, Terry. 1999. "Confucianism and Feminism." Pp. 110–48 in Arvind Sharma and Katherine Young, ed. *Feminism and World Religions*. Albany, NY: SUNY Press.

CHAPTER 5

Women in Indigenous Traditions

Dawn Martin-Hill

Makasa (Red Earth) Looking Horse, Hereditary Pipe Keeper.

Photo by Linsey Hill

Makasa Looking Horse

Makasa, my daughter, had a dream she was to become a woman. Her father said she must have an *Ishnati* (the Lakota "Preparing a Girl for Womanhood" ceremony). I worried, as a Mohawk mother, about her being in a tipi on a hill for four days, with rattlesnakes, black widow spiders, and other things any mother would worry about. The rules require that no men see her and that she stay inside day and night. The evening before she was to begin her *Ishnati*, another ceremony would be held, to pray for her—an *inipi*. Late at night, when we crawled out of the lodge, the Milky Way was so bright, it seemed to dip into her tipi, illuminating it—it was a sight for all of us to behold.

She was both scared and excited. We had prepared everything for her ceremony. The women had to bring food to her each day in a wooden bowl. Women from Six Nations had travelled to support her, and friends and family from all over came. We sat outside the tipi as the sun beat down on us; it was 43 degrees Celsius on the outside of her tipi; inside it was at least 50 degrees. Her face was so red and soaked with sweat. I asked if she could cool off for a while, fearing heatstroke, but her father refused to move her. Thankfully, some of my friends are medical doctors; a young Cree doctor took vigil by her tipi with another friend. We watched the Elder women climb the steep hill, some with gifts, and they would sit with her. Her adopted grandmother stayed with her, refusing to leave her side despite the heat. They told her about blue women, the Creation story, the story of the White Buffalo Calf Woman, and the Seven Sacred Rites. They told her how to carry herself and be compassionate and respectful. They spoke only of her powers as a woman. Midwife Katsi Cook explained the birthing prayers and her role in bringing her elder sisters' babies into the world. We all wanted to listen in, but it was her time, not ours.

While we suffered in the unbearable heat, she was dancing around the tipi at times in pure glee. That night the thunder beings came and tore her beautiful tipi—a generous gift to her from Katsi Cook, the midwife who "catched" her when she was born in my home. The strong wind snapped the three huge poles. We brought her down the hill in the storm and covered her with a blanket so no men could see her. I was delighted the thunder beings had blessed her and a bit terrified that she could have been hurt. Thinking it was over, her father quickly put up a tent and her uncle, Tom Cook, repaired the tipi. I asked her while she sat in her Aunt Gladys's air-conditioned room, eating fresh fruit, "Do you really want to go back up? It is still very hot." She said, "Yes! I want to go now and finish what we started. Why is it taking them so long?"

The fourth day, the feast and celebration would begin; she would be seen by the people again. We had a white buckskin dress made; she had to have this new dress covered with a red cloth dress. They bathed her in medicine, braided her hair, and painted her face with red ochre and later placed an eagle plume in her hair. We had all the gifts gathered to give away in her honour. Her father sat her in a chair and Elder women offered last words of praise, warnings, and encouragement. He prayed over her with the Sacred Pipe. He then stood her up and her eldest sister, Amber, pulled the red dress off her; and then the tears flowed. She was announced to the people and had finished her four days without one complaint or any words of self-pity. Her little brother seemed to be as elated as she; he beamed with pride. She emanated beauty and light, which brought tears to many eyes. There were tears of joy for her and, from many older women, tears of sorrow. We never had our rites of passage; the sorrow was the reminder of what had been denied to us. Many of us had no idea of what we had stolen from us until that moment. This ceremony was only one of many that had been outlawed by the government.

> *A Nation is not defeated until the hearts of its women*
> *are on the ground.*

—*Cheyenne proverb (St. Pierre and Long Soldier, 1995)*

Introduction and Overview

Indigenous women's spiritual traditions can be explored from a variety of sources. This chapter will focus on what those traditions can contribute to contemporary efforts to reclaim, restore, and revitalize contemporary Indigenous spirituality as a whole, by way of a review of literature, personal voice, and the testimonies of Indigenous women.

Many Indigenous ceremonies were made illegal in Canada under the Indian Act of 1884. At the same time, laws were passed that banned "Natives" from dancing and wearing traditional clothing (Steckley and Cummins, 2001: 172). The 1914 Act that condoned the active suppression of Indigenous spirituality through legal means was finally repealed in 1951. However, **Elders** today feel that the persecution of Indigenous spirituality, by governments and missionaries alike, embedded discriminatory attitudes in Indigenous communities across the country. The fact that traditional members of those communities have been persecuted by some Christian Indigenous leaders and government agents indicates that the stigma attached to traditional spirituality continues to influence community social and political dynamics today. As a result, a primary issue in many communities is the need to revive traditional spiritual practices that will help to restore the dignity and integrity of both Indigenous culture and Indigenous women (Martin-Hill, 2003b).

The holistic world view of Indigenous peoples sees spiritual knowledge as interrelated with all spheres of life. Representations of Indigenous women's spirituality are as complex and diverse as the many Indigenous cultures discussed in the literature. Since spirituality is thought of as a way of life rather than as a rigid, organized institution, it is manifested in values, beliefs, and world views as they are expressed in everyday actions rather than periodic rituals.

The objective of this chapter is to identify the symbols, cosmologies, and epistemologies that demonstrate the diversity of Indigenous women's spirituality while linking the underlying collective assumptions about the feminine nature of the earth and the universe. The **Indigenous knowledge** framework developed by Indigenous scholars identifies spirituality as a foundation of thought rather than a separate discipline of inquiry. The related issue of cultural survival through women is critical to Indigenous women, who are the cultural transmitters; anthropologist Wade Davis says that every time a mother does not sing Cree lullabies to her babies, that culture begins to die (interview with the author). Women play an instrumental role in preserving Indigenous cultures and spirituality in the ever-more threatening climate of hegemonic globalization. This is a matter not of returning to the past but of drawing on traditional wisdoms to transform the present. Indigenous theory is concerned with all aspects of the human condition of Indigenous women: emotional, psychological, and physical as well as spiritual. Thus spirituality is part of the intellectual process of Indigenous societies, not a process of intellectualism.

The role of gender in colonialism is a critical issue in the pursuit of decolonization. Métis author Kim Anderson demonstrates the significant role that colonial subjugation played in the loss of status and power experienced by Indigenous women, which in turn crippled or fragmented our societal structures, including those in which Indigenous women fulfilled their responsibilities:

It may seem incredible that this territory we now know as Canada once hosted societies that afforded significant political power to those currently most marginalized: older women. . . . For the first time in our history, our women found themselves on the margins, in ghettos of evolving culture. The exclusion of our women from decision-making in important political and community matters not only disempowered the women, it also disempowered Indigenous cultures. . . . As the church replaced Native spirituality and became a powerful agent in the structure of Indigenous communities, Native women's loss of both political and spiritual authority was achieved. . . . Through colonization and the work of missionaries, women were excluded and handed a marginal role (Anderson, 2000: 70–8).

The devastating impact that Western ideologies and practices had on Indigenous women's traditions is best summed up in Amnesty International's report on missing and murdered Indigenous women in Canada, *Stolen Sisters* (2004). These women—estimated to number more than five hundred as of 2004—are a non-issue for the Canadian state, because of the low value it places on Indigenous women. In the United States, according to Amnesty International's report *Maze of Injustice* (2007):

Native American and Alaska Native women are more than 2.5 times more likely to be raped or sexually assaulted than other women in the USA in general. . . . [I]n at least 86 per cent of the reported cases of sexual assault Native American and Alaska Native women, survivors report that the perpetrators are non-Native men. . . . Gender-based violence against women by settlers was used in many infamous episodes, including during the Trail of Tears and the Long Walk. Such attacks were not random or individual; they were an integral part of conquest and colonization (2, 4, 16).

In 1550, in Valladolid, Spain, the father of human rights, Bartolomé de las Casas, told the pope that "Indians" were in fact human and not animals. In response, a **papal bull** declared that Indians were human only if they were Christian (Berger, 1991; Newcomb, 2008). The history of European ideas about Indigenous people and their "evil" traditional practices can be traced to this document, which entrenched the degradation of Indigenous women and their traditions and ensured that those who refused to adopt Christianity were punished with death. The colonizers' valuation of Indigenous women is obvious in the statistics from Amnesty International outlined above.

In Canada, missionization and government-enforced assimilation policies resulted in a shift from respecting the authority of women to positioning them as subordinates. The representation of Indigenous women in Western literature is laden with patriarchal and sexist ideologies. To address these issues, contemporary Indigenous women authors have adopted an interdisciplinary approach and a framework that acknowledges the massive losses and suffering that Indigenous women have experienced. Intergenerational trauma is exacerbated by the fact that history has been denied by the dominant society, which perpetrated a peace-time genocide, resulting in "historical trauma" (Braveheart, 1998: 287–305). Indigenous women's desire to participate in the development of a discourse informed by their unique experience, identity, and diversity demonstrates their resiliency. Drawing on many cultures from a variety of academic disciplines, such a discourse must be steeped in Indigenous women's own spiritual traditions and culturally transmitted knowledge. The ceremonial traditions that the Indigenous women of the Americas hold common is a spiritual connection with the land and the cosmos. At the same time, their diverse cultures vary widely in political and social organization. For the purposes of this chapter I will focus on **Haudenosaunne** (Iroquois) and **Lakota** spiritual traditions.

A Unique Feature: Indigenous Knowledge

Today, Indigenous women are seeking to reconstruct their spirituality and relearn their traditional teachings as a means of improving their quality of life, from both an individual and a collective perspective. By contrast, Western feminism has sought to deconstruct traditional European views of women as a means of empowerment. The fact that, traditionally—unlike their Western counterparts—Indigenous women did exercise power and authority in many Nations pre-contact (Anderson, 2000; Gunn Allen, 1998) was dismissed by European intellectuals as evidence of their societies' primitive character. As one of the fathers of social science, Emile Durkheim, explained:

> The further we look into the past, the smaller becomes this difference between man and woman. The woman of past days was not at all the weak creature that she has become with progress of morality. . . . These anatomical resemblances are accompanied by functional resemblances. In the same societies, female functions are not very clearly distinguished from the male. Rather, the two sexes lead almost the same existence. There are even now a very great number of savage people where the woman mingles in political life. That has

been observed especially in the Indian tribes of America, such as the Iroquois, the Natchez; in Hawaii she participates in myriad ways in men's lives, as she does in New Zealand and in Samoa (1933: 58).

Both the Church and science perpetuated the notion of Indigenous "savagery" while promoting assimilation and subordination to patriarchy and Christianity. For this reason it is impossible to examine Indigenous women's spirituality without examining colonialism.

In developing an Indigenous knowledge framework, it is important to outline our holistic approach, which underscores the interdependence of all things in the universe; spirituality is entrenched in all aspects of a "way of life." Indigenous epistemology incorporates "mind," "body," and "spirit" as facets of being that seek balance. Indigenous knowledge is a form of spiritual and intellectual enlightenment and consciousness. For example, the relationship of Indigenous peoples with the earth is understood as spiritual; all living things embody spirit, and they make offerings to these spirits based on physical, spiritual, or emotional needs. At the same time it is important to understand intellectually how natural laws demand coexistence with nature as essential for human survival. Indigenous people have relationships with the land, and a dialogue exists between the people and their land. They speak to her and she answers.

Western epistemology defines science or knowledge as objective, independent of spirituality, values, beliefs, and irrational, subjective emotion. By contrast, the Indigenous holistic approach acknowledges that no human being is capable of "objectivity" or "neutrality," as demonstrated by the papal bull and Emile Durkheim. We are all culturally influenced by the place where we originated and the language we speak.

Indigenous epistemologies understand time and space in terms of circular motion, in contrast to the linear view of the West and of Christianity. Economic, social, and political systems all have a spiritual base. The key point here is that spirituality is interwoven with all aspects of human activity and therefore cannot be discussed in isolation.

Mohawk scholar Marlene Brant Castellano identifies three sources of Indigenous knowledge: spiritual revelation, empirical observation over time, and oral histories and teachings passed down through the generations (2000: 23). Because these multiple sources of knowledge do not conform to the Western model of social-scientific inquiry, an alternative paradigm is needed to explore Indigenous women's traditions.

To understand the complexity of Indigenous knowledge, it is also necessary to recognize how deeply Indigenous cultures are rooted in specific landscapes, and how integral those landscapes may be to their spirituality. For example, the Navajo tradition holds corn pollen to be sacred. Thus it is customary to offer the Holy Ones (deities) corn pollen for healing, blessing, or guidance, and some healing rituals involve the creation of intricate sand paintings of specific Holy Ones. These practices are inseparable from the landscape in which the Navajo culture has been rooted for millennia. The ability of the Navajo and Hopi to grow corn in the desert is attributed to their people's spiritual relationship with the land and the Holy Ones.

Another key aspect of Indigenous spiritual traditions is that they make no attempt to proselytize or convert others: people simply are Navajo or Hopi, Haudenosaunne or Lakota. Indigenous peoples have ancient religious practices and beliefs, but their only temples are the natural ones provided by the land, and their only doctrines are those of sustaining balance and reciprocal relationships, in keeping with the Creator's natural law (Alfred, 1999: 4; Cajete, 2000; Martin-Hill, 1992: 63).

The consciousness that existed prior to the arrival of Europeans can be seen in the principles that guided pre-contact Haudenosaunne society. They also illustrate how the philosophy of **Deganawida** the Peacemaker, whose visions led to the development of the Confederacy of the Iroquois, promoted a form of participatory democracy in which women were authority figures (Lyons and Mohawk, 1992: 1–13). The Haudenosaunne operated their society on intellectual principles. Emile Durkheim missed that point. It is only recently that scholars of the West have examined the First Americans as interdependent societies with autonomous political, social, and economic structures, and even more recently that they have begun to consider the historical authority and power of Haudenosaunne women.

Removing the shackles of stereotypes is part of the agenda of Indigenous women. They are rebuilding traditional structures in their communities and renegotiating the authority that was stripped from them through legal frameworks such as the Indian Act. Indigenous women are trying to rebuild traditional structures based on tribal egalitarianism and matriarchal lineage (Anderson, 2000; Green, 1998; Wagner, 2001).

Symbols, Rituals, and Interpretations

The bond among Indigenous women is rooted not only in their collective colonial experience but also in a spiritually based belief system. Their understanding of power differs from Western notions. For example, it would be erroneous for Indigenous people to define *power* in terms of wealth or material possessions. To be powerless is to be without the knowledge of *who you are*. To be weak is to display disrespect and ignorance (Deloria, 1992; Gunn Allen, 1998; Lyons and Mohawk, 1992).

To let go of the pain of colonialism and rebuild our families is a lifelong, daily process involving mind, body, and spirit. The foundations of Indigenous ideology are located in our languages, ceremonies, and ritual expressions. Ideas and beliefs originating with the divine are reinforced through participation in rituals. The interaction between the physical and spiritual realms includes the bringing together of clans or kinfolk, and sometimes whole communities; this gathering of people is critical to the collective bonding within the ceremonial circle. The natural law provided to the people by the Creator is the guide to seeking balance. While each Nation may approach this differently, it would appear that all hold the same philosophy regarding natural laws.

For example, in Haudenosaunne cosmology, a pregnant woman fell from the Sky World with strawberries in her hand. Blue herons caught her and placed her on a turtle's back because there was only water on earth at this time. Many animals tried to bring dirt up from the ocean floor to form land, but failed. Finally, the most unlikely animal, the muskrat, succeeded, and the woman placed the dirt on the turtle's back. That is how the earth started. Through the Creation story the energy of the universe is explained. The sun is male and the earth female, like Grandmother moon; things of water are female, and things of fire are male. The Creation story defines the world in both gender and kinship terms. It explains that small animals are as great as big animals, how strawberries and other seeds are gifts from the Sky World and the first medicine. The Haudenosaunne Creation story defines both the cosmos itself and the relationships, roles, and responsibilities that exist within it (Porter, 2008). The same can be said for the Lakota, Cree, and other Indigenous groups, each of which has its unique Creation story that explains the world and humans' place in it (Deloria, 1992; Porter, 2008).

A significant event in the history of the Haudenosaunne people was the arrival of Deganawida the Peacemaker and his message of the **Great Law of Peace** (Martin-Hill, 2007). All five Iroquoian Nations—the Onondaga, Oneida, Seneca, Mohawk, and Cayuga—were embroiled in terrible warfare against one another when the Peacemaker—a divine spiritual messenger—came to them and appointed a speaker known as Hiawatha (a man he found grieving over the loss of his daughters to an evil leader) to help him establish peace among the Nations. The Peacemaker healed his grief through the "**condolence** ceremony" (a ritual in which tears are symbolically wiped away, the lump in the throat is removed, and the veil of death is cleared from the eyes) and gave us the teaching that all leaders must possess clarity through spiritual wellness. This healing ceremony is still performed when appointing or burying leaders. The Peacemaker and Hiawatha helped establish the constitution known as the Great Law of Peace, which consisted of more than 100 laws or articles. The Peacemaker also appointed the first **Clanmother**, Jikonsahseh, who had a neutral home in the time of war among the five Nations that comprise the Haudenosaunne. She was deceitful, and harmed her male visitors, but he changed both her mind and her behaviour, and in appointing Jikonsahseh as the first female leader he acknowledged the important role that women play in decision-making. From this we learn that words, compassion, and healing can overcome the worst attributes of humans, and that the worst humans can become the greatest of leaders.

Under the Great Law, women have authority within their clans (social systems). "Clanmother" is a spiritual socio-political title that honours certain characteristics of women, especially compassion and the desire for peace. The Great Law gives women of each clan the power to appoint its male leader, the **Sachem**, because she would know best which of the children in her **longhouse** had the attributes of a leader (kindness, generosity, fairness, and so on). She could (and still can) also impeach her appointed Sachem if his conduct was unbecoming or immoral (Barreiro, 1992; Fenton, 1998; Porter, 2008).

The establishment of a united Confederacy Council to govern the five warring Nations created the first democracy in the Western hemisphere: one that would serve as a model for the constitution of the United States (Barreiro, 1992; Lyons and Mohawk, 1992), although the US constitution did not take up the Great Law's notion of female leadership and recognition of peace as the founding principle. Second, the Great Law incorporates a ritual whereby men being "stood up" as Sachems undergo spiritual healing so that they may have "good minds and good hearts" (Martin-Hill, 1992; Porter, 2008).

Family Structure and Sexuality

Haudenosaunne society is matrilineal, organized around clan affiliations. According to the Great Law, the Sachems chosen by the Clanmothers would carry the clan's decisions on matters of national interest to the grand council, which consisted of the clan Chiefs of the five original Nations (Mohawk, Cayuga, Seneca, Onondaga, and Oneida; the sixth Nation, Tuscarora, joined the confederacy in 1722).

The clan system involves numerous social regulations. The number of clans varies from one Nation to another, but three—the Wolf, Bear, and Turtle clans—are common to all six Iroquois Nations. All members of a clan form one family, even if they come from different Nations. Thus a Mohawk man and a Seneca woman who were both members of the Wolf clan would not be allowed to marry, since they would be considered brothers and sisters. This symbolic kinship created a spiritual bond that ensured peace and harmony among peoples who had a history of conflict.

Within each Nation, each clan lived in its own longhouse under the direction of its clanmother. When a man and a woman formed a union, the man would go to live in the woman's longhouse, but would continue to be involved in his own clan's business and assist in raising his sisters' children, while his children, both male and female, would became part of their mother's clan lineage and be raised by her and her brothers. In this system, a failed marriage had little impact on the children's way of life, since their mother's brothers continued to fulfill the responsibilities of a father.

Although colonialist agencies have tried to institutionalize patriarchy and undermine the matrilineal system (for example, by introducing Indian status cards that identify people by their father's last name and nation membership), the traditional understanding of family identity has continued through oral history. In spite of the state's efforts to undermine the matrilineal family structure, it has survived through oral transmission of Indigenous knowledge. My "Indian card" states I am Oneida, but my children and I know that our female lineage is Mohawk and identify ourselves as such. Even though households are now generally organized on the nuclear model, the extended family persists as daughters and sons still tend to live near their mothers.

Haudenosaunne Women Speak

I interviewed highly respected Elder Judy Swamp about women's roles in the Mohawk community of Akwesasne for the film "Mothers of our Nations." Reflecting on the fact that when women get married today, they tend to follow "the newer tradition" and go to live with the man rather than with her family, she thought that the older tradition would have provided greater security and peace for women:

> What man in his right mind would ever abuse a woman when she has her family right close, her aunts, her sisters, her grandmother, or even great grandmother if you're lucky enough . . . where would the violence be? . . . I don't hesitate to correct my sons if something they say or do . . . offends their wives. I say to them I remain your mother forever, like my mother told me. The day that you aren't answering to me, she says, is when I am in my grave (*Mothers of our Nations*).

Clanmothers serve as spiritual leaders, political authorities, and counsellors 24 hours a day, every day of the year, and receive no compensation for their work other than the knowledge that they are following the Creator's law. While many Indigenous Nations do not have matrilineal social structures, they all have female Elders who uphold the natural laws passed on from earlier generations and are intertwined with the socio-political spiritual life of their nations. To ensure that they are not exposed to the opposition that men face when they speak for the clan, Clanmothers normally communicate only through their appointed Chief, and it is rare for them to speak in public.

In the summer of 2004, however, the Clanmothers of the Six Nations of the Grand River agreed to be interviewed for the Confederacy-supported educational film, *The Dish with One Spoon*. In the following excerpts, two of them describe how they became Clanmothers:

> Cathy Smoke: When I was made a Clanmother, my grandmother who had been the Clanmother before had passed away . . . and they had put in my aunt as a benchwarmer. [But] she decided that she didn't want it, so the family came to me and asked me if I would take the title. . . . I began attending meetings and when the big condolence came up they put me in as Clanmother. . . . I've been a Clanmother since 2002.

Clanmother Bernice Johnson started out helping her grandmother, who would take her along to help out whenever she had to attend a death or a condolence ceremony. Eventually her grandmother began talking about what would happen when she could no longer fulfill her duties, asking Bernice to help the older cousin she thought would replace her as Clanmother. After her grandmother died, however, when the time came to choose a new Clanmother, Bernice's cousin told her to put on her longhouse regalia:

> And I thought then, oh no. . . . My cousin that they had picked . . . she had a spot there and she said come here, sit here. Oh my goodness, I thought . . . I bet you that's what this is all about and they didn't tell me. What I am going to do, I can't say no. So sure enough they did. I sat there and listened to the Chief speak and tell us . . . that we've picked somebody to take her spot, take her place for now; she's going to be the one. I just didn't know what to do, I was so nervous. I thought what am I going to say, what am I going to do? I know what I have to do, but what do I say now? . . . Every time I would try to stand up [my cousin] would say "Sit down, stay here." And finally I got over being nervous. Then they asked [the chief if he was ready]. . . . He said "Yes, I am." "Okay," he said, "now you can see her, this is who we picked." They had me stand up in front of the whole house full of people and I was just shaking. I didn't know, I guess I kind of expected it and yet I didn't know what to do.
>
> So finally, [my uncle] came and grabbed my hand and he said to me, "You're going to be alright, don't worry, you'll be okay, you're going to be alright, it's okay." He could tell I was just shaking so he held my

hand. . . . That's when they started saying that there little speech that they had to say, do I know what I have to do and will I accept it. Am I accepting what they want? And they said that this clan wants you, so are you ready and willing to do it? To carry on what your grandma did? I was just shaking at that moment. . . . So, I don't know why but it just came to me and I told them that I did, that I will accept . . . their words their wisdom that encouragement to me, that I will accept it and that I'll do my best. And then I said that's all I have to say, so I said *nya:wen* [thanks] to them and they all just smiled. And I felt good that I saw them smile, that they didn't say anything else and I didn't have to say anything else. And they said that's it now you can sit down, so I sat down, that was it. So, that's how I became Clanmother (*Dish with One Spoon*, 2007).

Under the Great Law, it is Clanmothers' duty to protect their lands. Thus in 2006 they supported several young Six Nations women who were protesting against the town of Caledonia's construction of a housing development on lands under legal claim by their community. The women's peaceful intervention resulted in an early morning police raid involving snipers, tear gas, and tasering of Elders, youth, and women. The Six Nations' swift response to the raid resulted in a peaceful end to the police state-sponsored terror, and demonstrated the power of women to the non-Native community.

Here two of the Clanmothers speak about the roles they played in the Caledonia negotiations and, more broadly, about relations with the dominant society:

RW: How we got involved was these girls, Dawn and Janie Jamieson, they were handing out pamphlets, they asked us if we'd come to their meeting about their having this protest and . . . if we could, you know, help support them, and give them advice. So we went over to Jeb's house and they had a meeting there. . . . Bernice and Ruby, and Myna and I, we went there to see what it was all about. . . . They said that they needed us to help support them. . . . I know we weren't supposed to be in front. We're not supposed to be out in public like that, but it was so, so scary after the police went in, so we thought that we would have to help them somehow. So we gave them support, guidance, and I was really, really scared. . . . All this violence, the police came in and . . . it was just like the army getting after our people. . . .

Bernice: Then all of a sudden . . . this guy came and made a big commotion . . .

RW: Myna and I went to over there to see what was wrong with him, and we just grabbed his hand [and told him] not to be shouting that way. That this wasn't the place to be carrying on like that and, I don't know, he calmed down; Myna and I both grabbed him because he was getting out of hand. . . . We just talked to him and he seemed to have settled down. . . .

RW: . . . We ran into all kinds of different things every day. And we were there quite a few hours every day; there was a lot of stress. A lot of people were getting tired out and they needed someone to talk to. Most of the time we were in . . . the trailer. And that's where they would bring people in who needed to talk and who needed settling down. Try to soothe whatever it is that was bothering them. And then there [were] things that maybe we couldn't allow them to do and we had to explain it to them, why. And they read us letters that [they wanted to send to the government or media] . . . they would read it to us first and we would decide whether they should or shouldn't. There was all kinds of people that wanted to talk to us, to meet us. . . . It was pretty stressful [what] people were going through there, fighting for something that I always say we owned. Why are we doing this when we own the land, you know? . . .

Then this one day . . . there was a bunch of news people up front there, between where the Caledonia people were and the Haudenosaunee people, and they wanted us up there. . . . And so we went up there and we were meeting . . . different people from different reservations, [and they were] telling us that they were behind us . . . which was good to hear.

. . . . We do need a place for our future, children and grandchildren . . . we need a place for them to live and to own. Yeah, it's really sad the way things are going. . . . I keep asking our Creator to help us and asking him to guide us, what else can we do? And where else can we turn for help and stuff like that.

To me, I think that he [the white man] gave us education but he didn't think that we were going to shoot it back at him. And that's where we are today. And they promised that as long as the grass shall grow the sun shines and rivers flow, and this is what we believe in strongly. . . . We're using all that against him now, and I'm hoping and asking the Creator to help us, that he will not . . . push us anymore. This is it, we've had it. Thank you (*Dish with One Spoon*, 2007).

Indigenous women have been invisible in the White man's epic settlement story except in the form of the two stereotypes dear to the writers of westerns:

the noble princess who helps the white man or the ignoble, obese, foolish, giggling, mindless woman (Berkhofer, 1979; Churchill, 1994; Green, 1998). Rarely speaking or showing any emotion, these women were often depicted as nearer to animals than human beings (Berkhofer, 1979), and their dehumanization was compounded by their depiction as beasts of burden or slaves to their owners—their husbands. And the western genre was not alone in dehumanizing Indigenous women: academia too tended to focus on Indigenous warriors, hunters, sages, and shamans while ignoring women and the family unit.

Social Change

The Literature

Authors including Linda Smith, Kim Anderson, Tom Porter, and Paula Gunn Allen have outlined the crucial role that colonialism and European cultural constructs have played in displacing Indigenous women from their former positions of respect. Indigenous women's ongoing resistance to the dominant culture's constructions of them as "Other" is found in both artistic and literary expressions. Their work is primarily concerned with, and stands as a response to, legal and social policies implemented in the context of colonization.

Paula Gunn Allen explores how the adoption of Christian values and ideologies through colonization subordinated the authority of Indigenous women and transformed traditional female cosmologies into male patriarchal epistemologies. The spiritual powers a woman possessed were directly related to her social status and decision-making authority. Colonial policy legislated by the Canadian government controls all aspects of Indigenous peoples' lives, including their religious beliefs.

Women suffered enormous losses through the imposition of the Indian Act, including loss of the right to raise their own children. The late grandmother of my two youngest children, Lakota Elder Cecelia Looking Horse, described that experience as "the stealing of our bundles, our power" (interview with the author, 1998). The emotional wounds suffered by Indigenous mothers whose children were ripped from their arms and forcibly carted off to **residential schools** (in the United States, boarding schools) are still unhealed in many communities today. Many of the pivotal stories are shared in books such as John Milloy's A National Crime (1999); Suzanne Fournier and Ernie Crey's Stolen from Our Embrace (1997); and Kim Anderson and Bonita Lawrence's Strong Women Stories (2003), a compilation of essays by women giving their personal testimonies. The personal histories of Indigenous women detail the roles and responsibilities they had in food production, healing, and controlling the distribution of wealth as well as spiritual leadership, and how colonialism marginalized them. These stories demonstrate that spiritual power was and continues to be connected to women's roles as mothers and grandmothers seeking to preserve a way of life. Stories of Indigenous women's spiritual traditions are also chronicled in texts such as *Walking in the Sacred Manner: Healers, Dreamers, and Pipe Carriers—Medicine Women of the Plains Indians* (St. Pierre and Long Soldier, 1995). *Medicine That Walks* (Lux, 2001) explores women's spiritual healing powers. *And Grandma Said . . . : Iroquois Teachings as Passed Down through the Oral Tradition* (Porter, 2008) explores the teachings of a Haudenosaunne grandmother. *In the Words of Elders: Aboriginal Cultures in Transition* (Kulchyski, McCaskill, and Newhouse, 1999) gives voice to Elders. And my own documentary *Mothers of Our Nations* (2004) visualizes women's power and pain. These voices and others provide personal accounts and first-person interviews with Elders, **healers**, and **medicine women**, sharing their spiritual searches and philosophy regarding women's roles and responsibilities. Contemporary accounts of Indigenous women's spirituality are part and parcel of the agenda to rebuild spiritual knowledge as a tool of decolonization. By reviving ancient knowledge, Indigenous women are bringing back the teachings that value women's traditions and their roles in society.

The White Buffalo Calf Woman's Gift of the Sacred Pipe

The Lakota people tell the story of the White Buffalo Calf Woman, who brought the Sacred Pipe to them 19 generations ago. As told by Black Elk in Joseph Epes Brown's *The Sacred Pipe* (1953) and by Arvol Looking Horse, the current Keeper of the White Buffalo Calf Pipe, this story begins with two scouts who had been sent out by their chief to look for buffalo. The people were starving and prayed for *Wakan Tonka* (Great Spirit) to help. The scouts saw a beautiful woman coming toward them, carrying a bundle. One scout had bad thoughts and wanted to force her to be a wife, but the other scout warned him that she was a spirit woman. She pointed to the ill-minded scout and a cloud enveloped him. When the dust cleared, he had been reduced to bones with snakes crawling about him. She then told the other scout to tell his people what he had witnessed, no more and no less. He was to tell the leaders to prepare a special area for her in their camp and await her arrival. The next day she appeared, singing a song and carrying a bundle in her arms. That song is still sung today. She gave the bundle, the Sacred Pipe, to Chief Standing Hollow Horn and instructed him on how to pray with the Pipe. Upon her departure she said that when the people are in very hard times, she would return as a white buffalo. She then walked away, turning into a white buffalo (Brown, 1953: 8–9; Martin-Hill, Fieldnotes from Arvol Looking Horse, 1998).

Martha Bad Warrior, Keeper of the eighteenth-generation White Buffalo Calf Pipe, and grandmother to Makasa Looking Horse.

The teachings of the story of the Sacred Pipe exemplify the power that women carry and give to the people. The notion of the female as sacred and powerful is reinforced by the fact that two of the Lakota's Seven Sacred Rites are for women: *Ishnati* (Preparing a Girl for Womanhood) and ***Tapa Wanka Yap*** (Throwing of the Ball). Both ceremonies celebrate womanhood and the powers of female energy. The story of *Tapa Wanka Yap* reveals a great deal about Lakota rituals and female energy. Holy man Black Elk tells the story:

> Moves Walking then picked up the painted ball and handed it to the young girl, telling her to stand and to hold it in her left hand and raise her right hand up to the heavens. Moves Walking then began to pray, holding the pipe in his left hand, and holding his right hand up to the heavens. "O Grandfather, Wakan Tanka, Father, Wakan Tanka, behold Rattling Hail Woman, who stands here holding the universe in her hand. . . . She sees her generations to come and the tree of life at the center. She sees the sacred path" (Brown, 1953: 133).

The notion of woman as central energy in the universe is both profound and simplistic. It is women who have the ability to give life. The **Lakota Star knowledge** reiterates the connections between earth and universe and the life-force energy that women hold. In fact, the Lakota creation story traces their ancestry from the "star nation" to under the earth. The journey from the stars was their beginning, and then they lived under the earth. Today, in the Black Hills there is a site known as Wind Cave. The Lakota believe this is where they were tricked by Ictomy (Spider) to come out from under the earth. They followed him through the hole known as Wind Cave. Immediately they saw predatory animals and wanted to return, but could not find their path. At this time, the thunder beings chased big predatory animals underground so humans could live. Today they cannot even access Wind Cave to pray unless they pay the fees for tourist guides, who quickly remind them not to touch anything. Spiritual oppression is still active; imagine how demeaning it is for Elders and spiritual leaders to pay the settlers to pray on their own lands. It is their temple, their mosque, their church; it belongs to them. The employees of the National Parks Service are paid well to tell their version of history, in which it was the White man who discovered Wind Cave, and then to footnote the Indian "folklore."

Another sacred site is Bear Butte, the location of another sacred rite, the vision quest. Today, the Sturgis motorcycles rallies are in full swing during the summer solstice; drunken, drug-filled partiers surround the Lakota people trying to hold ancient ceremonies in their sacred places. While my son will be trying to communicate with the Creator for his vision quest, he will hear thousands of motorcycles, and blaring music from bars built within earshot of these sacred sites. Tourists will stop and gawk at the "Indians praying." In the film *Paha Sapa: Struggle for the Black Hills* (1998), an Elder critiques how many evil things, such as gambling, sexual exploitation, and drinking, now occur in this holiest of places. *Mitakuye oyasin*. We are all related.

Indigenous women are tied to their grandmothers, who often act as spiritual guides, teachers, mentors, and healers. A grandmother's power is different from a grandfather's, especially when it comes to birthing and welcoming children into this world. Birthing is a spiritual experience, sacred in many traditional Indigenous cultures. Women are spiritually connected to their unborn children and often connect with their unborn's spirit through dream and vision. The actions of both the mother and father influence the child's well-being in many ways. Traditionally, there is careful ritual surrounding the birth, umbilical cord, afterbirth, and veil (or caul; a sign that means the child is an old soul returning and will be a seer or healer). While the Mayan, Navajo, Haudenosaunne, Lakota, and Cree interpretations of these elements may differ, all would agree on the spiritual significance of giving birth (Cook, in Bruchac, 1989; Meili, 1991; St. Pierre and Long Soldier, 1995). It is from the womb and ovaries that women's "power" flows—it is no wonder that there is such a predisposition in Western medicine to remove, stigmatize, or control these sacred female body parts.

Official and Unofficial Roles of Women

Medicine Women, Healers, and Spiritual Guides

The spiritual authority that Indigenous women once held in their societies has been severely eroded and undermined through colonialism. However, Indigenous women are working to repair and rebuild their families' lives and their traditional positions (Alfred, 1999; Anderson, 2000; Gunn Allen, 1986). The need for healing from decades of unjust policies and treatment has sparked a resurgence of traditional healing and spiritual recovery. Dorothy Rosenberg has this to say:

> In traditional matriarchal cultures, healing was associated with the life-giving capacities of women. . . . For most of human history holistic healing was practised largely by women. . . . For many women, knowledge of herbal preparations was as common as knowledge of cooking today. . . . In addition, Indigenous healing practices maintained by laywomen for thousands of years remain among the most important healing practices in most rural parts of the world. According to WHO [World Health Organization], these practices provide 95 per cent of the world's needs (2000: 140–7).

Eurocentric representations portray Indigenous people, spirituality, ritual, and ceremony either as mythology and "quackery" or, in the case of the current New Age movement, as ultra-mystical and secretive. The truth is far less glamorous than some "experts" suggest and more in line with Rosenberg's analysis. Spirituality is expressed in our actions and interactions, as a part of everyday life; this point cannot be overstated. As the Clanmothers quoted above make clear, their roles are to offer quiet support to families who have lost a loved one, to cook for ceremonies, and to counsel community members. Only in the case of conflict with Non-natives have their roles been made so public to everyone involved.

As Cecelia Looking Horse pointed out, "A **Sundance** is a powerful ceremony, a sacrifice for the people, unfortunately what people do not understand is life is a Sundance, it's what you do in between these ceremonies that counts as much as the ceremony itself" (Martin-Hill, Fieldnotes from Arvol Looking Horse, 1998). In *Medicine That Walks*, Maureen Lux (2001) cites numerous examples of historical records and archives documenting the traditional medicinal knowledge that women practised in Plains cultures. She quotes the account, given in the 1890s by Native American documentation enthusiast Walter McClintock, of a Blackfoot ceremony: "Ekitowaki began to brew herbs from her medicine pouch, and while purifying herself with incense, beseeched the bison spirit to help her find the source of the disease. . . . Her fingers danced over Stuyimi's body until she announced the illness was in his chest. . . [S]he danced in imitation of the bison" (Lux, 2001: 76). Lux discusses the spiritual nature of healing in Plains culture and how one Blackfoot woman, Last Calf, contracted tuberculosis and dreamed of a cure. She was instructed to boil pitch of the lodgepole pine and drink the brew. She was recorded as vomiting profusely until her chest was cleared. Last Calf's remedy was widely used for tubercular cough. Lux also elaborates on the high social standing of Plains midwives and how they performed not only prenatal but postnatal care for months for the woman and her child.

Sarah Carter's article "First Nations Women in Prairie Canada" (1996) elaborates on the traditional medicinal knowledge of Indigenous people of the plains. Historical documents suggest that medical doctors commonly used traditional midwives and healers. She cites a number of examples of Indigenous women assisting medical doctors with both Native and non-Native births, and administering medicinal brews for jaundice and other ailments (Carter, 1996: 62). A passage from the archives dated 1880 brings to life Indigenous women's historical role in healing:

The Indian woman took in the situation at a glance. She pushed aside the terrified mother and picked up the ailing child. By signs she indicated hot water from the kettle on the stove. Into it she put a pinch of herbs from the pouch slung around her waist. Soon the gasping subsided, and a sweat broke to cool the fevered skin. She cooled the brew and forced some of it between the blue lips of the infant. The baby relaxed into a peaceful sleep cradled in the arms of the crooning Indian woman. . . . That mother to her dying day remained grateful (Carter, 1996: 64).

Carter also notes that Indigenous women were marginalized both formally and informally through legal, social, and economic interference. Neither historians nor anthropologists have specifically addressed colonialism's impact on Indigenous women's practice of traditional medicine and ceremonial ritual (Anderson, 2000; Gunn Allen, 1986; Rosenberg, 2000; Smith Tuhiwai, 1999). Elder and healer Rose Auger sums up the reality that Indigenous women face today:

It's been less than one hundred years that men lost touch with reality. There's no power or medicine that has all the force unless it's balanced. The [woman] must be there also, but she has been left out! When we still had our culture, we had balance. The [woman] made ceremonies, and she was recognized as being united with the moon, the earth, and all forces on it. Men have taken over. Most feel threatened by holy women. They must stop and remember the loving power of their grandmothers (Auger, in Meili, 1991: 25).

Today, a debate is taking place across the continent about women's roles in ceremonies. There are many Elders, healers, and spiritualists who do not allow women to participate in healing rituals, pipe ceremonies, or any other spiritual activity. Indigenous writers such as Anderson and Lawrence suggest that Christian values played a role in transforming a matrilineal tradition into a patriarchal system that positions Indigenous women as servants rather than the spiritual leaders they once were (2003: 15).

The New Age Movement and Indigenous Spirituality

In recent years, some non-Indigenous "New Agers" have found financial reward in appropriating Indigenous spirituality, turning traditional ceremonies and healing practices into businesses targeting non-Indigenous consumers. Poverty leaves many esteemed Elders and spiritual leaders vulnerable to economic exploitation of their culture and tradition. The New Age movement is a multi-million-dollar industry that has displaced and exploited Indigenous spirituality (Battiste and Henderson, 2000) without benefiting the people from which it is taken. Thus, ironically, the revitalization of Indigenous spirituality and healing practices, and the lifting of the prohibitions that had prevented them from being practised openly, has presented new challenges for Indigenous women's spirituality. The appropriation of Indigenous spiritual knowledge can be referred to as the Last Frontier (Martin-Hill, 1992).

A number of articles have discussed the influence of Western culture and the commercialization of ceremonies and rituals attached to traditional healing practices. In Lisa Aldred's view, the "fetishization of Native American spirituality not only masks the social oppression of real Indian people but also perpetuates it" (2000: 329). Indigenous women are at the bottom of North America's socio-economic ladder, and now their own spiritual identity and authority are in serious jeopardy. Mohawk author Christopher Jocks elaborates on this point: "This issue of appropriation and intrusion by academics and the 'New Age' enthusiasts is . . . of the deepest concern to Native traditionalists these days . . . continuing economic and cultural invasion of Native communities, causing erosion of self-sufficiency and the decay of integrity in ceremonial work" (2000: 73).

New Agers who have the financial resources to promote and consume Indigenous practices compound Indigenous people's loss of authority over their own culture. This erosion of Indigenous participation is of grave concern to Elders and spiritual leaders. Indigenous women are being displaced both by New Agers themselves and by Indigenous spiritual leaders who became dependent on the financial support they provide. Many Indigenous women who as children were shipped off to mission-run residential schools and taught that their traditional ways were evil have suffered "spiritual trauma." These women are the ones most in need of spiritual healing, and yet they are alienated from the very ceremonies that might soothe their inner turmoil and help them achieve peace and healing. As one Elder confided to me, "I shook the first time I saw the pipe, every fibre of me believed it was evil, I had been told this from the time I can remember. I cried; there stood those White people smoking the very pipe I could not behold."

Revictimization

Cynthia Kasee substantiates the colonial culture's exploitation of Native spirituality. She denounces the ongoing marginalization of Indigenous women as their ancestral roles are appropriated by the dominant culture (Kasee, 1995). Cultural imperialism and marginalization are factors in the continuing victimization of Indigenous women.

As a result of colonial policies, Indigenous women are overrepresented in recent statistical data on issues such as domestic violence, imprisonment, suicide, and general poor health (Frideres, 2005). Now more than ever, they need help to heal the wounds inflicted by residential schools, forced removal of their children, and loss of land and culture. Yet as Kasee (1995) points out, they are revictimized when their lack of traditional knowledge and their marginal social status prevent them from gaining access to traditional healing and ceremonies. New Agers' ability to pay has launched a new wave of imperialist activity—the mining of Indigenous knowledge and spirituality—that leaves Indigenous women without privileges in either culture. The internalization of colonialism is far more dangerous than what governments have done to Indigenous women; our society continues to erode the spiritual integrity of Indigenous women, and the New Age movement's appropriating of our ceremonies is just one more violation of Indigenous women. Discrimination, destruction of our sacred sites, and mockery of our spiritual practices are just the tip of the iceberg. Over 50 per cent of Indigenous people identify themselves as Catholics, and another 20 per cent as Baptists, Anglicans, or other Protestants; few identify themselves as practitioners of Indigenous spiritual traditions (Frideres, 2005).

Summary

Historically, Indigenous women were constructed as powerful. In the Indigenous worldview, according to which all things in the universe were female and male, and the goal was to achieve balance between them, women had key roles to play. Women's power flowed from their spiritual knowledge, which gave them the authority to make decisions for the good of the people. Despite the negative impacts of colonialism, Indigenous women resisted oppression and continued to use spirituality as a major source of strength, courage, and guidance, and today, despite all obstacles, they are in fact rebuilding and revitalizing their spirituality. As the voices we have heard in this chapter show, many women are upholding the matrilineal Great Law. The authority of Clanmothers may be invisible to mainstream society, but when a crisis, such as a land dispute, erupts, it soon becomes clear to police, government, and media who are really in control. These women continue working to reclaim their traditional knowledge and restore the dignity and integrity stripped away by missionaries, the Indian Act, and residential schools.

The spirituality of Indigenous women today is focused on healing: healing historical trauma, healing families, healing communities, and healing themselves. They draw strength from sacred sites and their relationship to the land. Their practice of spirituality is an integral part of the intellectual and political efforts of other Indigenous women who are working to achieve well-being and a higher quality of life for themselves and their children. This is the spirit of our ancestors. True intellectual and emotional recovery, liberation, self-determin-ation, and decolonization require the reconstruction of women's traditional roles, responsibilities, and authority. The strengthening of Indigenous women will strengthen the Nation.

Glossary

Clanmother   A key political office in Indigenous societies; the woman who chooses the chief and has other sorts of political authority.

Condolence   A grieving ceremony for leaders of the Confederacy.

Deganawida the Peacemaker   A man, thought to be Huron/Wyandot, whose visions led to the development of the Great Law of Peace and thereby the Confederacy of the Iroquois.

Elders   People recognized for their learning over a relatively long life span, who are respected and cherished for their willingness to share their wisdom.

Great Law of Peace (Mohawk: *Gayanerengo:wa*)   Literally, "it is a great good." The name refers to the law that brought the five nations of the Iroquois (Haudenosaunne) together, sustained their confederacy for centuries, and is still in place today.

Haudenosaunne   The people of the Long House, also known as the Iroquois, who comprised five nations—Cayuga, Mohawk, Oneida, Onondaga, and Seneca—that formed a confederacy. The Tuscarora joined in the eighteenth century and the group then became known as the Six Nations.

healers   Gifted individuals who may use a variety of therapies, including ritual, to heal people spiritually, emotionally, or physically.

Indigenous knowledge   A complete knowledge system, with its own epistemology, philosophy, and scientific and logical validity, that can be learned through the pedagogy traditionally employed by Indigenous peoples.

Lakota   One of the three primary Nations that comprise the Sioux of the Plains in the United States and Canada; the other two are the Dakota and Nakota. The Lakota are concentrated in South and North Dakota.

Lakota Star knowledge   A culturally specific set of principles by which to live, thought to come from the heavens.

longhouse   An Iroquoian dwelling of the pre-contact era, now known as a place where ceremonies are conducted.

medicine man/woman   One who possesses sacred bundles, sacred pipes, sacred masks, and the rights to rituals, songs, and medicines inherited from parents or grandparents, or earned through apprenticeship with a respected medicine man or woman; in some Nations, also a conductor of community ceremonies.

papal bull   An official decree proclaimed or issued by a pope. The term *bull* comes from the authenticating seal (*bulla*) affixed to it.

residential schools (US: boarding schools)   Boarding schools for Indigenous students financed by the federal government and run by various churches. Not only did their students receive a lower standard of education than non-Indigenous children, but also many of them were abused—physically, emotionally, and sexually.

Sachem   A title often used to refer to the 50 chiefs of the League of the Iroquois, derived from an Eastern Algonquian word for "leader."

Sundance   One of the seven sacred rites of the Lakota; a healing ceremony that lasts for four days and includes fasting and dancing.

Tapa Wanka Yap (Throwing of the Ball Ceremony)   One of the Seven Sacred Rites of the Lakota; acknowledges the passage of childhood to womanhood marked by the first menses.

Further Reading

Carter, Sarah. 1996. "First Nations Women in Prairie Canada in the Early Reserve Years, the 1870s to the 1920s: A Preliminary Inquiry." Pp. 51–75 in Christine Miller and Patricia Chuchryk, eds. *Women of the First Nations: Power, Wisdom, and Strength*. Winnipeg: University of Manitoba Press.

Fournier, Suzanne, and Ernie Crey. 1997. *Stolen from Our Embrace: The Abduction of First Nations Children and the Restoration of Aboriginal Communities*. Vancouver: Douglas & McIntyre.

Gunn Allen, Paula, ed. 1990. *Spider Woman's Granddaughters: Traditional Tales and Contemporary Writing by Native American Women*. New York: Ballantine Books.

Films and Online Resources

The Dish with One Spoon. 2007. 75 mins. Directed by Dawn Martin-Hill. Hamilton, ON: Six Nations Confederacy of the Grand River 7 Indigenous Elders and Youth Council and McMaster University. Further information online at www .mcmaster.ca/indigenous/Sewatokwatsherat.html.

Jidwá:doh: Let's Become Again. 2005. 50 mins. Directed by Dawn Martin-Hill. Hamilton, ON: Six Nations Confederacy of the Grand River 7 Indigenous Elders and Youth Council and McMaster University. Further information online at www .mcmaster.ca/indigenous/Jidwadoh.htm.

Mothers of Our Nations. 2004. 48 mins. Directed by Dawn Martin-Hill. Hamilton: Six Nations Confederacy of the Grand River 7 Indigenous Elders and Youth Council and McMaster University. Further information online at www .mcmaster.ca/indigenous/Onkwanistenhsera.htm.

See "Women Make Movies," www.wmm.com, for a growing list of films about women in various religious traditions.

References

Aldred, Lisa. 2000. "Plastic Shamans and Astroturf Sun Dances: New Age Commercialization of Native American Spirituality." *American Indian Quarterly* 24: 329–52.

Alfred, Taiaiake. 1999. *Peace, Power, Righteousness: An Indigenous Manifesto.* Toronto: Oxford University Press.

———. 2007. *Peace, Power, Righteousness: An Indigenous Manifesto.* 2nd edn. Toronto: Oxford University Press.

Amnesty International. 2004. *Canada: Stolen Sisters: A Human Rights Response to Discrimination and Violence against Indigenous Women in Canada.* New York: Amnesty International. www.amnesty.ca/research/reports/stolen-sisters-a-human-rights-response-to-discrimination-and-violence-against-indig.

———. 2007. *Maze of Injustice: The Failure to Protect Indigenous Women from Sexual Violence in the USA.* New York: Amnesty International. www.amnestyusa.org/women/maze/report.pdf.

Anderson, Kim. 2000. *A Recognition of Being: Reconstructing Native Womanhood.* Toronto: Second Story Press.

———, and Bonita Lawrence. 2003. "Introduction." In Anderson and Lawrence, eds. *Strong Women Stories: Native Vision and Community Survival.* Toronto: Sumach Press.

Barreiro, Jose, ed. 1992. *Indian Roots of American Democracy.* Ithaca, NY: Akwe:kon Press.

Battiste, Marie, and James (Sa'ke'j) Young-blood Henderson. 2000. *Protecting Indigenous Knowledge and Heritage: A Global Challenge.* Saskatoon, SK: Purich.

Berger, Thomas R. 1991. *A Long and Terrible Shadow: White Values, Native Rights in the Americas 1492–1992.* Toronto: Douglas & McIntyre.

Berkhofer, Robert. 1979. *The White Man's Indian.* New York: Vintage Books.

Brant Castellano, Marlene. 2000. "Updating Aboriginal Traditions of Knowledge." Pp. 21–36 in George J. Sefa Dei, Budd L. Hall, and Dorothy Goldin Rosenberg, eds. *Indigenous Knowledges in Global Contexts:*

Multiple Readings of Our World. Toronto: University of Toronto Press.

Braveheart, Maria. 1998. "The Return to the Sacred Path: Healing the Historical Trauma Response among the Lakota." *Smith College Studies in Social Work* 68, 3: 287–305.

Brown, Joseph Epes, ed. 1953. *The Sacred Pipe: Black Elk's Account of the Seven Sacred Rites of the Oglala Sioux.* Norman: University of Oklahoma Press.

Cajete, Gregory. 2000. *Native Science.* Santa Fe, NM: Clear Light Publishers.

Carter, Sarah. 1996. "First Nations Women in Prairie Canada in the Early Reserve Years, the 1870s to the 1920s: A Preliminary Inquiry." Pp. 51–75 in Christine Miller and Patricia Chuchryk, eds. *Women of the First Nations: Power, Wisdom, and Strength.* Winnipeg: University of Manitoba Press.

Churchill, Ward. 1994. *Indians Are Us? Culture and Genocide in Native North America.* Toronto: Between the Lines.

Cook, Katsi. 1989. "The Women's Dance." Pp. 80–6 in Joseph Bruhac, ed. *New Voices from the Longhouse: An Anthology of Contemporary Iroquois Writing.* Greenfield Center, NY: Greenfield Review Press.

Deloria, Vine. 1992. *God Is Red: A Native View of Religion.* Golden, CO: Fulcrum Publishing.

Durkheim, Emile. 1933. *The Division of Labour in Society.* New York: The Free Press.

Fenton, William N. 1998. *The Great Law and the Longhouse.* Norman: University of Oklahoma Press.

Fournier, Suzanne, and Ernie Crey. 1997. *Stolen from Our Embrace: The Abduction of First Nations Children and the Restoration of Aboriginal Communities.* Vancouver: Douglas & McIntyre.

Frideres, James S. 2005. *Native Peoples in Canada: Contemporary Conflicts.* 7th edn. Scarborough, ON: Prentice Hall Canada.

Green, Rayna. 1998. "The Pocahontas Perplex: The Image of Indian Women in American Culture." Pp. 203–10 in Susan Lobo and Steven Talbot, eds. *Native American Voices: A Reader.* New York: Longman.

Gunn Allen, Paula. 1986. *The Sacred Hoop.* Boston: Beacon Press.

———. 1998. *Off the Reservation: Reflections on Boundary-Busting, Border-Crossing Loose Cannons.* Boston: Beacon Press.

Jocks, Christopher Ronwanièn:te. 2000. "Grim Spiritualities for Sale: Sacred Knowledge in the Consumer Age." Pp. 61–77 in Lee Irwin, ed. *Native American Spirituality: A Critical Reader.* Lincoln: University of Nebraska Press.

Kasee, Cynthia. 1995. "Identity, Recovery, and Religious Imperialism: Native American Women and the New Age." Pp. 83–93 in Judith Ochshorn and Ellen Cole, eds. *Women's Spirituality, Women's Lives.* New York: Haworth Press.

Kulchyski, Peter, Don McCaskill, and David Newhouse, eds. 1999. *In the Words of Elders: Aboriginal Cultures in Transition.* Toronto: University of Toronto Press.

Lux, Maureen K. 2001. *Medicine That Walks: Disease, Medicine, and Canadian Plains Native People, 1880–1940.* Toronto: University of Toronto Press.

Lyons, Oren, and John Mohawk. 1992. *Exiled in the Land of the Free: Democracy, Indian Nations, and the US Constitution.* Santa Fe, NM: Clear Light Publishers.

Martin-Hill, Dawn. 1992. *As Snow Before the Summer Sun.* Brantford, ON: Woodland Cultural Centre.

———. 2003a. "She No Speaks and Other Colonial Constructs of 'The Traditional Woman.'" Pp. 106–20 in Kim Anderson and Bonita Lawrence, eds. *Strong Women Stories: Native Vision and Community Survival.* Toronto: Sumach Press.

———. 2003b. "Traditional Medicine in a Contemporary Context." Report for the National Aboriginal Health Organization. www.naho.ca/documents/naho/english/pdf/research_tradition.pdf.

Martin-Hill, Dawn, dir. 2004. *Mothers of Our Nations.* 48 mins. Hamilton, ON: Six Nations Confederacy of the Grand River 7 Indigenous Elders and Youth Council and McMaster University.

———. 2007. *The Dish with One Spoon.* 75 mins. Hamilton, ON: Six Nations Confederacy of the Grand River 7 Indigenous Elders and Youth Council and McMaster University.

Meili, Dianne. 1991. *Those Who Know: Profiles of Alberta's Elders.* Edmonton: NeWest Press.

Milloy, John. 1999. *A National Crime: The Canadian Government and the Residential School System, 1879 to 1986.* Winnipeg: University of Manitoba Press.

Newcomb, Steven T. 2008. *Pagans in the Promised Land.* Golden, CO: Fulcrum Publishing.

Paha Sapa: Struggle for the Black Hills. 1998. 60 mins. Directed by Mel Lawrence. Williston, VT: Mystic Fire Video.

Porter, Tom. 2008. *And Grandma Said . . . Iroquois Teachings as Passed Down through Oral Tradition.* Bloomington, IN: Xlibris.

Rosenberg, Dorothy Goldin. 2000. "Toward Indigenous Wholeness: Feminist Praxis in Transformative Learning on Health and the Environment." Pp. 137–54 in George J. Sefa Dei, Budd L. Hall, and Dorothy Goldin Rosenberg, eds. *Indigenous Knowledges in Global Contexts: Multiple Readings of Our World.* Toronto: University of Toronto Press.

Smith Tuhiwai, Linda. 1999. *Decolonizing Methodologies: Research and Indigenous Peoples.* New York: Zed Books.

St. Pierre, Mark, and Tilda Long Soldier. 1995. *Walking in the Sacred Manner: Healers, Dreamers, and Pipe Carriers—Medicine Women of the Plains Indians.* New York: Touchstone.

Steckley, John, and Bryan Cummins. 2001. *Full Circle: Canada's First Nations.* Toronto: Prentice Hall.

Wagner, Sally Roesch. 2001. *Sisters in Spirit: Haudenosuanee (Iroquois) Influence on Early American Feminists.* Summertown, TN: Native Voices Book Publishing Company.

Allen, Paula. 1986. *The Sacred Hoop.* Boston: Beacon Press.

CHAPTER 6

Women in Christianity

Pamela Dickey Young

Woman in Vredehoek, South Africa, holding a rosary.

© Radius Images/Alamy

Ivone Gebara

In my view, the oppression of women was not some addendum or just one more theme for theology. It was at the heart of the unjust organization of our societies, and expression of our human sin, touching every aspect of existence....

Similarly, I would say that feminism, or the marginalization of women, is not just one more theme but that the appearance of women on the public stage of history had to change the very structure of the theological enterprise, taking this new problematic into account. Given the "explosion of women in the midst of the explosion of the poor," as feminists of the third world were saying, it is no longer possible to maintain the same trends of thought or to repeat the same theological formulas. Something very deep within the human person was beginning to awaken....

The concept of gender . . . helped me to understand how deeply a hierarchical, dualist structure was embedded in our theology, so integrally as to become almost its essence, its specificity....

I often heard that I was not really a theologian but a philosopher, because I held the title of doctor of philosophy and not doctor of theology. For some people this distinction explained the waywardness of my thought. It would seem that the academic title decides whether discoveries of thought are or are not legitimate. This is true also for men, I know, but for women the judgment is harsher and more cutting. I have often heard it said that women are only one subject among others in theology, and that today it is a fashionable subject. Often too I have heard that the theological claims of women have no basis in tradition. But what tradition is that? Must we, while keeping intact the good things of our patriarchal tradition, cling to its harmful aspects and forget the primacy of justice and love? Must we lack respect for the present in the name of the tradition of the past? Must we always glorify the past, the traditions of the fathers, as if their thought were to be useful for every situation and for all cultures? (Gebara, 2002: 52–3).

Ivona Gebara is an ecofeminist liberation theologian from Brazil.

Introduction and Overview

Christianity is a religious tradition that arose around Jesus, whom early followers began to call "the Christ," which means the Messiah, the one sent and anointed by God. Jesus was born around 4 BCE. He was Jewish, as were most of his early followers, those he seems to have attracted through his charisma. After Jesus' death, his followers continued to recount stories about him and his effect on them, and they tried to convert others to follow him as well. The existing sources about Jesus and his life are mostly from the Christian New Testament, which means that they are texts composed by followers who testify to his effect on them rather than recount historical facts. The gospels are not eyewitness accounts, and they are not history books. Traditions about Jesus circulated orally and in snippets of writing before they were finally compiled in their current forms as the gospels of Matthew, Mark, Luke, and John. Each gospel has its own particular emphasis.

The New Testament is a collection of books, including the four gospels, that appeared in written form between about 50 and 100 CE. Much of the rest of the collection consists of letters from early converts to Christianity, especially the apostle Paul, who wrote to instruct and advise various churches around the Mediterranean. The Christian churches also count the Hebrew Bible (which they call the "Old Testament") as sacred scripture.

Jesus' followers were men and women who gave up nearly everything, including their families, to go with him. Stories about him are many, and several tell us about interactions between Jesus and women. Remarkably, given the patriarchal times in which the stories were told, none portrays Jesus as teaching that women are lesser beings than men.

Christianity was, from early on, a missionary religion, seeking to win converts not only among Jews, but throughout the known world. Over the centuries, Christianity has taken a wide variety of historical and cultural forms, and some of these forms are the results of major splits within the church. In the first five centuries of Christianity, much effort was expended to define orthodoxy or right belief. Many of the traditional Christian ideas or doctrines date from this era.

The first major split in Christianity occurred in 1054, when the Eastern churches (now called "Orthodox") separated from the Western (Roman Catholic) church, mostly because of disagreement over the nature of the **Holy Spirit**. A second major division took place in the West in the sixteenth century, when "Protestant" reformers such as Martin Luther and John Calvin broke with the Church over what they saw as its economic, moral and doctrinal excesses. Further divisions among the various groups that launched the Reformation produced many different Protestant denominations.

One of the main differences between Roman Catholicism and Protestantism is the official locus of authority. For Roman Catholicism, authority is, finally, vested in the pope and the bishops (local religious authorities). For Protestantism, the supreme locus of authority is usually seen to be scripture. Governance is generally carried out by the people, although the degree to which this is the case depends on the type of Protestantism.

Christianity is not monolithic. There is never one single "Christian" way to believe or to act. Christianity takes a wide variety of social, historical, geographic, and cultural forms. Thus when feminists study "Christianity" it is always helpful to remember that they are studying particular forms of Christianity, not a single unified and univocal religious tradition. Any conclusion about, for example, whether Christianity is liberating or oppressive for women must recognize the particular context in which that particular judgment is situated.

To urge caution here is not for a minute to suggest that one should overlook how much in the history of Christianity has been oppressive to women. Historically, when Christians discussed the topic of women, they were mostly men talking about women: about women's nature and purpose, about whether or not women were in the image of God, about whether women could be saved, about what sorts of leadership roles women could and could not play. There has been a strong emphasis on differences between women and men and on the notion of male and female as **complementary**, which has usually meant that females are seen as needing to be completed by males.

Tertullian, a second-century "father" of the church, called women "the Devil's gateway" (1869: 1.1.2). Augustine, a famous and influential fourth- and fifth-century thinker, believed that males alone were made in the full image of God, and that women could be in the image of God only when joined to males as "helpers" (Ruether, 1974: 156). For Augustine, women were equated with the body and men with the mind. This made women sexually dangerous to men. According to Augustine, women were more carnal than men and therefore more subject to temptation and **sin**. As Rosemary Ruether, a prominent feminist theologian, explains, he believed that women could overcome their carnal nature and be rational only if they renounced sexuality completely:

> That woman has a rational mind equivalent to man's is never entirely denied, and indeed is assumed by the view that allows her to lead the monastic life. But since she is somehow made peculiarly the symbol of "body" in relation to the male (i.e., in a male visual perspective), and is associated with all the sensual and depraved characteristics of mind through this peculiar "corporeality" her salvation must be seen not as an affirmation of her nature but a negation of her nature, both

physically and mentally and a transformation into a possibility beyond her natural capacities (Ruether, 1974: 161).

For Augustine, before sin entered the world through the Fall (that is, before Eve ate the forbidden fruit and gave it to Adam), sexuality was dispassionate, for procreative purposes only. After sin, sinful carnality overcame rationality in the form of human sexual arousal. For Augustine, the male erection becomes the "essence of sin [and] woman, as its source, became peculiarly the cause, object and extension of it" (Ruether, 1974: 163). Thus, sin is transmitted throughout humanity by the sexual act, and woman as both original and continuing sexual temptress is primarily to blame.

Texts, Interpretations, and Rituals

The central texts of the Christian tradition are those of the Bible. The biblical texts include the texts of the Jewish Bible (usually referred to as the Old Testament by Christians) and the New Testament texts. The New Testament was written over a period from about 50 CE to the early second century by a variety of different authors who, as far as we know, were all male. Oral traditions preceded the writing down of the gospel texts. It took several centuries before the Christian church decided more or less definitively which texts were to be seen as authoritative. (This is known as the process of *canonization*.) There were other texts that could have been included in the New Testament canon but that were not, such as the gospel of Thomas or the various Gnostic gospels.

All the biblical texts are human documents, written for particular purposes in specific times and places. Those that were selected to make up the Bible were already interpretations of past events, and the centuries of interpretation that followed their selection can give a particular focus to the way they are read today. For example, the traditional Christian understanding of Eve as the temptress and the source of all sin in the world is only one possible interpretation of the text of Genesis 3, read back through Augustine's understanding of original sin. The text itself mentions disobedience, but the notion that there is an inherited sinfulness for which Eve is primarily responsible reflects a much later Christian reading of the text. The biblical texts, when they mention women (sometimes by name, but often not), present them through patriarchal male eyes. In the same way, the passages about Jesus and women reflect the interpretations both of those who told the stories and of those who eventually wrote them down, and not all the stories view women in the same way.

Even though feminists do not always agree about how to interpret New Testament texts, anyone who reads them with the question of women's status in mind will notice that the interactions between Jesus and women are in all cases presented as remarkably open. Women listen to Jesus, but they also teach him (Mark 7:24–30; John 4:1–39), and they are commissioned to preach (John 20:17–18). The purity laws that affected women's eligibility for public action do not seem to have mattered to Jesus (Mark 5:25–34). Although no women are named among the 12 central disciples, the actual listing of these names varies somewhat and the list is more dependent on the importance of the number "12" (after the 12 tribes of Israel) than on the specific names. But many people, including women, followed Jesus from place to place (Matthew 27:55–6), and this act of following is one of the central understandings of what it means to be a disciple.

There are also indications that women occupied many leadership roles in the early Christian community. Women are called "deacon" and "apostle" (Romans 16:1, 7). Women preach. They have churches in their houses, or are in other ways patrons of the new Christian community.

The early Christians formed what is usually called a "charismatic" movement, meaning one centred around a specific leader figure that did not have formal structures or organizational rules. For the most part, the roles of women and men in the early Christian movement seem to have been interchangeable. The earliest Christians tended to think that the end of history was at hand and that the second coming of Jesus Christ would take place in their own lifetimes. It was only as time went on and it began to seem that the apocalypse was not imminent after all that more formal structures were put in place, which did tend to exclude women (for example, 1 Timothy 3:2–13). Many of the passages most problematic for women are from this later period of New Testament composition, and although they come from books traditionally attributed to Paul (1 and 2 Timothy and Titus), most scholars today believe that they were actually written in the late first or early second century. The letters that are generally thought to be Paul's do include some passages calling on women to be silent in churches and referring to the husband as the "head" of the wife (see 1 Corinthians 11:2–16, Ephesians 5:22–33). There is no question that Paul was a person of his time who had a patriarchal understanding of women's place; nevertheless, at times he does seem to see the message of Jesus as abolishing traditional hierarchical distinctions (Galatians 3:27–9).

Since the eighteenth century, biblical scholars have understood the texts to be historical (as opposed to received directly from God), written for particular purposes in particular times and places. In the late nineteenth century, a group of female scholars led by Elizabeth Cady Stanton published a book entitled *The Woman's Bible*, in which they commented on the texts of particular interest and importance to women, beginning with the creation accounts and the stories of Sarah and Abraham and continuing through all passages in which women are either visible as actors (e.g., the leadership of women in Romans 16) or treated as second-class citizens (Stanton and the Revising Committee, [1898] 1974).

When, in the mid-twentieth century, feminists began interpreting the biblical texts, they did so using a variety of strategies and with a several purposes in mind. As Elisabeth Schüssler Fiorenza says,

> In the footsteps of Cady Stanton, women's biblical studies have developed a dualistic hermeneutical, or interpretive, strategy that is able to acknowledge two seemingly contradictory facts. On the one hand, the Bible is written in androcentric language, has its origin in the patriarchal cultures of antiquity, and has functioned throughout its history to inculcate androcentric and patriarchal values. On the other hand, the Bible has also served to inspire and authorize women and other nonpersons in their struggles against patriarchal oppression (1993: 5).

Thus those who seek to be feminists within the Christian tradition generally do not deny the patriarchal nature of the biblical texts and contexts; for the most part, however, they see the texts as potentially valuable beyond their patriarchal context and content.

One school of feminist thought argues that biblical texts need to be read in the light of their historical, patriarchal contexts and should be given the most charitable interpretations possible. This approach tends to be taken by feminists in more conservative denominations, which believe the biblical texts to have been divinely inspired.

A second school argues that one can look to the biblical texts for a liberating message, or support for a liberating movement, or some other liberatory features, but should not assume that every text will contain such a message: some texts may not be redeemable. Such an approach looks, perhaps, to the example of Jesus, or to stories such as that of the Exodus (the liberation of the people of Israel from Egypt).

A third school tends to read the biblical texts without regarding them as authoritative for the Christian tradition. It sees the Bible not as a set of normative texts but as "a cacophony of interested historical voices and a field of rhetorical struggles in which questions of truth and meaning are being negotiated" (Fiorenza, 1993: 8). Because the process of canonization itself inscribed the chosen texts and their traditional interpretations with certain values and visions, the texts and the canon must be questioned. Fiorenza argues for a **hermeneutics** of "suspicion" that approaches the biblical texts looking for evidence of patriarchy, for who benefits and who is injured. She also argues for a "hermeneutics of re-vision" that would take a broader view, looking for "values and visions that can nurture those who live in subjection and authorize their struggles for liberation and transformation" (1993: 10).

Since the earliest period of Christianity, when it seems that both men and women were ritual actors in roles that were defined as needs arose, it has been mostly men who have acted in official capacities in ritual. In most churches only ordained clergy can preach and administer the **sacraments** (e.g., baptism), and until various Protestant denominations began ordaining women, virtually all of those ordained were men. Thus for most of the church's history, sacraments and preaching have been almost exclusively male preserves. When women have served as ritual actors, it has usually been in small groups of women meeting for prayer or teaching on their own; rarely have they had official sanction.

Symbols and Gender

A symbol is a picture, word, thing, act, or concept that bears particular meanings for a particular group. Christianity employs a variety of symbols to convey its tradition and message. One central symbol for Christianity is the word and concept "God." Another is the concept of Jesus as Christ or saviour, which captures meaning and importance beyond simply seeing Jesus as a historical person who lived in a particular place and time. Mary, the mother of Jesus, is also a symbol as well as a character in the biblical texts. Actions such as the performing of the Christian sacraments of baptism and **eucharist** are symbolic. The cross too is a typically Christian symbol. This section focuses on two of the central symbols of Christian tradition: God, and Jesus as the Christ or saviour.

Although some scholars would argue that all religious symbols are projections of human needs and desires, rather than symbols that point to reality, adherents of the Christian tradition usually agree that the word "God" points to a transcendent reality. No single view of God is held by all Christians. That said, it is also generally agreed that whatever God is, God does not have any biological sex in the sense that humans do. Yet most Christian imagery for God has been male, and when pronouns are used to refer to God, they are almost invariably male.

Feminists have long raised questions about what it means to use primarily or only male language and imagery for God. Religious symbols function both as symbols *of* reality and as symbols *for* reality. That is, they purport to portray reality both as it is and as it ought to be (see Christ, 1979: 274–5; Geertz, 1966). Thus the use of male language and images to refer to God can give the impression that the "reality" of God is male. In turn, the apparent maleness of God can reinforce a social system that connects maleness to godliness. Mary Daly argues that "if God is male, then the male is God" (1973: 19). What she means is that male language for God associates God more closely with males than with females. It gives the impression that maleness is more godly than femaleness, hence that males have the right to exercise godlike power.

If language about God were simply a matter of convenience and convention for most Christians, there would be no resistance to the use of female imagery or pronouns instead of, or alongside, male ones. But many Christians have found the idea of "God-she" problematic, and for feminists this raises questions about the impact that the standard masculine language for God has on the status of women with respect to men. Some scholars, such as Daly, have argued that the Christian God is so inherently male that no change of language can alter the traditional view.

Yet there are some biblical images that do refer to God in female terms: as a midwife (Isaiah 66:9; Psalm 22:9–10), as a woman giving birth (Isaiah 4:14; Deuteronomy 32:18), as a mother hen (Matthew 23:27) (see Mollenkott, 1985). Most feminist Christians have argued that neither male nor female language for God is superior to the other, and that male language should simply be supplemented with female language. This argument often goes hand in hand with recognition that because Christians speak of a personal relationship with God, the language they use needs, at least in part, to be personal: to depersonalize all such language is not an option for most Christian feminists. Further, depersonalization could well mean that the appropriateness of exclusively male language would never be directly or fully challenged.

Elizabeth Johnson, for example, has developed a wide-ranging rethinking of the Christian God in terms of the biblical image of "Sophia" (wisdom). In both the Hebrew Bible and the New Testament, "Sophia" is sometimes used to refer to an aspect of God that is always personified as female. Johnson suggests that the traditional persons of the Christian **Trinity**—Father, Son, and Holy Spirit—could be renamed Mother-Sophia, Jesus-Sophia, and Spirit-Sophia (1992). It is important to note that feminist Christians caution against relying on "mothering" language to provide female images of God because that could simply reinscribe rather than challenge stereotypical views of parenting (Ruether, 1983: 69–70).

Jesus, whose maleness has often been emphasized, is central to the Christian tradition as the one who is claimed as Christ or Messiah, Saviour, Lord, and so on. Christian feminists question what it means to have a male figure at the centre of a tradition. Can a male saviour save women? (Ruether, 1983: 116). Is Jesus' maleness essential to his role as saviour? Here the question of the overlap between Jesus' historical maleness and his symbolic function of salvation comes to the fore.

Just as there is no single Christian view of God, so there is no single Christian view of Jesus and how he "saves" humans. Early on, Christians came to the agreement that salvation was offered to women as well as to men (Ruether, 1998). Thus women were welcomed as members of the Christian church. Yet the maleness of Jesus has had serious implications for women. For one thing, it reinforces and extends the notion of the maleness of God. If, as Christians claim, Jesus is the incarnation of God—God in human flesh—and if Jesus is male, then maleness is even closer to godliness than it is in Judaism, where the chief problem is male language.

Also problematic is the idea that if God "chose" a male rather than a female body in which to become incarnate, that must indicate something about the importance of maleness, or the normativity of maleness, as opposed to female-ness. In the Roman Catholic tradition, the maleness of Jesus is one of the justi-fications for an all-male priesthood (Paul VI, 1977); if the priests who celebrate the mass are to represent the male Jesus, then they must be male as well.

The influence of various postmodern theories has led some thinkers to destabilize the maleness of Jesus (for example, by exploring possibilities of Jesus as a transgendered figure or as one who presents gender roles beyond a simple binary of maleness and femaleness) and to show how this instability might pro-vide new avenues of thought about Christology (Alliaume, 2006; Isherwood, 2001; Sheffield, 2008; and Young, 2010). Even so, this cannot change the reality that the maleness of Jesus has been used in ways that subordinate women. And any feminist response must take these long-standing problems seriously.

Sexuality

Christianity has historically been far more ambivalent than Judaism about sexuality. There is no evidence that Jesus was married, although it would have been unusual for a Jewish man of his time to remain unmarried. One factor that may have led early Christians to place a lower value on procreation than Judaism did was the expectation that the world would end during their own lifetimes. Another might have been the fact that the first Christians joined the new faith through conversion rather than through birth into a Christian family. Thus procreation was not as essential to the propagation of Christianity as it was to the propagation of Judaism.

Christianity emerged under the influence of both Jewish apocalypticism and classical Neoplatonism (Ruether, 1979). Around the time of Jesus, many Jews were beginning to look less toward God's fulfillment of human hopes within history and more towards otherworldly fulfillment after the cataclys-mic destruction of the present world. In Neoplatonism, the intellect or soul longs to be separated from the body, which drags it down from its true spiritual home with God. The upshot of such influences was a Christian tradition that associated maleness with mind and soul as superior and femaleness with body as inferior. Although that tradition had other strands recognizing the goodness of creation, it tended to be fearful of the body and all its appetites. Rosemary Ruether (1979) argues that these "dualisms" (as she calls them) are at the root of traditional Christian attitudes towards both women and sexuality.

Virginity came to be seen as the preferred way of life for Christians, although it was clearly not everyone's calling. Today the tendency is to see the notion of virginity as the preferred choice for women as devaluing sexuality, especially in light of the interpretations of fourth- and fifth-century theologians such as Augustine, Ambrose, and Jerome. However, it is also possible to understand the choice of virginity on the part of some early Christian women as a way of avoiding submission to the authority of a man (Malone, 2000: 146–9). Women who chose to live as hermits avoided all male control, and those who chose to join a monastic community of women could still live their day-to-day lives in relative freedom from male control, even if such communities were under the official authority of bishops or priests.

Still, by the fourth century, sexuality, especially women's sexuality, had been made an object of fear and revulsion by the "fathers" of the church, who blamed women for the difficulty of controlling their own sexuality. Augustine, as we have seen, believed that lust began with the sin of Adam and Eve and was passed on to each new generation. As a young man, he had a concubine and a son; then after his conversion he renounced sexuality and, so far as possible, the company of women. But his works make it clear that he was troubled by his inability to control his own sexual urges.

Celibacy was not absolutely required of male clergy until the twelfth century. However, the life of virginity was officially established as the ideal by about the fifth century. The Virgin Mary—the asexual woman, born without lust, whose body was simply a vessel for the birth of Jesus and who remained forever a virgin—became the model of Christian life. Consequently, although all women were viewed as temptresses (because of their association with the body), women who chose virginity were considered to be somewhat more like men. Ever since, Christian churches have found it difficult to take an affirmative view of sexuality.

In the sixteenth century, Luther was an exponent of the positive value of marriage. But wives were still considered the property of their husbands, so it was not until the mid-twentieth century, when marriage began to be seen as a relationship between equals, that a central emphasis began to be placed on the quality of the marriage relationship. The result has been an emphasis on the goodness of marriage and, correspondingly, of sexuality.

In more contemporary times, different churches have held very different official views of sexuality. From the 1950s onward, many North American

Protestant churches began to laud birth control for married couples as a means to prevent unwanted pregnancy and thus eliminate undue strain on marriages. As the women's movement in North America developed, churches began to recognize the importance of allowing women to control their lives. One way of accomplishing this was to ensure that they had access to birth control.

In the 1970s and 1980s, churches had to struggle with premarital sex. In general, Protestant writing on sexuality began to focus less on marriage than on the quality of human relationships. In most North American Protestant churches today, official opinions on sexuality are based less on traditional "rules" than on consideration of the human relationship that should underlie and support sexual activity.

The focus of concern about sexuality in those churches has shifted to gay and lesbian sexuality. At the time of writing, there is a spectrum of official opinions concerning gay and lesbian sexuality in North American Protestantism. The Metropolitan Community Church was founded to welcome and minister with gay men and lesbians. The United Church of Canada and the United Church of Christ have broadened their perspectives on sexuality as relationship to include gay and lesbian sexuality, and have stopped speaking of heterosexuality as normative. Presbyterians, Anglicans, and United Methodists separate the person from the sexual activity, arguing that it is no sin to be gay or lesbian, but that to "act on" gay or lesbian sexuality is sinful. Most churches have not even begun to grapple with the issues posed by bisexual, transsexual, or transgender identities. Indeed, most Christian attitudes toward sexuality are still firmly anchored in a notion of male and female as complementary (though not necessarily equal) parts of one human whole. In this progression we can see that, in North American Protestantism, discussions about sexuality have reflected those in the broader culture.

Roman Catholicism is a different matter. Although it appeared to many in the 1960s that the Roman Catholic Church would embrace artificial birth control, the 1968 encyclical *Humanae Vitae* (Paul VI, [1968] 1969) explicitly forbade the use of any means of birth control except the rhythm method. Although the "Winnipeg Statement" issued by the Canadian Conference of Catholic Bishops (1968) in response to *Humanae Vitae* seemed to allow a range of pastoral responses to couples contemplating the use of birth control, it has never been highly publicized or read in Canada. Although *Humanae Vitae* identified the unitive dimension of sex in marriage as one of its goods (virtues), it still saw procreation as the primary goal. Sexual activity, in Roman Catholicism, does not have a place outside marriage. Divorce is still prohibited insofar as divorced Catholics may not remarry within the Church. Gay and lesbian sexuality is reduced to sexual activity and identified as sinful. Thus, a rules-based approach to sexuality is still in place in official Roman Catholicism.

Lesbian sexuality has never been of as much concern to churches as the sexuality of gay men. The Hebrew Bible makes no mention of sexual activity between women. In the New Testament the only mention of what might be seen as same-sex activity between women is in Romans 1:26, in the context of a discussion of those who worship idols instead of the true God:

> For this reason God gave them up to degrading passions. Their women exchanged natural intercourse for unnatural, and in the same way also the men, giving up natural intercourse with women, were consumed with passion for one another. Men committed shameless acts with men and received in their own persons the due penalty for their error.

Historically, most churches have extrapolated to lesbian activity from what they see as scriptural condemnations of male homoerotic activity. Such positions usually rely on a relatively literal interpretation of a handful of texts: Leviticus 18:22 and 20:13, Romans 1:26–7, 1 Corinthians 6:9ff., 1 Timothy 8:10. Churches that are opposed to gay and lesbian sexual activity often try to differentiate between the activity, which they see as sinful, and the individual who might have what they call a homosexual orientation but who does not act on it—that is, they say they condemn the sin, not the person.

The churches that are reinterpreting gay and lesbian sexuality in a positive light, such as the Metropolitan Community Church, do not treat those texts as establishing a set of rules to be followed. They argue that there are some biblical principles (for example, Jesus' teaching that people should love one another as God loves them) that are more central to understanding Christianity than others that have been identified (for reasons that are not always obvious) as authoritative. Second, they note that there are disputes about what sorts of activity are actually in question in these texts. Is all same-sex activity problematic, or only certain sorts? (Some, for example, have suggested that the "unnatural" relationships at issue in Romans were relationships of older with younger men, which were common in Roman circles at that time.) Third, they argue (with Michel Foucault) that "homosexuality" as a category is a relatively recent invention, as is the notion of sexual orientation and therefore that the biblical texts do not apply to contemporary understandings of sexuality. Most inclusive churches also argue that sexual orientation is a given and hence that gay men and lesbians cannot be expected to change. Most such churches therefore embrace gay and lesbian sexuality under the heading of sexuality in general and say that what is morally acceptable between two people is a function of the quality of their relationship.

Even the inclusive views of gay and lesbian relationships held by some churches depend in large part on the view that sexual orientation is a given (even a given-by-God) and cannot be changed. No church has even begun to deal with the view that sexuality, whether heterosexual or gay–lesbian, is socially constructed.

Family Structures and Traditions

Because Christianity developed an ambivalent, even negative, attitude to sexuality early in its history, attitudes to the family followed suit (see Ruether 2000). Thus although the family is sometimes idealized, it is sometimes seen in a negative light to the extent that it implies sexuality. At the same time, early Christianity saw the church itself as a form of family in which all Christians were "brothers and sisters in Christ." This "church as family" model saw commitment as more important than blood in the making of family. In some ways this granted women a certain independence as converts; nonetheless, married women were still expected to be subject to their husbands.

The fact that the church revered the "Holy Family" of Jesus, Mary, and Joseph does not mean that it held human families in the same regard. However, since the tradition of Jesus' virginal conception means that he is thought to have had no earthly father, sometimes the family grouping is presented as Jesus, with Mary his mother and Anne his grandmother. The Holy Family of Jesus, Mary, and Joseph cannot be interpreted as a model of licit sexuality, because Jesus was understood to be the son of God, not of Mary's husband Joseph, and Mary herself was said to have been not only a virgin, but free of the taint of original sin from the moment of her own conception. Thus women in families are subject to the Madonna/whore dichotomy and childbearing is the only way to redeem their sexuality.

Indeed, when celibacy was the Christian ideal, couples were counselled by early leaders such as Jerome (fourth century) to have celibate marriages (Jerome 1994: 1,7). Of course, Christians continued to have children and live in family groups that varied depending on the social customs of the time and place. Around the time of the Reformation, as marriage became the norm for Protestant clergy, the family was revalorized both in Protestantism and, as a result of the Counter-Reformation, in Roman Catholicism. The home came to be seen as the first site of Christian learning, and it was the responsibility of mothers to teach their children what it meant to be a good Christian. The expectation that Christian families would engage in daily devotions and attend church together continued in North America well into the 1960s and is still alive and well in some devout homes (see, for example, Ruether 2000).

Marriage assumed a central place in Christianity after the Middle Ages, when churches assumed control over some aspects of marriage and divorce (Young 2012) and marriage became a sacrament in the Roman Catholic Church.

Although some allowances are made for local cultural customs, monogamous heterosexual marriage remains the ideal (unless one embraces celibacy). The basic family structure is patriarchal, with a male at its head.

Since the late twentieth century, as questions first of women's rights and then of gay rights have come to the fore, churches have had to grapple once more with what constitutes a family. The Roman Catholic Church and more conservative Protestant churches have continued to emphasize the married heterosexual family, though in Europe and North America allowances have been made to accommodate the new roles that women have taken on as a direct result of the women's movement. More liberal churches have sought to move beyond the male-headed model to embrace a wide variety of family structures, often including gay and lesbian couples with or without children.

Social Change

Many people today see religion as a force that supports rather than challenges the status quo. Thus it is often assumed that Christianity cannot be a force for positive change in the lives of women. Yet there have been times when Christianity has promoted social change for the better in the roles of women.

In the late twelfth century in Europe, there arose a movement of women who were pious and dedicated to good works but who did not want the restrictive life of the cloister. These women, called beguines, did not follow any formal religious rule and were not directly subject to any male authority, although they made alliances with local Franciscans or Dominicans. In many cases they formed communities, though some lived alone. Beguines came from mixed class origins and supported themselves by teaching, nursing, working in trades such as weaving, and sometimes begging. (By contrast, cloistered women came largely from the upper classes and were not permitted to work outside their communities, many of which relied on the dowries brought by new members to support themselves.) Because the beguines lived in poverty and did not demand as much for their labour as their male competitors, they often ran afoul of men in the labour market (Simons 2011: 116).

Not surprisingly, the church did not approve of the beguines' independence. The Second Council of Lyons in 1274 declared that any religious order founded without papal approval must be dissolved, and in 1298 Boniface VIII decreed that all religious women must be cloistered. There followed countless edicts designed to bring the beguines under control. Often beguines were persecuted and killed. Some were among the targets of the witch craze.

A number of beguines are known for their mystic poetry and accounts of visions, but some also wrote critiques of the church. Several had "lives" written of them, among them Mary of Oignies (1177/8–1213), Marguerite Porete (d. 1310), Hadewijch (thirteenth century), and Mechthild of Magdeburg (1210?–1294?). In her book *The Flowing Light of the Godhead*, for example, Mechthild of Magdeburg in Germany criticized the corruption of the church and the clergy of her day, and, as a consequence, she had to flee from Magdeburg to a convent at Helfta. Marguerite Porete's book *The Mirror of Simple Souls* was read throughout the late Middle Ages despite her condemnation for heresy. In the book she argues that the institutional Church itself is not the final word on what is holy or loving (Porete, 1993: 122). Having refused to obey an ecclesiastical order to cease distributing her book, she also refused to answer to the Inquisition and burned as a heretic in 1310. Marguerite was not the only beguine to endure persecution and death as the price of the freedom she sought. By challenging the status quo and living independent, self-supporting lives, the beguines set an example for other women and attained a certain degree of social change for women in their time.

A second example of a Christian-inspired proponent of change was Nellie McClung (1873–1951). A first-wave feminist, she was an active supporter of social reform who worked for both temperance and women's rights, including women's suffrage; a Liberal member of the Alberta Legislative Assembly from 1921 to 1926; and one of the "Famous Five" women who in 1929 argued to the Canadian government that women, like men, were "persons." She was a member of the Women's International League for Peace and Freedom, and Canadian delegate to the League of Nations in 1930. She was also a Methodist and an advocate of women's ordination. She believed that women and men were equal and ought to be treated equally by state and church alike. McClung wrote, "Man long ago decided that woman's sphere was anything he did not wish to do himself, and as he did not particularly care for the straight and narrow way, he felt free to recommend it to women in general" ([1915] 1972: 70). She was a prolific writer who published books, novels, stories, speeches, and newspaper columns.

The main motivation in all Nellie McClung's activities was her understanding of the Christian message (Warne, 1993: 186). Although she was certainly aware that churches were not living up to her understanding of that message, she took her inspiration from it. "Christ," she wrote, "was a true democrat. He made no discrimination between men and women. . . . He applied to men and women the same rule of conduct" (McClung, [1915] 1972: 68). She thought that Christianity had a particular obligation to be concerned about those who were oppressed in society, and she argued that Christian women had a specific responsibility: "When Christian women ask to vote, it is in the hope that they may be able with their ballots to protect the weak and innocent, and make the world a safer place for the young feet" (McClung, [1915] 1972: 77).

McClung advocated theological ideas that have only recently been "rediscovered." For instance, she favoured the use of female as well as male imagery for God: "I believe the Protestant religion . . . lost much when it lost the idea of the motherhood of God" (McClung, [1915] 1972: 79).

McClung uses the biblical story of Martha and Mary (Luke 10:38–42) to argue that women are called not just to serve but to "think":

> The question of whether or not women should think was settled long ago. We must think because we were given something to think with, ages ago, at the time of our creation. If God had not intended us to think, he would not have given us our intelligence. It would be a shabby trick, too, to give women brains to think, with no hope for results, for thinking is just aggravation if nothing comes out of it (McClung, [1915] 1972: 32).

McClung was a liberal feminist and a product of her times, but she also gives us insight into the way Christian beliefs can inspire and sustain social reform, particularly reform for women.

Official and Unofficial Roles of Women

We noted earlier that women in the biblical Christian communities served in leadership roles that were later reserved for men alone. In the Priscilla Catacombs in Rome there is a fresco (dated to the early third century, but probably earlier) that shows seven women at a table where bread and wine and fish are visible. The woman at the far left has her hands raised in a gesture of eucharistic celebration. Here is pictorial evidence of women in liturgical leadership. Although some have argued that these figures are men, the body shapes, hairstyles, jewellery, lack of beards, and length of skirts all indicate females (see Denzey, 2007; Houts, 1999; Irvin, 1980).

Women were among those persecuted by the Roman Empire in the second and third centuries and revered by the Church for their martyrdom. By the end of the fourth century, Christianity had become the official religion of the Roman Empire, and persecution of Christians had ceased.

From the second century onward, women who dedicated themselves to lives of chastity and asceticism were given titles such as "**deaconess**," "widow," and "virgin." A fourth-century document called *The Apostolic Constitutions* includes a service for the ordination of deaconesses, who seem to have been entrusted with the pastoral care of married women and ministering to the poor and the infirm. Yet by the fifth century the role of deaconess seems to have virtually disappeared in the Western churches, and bishops were revising history, arguing that there had never been deaconesses at all (Malone, 2000: 126–8).

© Pontino / Alamy

The Revd Anne Le Bas, vicar of the church of St Peter and St Paul in Seal, Kent, England, celebrating the eucharist.

Some women in the first few centuries of Christianity retreated from the temptations of the world to live as ascetics in the desert alongside men who did the same. Although the ascetic movement in Christianity does tend to denigrate the body and sexuality, it also gave women a spiritual equality with men and a certain amount of freedom from the direct control of men.

Other Christian women, mainly of the well-to-do and educated class, established and led communities of women. Marcella was the leader of one such community in fourth-century Rome: "Under her guidance, the women learned to pray, to dispose of their possessions wisely, to live in utter simplicity, and to learn the art of governing their own lives" (Malone, 2000: 139). These were among the benefits that the religious life offered women, and over the next centuries women flocked to such communities, which soon became formalized as religious orders. Women in orders, although they were ultimately responsible to bishops and dependent on male priests for the sacraments, were fairly independent in their communal lives. The religious life offered women an alternative to marriage and the male dominance that came with it. In addition, the religious life could offer women the possibility of education, and it remains an option for Roman Catholic women.

Around the seventh century a number of "double monasteries" were established where men as well as women lived under the direction of an abbess. One famous abbess was Hilda (d. 680 CE) of Whitby, England. Hilda was a scholar and developed an enormous library that became an important teaching centre and gathering place for theologians.

The Protestant Reformation, which disavowed celibacy and tried to reclaim the positive value of sexuality within marriage, eliminated the possibility of pursuing a monastic vocation, thus also eliminating an option that allowed women to live without direct male control. Until the late nineteenth century, one of the main leadership callings for a Protestant woman was as a minister's wife. Protestant women in general were expected to live out the Christian callings of wife and mother.

In nineteenth- and twentieth-century North America, women's roles in churches changed, sometimes propelling, sometimes following societal changes. In Methodism, founded by John Wesley in the late eighteenth century, there was an emphasis on the gifts of the Holy Spirit, and consequently women who felt a calling to pray and testify to their conversions as well as to preach began to do so.

In the nineteenth century, Protestant women's groups began to do various kinds of charity work at home and abroad. This work was aimed at education, social reform, taking care of the poor, and mission. A whole class of women church workers known as "deaconesses" materialized. These deaconesses worked primarily for the underprivileged in cities, in social work and evangelism, but they were not considered to be members of the ordained clergy. This changed in the mid-nineteenth century with the movement for women's ordination.

The first woman ordained in modern times was Antoinette Brown (later Antoinette Brown Blackwell), who became a minister in the Congregationalist Church in East Butler, New York, in 1853. Ordination was possible in Congregationalism sooner than in other denominations because local Congregationalist churches made their own decisions regarding matters such as ordination. Some Methodist groups also ordained a few women in the late nineteenth century. The first woman to be ordained in the United Church of Canada was Lydia Gruchy, in 1936.

Even so, it was not until the 1960s and 1970s that most mainline Protestant churches in the United States and Canada began either to ordain women or to accord them equal status to ordained men. By the 1990s the numbers of women in Protestant theological schools exceeded the numbers of men.

The Roman Catholic Church does not ordain women. The argument against the ordination of women, stated in detail by Pope Paul VI in 1976 and reaffirmed by Pope John Paul II, makes three main points. First, tradition, assumed to have been dictated by God, has always affirmed that only men can be priests. Second, Jesus had an open attitude toward women and could have chosen women to be among the 12 disciples, but he did not. This decision applies to all times and places. Third, when the priest celebrates the mass he is called to represent Jesus Christ to the people; this representation requires a "natural resemblance" between the priest and Jesus Christ, and this natural resemblance must be the resemblance of maleness.

Many people, including many Roman Catholics, have refuted all three arguments on the following grounds. First, the Church has changed in a variety of ways over time. Why not in this way, too? Second, the names on the lists of the 12 disciples or apostles are not uniform in the biblical sources (compare Mark 3:14–19 and Acts 1:12–13). Many other people, including women, followed Jesus from place to place, and there is no indication that these 12 individuals alone were important in Jesus' life and ministry. On the other hand, 12 was a significant number to the Gospel writers because of the 12 tribes of Israel. As well, there is no evidence that Jesus, as the leader of a charismatic movement, believed he was founding an institution that would remain in existence for all time. Third, why is it the "natural resemblance" of maleness that is all-important? Jesus was Jewish; he probably had brown eyes; he probably had dark skin. Why are genitalia more important than those characteristics in establishing "natural resemblance"?

Even though some find Pope Francis open to possible change, these refutations of the official arguments against the ordination of women are still not likely to sway current practice. The fact that fewer and fewer men are choosing the calling of celibate priesthood, especially in North America and Europe, will probably also eventually have an impact on this matter.

Throughout history Christian women have banded together both as nuns and as lay women. Beginning in the nineteenth century, North American and European women organized study groups and missionary endeavours to other parts of the world. Women's organizations also developed world-wide to provide social betterment in their own communities as well as nationally and globally. Such all-female groups have always given women a chance to develop their own approaches to Christianity, independent of the men in their lives.

The religious lives of Christian women today are as varied as the lives of women in any other way. Women live their religious lives as part and parcel of the interconnected webs that structure their lives as a whole. They may be single, married, or in lesbian relationships. They may be part of local, national or global women's religious groups. They may play leadership roles as scholars, theologians, or ordained ministers. They may aspire to full formal equality with men in religious life, or they may be part of patriarchal families with men as acknowledged heads. They may accept the religious roles dictated by their tradition, geography, and culture or they may challenge those roles. They may pray and worship as directed by the hierarchy of their churches or they may develop new forms of prayer and new feminist rituals.

In her work with evangelical Christians in Britain, Kristin Aune interviewed "Jane":

An educated creative professional, Jane had made career sacrifices in favour of family life during her twenties, declining an interview for a prestigious job because it would mean moving away from her local church and fiancé. In her early thirties . . . she gave up full-time employment on having children and does periodic paid work as an artist. . . . But Jane was also critical of contemporary Christian idealizations of full-time motherhood. "Lots of Christian women feel guilty because they feel they have to be at home with their children, like their mothers were for them," she said, adding that in Christian contexts "there's also this pressure to be a superwoman and to do all the housework perfectly" (Aune 2008: 284–5).

For a project on violence against gay and lesbian parishioners, I interviewed "Eileen," a lesbian minister in her fifties who has been ordained more than 20 years. Eileen lives with her partner and ministers in a large downtown church in urban Canada that welcomes gay and lesbian members. She is theologically liberal, calls herself a feminist, and is well regarded in her denomination and congregation. Her congregational leadership is creative and forward-thinking. Her ministry as a lesbian feminist has developed alongside the developments in her own church in accepting the full leadership of women and of sexual minorities.

In her book *God Gave Us the Right: Conservative Catholic, Evangelical Protestant and Orthodox Jewish Women Grapple with Feminism*, Christel Manning interviews "Barbara," a Roman Catholic woman who would not call herself a feminist but who does think women are equal to men and that they can be spiritual leaders. Although she handles most of the child care in her family, she does not necessarily think that is women's given role, and she uses birth control despite her church's ban on contraception. However, she is not in favour of women's ordination to the priesthood (Manning 1999; see also Spickard, Landres and McGuire 2002).

Even these three brief vignettes, all from the global north, show how varied Christian women's lives can be from one another. Women from other parts of the world would show even more variation.

Backlash

In the words of Letty Russell, backlash is "a powerful counterassault on the rights of women of all colors, men of color, gay, lesbian and bisexual persons, working-class persons, poor persons and other less powerful groups both in the US and abroad" (1996: 477). In other words, backlash is a strategy for the traditionally powerful and privileged to retain their power and privilege against arguments for full inclusion of others in the church and in society. Backlash is the enemy of diversity and of those who are marginalized. In North America, backlash against women is often supported by Christians who, theologically or politically or both, are opposed to changes in the status and roles of women and to theologies that support such changes.

One common form of backlash blames societal woes on the breakdown of "traditional" families. The idea is that before women worked outside the home, before divorce and single parenthood became so common, before gay and lesbian relationships were considered socially acceptable, families were more stable, children were better raised, and everyone knew his or her place in the social structure. One problem with this argument is that it is not historically supportable. In fact, according to Hunt, "[b]acklash rewrites history" (1996: 50). The whole notion of separate private spheres for women, away from the public and especially away from economic production, is largely a product of the Industrial Revolution, when the family ceased to be the fundamental economic unit and men became wage earners. Although this separation of spheres actually applied only to upper-class women—poor women, especially poor women of colour, have always had to work for pay—women become the guardians of the private sphere, including family piety (Rudy, 1997: 26).

The idea that Christianity supports this ideology of the family has serious limitations. The New Testament does not teach anything like the modern notion of family. People at that time lived in extended kinship groups; Jesus called on his followers to leave their families; and Paul thought that celibacy was better than marriage for Christians.

Yet the idealized non-historical view of family has had a powerful impact on church and politics, precisely because it allows those who have traditionally held power and privilege to retain it. In the United States, the Christian right has been strongly allied with the Republican Party, and successive Republican presidential candidates since Ronald Reagan have enlisted conservative Christian preachers and "biblical" arguments to bolster their appeal. Even Democratic politicians seek to capture the conservative Christian part of the political spectrum because it is so powerful. In Canada, where the population as a whole is less susceptible to claims of religious authority, only the Conservative Party makes any overt use of the "Christian values" argument; and that use is subdued, in recognition of the realities that not all Conservative supporters are Christian and that Canadians expect their politicians at least to pay lip service to cultural diversity.

Often when religious institutions seek to put forward or defend positions that are detrimental to the interests of women, they use female spokespersons to assure listeners that there are women as well as men who oppose advances such as ordination, access to safe, legal abortions, or increases in social funding for women raising children alone. Suggesting that only "radicals" or those on the "far left" favour such changes, this strategy is designed to pit women against each other. It is also deceptive in that it shifts the focus from the needs of marginalized women by arguing that not "all women" want these changes.

Those who would restrict women's roles in church and society often bolster their position by referring to particular biblical passages and theological inter-pretations that are sometimes described as "fundamentalist." But "fundamen-talism" is hard to define. The term was first used in the American Christian context of the early twentieth century, when a series of pamphlets called "The Fundamentals" was published. But more recently it has been used to describe particular movements within many world religions that oppose, among other things, the Enlightenment values of critical and rational inquiry and support a highly structured and authoritarian view of the particular religious tradition. All major leadership roles in Christian fundamentalist groups are taken by men (Lawrence, 1989; Marty and Appleby, 1991–5).

Christian fundamentalists believe that the Bible is the literal and inerrant word of God. Statements from 1 Corinthians, Ephesians, Timothy, and Titus are often used to substantiate their positions on women. One hallmark of such argu-ments is that the passages in question are interpreted as if they were literal words of God that can be taken directly out of their first-century context and applied in the twentieth-first century. It is also important to note that not all biblical pas-sages are accorded equal authority. In fact, as we noted above, the selection of bib-lical passages is informed by views of women and the family that are themselves relatively recent and originated in a particular historical and cultural context.

Unique Features

Some symbols, movements, and themes are unique to Christianity, or take spe-cifically Christian forms. The following pages will explore a few of these.

Mary

Mary, the mother of Jesus, has been an ambiguous figure for Christian fem-inists. She is one of the few biblical women whose name is known and about whom we have more than just a few words of text. She has not figured as prom-inently in Protestant Christianity as she has in the Roman Catholic tradition, as the early Protestant Reformers thought that veneration of Mary could too easily lead to worship of her. According to the tradition fostered by the Roman Catholic Church, Mary was chosen to serve as the vessel for God's plan pre-cisely because of her perfect obedience. The demure, passive, obedient Mary is often contrasted with the disobedient Eve and held up to women as the model for their lives. The Roman Catholic doctrines of the Immaculate Conception, according to which Mary herself was without original sin from the moment of her own conception, and the Virgin Birth, according to which she remained a virgin through her son's conception and birth, and through her entire life, were set in place to reinforce the doctrine of Jesus' sinlessness. But they also served to create an ideal of womanhood that is unattainable for any actual woman: the ideal of the virgin-mother, untainted by sexuality.

Yet Mary has not been confined to the role of unattainable ideal. For Catholic women around the world, Mary has also been a powerful support in the struggle to stand up for their rights. Those who see Mary in that light often quote a passage known as the Magnificat (Luke 1:46–55), in which Mary says that God has "brought down the powerful from their thrones, and lifted up the lowly" and has "filled the hungry with good things and sent the rich away empty." Mary is the one who understands their problems even when God and Jesus seem far away. In fact, because the line between devotion to and worship of Mary does get blurred, Mary at times seems very much like God, only nearer and more accessible. For many Roman Catholic women, Mary effectively functions as a goddess (see Daly, 1973: 90–2).

Women as Missionaries

In the nineteenth century, both Catholic and Protestant women became heavily involved in the missionary enterprise of extending Christianity to all parts of the world. At first, Protestant women raised funds and organized support for missionary efforts without becoming missionaries themselves, though many wives accompanied their missionary husbands into the field. In time, however, the churches came to realize that male missionaries were not always allowed contact with the women of the peoples among whom they were supposed to work, and so, by the mid-nineteenth century, Protestant churches began to send single women as missionaries. Indeed, many single women who were professionally trained, such as early female doctors, often found that they were more accepted in the mission field than back at home (Grant, 1972: 57–8; MacHaffie, 1986: 93–106).

Roman Catholic nuns also undertook mission work in the nineteenth century. Pope Pius XI ordered that all congregations of nuns should have missionary communities to convert non-Westerners to Christianity, and some new religious orders were founded specifically to pursue missionary work (McNamara, 1996).

Development of Feminist Theologies

As the women's movement developed in North America in the 1960s and 1970s, women within the churches began to articulate feminist critiques of both the institutional church and the patriarchal theologies that supported it. Further, they began to propose new ways of thinking about theology (see Young, 1995).

In 1960, Valerie Saiving wrote what is usually considered the first article in contemporary feminist theology, "The Human Situation: A Feminine View," in which she raises the question of experience that becomes central to feminist theology. She opines that women do not experience the world in the same way that men do and that, therefore, traditional theological definitions of sin and salvation do not apply to women in the same way as to men (Saiving, 1979). In 1968, Mary Daly's *The Church and the Second Sex* raised questions about the status and roles of women in the history of the church. As other women responded to these writings, and others like them began to appear, a whole set of questions emerged. There were questions about the biblical texts and interpretations. There were historical questions. Where were the women in the Bible and in church history? Could their stories be recovered? What is the importance of noticing that the biblical texts and the history of the church are told from a male/patriarchal point of view? And there were theological questions. Why is God always portrayed as male? Why are women considered to be primarily responsible for sin?

Feminists who wanted to stay within the church began to write biblical commentaries, histories, and theologies that took women's experience into account and considered with utmost seriousness the full humanity of women. Thus feminist theology quickly moved beyond critique to the construction of new ways of thinking about history and theology. Feminist theologies were written by both Roman Catholic and Protestant women who did not accept that the patriarchal institutional church was the only or best interpreter of Christianity. Although some feminist theologians, like Mary Daly (1973, 1975) and Daphne Hampson (1990, 1996), left the Christian church behind as irretrievably patriarchal, many other feminist theologians have decided that there are liberating strands within Christianity that can be woven into a nonpatriarchal whole (Young, 1990).

The work of feminist historian and theologian Rosemary Radford Ruether has spanned more than three decades. It was she who brought attention to the construction of Christianity in hierarchical dualisms such as mind/soul over body and humans over nature (Ruether, 1975). She wrote one of the first books of constructive theology, going beyond criticism of the patriarchal theologies to formulate a theology from a feminist starting point (Ruether, 1983; see also Ruether, 1998, 2007). Letty Russell, whose work paralleled Ruether's, developed the idea of "partnership" as a way to organize and live out Christianity rather than simply accept traditional hierarchical thinking (1974, 1979, 1993). Today, feminist theologies are many and varied, arising from new contexts to speak to new experiences.

Christian feminism has a variety of global and cultural forms. Early Christian feminist theologies were rightly criticized for speaking from what was basically a single point of view—that of white, educated, heterosexual, and relatively privileged women—yet using "woman" as a generic term. Women of colour, women from geographic locations outside North America and Europe, and lesbian and other sexual-minority women began to raise questions about the assumption that all women's experiences were alike. They raised new questions and explored new outlooks. Lesbian women began questioning the construction of sexuality as focused on heterosexual pairs (Heyward, 1989). In North America there are womanist theologies written from an African American perspective, and *mujerista* theologies written from a Hispanic perspective. There are also *mujerista* theologies from Central and South America, African feminist theologies, and Asian feminist theologies (see, for example, Aquino, 1993; Chung, 1990; Fabella and Oduyoye, 1988; Fabella and Park, 1989; Isasi-Díaz, 1996; Oduyoye, 1995; Russell, Kwok, Isasi-Díaz, and Cannon, 1988). Each of these theologies takes its own cultural context and its own particular version of patriarchy into consideration. For example, Maria Pilar Aquino, writing of Latin America, specifically addresses not only issues in the Roman Catholic Church, the dominant church in the region but issues of colonialism and capitalism as they affect women. She also examines the cultural specificity of *machismo*:

> *Machismo* does not derive or have its origin in capitalism, although it converges and combines with it in mutual reinforcement. But it can also combine with socialist structures in which unequal relationships persist between men and women, if there is insufficient criticism of women's double workload, the sexual division of labor, and inequalities between the sexes in general (1993: 23).

Aquino suggests many contributions that a specifically feminist Latin American theology can make to theological understanding. One such contribution is to portray God as a God of life:

> The starting point for this new experience of faith is the general context of suffering and oppression of the Latin American masses. In the light of faith this situation is *unnatural*, and God is not indifferent to it. On the contrary, realizing that this immense suffering is against God's plan for fullness of life for humanity has led to the discovery of God in the suffering faces of the oppressed. . . . This encounter with God in the faces of the poor, of women, and all the oppressed has given faith a new meaning. . . . [P]recisely because life is preeminent to women, they feel called by God—like the biblical prophets—to denounce every threat to it (Aquino, 1993: 132–3).

Chung Hyun Kyung is a Korean feminist theologian who has sought to integrate traditional Korean women's shamanistic practices and beliefs and other expressions of women's popular religion in Asia into her feminist Christianity. When she invoked the spirits of her ancestors in a speech to the World Council of Churches in 1991, she was denounced by many of the more conservative members of the audience as a syncretist (one who indiscriminately combines or collapses two or more religions into one; see Chung, 1988, 1990). She writes:

> We Asian women theologians must move away from our imposed fear of losing Christian identity, in the opinion of the mainline theological circles, and instead risk that we might be transformed by the religious wisdom of our own people. We may find that to the extent that we are willing to lose our old identity, we will be transformed into truly *Asian* Christians. . . . Who *owns* Christianity? (Chung, 1990: 113)

Chung notes that because most shamans in Korea have been women, Korean women relate to Jesus best in the image of a woman. To make her point, she quotes from the poem "One Day I Shall Be Like a Banyan Tree," by Indian theologian Gabriele Dietrich:

> I am a woman
> > and the blood
> > of my sacrifices
> > cries out to the sky
> > which you call heaven.
> I am sick of you priests
> > who have never bled
> > and yet say:
> This is my body
> > given up for you
> > and my blood
> > shed for you
> > drink it.
> Whose blood
> > has been shed
> > for life
> > since eternity? (Dietrich, 1986: 73–4, in Chung, 1990: 69)

Recent feminist theologies have been influenced by postmodernism, postcolonialism, ability studies, studies in sexuality, and ecofeminism (see Althaus-Reid 2003; Althaus Reid and Isherwood 2007; Fulkerson, 1994; Gebara, 1999; Gudorf, 2001; Isherwood and McPhillips 2008; Kamitsuka 2007; Kwok, 2005; Ruether, 1992). Many feminist theologians have begun to argue that the male–female binary is, by definition, hierarchical and that we therefore need to begin thinking beyond sex and gender categories (see, for example, Gudorf 2001). The category "woman" is no longer a stable and univocal category, even though it may continue to be used for strategic reasons to highlight the oppression of sexism and patriarchy. Once it was simply assumed that gender was socially constructed but firmly rooted in biological sexual differences. Now there are many feminist scholars who argue that such differences are made important and central because they keep the male-dominant power structure in place (see Delphy 2001). However disparate and diverse the category "woman" is taken to be, it is still useful to study women in Christianity because so much of Christian tradition and thought has used the male–female dichotomy to accord power, prestige, and privilege to men.

Christian Feminist Anti-Semitism

One of the temptations of Christian feminist theology is to portray Christianity as superior to Judaism with respect to the status of women. When Christian women began to express concern about the patriarchy endemic to the Christian tradition, they often began with Jesus' teachings and acts as recorded in the New Testament. Often a contrast was too quickly drawn between "Christianity," with its non-patriarchal roots, and "Judaism" as patriarchal. This characterization fails to recognize that Jesus was himself a Jew and that what became Christianity was in its beginnings a movement within Judaism. It also fails to take seriously the official Judaism of Jesus' time and place (centred on the temple and on ritual practices by a priestly caste), which was no more a monolithic representation of all Judaism than the Christianity of any particular time and place is of all Christianity. In Jesus' time there was reaction against this official Judaism from a number of Jewish quarters (see Ruether, 1998: 14–15). The aims of Christian feminism cannot be met if "rescuing" Christianity for women means denigrating another religious tradition. Christian feminists can draw on Jesus' acts and teachings without having to find them superior to all other religious movements of the period (see Fiorenza, 1994: 67–73).

Conclusion

There is no singular way to talk about women in the history of Christianity. Women's roles have been varied and variable. Patriarchy has been a given, but women have worked around it to discern roles for themselves and others. For many women, Christianity has offered more than its patriarchal forms would seem to suggest. There is also no singular way to talk about the prospects for reforming Christianity in a non-patriarchal manner. Like all other cultural forms, Christianity is closely related to the values of the cultures in which it exists. Sometimes forms of Christianity lag behind those values, sometimes they forge ahead, and sometimes they simply keep pace.

The question of whether one can be Christian and feminist at the same time does not allow for an easy answer. One response is that there are lots of women in a variety of social and geographical contexts who identify themselves as both. They see liberating potential in some forms of Christianity even as they recognize the patriarchy. They see the possibility of reform.

It will be crucial to examine how Christianity changes as scholars begin to take seriously the critiques of feminist theory on issues that once seemed simple and straightforward, such as whether "women" is a category defined only or fully by biology or whether Christians, regardless of their biology, can perform (or refuse to perform) the gender role "women." It is clear that ongoing feminist reflection will continue to be a necessary part of the academic study of Christianity.

Glossary

complementary In the context of religious traditions, a view that sees men and women as sexual opposites to one another who together make up the wholeness of humanity.

deaconess A female religious leader in the Christian church; deaconesses have had different roles in different times and places.

eucharist The Christian sacrament that re-enacts the last meal of Jesus with his followers.

hermeneutics A theory of interpretation.

Holy Spirit A name for the third person of the Christian Trinity.

sacrament A rite thought to confer benefits on the recipient. In the Roman Catholic tradition there are seven sacraments: baptism, confirmation, eucharist, penance, ordination, marriage, and anointing of the sick. In most Protestant churches there are two: communion (eucharist) and baptism.

sin Wrongdoing in God's sight; the Christian idea of "original sin" means that all humans are born sinful.

Trinity The Christian conception of God as three persons in one nature. The three persons are traditionally named Father, Son, and Holy Spirit.

Further Reading

Fiorenza, Elisabeth Schüssler, ed. *Searching the Scriptures*. 1993, 1994. Vol. 1. *A Feminist Introduction*. Vol. 2. *A Feminist Commentary*. New York: Crossroad.

Haker, Hille, Susan A. Ross, and Marie-Theres Wacker, eds. 2006. *Women's Voices in World Religions*. London: SCM.

King, Ursula, and Tina Beattie, eds. 2005. *Gender, Religion and Diversity: Cross-Cultural Perspectives*. New York: Continuum.

Kirk-Duggan, Cheryl A., and Karen Jo Torjesen, eds. 2010. *Women and Christianity*. Santa Barbara: ABC-CLIO LLC.

Kwok, Pui-Lan, ed. 2009. *Women and Christianity*. 4 vols. New York: Routledge,

Malone, Mary. 2000, 2001. *Women and Christianity*. Volume 1: *The First Thousand Years*. Volume 2: *From 1000 to the Reformation*. Ottawa: Novalis.

Ruether, Rosemary Radford. 1983. *Sexism and God-Talk: Toward a Feminist Theology*. Boston: Beacon.

——, ed. 2007. *Feminist Theologies: Legacy and Prospect*. Minneapolis, MN: Fortress.

Russell, Letty, and J. Shannon Clarkson, eds. 1996. *Dictionary of Feminist Theologies*. Louisville, KY: Westminster John Knox.

Films and Online Resources

Divine Women. 2012. Three programs. Directed by Bettany Hughes. BBC Television. Further information online at www.bbc.co.uk/programmes/b01g8ck1.

Four Women of Egypt. 1997. 89 mins. Directed by Tahani Rachid. Montreal: National Film Board of Canada. Four women of different backgrounds debate social and political issues.

Mystic Women of the Middle Ages. 2000, 2003. Series 1 and 2. Six videos per series. Directed by Kate Gillen. Hamilton, ON: Redcanoe Productions. Further information online at http://mw.mcmaster.ca/tvseries/tvcredits.html and http://mw.mcmaster.ca/tvseries/.

Pink Smoke over the Vatican. 2011. 64 mins. Directed by Jules Hart. Further information online at: http://pinksmokeoverthevatican.com.

Religions of the Book: Women Serving Religion. 2003. 29 mins. Produced by Michael J. Doyle. Princeton, NJ: Films for the Humanities and Sciences. Jewish, Christian, and Muslim women discuss the position of women in their religious traditions.

Women and Spirit: Catholic Sisters in America. 2009. 56 mins. Leadership Conference of Women Religious. Further information online at http://womenandspirit.org/dvd.html.

Women and the Christian Tradition, Women and Islam, The Goddess and Other Women of Power. 1988–2006. Directed by Bill Moyers. Perspectives on Gender & Religion. New York: PBS. Further information online at www.pbs.org/moyers/faithandreason/perspectives3.html.

Women of Faith: Women of the Catholic Church Speak. 2009. 60 mins. Directed by Rebecca M. Alvin. Further information online at www.wmm.com/filmcatalog/pages/c774.shtml.

See "Women Make Movies," www.wmm.com, for a growing list of films about women in various religious traditions.

References

Alliaume, Karen Trimble. 2006. "Disturbingly Catholic: Thinking the Inordinate Body." Pp. 93–119 in Ellen T. Armour and Susan M. St. Ville, eds. *Bodily Citations: Religion and Judith Butler.* New York: Columbia University Press.

Althaus-Reid, Marcella. 2003. *The Queer God.* London: Routledge.

——— and Lisa Isherwood. 2007. *Controversies in Feminist Theology.* London: SCM.

Aquino, Maria Pilar. 1993. *Our Cry for Life: Feminist Theology from Latin America.* Maryknoll, NY: Orbis.

Aune, Kristin. 2008 "Evangelical Christianity and Women's Changing Lives." *European Journal of Women's Studies* 15, 3: 277–94.

Canadian Conference of Catholic Bishops. 1968. "Canadian Bishops' Statement on the Encyclical *Humanae Vitae.*"

Christ, Carol P. 1979. "Why Women Need the Goddess: Phenomenological, Psychological and Political Reflections." Pp. 273–87 in Carol P. Christ and Judith Plaskow, eds. *Womanspirit Rising: A Feminist Reader in Religion.* San Francisco: Harper & Row.

Chung Hyun Kyung. 1988. "Following Naked Dancing and Long Dreaming." Pp. 54–74 in Letty Russell, Kwok Pui-lan, Ada María Isasi-Díaz, and Katie Geneva Cannon, eds. *Inheriting Our Mothers' Gardens: Feminist Theology in Third World Perspective.* Philadelphia: Westminster Press.

———. 1990. *Struggle to Be the Sun Again: Introducing Asian Women's Theology.* Maryknoll, NY: Orbis.

Daly, Mary. 1968. *The Church and the Second Sex.* New York: Harper & Row.

———. 1973. *Beyond God the Father: Toward a Philosophy of Women's Liberation.* Boston: Beacon.

———. 1975. *The Church and the Second Sex, with a New Feminist Postchristian Introduction by the Author.* New York: Harper Colophon.

Delphy, Christine. 2001. "Rethinking Sex and Gender." Pp. 411–23 in Darlene Juschka, ed. *Feminism in the Study of Religion: A Reader.* New York: Continuum.

Denzey, Nicola. 2007. *The Bone Gatherers: The Lost Worlds of Early Christian Women.* Boston: Beacon.

Dietrich, Gabriele. 1986. *One Day I Shall Be Like a Banyan Tree: Poems in Two Languages.* Belgaum, India: Dileep S. Kamat.

Fabella, Virginia, and Mercy Amba Oduyoye, eds. 1988. *With Passion and Compassion: Third World Women Doing Theology: Reflections from the Women's Commission of the Ecumenical Association of Third World Theologians.* Maryknoll, NY: Orbis.

Fabella, Virginia, and Sun Ai Lee Park, eds. 1989. *We Dare to Dream: Doing Theology as Asian Women.* Hong Kong: Asian Women's Resource Centre for Culture and Theology.

Fiorenza, Elisabeth Schüssler. 1993. "Transforming the Legacy of *The Woman's Bible.*" Pp. 1–24 in Fiorenza, ed. *Searching the Scriptures: A Feminist Introduction.* Vol. 1. New York: Crossroad.

———. 1994. *Jesus: Miriam's Child, Sophia's Prophet: Critical Issues in Feminist Christology.* New York: Continuum.

Fulkerson, Mary McClintock. 1994. *Changing the Subject: Women's Discourses and Feminist Theology.* Minneapolis, MN: Fortress.

Gebara, Ivone. 1999. *Longing for Running Water: Ecofeminism and Liberation.* Minneapolis, MN: Fortress.

———. 2002. *Out of the Depths: Women's Experience of Evil and Salvation.* Minneapolis, MN: Fortress.

Geertz, Clifford. 1966. "Religion as a Cultural System." Pp. 1–42 in Michael Banton, ed. *Anthropological Approaches to the Study of Religion.* London: Routledge.

Grant, John Webster. 1972. *The Church in the Canadian Era: The First Century of Confederation.* A History of the Church in Canada 3. Toronto: McGraw-Hill Ryerson.

Gudorf, Christine. 2001. "The Erosion of Sexual Dimorphism: Challenges to Religion and Religious Ethics." *Journal of the American Academy of Religion* 69: 863–92.

Hampson, Daphne. 1990. *Theology and Feminism.* Oxford: Basil Blackwell.

———. 1996. *After Christianity*. London: SCM.

Heyward, Carter. 1989. *Touching Our Strength: The Erotic as Power and the Love of God*. San Francisco: Harper & Row.

Houts, Margot G. 1999. "The Visual Evidence of Women in Early Christian Leadership." *Perspectives* 14: 7–11.

Hunt, Mary. 1996. "'Reimagining' Backlash." Pp. 45–52 in Elisabeth Schüssler Fiorenza and M. Shawn Copeland, eds. *Feminist Theology in Different Contexts*. London: SCM.

Irvin, Dorothy. 1980. "The Ministry of Women in the Early Church: The Archaeological Evidence." *Duke Divinity School Review* 45: 76–86.

Isasi-Díaz, Ada María. 1996. *Mujerista Theology: A Theology for the Twenty-First Century*. Maryknoll, NY: Orbis.

Isherwood, Lisa. "Queering Christ: Outrageous Acts and Theological Rebellions." *Literature and Theology* 15 (2001): 249–61.

———, and Kathleen McPhillips, eds. 2008. *Post-Christian Feminisms: A Critical Approach*. Burlington, VT: Ashgate.

Jerome. 1994. "Against Jovininaus." Pp. 346–416 in Philip Schaff and Henry Wace, eds. *Jerome: Letters and Select Works*. Nicene and Post-Nicene Fathers Volume 6. Peabody, MA: Hendrickson, 1994.

Johnson, Elizabeth. 1992. *She Who Is: The Mystery of God in Feminist Theological Discourse*. New York: Crossroad.

Kamitsuka, Margaret D. 2007. *Feminist Theology and the Challenge of Difference*. New York: Oxford University Press.

Kwok, Pui-lan. 2005. *Postcolonial Imagination and Feminist Theology*. Louisville, KY: Westminster John Knox.

Lawrence, Bruce. 1989. *Defenders of God: The Fundamentalist Revolt against the Modern Age*. San Francisco: Harper and Row.

MacHaffie, Barbara J. 1986. *Her Story: Women in Christian Tradition*. Philadelphia: Fortress.

Malone, Mary. 2000. *Women and Christianity, Volume I: The First Thousand Years*. Ottawa: Novalis.

Manning, Christel. 1999. *God Gave Us the Right: Conservative Catholic, Evangelical Protestant and Orthodox Jewish Women Grapple with Feminism*. New Brunswick, NJ: Rutgers.

Marty, Martin, and Scott Appleby, eds. 1991–5. *The Fundamentalism Project*. 5 vols. Chicago: University of Chicago Press.

McClung, Nellie L. [1915] 1972. *In Times Like These*. Toronto: University of Toronto Press.

McNamara, Jo Ann Kay. 1996. *Sisters in Arms: Catholic Nuns through Two Millennia*. Cambridge, MA: Harvard University Press.

Mollenkott, Virginia Ramey. 1985. *The Divine Feminine: The Biblical Imagery of God as Female*. New York: Crossroad.

Oduyoye, Mercy Amba. 1995. *Daughters of Anowa: African Women and Patriarchy*. Maryknoll, NY: Orbis Books.

Paul VI. [1968] 1969. "*Humanae Vitae*: On the Regulation of Birth." *Journal of Church and State* 11: 16–32.

———. 1977. "Vatican Declaration: Women in the Ministerial Priesthood, 1976." *Origins* 6, 33: 517–24.

Porete, Marguerite. 1993. *The Mirror of Simple Souls*. Translated by Ellen L. Babinsky. New York: Paulist Press.

Rudy, Kathy. 1997. *Sex and the Church: Gender, Homosexuality and the Transformation of Christian Ethics*. Boston: Beacon.

Ruether, Rosemary Radford. 1974. "Misogynism and Virginal Feminism in the Father of the Church." Pp. 150–83 in Ruether, ed. *Religion and Sexism: Images of Women in the Jewish and Christian Traditions*. New York: Simon and Schuster.

———. 1975. *New Woman, New Earth: Sexist Ideologies and Human Liberation*. New York: Seabury Press.

———. 1979. "Motherearth and the Megamachine: A Theology of Liberation in a Feminine, Somatic and Ecological Perspective." Pp. 43–52 in Carol P. Christ and Judith Plaskow, eds. *Womanspirit Rising: A Feminist Reader in Religion*. San Francisco: Harper & Row.

———. 1983. *Sexism and God-Talk: Toward a Feminist Theology*. Boston: Beacon.

———. 1992. *Gaia and God: An Ecofeminist Theology of Earth Healing*. San Francisco: HarperSanFrancisco.

———. 1998. *Women and Redemption: A Christological History*. Minneapolis, MN: Fortress.

———. 2000. *Christianity and the Making of the Modern Family*. Boston: Beacon.

Ruether, Rosemary Radford, ed. 2007. *Feminist Theologies: Legacy and Prospect*. Minneapolis, MN: Fortress.

Russell, Letty. 1974. *Human Liberation in a Feminist Perspective: A Theology*. Philadelphia: Westminster Press.

———. 1979. *The Future of Partnership*. Philadelphia: Westminster Press.

———. 1993. *Church in the Round: Feminist Interpretation of the Church*. Louisville, KY: Westminster/John Knox.

———. 1996. "Practicing Hospitality in a Time of Backlash." *Theology Today* 52: 476–84.

Russell, Letty, Kwok Pui-lan, Ada María Isasi-Díaz, and Katie Geneva Cannon, eds. 1988. *Inheriting Our Mothers' Gardens: Feminist Theology in Third World Perspective*. Philadelphia: Westminster Press.

Saiving, Valerie. 1979. "The Human Situation: A Feminine View." Pp. 25–42 in Carol P. Christ and Judith Plaskow, eds. *Womanspirit Rising: A Feminist Reader in Religion*. San Francisco: Harper & Row.

Sheffield, Tricia. 2008. "Performing Jesus: A Queer Counternarrative of Embodied Transgression." *Theology and Sexuality* 14: 233–58.

Simons, Walter. 2011. *City of Ladies: Beguine Communities in the Medieval Low Countries, 1200–1565*. Philadelphia: University of Pennsylvania Press.

Spikard, James V., J. Shawn Landres, and Meredith B. McGuire, eds. 2002. *Personal Knowledge and Beyond: Reshaping the Ethnography of Religion*. New York: New York University Press.

Stanton, Elizabeth Cady, and the Revising Committee. [1898] 1974. *The Woman's Bible*. Seattle, WA: Coalition Task Force on Women and Religion.

Tertullian. 1869. "On the Dress of Women." Pp. 304–9 in Alexander Roberts and James Donaldson, eds. *Ante-Nicene Christian Library*. Vol. 11. Edinburgh: T. & T. Clark.

Warne, Randi R. 1993. *Literature as Pulpit: The Christian Social Activism of Nellie L. McClung*. Waterloo, ON: Wilfrid Laurier University Press.

Young, Pamela Dickey. 1990. *Feminist Theology/Christian Theology: In Search of Method*. Philadelphia: Fortress.

———. 1995. "Feminist Theology: From Past to Future." Pp. 71–82 in Morny Joy and Eva K. Neumaier, eds. *Gender, Genre and Religion: Feminist Reflections*. Waterloo, ON: Wilfrid Laurier University Press and Calgary Institute for the Humanities.

———. 2010. "Neither Male nor Female: Christology beyond Dimorphism." In Ellen M. Leonard and Kate Merriman, eds. *From Logos to Christos: Essay in Christology in Honour of Joanne McWilliam*. Waterloo, ON: Wilfrid Laurier University Press.

———. 2012. *Religion, Sex and Politics: Christian Churches and Same-Sex Marriage in Canada*. Winnipeg: Fernwood.

CHAPTER 7

Women in Islam

L. Clarke

Women attending the Hartford Seminary in Hartford, Connecticut.

Sumayya Ayoub

Interpreting the Quran

One way for Muslim women to gain religious authority and potentially bring about change is through interpretation of the Quran. Quranic exegesis is particularly powerful because the Quran is regarded as the literal Word of God, revealed to the Prophet Muhammad in the seventh century CE. A number of **hadiths** (sayings attributed to the Prophet and stories about his actions and judgments) credit his wife Aishah with exegesis of important verses of the Quran; and whether or not these sayings actually reflect a historical reality, later scholars clearly regard her as an exegetical authority (Geissinger, 2011). Until very recently, however, women did not write books of exegesis. Since production of major written texts implies great authority and prestige, it remained the preserve of men. This is changing only slowly. A few women have now produced *tafsir* (Arabic for "exegesis"), although in a concise, somewhat popular form focusing on selected verses rather than the comprehensive, scholarly style that is still most esteemed.

One passage of the Quran that has attracted attention from female exegetes is verse 34 of Chapter 4, titled "Women." Much ink has been spilled over this famously problematic verse, which is quite out of tune with the egalitarian spirit of the rest of the revelation:

> Men are set over women because God has favoured one over the other and because men maintain them with their wealth; thus righteous women are devout and guard what God would have them guard in [their husbands'] absence. As for those women from whom you fear bad behaviour, admonish them, refuse to share their beds, and hit them. But if they obey you once again, do not try to vex them; surely God is Most High, Most Great.

The verse is taken up by the Egyptian activist Zaynab al-Ghazali in her volume of *tafsir, Reflections on the Book of God* (1994). Al-Ghazali, who died in 2005, was the founder of a "Muslim Women's Association" connected with the Muslim Brotherhood, the religiously conservative group that came to power in Egypt following the "Arab Spring." The following abridged excerpt from *Reflections* treats Quran 4:34 in a way that accepts the premise of male authority and even right of a husband to discipline his wife, but also reproaches men for bad behaviour and argues for balance between the roles of men and women:

> In this Noble Verse, God confirms that men are "set over" women and that they have the right to leadership in the family. . . . The essence of the "setting over" spoken of in the verse is responsibility, in the sense that the man has full financial responsibility for his wife and children. He is also responsible for cooperating with his wife in all domestic affairs, in the manner laid down in the Noble Quran and exemplary Custom (**Sunnah**) of our beloved Prophet. . . . The wife, on the other hand, has independent authority inside the house and is responsible before God for the well-being of her husband and children. This [model of family life] can only be achieved if the wife accepts, out of love and obedience to God and contentment with His will, that the setting of the man over her is perfectly just and in her best interest, since it obliges him to deal with her justly . . . and protect her honour and humanity. . . . By "disobedience," the verse means making one's position higher than it should be (*irtifa*); a disobedient wife is one who tries to place herself higher than her husband by not listening to him. . . . We should "admonish" such women and warn them of God's punishment for disobeying Him. And if they will not be admonished . . . it is fitting to "refuse to share their beds," that is to turn one's back to them and not have intercourse. . . . And if that has no effect, "hit them," but lightly and not so as to cause pain . . . ; and even then, the Prophet once added while reciting this verse: "Only the most evil of you hit." But the behaviour of some men toward their wives represents a kind of degraded mentality due to their extremely deficient understanding of the true nature and spirit of Islam. And [the conclusion of the verse], "God is Most High, Most Great," is in fact a warning from God to those who go against His command, whether a wife disobeying her husband or a man oppressing his wife. (Ghazali, [1414] 1994: 297–8).

Ghazali's determined activism, which earned her a long prison term and torture under the secular Nasser regime (1956–70), has led some Western scholars (e.g., Cooke, 1995) to see a strain of feminism in her thinking, but her interpretation of Quran 4:34 is profoundly conservative. A somewhat more progressive reading of the verse is offered by Laleh Bakhtiar in her *Sublime Quran* (2007), presented as "the first English translation of the Quran by an American woman" (www

.sublimequran.org). Eschewing the literalism of Ghazali, Bakhtiar translates the Arabic word *daraba* as "to go away," instead of "to hit," so that the man is not told to discipline a wife he cannot get along with, but rather to leave her or turn away. The African-American scholar Amina Wadud takes a more radical approach, asserting that while the immediate purpose of the rule was to improve the rather low "marital norm" that existed in seventh-century Arabian society, the ultimate intent was to establish an equal relation between the spouses, a goal that should now be realized in a different way in light of the "changing needs of developing civilizations" (Wadud, 1999: 70–8 and 2006: 192 ff.). These are only a few of many recent attempts (see also Barlas, 2002: 184–9) to deal with this controversial passage.

Introduction and Overview

Islam arose in the Arabian Peninsula, the area now largely occupied by the modern state of Saudi Arabia, in the early seventh century. The religion was founded by the Prophet Muhammad, who spurned the cult of idols in his native town of Makkah (Mecca) and finally succeeded, after much struggle, in establishing the worship of one God—known in Arabic as Allah, or *the* God. Following the death of Muhammad in 632 CE, his successors, the **caliphs**, conquered the entire Middle East. Islam continued to spread over the following centuries to such diverse regions as Africa, Spain, the Indian subcontinent, Central Asia, and Indonesia, and eventually to Europe, Australia, and the Americas. Islam is currently said to be the fastest-growing religion in the world.

Muslims are linked together by basic beliefs, such as belief in a Day of Judgment and a continuous line of prophets culminating in the last Prophet, Muhammad. They are united by faith in the Quran as the Word of God sent down to His Prophet through the angel Gabriel. As heirs to a rich culture and glorious history, Muslims are also joined by their desire to see the place of Islam and Islamic nations in the modern world recognized and secured.

Islam is, at the same time, a highly diverse and dynamic tradition. Because the daily lives and customs of Muslims living in disparate parts of the world are very different, they express their Islam in different ways. There is also a wide spectrum of Islamic thought on doctrinal, societal, and political issues. One of the most intensely debated issues is the position of women.

Since only a limited number of views and attitudes can be represented in this short chapter, I will use the categories "conservative" and "liberal" heuristically to refer to two broad streams of thought on gender. Those I call conservative believe that Islam guarantees women respect and protection within a system of gender relations that is essentially dominated by men. Conservatives believe that proper gender roles and correct female behaviour are vital to the social fabric and strength of Islam, and that the Muslim community must preserve and restore that ideal system. Liberals, on the other hand, believe that while the Quran and the Prophet attempted to secure the position of women, their intentions were neglected and obscured by later generations, including the religious scholars. In the view of liberals, extensive reinterpretation of the texts and rereading of history is needed to discover the original Islamic ideal and bring it into modern times. This position resembles the feminist critique of patriarchal religion.

Official and Unofficial Roles of Women

The period before Islam in the Arabian Peninsula is known as **Jahiliyah**, the "Time of Ignorance." Islam, by contrast, means literally "Submission [to God]." Women were instrumental in founding the new religion. As Islam grew and flourished, they also exercised political power, reached the station of mystics and saints, and became scholars. It is true that women's activities and renown in these areas were much less than those of men—a circumstance that is not peculiar to Islam. The basic position of women has always been on the margin, but they have nevertheless found openings through which they could move toward the centre. The questions that therefore need to be asked are: Where were the openings and how were they used? What were the limitations? And what does all this mean for Muslim women today?

Women and the Advent of Islam

The Prophet's first revelation came to him in 610 CE, when he was 40 years old. According to Ibn Hisham's ninth-century Biography of Muhammad, his wife Khadijah played a crucial role in his life at this time. Ibn Hisham describes her as "a woman of dignity and wealth . . . determined, noble, and intelligent" (1955: 82). Having employed Muhammad as overseer of her trading caravans, she proposed marriage to him, and he accepted. Khadijah was able to reassure Muhammad of the truth of his mission, even verifying that his inspiration came from an angel; as the Biography declares, "She was the first to believe in God and His apostle, and in the truth of his message" (111). Their monogamous marriage lasted 24 years, and the four daughters borne by Khadijah were the only offspring of the Prophet to survive. **Bukhari's** Sahih, the most prominent of the canonical hadith collections quoted throughout this chapter, tells how after her death in 620 God reassured Muhammad that she had been granted "an abode in heaven" (Bukhari, Book of Virtues, Muhammad's Marriage with Khadijah).

Despite persecution by the wealthy merchants of Makkah, "both men and women" (Ibn Hisham, 1955: 117) were attracted to the new religion. Among the women were Fatimah, the sister of the second caliph, Umar, whose reading of the Quran inspired his conversion; and Sumayyah, who became Islam's first martyr when she died of exposure to the midday heat after refusing to recant her faith. A woman called Nusaybah was among those who travelled from Madinah to secretly pledge allegiance to Muhammad; and after his death she suffered "twelve wounds from spear or sword" (203, 212) in battle against the tribes who rose up against Islam. Another early convert was Muhammad's widowed aunt Safiyah, who twice rushed into battle ahead of the men.

Laila Ahmed argues (1992) that the active roles played by women in the early days of Islam reflected the freer life and more relaxed gender norms of pre-Islamic Arabia. According to Ahmed, these began to wear away after the **Hijrah** ("migration") of the Muslim community to Madinah in 622. Having married two other women following Khadijah's death, the Prophet established a polygamous household in Madinah with increasingly secluded quarters for his wives and received the Quranic revelations about marriage and divorce that would lay the framework for gender relations in the new community. Many parts of the Quran are thought to have been sent down in response to issues in the community, and Ahmed's view that the advent of Islam brought about a more restrictive organization of gender in Arabia seems to be confirmed by traditions that attribute two Quranic verses imposing restrictions on Muhammad's wives to the influence of Umar. It is said that the verses in which God orders that Muhammad's wives be spoken to only from behind a partition (53:33) and in which they are threatened with divorce (66:5) were both sent down because Umar had disapproved of their behaviour. Umar also reportedly urged that women pray at home, ordered segregation in the mosque, tried to prevent the Prophet's widows from making the annual *hajj* pilgrimage to Makkah (citations in Abbott, 1942: 114–15) and favoured hitting recalcitrant wives (reported in the hadith collection of **Ibn Majah**, Book of Marriage). The sources paint Umar as a great and stern organizer of government and religion, and here he is depicted as playing the same role in relation to women.

On the other hand, the hadiths and other early Islamic texts record objections to Umar's views, not only by the women of the community, but by the Prophet himself. Such accounts were no doubt circulated by those who believed that God had meant women to have more autonomy and play a more active role. We even have stories about the revelation of the Quran parallel to those involving Umar that have God intervening in favour of women, rather than against them. For example, the books of exegesis say that Quran 33:35, in which women are specifically and repeatedly addressed as believers in addition to men (a feature also seen in many other passages), was sent down after a group of women noticed the exclusive use of the male gender in the language of the revelations and asked: "Is it possible that we [females] are not mentioned?" (*Tafsir* of Tabari). It is also recounted that a woman went to the Prophet to complain that her husband had abruptly divorced her after she had grown old. God subsequently sent down the verses that open Chapter 58, titled "She Who Disputes," in which such treatment is condemned.

There are many other stories of disagreements over the position of women in the early days. These have come down to us from a collective oral tradition in which persons with different views—including, possibly, women—were able to make their voices heard by contributing their own versions. Thus the time of the original Muslim community seems to have been marked by lively gender controversy, rather than steady decline from a freer pre-Islamic era as Ahmed asserts.

The community also had a vivid memory of the first female Muslims converting against the will of their male relatives. For instance, Umm Habibah, the daughter of Muhammad's deadly enemy Abu Sufyan, not only enraged her father by converting to Islam, but remained a Muslim even after her husband became a Christian. When the relatives of women who had fled Makkah for Madinah demanded that they be sent back, God revealed Quran 60:10, commanding that the women be examined to verify their faith so they could stay; the Chapter in which the verse appears is thus called "She Who Is Examined." One of the earliest Madinans to become a Muslim was a woman named Umm Sulaym, who converted despite her husband's disapproval and further defied him by teaching their son about Islam. It is true that some women bitterly opposed the Prophet. Nevertheless, the tales of female converts seem to point to a time before the institutionalization of gender hierarchy when Islam represented an opportunity for women to defy convention and act with relative freedom. A similar pattern can be seen in the early days of many new religious movements.

The prominence of women in this early period is extolled by all Muslims, but for different purposes. Conservatives take the example of the first female Muslims to mean that women should be active in the cause of their religion, but only within prescribed limits. They do not conclude that women may occupy positions of authority or venture outside the family for their own purposes. Thus while they admire the Muslim women who went to war as combatants, they maintain that this occurred under exceptional circumstances that do not establish a norm. Liberals, on the other hand, see the first female believers as forerunners of the modern, independent Muslim woman who is both rooted in her religion and reaching toward the goal of full participation in society.

The question of the relative position of women before and after Islam is treated in a similar way. Most Muslims believe that Jahiliyah society was degrading for women until Islam came to give them "dignity" and "respect." This common Muslim view is supported by passages of the Quran such as 16:59, 43:17, and 81:8-9, which condemn the killing of infant girls; 16:59 and 42:49, which reproach those who prefer sons to daughters; and 4:19, which forbids taking a widow as part of an inheritance in order to keep her wealth. Verses like these help to explain the widespread Muslim belief that Islam, if properly understood, guarantees a high position for women. Yet the force of the idea that Islam improved the position of women depends on the attitude believers bring to the text. In the liberal view, God meant the Prophet's reforms to be an initial stage in the gradual achievement of more complete gender equality. In the eyes of conservatives, on the other hand, the advances made in the Quran and the existence of certain rights in the **Shariah** (Muslim law) mean that the position of women in Islam is already ideal—better than in Judaism and Christianity—and should not be changed. Advocates of both perspectives tend to use similar "rights of women" language, however, and it is necessary to pay close attention to understand what is being said.

The Example of the Prophet's Family

The establishment of the Muslim community in Madinah marked a change in the Prophet's family life. Following the loss of his beloved first wife, Khadijah, Muhammad had married Sawdah and Aishah; and now in Madinah he contracted additional marriages. He is said to have had between 9 and 12 wives (the number varies depending on the source), of whom his favourite was apparently Aishah, the daughter of his close companion Abu Bakr (later the first caliph). The wives came to him under a variety of circumstances. Sawdah was a widow of about 50 years of age, whereas Aishah was very young and may have been the only virgin among the wives. Juwayriyah was captured when her tribe was defeated by the Muslims, and her marriage to the Prophet served to cement the tribe's allegiance to Islam. Safiyah was originally a Jewish captive, while Mariyah, probably a concubine instead of a wife, was a Copt (Egyptian Christian). Some of the wives were reputed to be beautiful, such as Juwayriyah, and some, such as Sawdah, were not.

Muslims often argue that Muhammad's marriages after Khadijah were contracted not for pleasure, but for practical reasons, to confirm alliances and to give unprotected women, such as widows, a home. This was the case, for instance, with Umm Habibah, whom the Prophet took in after her marriage to her Christian husband had ended (some stories say she divorced him; others, that he died). In any event, Muslims have not been overly concerned with the

Prophet's marrying many wives except as the question has been raised by out-side critics. More important for them are the personalities of the wives and the nature of the Prophet's relations with them.

The wives of Muhammad, honoured with the epithet "Mothers of the Believers" (after Quran 33:6: "The Prophet is closer to the believers than their selves, and his wives are as their mothers"), are highly respected by Muslims, largely because of their closeness to the Prophet. They are also, however, cred-ited with their own personal virtues. Aishah is reputed to have spent much time reading the Quran, fasting, and praying; to have freed slaves (an import-ant religious act); and generously given her income in charity. Zaynab bint Khuzaymah was so well known for her charity that she was called "Mother of the Poor." Muslims' reverence for the wives may be gauged by the fact that the violent reaction to Salman Rushdie's 1989 novel *The Satanic Verses* was stirred as much by the perception that it had insulted them as that it had insulted the Prophet himself.

Anecdotes about Muhammad's relationships with his wives are useful for purposes of Sunnah, since they provide models and precedents for marital rela-tionships. They are also much appreciated by Muslims, who discern in the tales of Muhammad and his family an image of tolerance and kindness. In his rela-tions with the women of his family, Muhammad does not appear as a stern patriarch, but rather the opposite. Faced with bickering among his wives, he simply withdraws until the more authoritarian Umar intervenes. When he real-izes he is dying and wishes to spend his last hours with his beloved Aishah even though it is not her turn to be with him, he only hints indirectly that he wants to skip over the turns of the other wives. Though the Quran lays down the law of divorce in some detail, the Prophet himself is not believed to have exercised this male prerogative.

Aishah is the best known of the wives. Married, according to most sources, at the age of nine, she lived with Muhammad for the last nine years of his life and was widowed at 18. Her fame was nevertheless guaranteed by her long life thereafter (she died in her 65th year), during which she recounted—or there were recounted in her name—many hadiths concerning the Prophet's words and actions. Thus Aishah, along with, to a lesser extent, her co-wife Umm Salamah, is a great source of hadiths—the second most important Islamic scriptures after the Quran. The canonical collection of Bukhari preserves more than 200 texts judged to be authentically from Aishah out of many more attrib-uted to her in the hadith corpus.

Aishah is depicted as actively enquiring about the Prophet's pronounce-ments: "she would never hear something she didn't understand without reviewing it until she did" (Bukhari, Book of Knowledge). Several hadiths attributed to Aishah even have her deciding herself what the Prophet would have ruled in a particular situation—as in the following statement: "Were Muhammad to see what we see of women today, he would prohibit them from going to the mosque" (Bukhari, Book of Call to Prayer). In a few hadiths, Aishah draws on her knowledge to correct the misperceptions of later generations regarding women. For instance, when a man thought it was forbidden for his wife to serve him during her menses, Aishah told him that she used to comb the Prophet's hair while she was menstruating, even as he prepared to go to the mosque (Bukhari, Book of Menstruation).

Aishah was finally unable to extend her influence to include political power. Later in her life, she joined a movement opposing the fourth Caliph, Ali ibn Abi Talib, which culminated in 656 in a battle near the Iraqi town of Basrah. The incident is known as the Battle of the Camel because Aishah, mounted on a camel, urged on the troops as the battle raged about her. She and her allies were defeated. Although, as a mark of respect, she was then escorted back to Madinah and allowed to continue her life there, her defeat was taken to show that women should not interfere in politics.

The other female figure associated with Muhammad who stands out is his daughter Fatimah, the only child of his to receive much attention in the sources. Muhammad and Fatimah are portrayed as having an ideal father–daughter relationship. We are told how she shielded the Prophet as she ministered to his wounds (Bukhari, Book of Ablutions), and he is said to have declared her "mistress of the women of Paradise" (Bukhari, Book of the Virtues of Fatimah). A well-known hadith (sometimes connected to the Prophet's forbidding her husband, Ali ibn Abi Talib, to take additional wives) has Muhammad say, "Fatimah is a part of me; who angers her, angers me" (Bukhari, Book of Virtues).

Fatimah is particularly beloved by the **Shiites** because of her marriage to Ali, the cousin of the Prophet revered by this minority group. Tales of her poverty, constant prayer, and charity are magnified in the Shiite literature. Shiite legend also links Fatimah to the supernatural: her birth is accompanied by a light that illuminates the earth, she has tragic visions of the future martyrdom of her sons Hasan and Husayn, and she plays a prominent role on the Day of Judgment, surrounded by hosts of angels, demanding revenge for her murdered sons and interceding for those who remained loyal to her descendants. In the eyes of Shiites, Fatimah is a celestial figure, somewhat parallel to the Christian Mary; she is immune from sin, does not menstruate, and is called "Luminous" (*Zahra*) and "Virgin" (*Batul*).

Images of women from the Prophet's family have undergone some change in modern times. The **Sunnites**, the majority Muslim group for whom the wives are most important, now emphasize Khadijah's independence and Aishah's learning, although Aishah's participation in the Battle of the Camel tends to be either not mentioned or (as in the classical sources) treated as an unfortunate mistake. For the Shiites, Fatimah's strength and courage in standing up to her enemies have become more important than in the past. Still, these changes are no more than shifts in emphasis: they do not reflect any questioning of traditional roles and ideals. The difficulty of re-imagining traditional female figures is illustrated by the effort of Ali Shariati (d. 1977) to go beyond conventional womanly virtues in his famous tract *Fatimah Is Fatimah*. A thinker who helped to lay the groundwork for Iran's Islamic revolution (1979), Shariati set out to create a Fatimah who refuses to be defined solely as daughter or wife, and is engaged in a struggle to realize herself as a person: "Fatimah must become Fatimah on her own; if she does not become Fatimah, she is lost." This Fatimah, Shariati thought, would be the model for the modern Muslim woman who "wants to build herself, wants to be reborn." Yet his Fatimah is finally unable to transcend her domesticity, uncomplaining suffering, and devotion to the males in her life. Shariati also somewhat patronizingly disapproves of traditional Shiite women's religiosity for its supposed passivity (Kashani-Sabet, 2005).

Writing on the founding women of Islam has been produced almost exclusively by men. In order to understand how women themselves relate to potential role models, it is necessary to seek out non-textual sources. Some young women in Saudi Arabia who want to start their own businesses have spoken of following the example of Khadijah (Coleman, 2013). One researcher who interviewed Lebanese Shiite women, including some associated with the militant Hizbullah movement, found that Fatimah's daughter Zaynab, who survived the great battle at Karbala, Iraq, in 680 in which her brother Husayn was killed, had become more important than Fatimah. Zaynab is admired for taking up arms in the battle and defying her captors, deeds that resonate deeply with women who feel that they and their families are under assault (Deeb, 2005). Shiite women also relate to the founding figures of their faith through mourning ceremonies, including exclusively female gatherings dedicated to remembering the women and infants who appear in the Shiite martyrology. These ritual occasions allow the participants to appeal to the martyrs as intercessors and identify with them by connecting their tragic experience to the sorrows of everyday life.

Women and Political Power

Madinah remained the centre of the expanding Islamic empire until the founding of the Umayyad Dynasty in the later seventh century, when the capital was moved to Damascus. With the overthrow of the Umayyads by the Abbasids in 750, the focus of the ever-expanding Islamic world then shifted to Baghdad. Abbasid rule survived in Baghdad until 1258, when the Mongols destroyed the caliphal line. But the banner of Islam had already been taken up by a host of other tribes and states—not only Arab, but Turkic, Iranian, Indian, and Berber.

The caliphate, which had once symbolized the unity of Islam, was gone; Islam as an international creed and civilization went on to win new peoples and territories.

Khayzuran, mother of two successive Abbasid caliphs, the short-lived al-Hadi (reigned 785–6) and legendary Harun al-Rashid (reigned 786–809), is one example of women's political influence in this "classical age" of Islam. Khayzuran was a favourite concubine of the caliph al-Mahdi. Both beautiful and cultured, as the most expensive slave girls were expected to be, she recited poetry and had some religious learning. She is suspected of having poisoned her son Hadi, since he had tried to limit her influence; with the succession of her other son, Harun al-Rashid, she was able to maintain a high position until her death. In the course of her climb, Khayzuran amassed great wealth and became noted for her charity, including the restoration of sites around Makkah.

Themes in the story of Khayzuran—concubinage, manipulation, and good works—are repeated throughout the classical period. Some females, however, did manage to exercise a degree of independent power. In Yemen in the twelfth century, the queens Asma and Arwa shared power with their husbands, members of a dynasty connected with the **Isma'ili** branch of Shiism. Shajarat al-Durr (her name means "Tree of Pearls") conspired with the Mamluk army in Egypt to keep the death of her husband secret while she repulsed a besieging Crusader army. In 1250, the military placed Shajarat al-Durr herself on the throne to secure their position. But she reigned for only a few months. As the Abbasid caliph refused to recognize a female ruler as legitimate, she was deposed and eventually murdered. A few women even managed to rule directly rather than as associates: for instance, al-Sayyidah al-Hurrah ("Free Lady," a title also held by other female rulers) held the position of governor of Tetouán, Morocco, for some decades in the sixteenth century and engaged in both piracy and diplomacy until she married the king of Morocco.

What can the influence and occasional rule of women mean? Nabia Abbott, a pioneer in the study of women in Islam, believes the role of women to have been even greater than admitted in the classical sources, since "[Muslim] historians tend to pass over unpalatable references to women's rule as briefly as possible, frequently ignoring it altogether" (1946: 55). Certainly, women's contributions to history tend to be undervalued when the records are drawn up; from that point of view, the recovery of these figures is a necessary corrective. Abbott also expresses the hope that highlighting the roles played by women in Muslim politics will provide examples and precedents for modern times.

From a strictly historical point of view, however, the influence or rule of women in the Islamic past is not so remarkable. Throughout the classical period, political power was centred at the ruler's court. Concentration of power in the court often opens a path to power for women, both because command depends on shifting alliances within a relatively small family group and because outside players may choose to use females connected to the court in their manipulations, as happened to Shajarat al-Durr. The rule behind the exceptions is brought home in misogynistic remarks about women's political power. Khayzuran is said to have been warned by her son al-Hadi not to "overstep the essential limits of womanly modesty . . . [for] it is not dignified for a woman to enter upon affairs of state" (Abbott, 1946: 89–90). The theme of disastrous women's rule even received scriptural authority. A famous hadith, sometimes linked to Aishah's part in the Battle of the Camel and still quoted today, declares that "A people who place women in charge of their affairs shall never prosper" (Bukhari, Book of Sedition).

A number of women have ruled Muslim states in modern times. Benazir Bhutto of Pakistan, Tansu Çiller of Turkey, Khaleda Zia and Sheikh Hasina Wajed of Bangladesh, Megawati Sukarnoputri of Indonesia and Mame Madior Boye of Senegal have all served as president or prime minister. Except for Çiller and the very short-lived Boye, however, these women were wives and daughters of previous rulers. The election of women still seems to be an outcome of political dynamics related to family rule, rather than a demonstration of preference for the candidates in their own right. Moreover, when we consider that, even today, most women who gain high political office do so in the midst of some kind of disorder (for instance, the death of male relatives who held power before them), it becomes clear that women's rule in general is more likely to point to political instability than gender equality.

A more lasting influence on decision-making requires participation in the political system at the level of voting, lobbying, and running for local and national positions. Although Muslim-majority countries overall continue to lag on such indicators, gradual improvement over the last half-century has affected even the most traditional societies. A notable example is Saudi Arabia, where King Abdullah has decided to include women in the national Consultative Council and promised that women will be able to vote and stand for office for the first time in 2015. The King cited both the need for "balanced modernization" and the example of Umm Salamah, the eldest of the Prophet's wives, whose advice he sought on important matters. The Saudi decision was also due in part to the long and ongoing campaign by women in the Kingdom for autonomy and basic social rights.

Legitimating women's political participation in Islamic terms is an important step. Here we see two opposite trends. On one side, some Islamist movements believe that women should not play any active role in government. In his famous *Purdah and the Status of Women in Islam*, written in Urdu in 1935, the Indo-Pakistani Islamist Abu al-Ala Mawdudi (d. 1979) ruled out women's participation in politics and any other activities that would take them into the public sphere and so prevent them from developing their feminine "natural gifts." Following Egypt's 2011 Arab Spring revolution, representatives of the radically conservative "Salafi" movement rejected the idea of a female vice-president; one reason given was that women are too emotional for politics.

On the other side, some argue that women's participation in the political process is actually an Islamic standard. The respected, though controversial, Egyptian scholar and journalist Muhammad Khalaf Allah states that women in the time of the Prophet shared in political consultation (*shura*) and that this is a right specified in the Quran itself (1977: 189–93), while Amina Wadud argues that the Quranic story of the Queen of Sheba should be taken as an example of a wise ruler who was only incidentally female, and who can serve as a model for both women and men (1999: 40–2). The pro-politics stance is taken even by a few traditional authorities, although always with the caution that family duties come first. Ayatollah Fadlallah of Lebanon (d. 2010) regards Fatimah's resistance to the caliphs who denied the rights of her family as proof that she was a "revolutionary" who "legitimized the political participation of women" (2000: 321–2), while Shaykh Yusuf al-Qaradawi, who is often seen on the Arabic satellite channel al-Jazeera and has a worldwide following, has issued **fatwas** declaring that women are entitled to become ministers, judges, and presidents (Stowasser, 2001).

Legitimation may also be achieved through the hard work of participation and determined activism. Tawakkol Karman, the young journalist and winner of the Nobel Peace Prize who has been prominent in the Arab Spring movement in Yemen, is one of more than a dozen members of the opposition Islamist *al-Islah* party sitting in the Yemeni parliament. Like their counterparts in the Majlis (Parliament) of the Islamic Republic of Iran, the Yemeni MPs have advanced their cause by adopting a religious discourse while building grass-roots support and cultivating potential allies.

Woman Mystics

Women have actively participated in Islamic mysticism, called Sufism after the rough woollen (*suf*) cloaks worn by the early ascetics. It is often said that mysticism is more open to women than more conventional expressions of religion, and to some extent this seems to hold true for Islamic mysticism. It is surely unrealistic to say, as the German scholar Annemarie Schimmel does, that in Sufism "woman enjoys full equal rights" (1997: 15). Nevertheless, in Sufism, as in mysticism generally, individual charisma is very important and the values and hierarchies of this world are often altered or reversed. This results in a certain flexibility of doctrine and authority, which has been exploited not only by women but also by others on the social margins, such as devotees of folk religion.

Islam recognizes numerous female saints, although, as we have come to expect from women's history, many fewer than male saints. The most famous female saint is, without doubt, Rabiah al-Adawiyah, who lived in southern Iraq in the early eighth century. Rabiah's story touches on common themes of saints' lives: a humble beginning (she was said to have been a slave girl), sudden conversion (she repented of singing and entertaining), and asceticism. She appears in Sufi lore as an early exponent of love mysticism. Perhaps the most famous anecdote in all of Sufism centres on Rabiah: when asked why she was running through the streets with a torch in one hand and a bucket of water in the other, she replied that she wished to put out the fires of hell and destroy paradise, so that God would be worshipped not out of fear but for His sake alone.

Rabiah's femaleness gives her legend a special colouring. Her physical characteristics are noted (she is supposed to have been beautiful), she refuses offers of marriage, and there are several tales in which she bests Hasan al-Basri, an equally famous male mystic. This emphasis alerts us to a shadow of ambivalence toward female sainthood. It is true that the esteem in which female saints were held was not less than that of males. This is a consequence of the very nature of sainthood, which involves mysterious qualities that cannot be evaluated according to conventional standards. We might, however, read Rabiah's story in another way. The basic mystical lesson Hasan al-Basri must learn—the danger of creeping pride—is driven home by the fact that it is delivered by a mere female. Rabiah's legend in general intimates that her accomplishment is all the more remarkable and unexpected because she is a woman. She is doubly exceptional; we do not expect all people to be like that, but especially not many women.

Residual discomfort with female sainthood can also be seen in the idea that women saints transcend their gender and become essentially men. Thus the twelfth-century Persian mystical poet Farid al-Din Attar in his "Memorials of the Saints" places Rabiah with the men rather than the women, explaining that "[w]hen a woman becomes a man in the path of God, she is a man and one cannot any more call her a woman" (1966: 40). The American scholar Valerie Hoffman reports that during her fieldwork among Sufis in Egypt she sometimes received the "compliment" that she was not a woman but a "brother," and that some shaykhahs (the feminine equivalent of shaykh, meaning "esteemed authority") simulated the behaviour of their male counterparts with their followers (1995: 45–6, 227, 249, 292).

Some Sufi theosophists incorporated the feminine principle into their cosmological speculations. Consideration of the feminine emerges in a fascinating way in the work of the most influential theosophist of Islam, Muhyi al-Din Ibn Arabi of thirteenth-century Andalusia. Ibn Arabi declares love for woman to be "one of the perfections of the gnostic . . . for this is a prophetic heritage [the Prophet having declared in a famous hadith that the three things most dear to him were perfume, women, and prayer] and a divine love" (Murata, 1992: 178ff). He not only acknowledges the complementary roles of male and female principles in structuring the universe, but proposes that God is seen most fully in woman, since she reflects His beauty and gives birth to the perfect human form. Ibn Arabi's attitude toward women as persons seems to have been aligned with his idealization of the feminine as a cosmic principle. He revered his female mystical teachers and stated repeatedly (Chodkiewicz, 1993: 72) that women could occupy any rank in the universal hierarchy of saints. Ibn Arabi does speak of women mystics acquiring spiritual "virility" (*rujuliyah*; 153), but this seems to have been part of a complex play on gender rather than a sign that he believed femininity is a bar to high spiritual achievement.

Ibn Arabi is an exception, however. Most Islamic mysticism conforms to the usual pattern of human religious thought in separating the sacred feminine from the profane human woman. For example, the *Tariqah*s (Orders) of institutionalized Sufism follow the conventional gender hierarchy in which men are founders and leaders and women auxiliaries and followers. The "blessing" (*barakah*) that flows through the largely hereditary line of Sufi *shaykh*s comes to females only under exceptional circumstances: for instance, when there is no male in the family to take up a position. Nevertheless, women in some Sufi Orders have been able to use the relatively flexible norms of mysticism to gain charisma and authority. In Senegal (Hill, 2010), for instance, as well as other places in sub-Saharan Africa, women are appointed to mid-level positions in their Orders that allow them to guide and even initiate disciples; although they must still negotiate gender expectations by displaying modesty, casting themselves in the familiar role of a wise and aged "mother," and leading only other women or younger males.

Saints outside the structure of the Orders who transcend their femaleness through athletic spirituality, as the legendary Rabiah did, have been very rare. One was Hazrat Babajan, who fled from a marriage arranged by her wealthy Afghan family to live as an itinerant fakir, and is said to have visited Makkah disguised as a man. By the time Babajan died in 1931 aged nearly a hundred in a slum in Pune, India, she had become famous for her asceticism, *barakah*, and miracles.

Texts and Rituals

The first part of this section focuses on women's long-standing participation in the tradition of Islamic learning. We see that religious learning has given women opportunities, but that the authority conferred by their learning has been limited. The second part of the section, on women's participation in rituals, involves a similar pattern of opportunities and limitations.

Religious Learning and Authority

In classical times, the pre-eminent learned pursuit for women was transmission of hadiths, a role believed to have been initiated by women who had witnessed Muhammad's words and actions. The hadiths are crucial for establishing the Sunnah, the model life-pattern of the Prophet and early community. Doubts raised by Western scholars about the authenticity of the hadith corpus need not concern us here. What is significant for our purpose is that, despite a few dissenting opinions (Sayeed, 2009), women were accepted as equal to men in hadith transmission: the proportion of women in the first generation of Islam who are considered "trustworthy"—the highest rating given by the hadith scholars—is equal to the proportion of men (Roded, 1994: 65–6).

Women continued to participate and even excel in hadith transmission in later centuries. More than one-quarter of 130 hadith authorities listed by the fifteenth-century scholar al-Suyuti are women—an outstanding example but not an exceptional one in the Muslim scholarly tradition (Berkey, 1991: 151). Transmission of hadith, moreover, involved not merely the relaying of texts but active teaching and scholarship in which the *muhaddithah* (the feminine form of *muhaddith* or "hadith expert") analyzed and explained the material while discussing its implications for related matters such as law. Nor were women limited to the study and teaching of hadith. They were also learned in fields such as poetry and history, and commonly obtained and granted *ijazahs*, "licences" attesting to their scholarly expertise. The Islamic biographical dictionaries, always a rich source for women's history, praise female scholars in the same terms as males, calling them "intelligent," "judicious," "patient," and "influential" (Abou-Bakr, 2003).

There are, nevertheless, many fewer women scholars mentioned in the biographical literature than men, and the proportion declines steadily after the second generation. For example, according to the twelfth-century *History of the City of Damascus* of Ibn Asakir, about 4.5 per cent of scholars belonging to the first century of Islam were female, while for the third century, the proportion falls to 2 per cent—13 women against 627 men (Abyad, 1981: 183). The diminishing number may have been due to formalization of learning, since women tend to be excluded from religious activities as they become more structured. Women did not, for instance, hold positions in the system of colleges or madrasahs that became a focus of Islamic learning beginning in the eleventh century. Aspiring woman scholars may have also been limited by space. The activities of those whose names we know appear to have taken place mostly in homes and study circles in the mosque. Although women did occasionally mix with men to some degree, for instance in a mosque lesson if accompanied by a male relative, and a few struck out on journeys to meet great teachers, they generally had less opportunity to seek knowledge, even if exceptional individuals, some of them aged or widows, succeeded just the same.

It should be kept in mind that the biographical literature captures only female learning that intersected with that of males and was public to some degree. There may have been a larger world of private study, including study with female teachers, that did not seem important to male biographers and therefore was not recorded. That world, if it existed, might have been visible in the letters and other writings produced by women that are mentioned in a few biographical entries (Abou-Bakr, 2003: 321–2), but those documents either were not preserved or have yet to be identified.

Although women's religious learning was widely accepted in Islam, the idea that women might use such learning to occupy positions of authority was not. In most societies even today, for women to exercise authority over men violates the traditional gender hierarchy. Men may admire women's accomplishments and knowledge, but they will not be dictated to. This was also the case in medieval Islam. It was widely agreed, for example, that a woman cannot be a judge. Legal rulings often vary between the different Islamic legal schools, and the Hanafis (one of the four Sunni schools) argue that women should logically be able to judge the kinds of cases in which they are allowed to serve as witnesses (which would still exclude some serious crimes such as adultery and theft). Since women did not actually serve as judges, however, the Hanafi position seems purely theoretical (for details of the controversy, see Bauer, 2010). Majority Sunni opinion allowed that women could issue fatwas. This view demonstrates respect for women's learning and spirituality. However, since fatwas in Sunnism are deemed to be merely advice about the law rather than rulings that must be obeyed, the ability to issue them does not give women—or slaves, who were thought to have the same capacity—authority over free men. Nor did it allow women to penetrate formal institutions. Women did not become famous as muftis (givers of fatwas) or gain appointments as muftis in courts. Supposing that the permission for women to issue fatwas was not merely theoretical, it may have been limited to activities such as dispensing informal legal advice in the family, neighbourhood, or among women. Even today, there is reluctance to allow women to issue fatwas in a formal, public way, and it is widely believed that they should give Shariah advice only to other women, and particularly in relation to feminine concerns.

The tension between respect for women's learning and reluctance to give them authority over men is clear in the Shiite school. In Shiite law, fatwas are issued by only a limited number of Grand Ayatollahs, and are binding rather than merely constituting advice. It is probably because of these features that women cannot, according to the traditional Shiite view, give fatwas. A woman who is sufficiently learned may deduce legal rulings, but only for herself to follow: her rulings cannot be binding on others, apparently because this would give her too much authority, over men in particular. In the last two decades, several reformist Ayatollahs have declared that women may deduce legal rulings for others to follow—that is, may become Grand Ayatollahs. The truly radical implication of this view is that men would be compulsorily bound by the opinions of women; however, this remains merely a theoretical possibility, as it is unlikely that a woman could receive the approval of the clerical apparatus and the wide popular acceptance necessary to secure such a position.

The reality of women's situation with respect to the authority conferred by learning in contemporary Islam is similar to their situation in the Sufi *Tariqah*s. The advances that women have made in many Muslim-majority societies, together with changes in society such as urbanization, have allowed them to enlarge their roles and influence; but these still tend to be confined to sub-networks in structures defined and dominated by males. At the same time, the ability of women within these structures to exert influence should not be underestimated. Two examples among many can be seen in Turkey, where numerous female preachers and "vice-muftis" are employed by the Directorate of Religious Affairs to minister to both women and men (Hassan, 2012), and in Indonesia, where women's study circles have succeeded in improving public understanding of gender issues (Van Doorn-Harder, 2006).

Rituals, Purity, and Space

The common, legislated rituals that all Muslims must perform are daily prayer, fasting during the month of **Ramadan**, and the *hajj* (pilgrimage to Makkah), which must be completed once in one's lifetime. (The other two of the five "pillars of Islam" are recitation of the **shahadah**—"There is no god but God and Muhammad is His Messenger"—and payment of *zakat*, a tax used to assist the poor.) There is no ritual required of women specifically, and females' performance of the standard rituals differs from that of males in only some details. This might be a legacy of the spiritual equality between men and women that was assumed in the early days when the rituals were laid down, or it could simply be in keeping with the very spare character of ritual in Islam in general.

Nevertheless, women's practice of those rituals is affected by concerns with the female body related to purity and space. A woman is not to pray or fast while she is menstruating; though she should make up the missed fast days. If she begins to menstruate during the *hajj*, she should not circumambulate the Kaabah (the small, cube-shaped building, on the grounds of the Great Mosque, toward which all Muslims in the world pray) until her period has finished; if she has to depart before then, she should pad herself well and perform the circumambulation, since it is required for the pilgrimage to be valid. (Opinions here are diverse and complicated, and some women take pills to prevent menstruation.) Permission to complete the pilgrimage is necessary from a practical point of view, since most believers cannot afford to undertake the journey to Makkah more than once in a lifetime; but it is also consistent with Islam's relatively moderate attitude towards menstruation. The basic principle is that only the blood is impure; a menstruating woman's body is not impure, and she does not contaminate persons or things she touches. This position may reflect a desire to free women from the purity restrictions found in other religions; the hadiths that tell women not to follow certain rules related to menstruation seem to be aimed at differentiating Islam from Judaism in particular, since those rules are found in Judaic law (Mazuz, 2012). The result is that, with one exception (prohibition of intercourse, laid down in Quran 2:222), a menstruating woman continues to function fully in society, including in spaces where ritual is being carried out.

Even so, there are still differences of opinion. Some present-day fatwas prohibit a menstruating woman from both touching a Quran and reciting from it, while others allow silent reading only, limit the amount of text that may be recited, or permit handling of the text as long as the actual writing is not touched. The range of opinion regarding the presence of menstruating women in the mosque is similarly wide, include prohibition, permission to enter while avoiding the place of prayer, and permission to circulate anywhere. One argument for the last position, which is held by some conservatives as well as liberals, is that women must always be allowed to attend the mosque in order to learn about religion. Fatwas laying out all these positions can be seen in English on the web.

Some lesser authorities and local traditions (for instance in Africa and the Indian subcontinent) have formulated even more elaborate rules, perhaps under the influence of cultural traditions in which menstruation is taboo, or symbolic pollution: for instance, that women should not simply wash thoroughly but undergo a complicated purification at the end of their flow. Although the high tradition of Islam resists this tendency, beginning in the hadiths (see the statement from Aishah cited earlier), it is sometimes suggested that women may be disqualified for work and positions of responsibility because of physical and mental weakness caused by menstruation (these arguments may have been picked up from Western pseudo-science of the nineteenth and early twentieth centuries). It is worth noting that men are not the only ones to have negative feelings about menstruation. Questions submitted to religious authorities by women through online fatwa forums reveal great anxiety: Is it a violation if an unrelated male sees a woman's menstrual blood? Is it necessary to wash menstrual pads before disposing of them? The issue of menstruation illustrates how real-life religious discourse and practice is shaped by influences other than official texts.

A similar tension between recognition of women's spirituality and caution regarding the female body can be seen in the rule that women stand behind men in prayer. (One sometimes also sees men and women side by side with a cloth or other division down the middle.) It does not seem logical that the original purpose of having women stand directly behind men was to separate the sexes, since the arrangement does not accomplish that. Perhaps the women stood behind because this was how the tribe migrated or went to war; the emphasis in ritual law on forming straight and compact rows seems to suggest a military formation. Nevertheless, the reason very soon given by the tradition for the division was that it helped the participants avoid distracting sexual thoughts.

Some hadith traditions even asserted that women should perform their prayers at home and not attend the mosque at all, lest their presence stir up sexual thoughts (see, for example, **Abu Dawud**, *Salah*); here the theme of sexual distraction during prayer is used to limit space absolutely. A contrary hadith tradition continued to insist on the right of women to pray in the mosque (e.g., Bukhari, *Adhan*). Still other statements attempted to find a compromise, allowing women to go to the mosque, but only if absolutely unadorned and knowing that it is more meritorious to pray at home (Clarke, 2003). (The controversy centres on the Friday congregational prayers and two annual Eid festivals, since gathering together for prayer on these occasions is considered either highly recommended or obligatory.)

Disputes over where women should pray are much sharper than disputes over menstruation because there is more at stake. Division of space has been the great exclusionary principle of the Islamic tradition; mixing in the mosque, it seems, is a symbolic blow at that principle. Actual practice today varies. In some countries, women do go to the mosque, especially if it is not very grand and located near where they live; in others, it is firmly believed that women should not go to the mosque or women themselves prefer the privacy and convenience of praying at home. Women's attendance at mosques and participation in mosque activities such as study circles has increased in the last decades in some parts of the world, a development that has been welcomed not only by liberals, but also many conservatives. Space within the mosque, however, still tends to be segregated, and prayer in which men and women actually intermingle in the rows is very rare except among a small avant-garde in the West.

Rituals practised by Muslim women sometimes become established in separate space, where they may develop distinctive features. For instance, some minor Sufi and Shiite shrines have been colonized by women, who gather there for mutual support and appeal to the saint for their special concerns. The exorcism rituals loosely connected to popular Sufism practised in Upper Egypt and Sudan are conducted only by women. Women in Turkish villages celebrate the birthday of the Prophet differently than men, emphasizing the moment of the infant Muhammad's birth and the experience of his mother (Tapper, 1987). Shiite women in Northwest Pakistan undermine their clergy's characterization of females as frivolous and weak-minded by contributing substantially to the organization of ritual mourning ceremonies and vigorously chanting for hours on end (Hegland, 2003). Among the approximately 25 million Muslims of China, separate women's mosques, first developed in the late eighteenth century, not only give women a measure of collective strength and independence, but also serve as centres for religious and health education, sometimes under the guidance of ordained female ritual experts (Jaschok and Shui, 2000).

There has not, however, been any parallel in Islam to the movements in Judaism and some other traditions to revive or create rituals to express the concerns of women. This is because the tradition lays great stress on correct practice. "Correct" means established by the Sunnah of the Prophet and early community; anything not legitimated in this way is liable to be viewed as reprehensible *bid'ah* ("innovation"), the opposite of Sunnah. Women's ritual is also hobbled by a long-standing view, seen in classical literature and even the hadith (though not the Quran), that the female psyche makes it dangerous for women to engage in unsupervised activity. For example, women have been thought to be naturally superstitious, and prone to engage in un-Islamic practices. They should not visit graves, as that might become an outlet for frivolous dressing up and socializing (Lutfi, 1991). Even now, it is recommended that women not attend funerals, as their lack of emotional control might spoil the dignity of the occasion.

Women's Sexuality

This section begins by outlining some of the traditional rules of Shariah relating to marriage and divorce. Marriage is central to the regulation of woman's sexuality, since intimate relationships must take place exclusively within that legal framework. The rules described were formulated in the classical period of Islam and are no longer entirely in place in any Muslim state. Since family law is regarded as the heart of God's plan for society, however, Muslims have been reluctant to see it openly cancelled; thus almost all governments, including avowedly secular ones, have been obliged to ensure that their law codes can be justified in Islamic terms. Revival of family law is also central to the platform of Islamist groups. Where these groups succeed in gaining influence or power, traditional Shariah, or a certain understanding of it, suddenly becomes very relevant. Shariah is of concern even for some liberal Muslims and Muslims living as minorities in the West, who may try to extract religious ideals from the law to guide them in their lives and personal relations.

The basic structural characteristic of the traditional law of marriage and divorce is gender hierarchy. This is suggested in the verse (Quran 4:34) stating that men are "set over" women and that husbands have the right to discipline their wives in various ways, "unless they [again] obey you." Islamic law builds on this verse to make "obedience" a legal duty of a wife, who may lose her right to support if she disobeys; one example of disobedience according to the law is leaving the marital home without a husband's permission. The legal rule of hierarchy in marriage is not absolute, however. It is mitigated by regard for women as individuals with their own standing and rights: for instance, a wife may sue her husband for non-payment of maintenance if he has no legal right to withhold it. The Quran, hadiths, and books of law also contain many moral exhortations to men to behave fairly and equitably despite their greater legal power. Thus, although a man is allowed to withhold sex if a woman is "disobedient," one twelfth-century authority points out that sexual intercourse is a right shared between the spouses, and that both would be harmed if it were discontinued (Kasani 1989: II, 334). The husband has a legal right derived from Quran 4:34 to physically discipline his wife if she is disobedient; but a series of hadiths also says that the Prophet cautioned that this discipline should consist of a light blow "not causing pain" (e.g., Bukhari, Book of Marriage), and it is said that he himself set the best example by never hitting any person or even animal (reported in the hadith collection of Muslim, Book of Excellences).

A similar pattern of gender hierarchy balanced by regard for the rights of women is seen in the marriage contract. The contract has the wife grant the husband exclusive access to her person, while the husband undertakes to deliver an appropriate dower (**mahr**) to his wife and support her as long as the marriage lasts. The husband, for his part, is given considerable legal authority over his wife and has a legal right to enjoyment of any part of her body, with the exception of contact forbidden by the law, such as intercourse during menstruation. Thus she apparently cannot refuse him sex (this is a point that has become somewhat controversial in modern times). On the wife's side, the Quran (for example, 4:4) and law emphasize both the bride's right to her dower, which is entirely her own property, and the duty of the husband to properly support her.

This is the legal framework of the marriage relationship. But the Law also has a moral or ethical voice, heard—to give just one example—in the numerous hadiths that speak of the special virtue of caring for daughters and the rewards that such care earns (Bukhari, Book of Singular Conduct). The marriage contract is framed in a way that suggests an exchange of the woman's body for payment by the man; but the jurists emphasize that marriage is not a matter of buying and selling. Of course, marriage all over the world is partly an economic institution.

Gender hierarchy is also manifested in the law, which makes it difficult for a woman to escape her marriage, but allows a Muslim husband to divorce freely without having to give any reason. The law does, however, impose some modest rules on the husband's power to repudiate his wife. For example, a divorce does not become final until the wife has completed three menstrual periods (Quran 2:228): during this time she remains, fully supported, in the marital home. This rule is designed not only to forestall hasty divorce, but also to guarantee paternity in the event that the wife is pregnant. The man's obligation to pay his wife any dower still owing at the time of divorce can also act as a restraint, if the dower was large and payment can somehow be enforced. The Quran (4:35) suggests mediation between the couple before divorce, and although this was taken by all schools except the Malikis to be a moral recommendation rather than actual law, court-supervised mediation is now compulsory in some jurisdictions. Finally, there are moral constraints. Moral condemnation of divorce is very strong. The most famous of several hadiths on this subject says, "Of all things permitted, divorce is in the eyes of God the most detested" (collection of Abu Dawud, Book of Divorce). Husbands are urged to exercise their prerogative justly and kindly: "either retain them [your wives] with kindness, or dismiss them honourably" (Quran 65:2; also 2:231), "compensate them, and dismiss them in a becoming manner" (Quran 33:48).

Again, it is important to understand that these are traditional norms, and that knowledge of them varies greatly. A good number of Muslims in the West, for instance, have little awareness of Shariah and arrange their family affairs according to other principles they believe to be consistent with their faith. Though the spirit and basic patterns of traditional law still influence legislation in most modern Muslim-majority states, many features of the law governing marriage and divorce have been subject to legislative reform since the nineteenth century. Polygamy is one example. Polygamy is not widely practised in the Muslim world, and most Muslims now adhere to the view, advanced by the famous Egyptian reformer Muhammad Abduh in the late 1800s, that the Quran actually disapproves of multiple wives except in very restricted circumstances. Abduh based his interpretation on the Quran's emphasis on treating multiple wives equally, pointing out that while one verse (4:3) says, "If you fear that you shall not be able to deal equally with them, then [take] one only" another declares, "You will never be able to deal equally between women, no matter how much you wish to do so" (4:129). Nevertheless, the difficulty of forbidding what seems to be permitted by God has prevented an outright ban on polygamy. Most countries have resorted instead to rules that severely restrict it. One common rule is that the first wife must either give her consent or be granted a divorce; another is that the man must prove that he has a valid reason for taking a second wife and sufficient means to support both in separate households. Where polygamy is more common and not legally restrained, such as in some Persian Gulf countries, it has become a live issue for women's groups, who regard it as a social ill.

Women's grounds for divorce, which were limited in most classical schools to fundamental faults in the husband such as proven impotence and lengthy desertion, have also been subject to reform. Most countries now include grounds such as failure to support the family and serious abuse. However, the idea of women divorcing without having to prove grounds before a judge has met with determined resistance. An argument often made against allowing women to divorce more easily is that it would destabilize families and society, since women are more emotional than men and might rush to divorce without thinking. The real problem, of course, is that it would undermine the dominance of the husband and thus, ultimately, the male authority so essential to traditional views of gender.

Even so, it is not the legitimate exercise of Shariah that causes women the most trouble. Islamic law is fitted to a patriarchal society; but it is also concerned with setting limits and preserving the order and functioning of society. And Muslim law is actually quite attentive, within the limits of patriarchy, to women and their concerns. It is when patriarchy oversteps the limits of the law that the worst abuse occurs.

Quick divorce—effected by three declarations uttered in one instant—is one example. Quick divorce violates the explicit instruction of the Quran (65:1) to wait for some time before making a divorce final. But it seems to have forced its way into the law—where it is still described as *bid'ah*, "reprehensively innovative"—through practice. In other words, since men were instantaneously divorcing their wives regardless of the Islamic standard, the law was compelled to recognize it. Shiite law, however, has never allowed instantaneous divorce, and many Muslim countries have now banned it.

Nonpayment of *mahr* (dower) has also been a persistent problem. Although divorce is chiefly the prerogative of men, the Quran (2:229) and law do allow a woman to ask her husband for a divorce in exchange for giving up some or all of her dower. This negotiated divorce, called in Arabic *khul*, seems to have been designed to allow women to escape unhappy marriages, but it has been widely used by men to force women to give up their *mahr* and other divorce benefits in order to gain their freedom or custody of the children.

Here we enter the territory of the entire dissolution of law and legal norms. Threats against couples who marry against the wishes of their families and denial of the inheritance rights explicitly given to females by the Quran (see 4:11–12) are two such instances. Knowledgeable Muslims condemn such practices as un-Islamic; but where they are part of local custom, people may imagine them to be sanctioned by religion. The claim often made by Muslims that liberation begins with the reclamation of "Islamic rights" begins to seem quite credible.

The phenomenon of so-called honour killings belongs to this category of un-Islamic practice. It seems to have some connection with tribal society; it is found, for instance, among tribal populations in Jordan and the North West Frontier Province of Pakistan. Honour killing is sometimes used to cover up simple murder or rape. Honour violence must have been known among the pre-Islamic Arab tribes, as the Quran itself attempts to block it. For instance, the Quran demands that illicit sexual relations be established through an open and formal accusation, and the standard of proof is very high: four witnesses are required (Quran 4:15) instead of the usual two, and they must have seen the actual act of penetration. In addition, false accusation, which the Quran assumes to be directed against women, is to be punished by lashing of the accusers (24:4). The only way a husband can bring an accusation of adultery against his wife is by solemn oath, which she then refutes by her own oath (24:6–9), so that she is not punished, but only divorced.

The Quran recognizes the danger of random violence sparked by sexual defamation, and the likelihood that such violence will be directed at women. The Quranic principle of constraint on honour violence was strong enough that the jurists did not allow it to make inroads into Shariah. Thus many argue that honour killing is at odds with Muslim legal norms. Yet honour crimes are often not prosecuted, and in some Muslim-majority countries the penalty for them is very low. (The jurists did introduce the penalty of death by stoning for fornication committed by anyone, of either sex, who had ever been married, even though the Quran makes no mention of any death penalty.)

Failure to prosecute honour killing results from the belief that cherished social values ultimately depend on the good behaviour and therefore the discipline of women. Women are caught in a similar predicament by Shariah revivalism in places such as Iran and Somalia, where the Islamic regime and the al-Shabaab militia respectively use Shariah to legitimate their power. Shariah is effective for legitimation not only because it is often seen as equivalent to Islam itself, but also because many think it is the best way to secure social order—the bedrock of which is believed to be sexual morality. The "Islamic" regime or group then answers to the expectations it has raised by imposing a set of corporal punishments (hudud; said to have been fixed by God Himself). As the symbols and bearers of morality, women play a central role in this drama. Punishment for sexual crime is typically aimed almost exclusively at females. In the case of rape, this may be accomplished by considering the woman' s accusation or pregnancy to be evidence of fornication, while rapists are less likely to be convicted due to the requirement that four witnesses testify to having seen the actual penetration. All this is difficult to justify in Islamic law, and the result is exactly the victimization of women the Quran tries to forestall.

Although Muslims living in the West are not governed by Muslim law, many are affected indirectly by the memory of Shariah gender norms. Divorce continues to be an issue. Although many religiously conscientious men will release their wives as the Quran recommends and pay the *mahr* in addition to whatever support the state requires, some women do have trouble obtaining a religious divorce. Incidents of abuse, including honour killing, have also occurred.

Because gender is deeply embedded in social structures, it is not surprising that most debates concerning Islam in the West have to do with the status of women. Two examples can be seen in controversy over the use of Muslim family law for alternative dispute resolution in Great Britain and the Canadian province of Ontario. In each case, the controversy ultimately revolved around how advantageous (for the purpose of obtaining a divorce) or disadvantageous "Shariah tribunals" would be for women. Shariah arbitration was decisively excluded from the Ontario legal system in 2005, while the situation in Britain remains ambiguous. The focus on Muslim women in these and other debates is certainly heightened by the deep entanglement of Western discourse about Islam with gender. For many if not most non-Muslims today, mention of Islam evokes images of the oppression of women; indeed, such images have become *the* outstanding example of "third-world" women being used to confirm a Western self-image of progress and virtue. The Western preoccupation with Muslim women will be seen again in the next section in relation to veiling.

Conservatism, Backlash, and Social Change

Law reform and Shariah revivalism are important barometers of change in the Muslim world. This section will consider two other indications of the situation of Muslim women today. One is the very extensive modern literature devoted to establishing the ideal position of women in Islam. The other is the lived reality of Muslim women themselves.

Most modern literature on women in Islam, especially in non-Western languages, is conservative and apologetic. Conservative discourse usually dwells on the wisdom of Islam and Shariah as they are, highlighting favourable features such as a woman's right to own property and seeking to show how the patriarchal Shariah system provides for and protects her. "The Rights of Women in Islam" is a popular title in this kind of writing. Unfavourable features, such as women's lack of grounds for divorce, are either skirted or justified in terms of the welfare of family and society. This approach may be illustrated by conservative treatment of the controversial phrase from Quran 4:34 (quoted in full at the beginning of the chapter): "Men are set over women because God has favoured one over the other and because men maintain them with their wealth." The classical exegetes say that this means men should correct women's behaviour and "take them by the hand" (*Tafsir* of Tabari) in matters involving religious duties. Modern conservatives generally agree, although they often soften their statements by adding that men and women have equal spiritual potential. Outright misogyny is uncommon in current conservative discourse, since women themselves are part of the audience for writings about Islam and woman-friendliness has become an important element in the self-presentation of all religions.

Liberal discourse on women and Islam has undergone a change in the last few decades. Many early feminists—such as Huda Sha'arawi of the Egyptian Feminist Union in the early twentieth century—believed that the path to progress for Muslim women lay in following the example of their Western sisters, including casting off the veil. This idea is now outmoded. Most Muslim women today want to find a path forward that preserves values they feel to be characteristically Islamic, such as the centrality of the family and male–female harmony. This approach tends to rule out the radical and secular theories of Western feminism. (In fact, female Muslim activists are usually reluctant to call themselves "feminists" because they feel that the term connotes an aggressive Western approach.) Most Muslim women do not favour gay rights, although there is a growing movement among gay Muslims of both sexes to find a place for themselves in Islam. The more modest and cautious project of the majority of Muslim liberals is to promote understandings of Islamic scriptures and history that undermine gender hierarchy and bring women into the public space.

The liberal argument against gender hierarchy is based on the premise that the spiritual equality believed to be established by God in the Quran also implies social equality. Proof verses for spiritual equality include Quran 4:124, 33:35, 49:13, and 3:195. The last verse reads: "Never shall I allow the deed of any of you, whether male or female, to be lost"; whereas "deed" (*amal*) is taken by the classical exegetes to mean religious deeds, some liberals interpret it as referring to the equal worth of men's and women's work and daily activities. The few problematic verses that clearly confer social privileges on men (in addition to Quran 4:34, quoted above, see 2:228, 2:282, 4:3, and 4:11) are explained in various ways: for instance, by asserting that they were directed to a male-dominated society that no longer exists, whereas the basic Quranic principle of equality was meant to endure. Thus Amina Wadud concludes that the "setting over" referred to in Quran 4:34 actually signifies men's responsibility to care for women, this being the counterpart of women's responsibility to bear children (1999: 73–4).

To demonstrate that women should share public space and play an active role in society, liberals cite examples from history. Emphasizing the roles that women played in establishing Islam, they argue that women's participation in politics and learning shows that many of them were independent and possessed of rights, despite the overall decline in women's status they believe took place after the time of the Prophet. Cases from the classical period in which women financed trading activities and endowed charitable foundations are highlighted, and court records showing that they sued for their rights in divorce and inheritance are given as evidence that the legal system was flexible in practice and that the traditional legal texts should not be taken literally, as some conservatives do. Muslim society, liberals insist, should search for and build on these positive precedents.

The idea of Muslim women moving freely in public space and participating fully in society raises the question of the hijab. Some liberal Muslims argue that the verses of the Quran usually taken as requiring women to veil were actually meant only to prescribe modesty, not a particular type of dress or head-covering. They also point out that modesty applies to men as well as women, since Quran 24:30–31 first tells men that they should "lower their gaze and guard their private parts" before addressing the same command to women. Although liberals used to regard the veil as a sign of oppression and its removal as a sign of liberation, most now focus on the issue of free choice and say that Muslim women should be able to choose whether or not to veil, as they see fit. This change in focus has been prompted by the fact that many Muslim woman, including those living in the West, freely choose to wear hijab, whether as a sign of their own personal devotion to Islam, a proud announcement of their Muslim identity, or because they feel it liberates them from the male gaze and gives them freedom to move, properly covered and respected, in any space.

Conservatives, by contrast, argue that the Quran makes veiling compulsory, since 24:31 says that women should "not display their beauty" and should "draw their clothing over their bosoms," while 33:59 commands them to "bring down over themselves part of their garments." The meaning of these verses, conservatives say, is clear, and is confirmed by hadiths as well as the long-standing consensus of the community. Although today *hijab* generally means a headscarf or veil, the Arabic word also means "screen" or "partition," and in classical sources it refers to the seclusion of women in the home. Many conservatives continue to adhere to this meaning and insist that women must keep their bodies out of sight to keep sexual energy under control and preserve social order. There is a great difference between hijab as a freely chosen mode of dress and hijab as a mode of confinement and social control. When listening to intra-Muslim debates about hijab, therefore, it is important to know which sense is in question.

Western perceptions of Muslim women's dress add further layers of meanings to hijab. Westerners who believe the treatment of the female body in their own culture to be an un-conflicted sign of women's freedom tend to see veiling as an unmistakable sign of Muslim women's inferior status. Presentation of the female body thus serves to encapsulate a supposed civilizational divide in gender ideals, with the long, loose robe and niqab (face covering) suggesting the greatest difference and incompatibility of values. This is the basic impulse behind anti-hijab and -niqab measures introduced or proposed in some European countries, as well as in the province of Quebec in Canada.

The Western preoccupation with the supposed oppression of Muslim women has tended to obscure the fact that the overall trend in the Muslim world today is actually towards gradual but steady progress led by Muslim women themselves. The first thing to notice is the impact of the incremental social changes that have come about as a result of increased urbanization and demographic shifts toward younger populations. There has been a steady rise in literacy rates for women in most Muslim countries in the last few decades. For example, according to UNESCO figures published in 2012, Indonesia and Iran are projected to reach gender parity by 2015, and substantial increases in overall literacy rates in Egypt, Yemen, and Pakistan are due largely to female education. In some Muslim countries, women outnumber men in higher education (UNESCO, 2012). Of course, to make this picture really meaningful, information is needed about the reasons women are pursuing higher education, the fields they enter, and career opportunities after college. Muslim women also continue to form philanthropic and activist organizations to aid their sisters and articulate women's concerns. The anti-Taliban Revolutionary Association of the Women of Afghanistan, the International Network for the Rights of Female Victims of Violence in Pakistan, Malaysia-based Sisters in Islam, and, in America, the association of Muslim woman lawyers for human rights known as Karamah ("Dignity") are but a few of hundreds such organizations around the globe. The vigorous activity of Muslim women on their own behalf is not often acknowledged in the West, where the preferred media image is that of the helpless victim in need of rescue.

The task for the future, at least from a liberal point of view, is to help the tradition catch up with these realities. The facts of education, state law reform and political participation are well ahead of establishment religious thought, despite the efforts of a few innovative clerics. Obstacles to progress are very basic. The fact that women have limited formal religious authority makes it difficult to have their views heard, let alone accepted. Gender hierarchy continues to be affirmed as an ideal, even if in the more moderate form of a complementarianism similar to that seen in conservative Christian movements. Male privilege in personal and social relations and the universal rule of patriarchy

University students in Mardin, Turkey.

enshrined in traditional Islamic law are rarely questioned, and conservative authorities continue to promote ideas about female sexuality and psychology that justify surveillance of women's space and behaviour. Religious discussions of women rarely address real problems such as violence, focusing instead on idealized images of harmony between husband and wife. None of this is unique to Islam, of course. Most institutionalized religions are slow to respond to change; indeed, most resist it.

Issues related to women in the Muslim tradition are also closely bound to politics. Again, this is not unique to Islam: the status of women has a political dimension everywhere on the globe. Still, the link between gender and politics has become particularly conspicuous in Muslim contexts since the rise of Islamism. Thus, backlash can occur as rulers try to placate the religious establishment and religious parties look for support. A leading example is Saudi Arabia, where the royal family is tied to the conservative clerics of the Wahhabi sect. Motivated by a desire to modernize the Kingdom, as well as a growing women's movement, the Saudi authorities show signs of wanting to loosen strictures on women; but their Wahhabi power base is reluctant even to allow women to drive (see Kéchichian, 2013: 43–53, 274). In Pakistan, right-wing religious parties are able to gain influence through the shifting coalitions that characterize Pakistani politics. Among those parties is the Jamaat-e Islami, founded by the Abu al-Ala Mawdudi quoted earlier. The Jamaat staunchly opposed the "Women's Protection Bill" passed in 2006 that made it easier to prosecute rape by removing it from the purview of Shariah (see Mehdi, 2010).

In 2014, the situation of women in countries that experienced Arab Spring revolutions remains fluid. The revolutions have opened space for organizations with conservative views on women, such as the Muslim Brotherhoods of Egypt and Syria, while also giving political opportunities to the smaller but more radical and puritanical Islamist or "Salafi" factions. All these groups consider control of women and restoration of traditional male–female relations central to the establishment of an authentically Islamic society. Society is to be corrected at the most fundamental level by being re-genderized. Islamists are sometimes, however, faced with different views from women. To take one instance, the announcement in 2011 by Chairman of the Libyan National Transitional Council Mustafa Abdul-Jalil that laws restraining polygamy would be repealed because they were "contrary to Shariah" was widely reported to have made women apprehensive (Nossiter, 2011). This is not to say that all Arab Muslim women oppose religiously coloured government or society. Many support it, as seen in a strong vote for Islamic parties; but their vision of Islam and understanding of their place within it does not always match that of the Islamists. Comments made by conservative political figures in Egypt about the rising incidence of rape throw stark light on basically different assumptions. Though women turned out in public squares to support the revolution and some also then demonstrated in favour of Islamic groups, the rapes were blamed by Salafists as well as some elements in the Brotherhood on women lacking "shame" and "femininity" going out to "stand among men" (El Sheikh and Kirkpatrick, 2013). It seems that religiously committed Egyptian Muslim women believed they had the right to move in public space, especially if veiled, and were not fully aware of different views held by the rising powers and strict rules of the traditional legal texts that back them up.

The course of the Arab Spring recalls events in Iran in the late 1970s. In the months leading up to the 1979 Revolution, tens of thousands of women draped in black chadors poured into the streets to call for the overthrow of the Shah. Once the Islamic regime was installed, it set about restoring traditional Shariah norms by repealing the "Family Protection" legislation that had limited polygamy, given women more equal rights in divorce, and raised the age of marriage. Women were compelled to completely cover their bodies and hair. It became clear that the conservative clerics were committed to establishing what they envisioned as an ideal Islamic society, with separate spheres and roles for women and men. Yet this ambitious project was at odds with the realities of a modern society in which women were widely engaged in work outside the home, many were educated, and public space, especially in large cities, was clearly mixed. Nor did it accord with the views on women of the philosopher of the Revolution, Ayatollah Mutahhari, who had done much to attract women to the cause. Many ordinary women were "astonished" and "incredulous" (Mir-Hosseini, 2006: 635) at measures that included a preference for fathers in child custody disputes and a provision that made the monetary compensation payable to the family of a murdered female half the amount payable for a murdered male.

Disappointment at these post-revolutionary developments was the catalyst for a rival Islamic discourse of woman's rights in Iran. Islamic feminism, as it is sometimes called by outside observers, is committed to the idea that gender justice can be delivered by transforming the tradition from within. The achievements of the Iranian movement include turning conversations about women in more critical and positive directions (Mir-Hosseini, 1999) and contributing to reformed laws, such as legislation placing limits on men's traditionally free right to divorce and a moratorium on execution by stoning for extra-marital sex.

The very forces that would deny women rights in the name of Islam are impelling women across the Muslim world to exchange interpretations and strategies, resulting in something like an Islamic "global feminism." One example can be seen in the activities of Musawah, an organization based in Malaysia that describes itself as a "global movement for equality and justice in the Muslim family" embracing "activists, scholars, legal practitioners, policy makers and grassroots women and men" from around the world. Advocates of a global Muslim women's movement argue that speaking the language of Islam and drawing on the positive resources of the tradition can be more effective than seeking secular reform, since it would take into account Muslim women's deep commitment to their religion. If this is the path Muslim women will take, it is a challenging one. Iran is often cited as a leading example of change being brought about through Islam; but the stoning penalty is again part of Iranian law, and some gender quotas have been re-imposed in higher education with the aim of keeping females out of traditionally male-dominated fields and preventing women from becoming more educated than men (Shahrokni and Dokouhaki, 2012). On the other hand, Iranian women's persistence has contributed to some re-thinking of traditional laws and norms not only by a number of political figures, but also by some religious authorities (Mir-Hosseini 2002). Discourse has shifted even in the ranks of the Pakistani Jamaat, so that the party that once stood for strict veiling and confinement now includes voices that encourage women to take up active roles outside the home and even practise some professions (Ahmad, 2008). Nevertheless, it will be decades before the success of the new Muslim women's movement can be assessed.

Glossary

Abu Dawud   One of the six canonical books of hadith for the Sunnites.

bid'ah   "Reprehensible innovation," illicit because it does not conform to *sunnah*, the accepted practice of the Prophet and early community.

Bukhari   One of the six canonical books of hadith for the Sunnites.

caliphs   Islamic rulers with special religious prestige; for instance, the four caliphs (Abu Bakr, Umar, Uthman, Ali) who ruled immediately after Muhammad.

fatwa   Advice or a ruling given in response to a question about Islamic law.

hadith   An anecdotal report of the sayings and exemplary action of the Prophet, or the early Muslim community, that is considered authoritative. Collectively, the hadith constitute the second body of Islamic scripture, after the Quran.

hajj   Pilgrimage to Mecca; one of the five pillars of Islam.

Hijrah   The migration of the Prophet Muhammad and his first followers from his birthplace, Makkah, to found an Islamic community in Madinah.

Ibn Majah   One of the six canonical books of hadith for the Sunnites.

Isma'ilis   A branch of Shiite Islam that includes the followers of the Aga Khan.

Jahiliyah   "Time of Ignorance" or "Time of Unrestraint"; a Muslim term for Arab culture before the rise of Islam.

mahr   Dower; an amount of wealth due to a bride from her husband.

Muslim   A follower of Islam; one of the six canonical books of hadith of the Sunnites.

Ramadan   The month-long fast that is one of the five pillars of Islam; the timing of Ramadan varies because it follows the lunar calendar.

shahadah   The declaration that "There is no god but God and Muhammad is His Messenger"; one of the five pillars of Islam.

Shariah   Muslim law, meaning literally "path."

Shiites   The smaller of the two main divisions in Islam, the other being the Sunnites. The Shiites have distinctive ideas about religious and political authority, theology, and law.

sunnah   "Accepted custom"; the ideal pattern of the life of Muhammad and the early community. The *sunnah* is largely derived from hadiths.

Sunnites   The largest division of Islam. The largest minority group is the Shiites.

tafsir   Arabic, "Quranic exegesis."

Further Reading

Ahmed, Leila. 2011. *A Quiet Revolution: The Veil's Resurgence, from the Middle East to America*. New Haven: Yale University Press.

Ali, Kecia. *Sexual Ethics and Islam: Feminist Reflections on Qur'an, Hadith, and Jurisprudence*. Oxford, UK: Oneworld, 2006.

Awde, Nicholas, trans. and ed. *Women in Islam: An Anthology from the Qurān and Ḥadīths*. Revised and expanded ed. London: Bennett & Bloom, 2005.

El-Azhary Sonbol, Amira, ed. *Beyond the Exotic: Women's Histories in Islamic Societies*. Syracuse, NY: Syracuse University Press, 2005

Badran, Margot. *Feminism in Islam: Secular and Religious Convergences*. Oxford: Oneworld, 2009.

Encyclopedia of Women and Islamic Cultures. 6 vols. Leiden: Brill, 2003–7.

Haddad, Yvonne Yazbek, and John L. Esposito, eds. *Daughters of Abraham: Feminist Thought in Judaism, Christianity, and Islam*. Gainesville: University Press of Florida, 2001.

Mahmood, Saba. *Politics of Piety: The Islamic Revival and the Feminist Subject*. 2d ed. Princeton, N.J.; Oxford: Princeton University Press, 2012.

Piela, Anna. *Muslim Women Online: Faith and Identity in Virtual Space*. Abingdon, Oxon; New York: Routledge, 2012.

Shehadeh, Lamia Rustum. *The Idea of Women in Fundamentalist Islam*. Gainesville: University Press of Florida, 2003.

Films and Online Resources

Children of Srikandi. 73 mins. Directed by the Children of Srikandi Collective. Srikandi Films/ Celestefilms, 2012. Billed as "the first film by queer women about queer women from Indonesia."

International Network for the Rights of Female Victims of Violence in Pakistan: http://ecumene.org/INRFVVP/index.htm.

Karamah ("Dignity"): www.karamah.org.

The Light in Her Eyes. 87 mins. Directed by Julia Meltzer and Laura Nix. Cinemaguild, 2011. Filmed in Damascus on the eve of the Syrian uprising, depicts a Quran school for girls founded by a female preacher.

Me and the Mosque. 52 mins. Directed by Zarqa Nawaz. National Film Board of Canada, 2005. A Canadian Muslim journalist travels across Canada to investigate women's place in mosques.

Musawah: www.musawah.org/about-musawah.

Muslim: Behind the Veil. A growing series of films examining women's issues in locations ranging from Afghanistan to North America. Further information on this series from 'Women Make Movies' at www.wmm.com/filmCatalog/collect9.shtml; the WMM list also includes material on women in other religious traditions.

Religions of the Book: Women Serving Religion. 29 mins. Produced by Michael J. Doyle. Films for the Humanities and Sciences, 1991. Jewish, Christian, and Muslim women discuss the position of women in their religious traditions.

Revolutionary Association of the Women of Afghanistan: www.rawa.org

Shifting Prophecy. Directed by Merajur Rahman Baruah. 30 min. Public Service Broadcasting Trust, 2007. A group of women in Tamil Nadu attempt to challenge the local male-dominated elder's council and create their own space for worship.

Sisters in Islam: www.sistersinislam.org.my

Sisters in Islamic Banking: Female CEOs and Sharia-Compliant Finance. 50 min. Directed by Suchen Tan. VPRO Television, 2011. Focuses on women heading banks in Malaysia that specialize in adhering to Islamic law.

Veiled Voices. 59 mins. Directed by Brigid Maher. Typecast Releasing, 2009. Presents the profiles of three female Islamic leaders in Syria, Lebanon, and Egypt.

Women of Islam: Veiling and Seclusion. 51 mins. Directed by Farheen Umar. Pasha Productions, 2004. A worldwide view of veiling that attempts to de-exoticize Muslim women; presents veiling as a matter of choice.

Women of the Holy Kingdom. 42 mins. Directed by Sharmeen Obaid. Sharmeen Obeid Films, 2005. Conversations with Saudi women reveal both advances and continuing problems.

References

Abbott, Nabia. 1942. "Women and the State in Early Islam." *Journal of Near Eastern Studies* I, I: 106–126.

———. 1946. *Two Queens of Baghdad.* Chicago: University of Chicago Press.

Abou-Bakr, Omaima. 2003. "Teaching The Words of the Prophet: Women Instructors of the Hadith (Fourteenth and Fifteenth Centuries)." *Hawwa: Journal of Women of the Middle East and Islamic World*, Vol. I Issue iii: 306–328.

Abyad, Malakah. 1981. *Culture et éducation arabo-islamiques au Shām pendant les trois premiers siècles de l'islam.* Damascus: Institut français de Damas.

Ahmad, Irfan. 2008. "Cracks in the 'Mightiest Fortress': Jamaat-e-Islami's Changing Discourse on Women." *Modern Asian Studies* 42, 2/3 (Mar.–May): 549–75.

Ahmed, Leila. 1992. *Women and Gender in Islam: Historical Roots of a Modern Debate.* New Haven, CT: Yale University Press.

Attar, Farid al-Din. 1966. *Muslim Saints and Mystics.* Translated by A.J. Arberry. Chicago: University of Chicago Press.

Bakhtiar, Laleh, trans. 2007. *The Sublime Quran.* Chicago: Kazi Publications.

Barlas, Asma. 2002. *"Believing Women" in Islam. Unreading Patriarchal Interpretations of the Quran.* Austin: University of Texas Press.

Bauer, Karen. 2010. "Debates on Women's Status as Judges and Witnesses in Post-Formative Islamic Law." *Journal Of The American Oriental Society* 130, no. 1: 1–21.

Berkey, Jonathan P. 1991. "Women and Islamic Education in the Mamluk Period." Pp. 143–57 in Nikki R. Keddie and Beth Baron, eds. *Women in Middle Eastern History: Shifting Boundaries in Sex and Gender.* New Haven, CT: Yale University Press.

Chodkiewicz, Michel. 1993. *An Ocean Without Shore: Ibn 'Arabî, the Book, and the Law.* Albany, N.Y.: State University of New York Press.

Clarke, L. 2003. "Hijáb According to the Hadith: Text and Interpretation." Pp. 214–86 in Sajida Sultana Alvi, Homa Hoodfar, and Sheila McDonough, eds. *The Muslim Veil in North America: Issues and Debates.* Toronto: Women's Press.

Coleman, Isobel. 2013. "Channeling Khadijah." Chapter in *Paradise Beneath Her Feet: How Women Are Transforming the Middle East.* 2d ed. New York: Random House.

Cooke, M. 1995. "Ayyám min hayátí: The Prison Memoirs of a Muslim Sister." *Journal of Arabic Literature* 26, 1–2: 147–64.

Deeb, Lara Z. 2005. "From Mourning to Activism: Sayyedeh Zaynab, Lebanese Shi'i Women, and the Transformation of Ashura." Pp. 241–66 in *The Women of Karbala: Ritual Performance and Symbolic Discourses in Modern Shi'i Islam*, ed. Kamran Scot Aghaie. Austin: University of Texas Press.

Fadlallah, Ayatollah Muhammad Husayn. 2000. *al-Zahra' al-qudwah.* Edited by Husayn Ahmad al-Khashin. Beirut: Dar al-Malak.

Geissinger, Aisha. 2011. "'A'isha bint Abi Bakr and her Contributions to the Formation of the Islamic Tradition." *Religion Compass* 5, 1 (January): 37–49.

al-Ghazali al-Jubayli, Zaynab. [1414] 1994. *Nazarat fi Kitab Allah*. Vol. 1. Cairo: Dar al-Shuruq.

Hassan, Mona. 2012. "Reshaping Religious Authority in Contemporary Turkey: State-Sponsored Female Preachers." Pp. 85–103 in Masooda Bano and Hilary Kalmbach, eds. *Women, Leadership and Mosques: Changes in Contemporary Islamic Authority.* Leiden; Boston: Brill.

Hegland, Mary Elaine. 2003. "Shia Women's Rituals in Northwest Pakistan: The Shortcomings and Significance of Resistance." *Anthropological Quarterly* 76, no. 3 (Summer): 411–42.

Hill, Joseph. 2010. "'All Women are Guides': Sufi Leadership and Womanhood among Taalibe Baay in Senegal." *Journal of Religion in Africa* 40: 375–412.

Hoffman, Valerie J. 1995. *Sufism, Mystics, and Saints in Modern Egypt.* Columbia: University of South Carolina Press.

Ibn Hisham. 1955. *The Life of Muhammad.* Translated by A. Guillaume. Lahore, Pakistan: Oxford University Press.

Jaschok, Maria, and Jingjun Shui. 2000. *The History of Women's Mosques in Chinese Islam: A Mosque of Their Own.* Richmond, UK: Curzon.

Kasani. [1409] 1989. *Bada'i al-sana'i.* 7 vols. Pakistan.

Kashani-Sabet, Firoozeh. 2005. "Who Is Fatima? Gender, Culture, and Representation in Islam." *Journal of Middle East Women's Studies* 1, 2 (Spring): 1–24.

Kéchichian, Joseph A. 2013. *Legal and political reforms in Sa'udi Arabia.* Milton Park, Abingdon, Oxon; New York: Routledge.

Khalaf Allah, Muhammad. 1977. *Dirasat fi al-nuzum wa-al-tashri'at al-Islamiyah.* Cairo: Maktabat al-Anjlu al-Misriyah.

Lutfi, Huda. 1991. "Manners and Customs of Fourteenth-Century Cairene Women: Female Anarchy versus Male Shar'i Order in Muslim Prescriptive Treatises." Pp. 103–15 in Nikki R. Keddie and Beth Baron, eds. *Women in Middle Eastern History: Shifting Boundaries in Sex and Gender.* New Haven, CT: Yale University Press.

Mawdudi, Abu al-Ala. [1935] 1991. *Purdah and the Status of Women in Islam.* Chicago: Kazi Publications.

Mazuz, Haggai. 2012. "Menstruation and Differentiation: How Muslims Differentiated Themselves from Jews regarding the Laws of Menstruation." *Der Islam* 87, 1–2: 204–223.

Mehdi, Rubya. 2010. "The Protection of Women (Criminal Laws Amendment) Act, 2006 in Pakistan." *Droit et cultures* 59, 1: 191–206.

Mir-Hosseini, Ziba. 1999. *Islam and Gender: The Religious Debate in Contemporary Iran.* Princeton, N.J.: Princeton University Press.

———. 2002. "The Conservative–Reformist Conflict Over Women's Rights in Iran." *International Journal of Politics, Culture and Society* 16, 1 (Fall): 37–53.

———. 2006. "Muslim Women's Quest for Equality: Between Islamic Law and Feminism." *Critical Enquiry* 32 (Summer): 629–45.

Murata, Sachiko. 1992. *The Tao of Islam: A Sourcebook on Gender Relations in Islamic Thought.* Albany: State University of New York Press.

Nossiter, Adam. 2011. "Hinting at an End to a Curb on Polygamy, Interim Libyan Leader Stirs Anger." *New York Times.* 30 Oct. www.nytimes.com.

Roded, Ruth. 1994. *Women in Islamic Biographical Collections: From Ibn Sa'd to Who's Who.* Boulder, CO: Lynne Reinner.

Sayeed, Asma. 2009. "Gender and Legal Authority: An Examination of Early Juristic Opposition to Women's Hadith Transmission." *Islamic Law and Society*, Vol. 16, Issue ii: 115–50.

Schimmel, Annemarie. 1997. *My Soul Is a Woman.* Translated by Susan H. Ray. New York: Continuum.

Shahrokni, Nazanin, and Parastou Dokouhaki. 2012. "A Separation at Iranian Universities." *Middle East Research and Information Project* Published online 18 October. www.merip.org/mero/mero101812.

Shariati, Ali. 1981. *Fatima Is Fatima.* Translated by Laleh Bakhtiar. Tehran: Shariati Foundation.

El Sheikh, Mayy, and David D. Kirkpatrick. 2013. "Rise in Sexual Assaults in Egypt

Sets Off Clash Over Blame." *New York Times*. 26 March. www.nytimes.com.

Stowasser, B. 2001. "Old Shaykhs, Young Women, and the Internet: The Rewriting of Women's Political Rights in Islam." *The Muslim World* 91: 99–120.

Tapper, Nancy, and Richard Tapper. 1987. "The Birth of the Prophet: Ritual and Gender in Turkish Islam." *Man*, New Series, 22, 1 (March): 69–92.

UNESCO. 2012. *Education For All Global Monitoring Report*. Online at http://unesdoc.unesco.org/images/0014/001489/148972e.pdf.

Van Doorn-Harder, Pieternella. 2006. *Women Shaping Islam: Indonesian Women Reading the Qur'an*. Urbana: University of Illinois Press.

Wadud, Amina. 1999. *Quran and Woman: Rereading the Sacred Text from a Woman's Perspective*. [2nd ed.] New York: Oxford University Press.

——. 2006. *Inside the Gender Jihad: Women's Reform in Islam*. Oxford: Oneworld.

CHAPTER 8

Women in Sikhism

Doris R. Jakobsh

At the Golden Temple.

Doris Jakobsh

Nikky-Guninder Kaur Singh

5 May 2009

Today was the final class for our seminar on Sikhism at Colby College. My students were scheduled to make their presentations. As I was walking toward my class, I heard Guru Nanak's morning hymn melodiously resounding in the corridor and found my students respectfully listening to it. It was a real jolt to my system. My deep unconscious associates these sounds with sacred moments at my home and in gurdwaras back in the Punjab—not in the academic corridors in central Maine, where I am probably the only Sikh resident. With this Sikh sacred music as a prelude, my students went on to make impressive scholarly presentations on different aspects of Sikh tradition. With their comparative insights and nuanced explorations, the "forgotten tradition" becomes a vital part of mainstream curriculum.

The day is over but those melodies still linger on, integrating the personal and professional aspects of my life. I grew up in a Sikh home in the Punjab, where I attended a convent school and had Hindu, Jain, and Christian friends. Sikhism, of course, was as natural for me as breathing and eating. Later, however, when I came to the USA to attend a girls' prep school, I was the only "foreigner." I was frequently asked about my religion and culture. My southern friends wondered why I could not have my hair short. As a Sikh woman I could not cut my hair, so one of them offered to singe it for me! It was at Stuart Hall that I started to wear salwar kameez for evening dinners, and became curious about my own faith. That curiosity accompanied me to Wellesley College—an intellectual paradise for me. I also met my host family, the O'Neils, who have been my lifelong friends. At Wellesley I started an in-depth study of Sikh scripture, and have been pursuing it ever since.

So at Colby I am back to the liberal arts environment that I loved as an undergraduate. Here I have the opportunity to share my literary heritage with my students and to learn from them. The personal and the academic come together harmoniously. Their questions prompt me to enter new areas of research, which I can then share with the academy and my Sikh community across the continents. Over the years I have been reading, interpreting, and translating Sikh sacred text from my own feminist perspective. Each time I analyze a verse I first heard from the lips of my mother, the distance between East and West is bridged and the past becomes magically alive. The singular Divine at the root of Sikhism is an opening for new encounters: it promotes embracing friends from different religions and being with them at a profoundly human level. A walk in the shimmering snows of Maine with my husband and daughter brings home Guru Nanak's quintessential experience: *"Waheguru!"* Being a Sikh woman is living life to its fullest—enjoying the wonder in all aspects of daily life. Ultimately,

> *hasandia khelandia painandia khavandia*
> *vice hovai mukat* (Guru Granth 522)
> While laughing, playing, dressing up, and eating,
> We attain liberation.

Nikky-Guninder Kaur Singh is the Crawford Family Professor of Religion at Colby College in Maine, USA. She has written extensively on women in Sikhism.

Introduction and Overview

Sikhism is one of the youngest of the world religions, but in terms of the numbers of its adherents the tradition has gained increasing importance as the fifth-largest religion worldwide, with about 23 million followers. As a largely regional tradition, with the majority of adherents residing in Punjab, in the northwest of India, Sikhism has often been neglected in the study of religions. However, Sikhs are also true citizens of the world as a result of extensive migration patterns that have made their presence known in virtually all parts of the globe.

The state of Punjab is where the first Guru of the Sikhs, Guru Nanak (1469–1539), was born. Nine other Gurus followed, until the living Guru lineage ended with the death of the tenth master, Guru Gobind Singh, in 1708. Guru Gobind Singh, before his death, bestowed ultimate authority on the sacred writings of the Sikhs, the **Adi Granth** (literally, "first book"). Sikh sacred scripture is understood as the actual embodiment of the Sikh Gurus and is thus regarded as the eternal Guru. From a confessional standpoint, Sikhs refer to their scriptures as the Guru Granth Sahib. Both terms, Adi Granth and Guru Granth Sahib, will be used throughout this chapter.

As an area of study, Sikhism offers a rich developmental history and unique rituals and devotional approaches to the Divine. Sikhism is also a heterogeneous tradition. While for mainstream Sikhs, ultimate authority rests with the eleventh Guru, the Guru Granth Sahib, sectarian groups such as the Namdhari and Nirankari Sikhs also follow their own lineages of living Gurus. Other Sikh organizations, such as the Akhand Kirtani Jatha, offer variants of the Sikh code of conduct, identity markers, and styles of devotional singing. While detail regarding all the varieties of Sikhs is beyond the scope of this chapter, it is important to understand that there are varied ways of "being Sikh."

Sikhs often proclaim their tradition to be uniquely egalitarian with regard to the status and role of women, based on a number of central references to women in Sikh scripture. In particular, the following verse from the Adi Granth is often heralded as unequivocally laying down the foundation to women's full equality in Sikhism:

> From woman, man is born; within woman, man is conceived; to woman he is engaged and married. Woman becomes his friend; through woman, the future generations come. When his woman dies, he seeks another woman; to woman he is bound. So why call her bad? From her kings are born. From woman, woman is born; without woman, there would be no one at all. O Nanak, only the True Lord is without a woman (AG 473).

Clearly, this and other scriptural references must indeed be upheld as breaking down boundaries that barred women from attaining liberation, especially with regard to women's bodies and notions of pollution. However, a gendered analysis of Sikhism offers a far more nuanced and complex understanding of Sikh women's religious roles and of their ritual inclusion and exclusion based on gender alongside attitudes that may liberate, and in other cases devalue, Sikh women.

Texts and Interpretations

The Adi Granth / Guru Granth Sahib

The Adi Granth is a voluminous body of work that contains the collected writings of six of the Sikh Gurus as well as compositions by other poet-saints, both Muslim and Hindu. It is highly organized and systematic, beginning with the hymns of the Sikh Gurus and ending with the compositions of the additional poet-saints. Numerous names for the Divine, the most predominant being **Akal Purakh** (Eternal Being), Parmeshur (Ultimate Reality), and Karta Purakh

(Creator), can be found throughout its 1,430 pages. Other names correspond to predominant Hindu beliefs (Rama and Hari, among others) and Muslim understandings (Allah and Khuda). According to Guru Nanak, no one name or character of the Divine, in and of itself, could be sufficient to fully capture that divine essence that is beyond all names, all words, all conceptions.

Sikhs refer to their scripture as the Guru Granth Sahib or Sri Guru Granth Sahib, for they understand it to be much more than a mere book. It is the actual abode of the Gurus in that it is the repository of the revealed thoughts of Akal Purakh that were put into textual, material form by their Sikh masters. As such, the text itself is understood as the eternal and living Guru of the Sikhs. The notion of Guru Granth Sahib then can be understood as a confessional statement. The Adi Granth is unique among the scriptures of the major world religions in that, for the most part, it is a collection of hymns intended to be sung rather than texts to be read quietly or recited. It is not a series of stories, parables, historical accounts of the Gurus, their wives or children, or philosophical statements; nor is it a set of ethical precepts or arguments. Indeed, music is integral to its very essence. These are hymns of praise to Akal Purakh, and in singing them, devotees are believed to be brought into a mystical union with the divine.

Importantly, the Gurus did not restrict their conceptions of Akal Purakh to masculine terms. Both male and female metaphors were used, reflecting a personal, loving relationship of the Divine. Akal Purakh is like a father, like a mother, like a kinsman, like a brother. At the core of Sikh theological underpinnings, based on Sikh sacred scripture, is an understanding that the Ultimate Being as formless One (*nirguna*) is inherent in all forms of being (*saguna*) yet remains transcendent (N.G.K. Singh, 1995: 2). Thus the Sikh mystical journey is grounded in the everyday workings of the world, for the Divine is to be found everywhere, in every being, in every aspect of creation. Above all, the Adi Granth is a collection of hymns praising the Divine and communicating a message of spiritual liberation for all, through loving devotion to God and the practical meditative techniques taught by the Gurus.

Scholar Nikky-Guninder Kaur Singh has done the most substantial work in uncovering feminine elements in the Guru Granth Sahib. She insists that while the sublime message of the Guru Granth Sahib underscores egalitarian principles, its interpreters and translators have skewed that foundational understanding in androcentric directions. Generally, Ultimate Reality is presented as male (N.G.K. Singh, 1993: 243–4). Singh's groundbreaking exegesis of Sikh scripture has offered new possibilities for highlighting the feminine in Sikh understandings of Ultimate Reality. Nonetheless, the central image offered by the Gurus with regard to the relationship between humanity and the Divine, the marital union between husband and wife, offers important gendered insights into the persistence of masculine imagery. For in the mystical language of striving for union with the Divine in conjugal bliss, true devotees of God are presented as brides to be enjoyed by the Divine. From this perspective, while there are also instances of feminine Divine imagery, the maleness of the Bridegroom has tended to remain steadfast. The Gurus freely took on the female voice in seeking to describe their devotion to the ultimate in all its fullness. According to Punjabi scholar Gurnam Kaur, "God alone is Man, the Purusha and all other are His bride or female" (Kaur, 2004). The Gurus too were "brides" separated from the Ultimate Man. The centrality of the marriage metaphor reinforced a deep perception of God as male.

Moreover, as *gurbani* (utterances of the Gurus) came to be understood as an alternative to the sacred scripture of others as the means of divine revelation, the male Gurus themselves gained a parallel prominence. While the Gurus refused all intimations of divinity, their message was so closely aligned to the Divine that their followers saw them as representatives of the Divine. In this regard, the male voice continues to hold a dominant place in Sikh scripture. While they used both male and female images, the Gurus' preference in addressing the divine was to use masculine epithets, including "Master" and "Lord" (Shackle and Mandair, 2005: l). Indeed, the very name given to the Guru Granth Sahib denotes a male perspective: "Sahib" is a masculine honorific.

The Dasam Granth

Another important text for Sikhs is the Dasam Granth (*dasam* means "tenth"). The Dasam Granth contains the writings of the tenth guru, Guru Gobind Singh, as well as, by most accounts, compositions by other writers at the Guru's court. While the bulk of the Dasam Granth plays a lesser role in the devotional lives of Sikhs, specific hymns from it are recited daily, especially those attributed to Guru Gobind Singh. For most Sikhs, however, the Dasam Granth does not have the same status as the Guru Granth Sahib.

Extensive references to Hindu deities, and invocations thereof, are among the aspects of the Dasam Granth that are problematic for Sikhs. By contrast, at the core of the Adi Granth is a decisive statement of monotheism. While the Sikh Gurus used varied names for the Divine, they clearly understood God to be One. Moreover, the Dasam Granth at times portrays the goddess Devi as Ultimate Reality, and for some Sikhs, this is cause for discomfort. Further, a substantial portion of the Dasam Granth called *Charitropakhian*, or "Wiles of Women," consists of stories about men and women who are engaged in illicit relationships. It has a particular emphasis on deceitful women. Many Sikhs are troubled by the explicit nature of this material and believe that, given these controversial elements, the Dasam Granth cannot be understood as scripture (Rinehart, 2010). Nonetheless, at two of the five principal centres of Sikh temporal authority, Hazur Sahib and Patna Sahib, the Dasam Granth is installed on a separate throne alongside that of the Guru Granth Sahib and offered obeisance, signalling its importance as Sikh scripture.

The *Janam-Sakhis*

Other important texts are called *Janam-sakhis*, also called *sakhis*, which are hagiographic (idealized and biographical) collections of anecdotes focusing on the life of the first Guru, Guru Nanak. The form and style of the earliest *Janam-sakhis* were later reproduced to include stories focusing on the later Gurus as well. This form and style of writing is known as the **janam-sakhi** genre. While the *Janam-sakhis* and subsequent narratives are not understood to be sacred, they hold an important place in Sikhism. Through these stories Sikhs can learn a great deal about the actual lives of the Gurus, their wives, and their children; miraculous occurrences surrounding them; and the difficulties caused by the Gurus' political and religious opponents. While they are questionable as historical sources, given that they were written well after the lifetimes of the Gurus they focus on and that the various versions of the *Janam-sakhis* are not consistent with one another, they do offer important insights into the development of the early Sikh tradition. Most importantly, they are testaments to how the early Sikh followers viewed and understood the life and mission of Guru Nanak and later Gurus.

The *Sikh Reht Maryada*

Another important, though more recent, text that plays a central role in Sikh religious life is the **Sikh Reht Maryada**, or the Sikh Code of Conduct. It outlines definitions for Sikh religious identity, including correct Sikh behaviour and avoidances; proper ways of conducting rituals surrounding birth, marriage, and death, and a large number of other personal and community disciplines. The version that is authoritative for Sikhs today dates from 1950, though it incorporates various earlier codes of discipline that were developed during and after the time of the Gurus.

Central Beliefs and Practices

The Divine

Central to Sikh teachings is the belief in the Oneness of God. However, the Sikh Gurus used a variety of names for the divine from both Hindu and Muslim traditions. In Sikh understandings, the Divine is the Formless One (Nirgun) or

Akal Purakh, the Eternal Being. However, Akal Purakh is also manifested in the world as well as within the human heart. From this perspective, Akal Purakh can be understood as both *nirguna* (without attributes) and *saguna* (with attributes). Importantly, the Sikh Gurus did not subscribe to the polytheistic understanding of the Divine in terms of multiple gods. The Gurus also taught that while the essence of Akal Purakh is beyond human comprehension, that same essence can be found everywhere, in every object, in every experience, in every relationship.

Humanity

The Sikh Gurus taught that humans have a close connection with the Divine. They spoke of the human soul as emanating from the light of God. For this reason, humanity is essentially good. The "problem" with humanity is that it does not recognize its true essence as emanating from God. In other words, human beings are unaware that the presence of God is within them and surrounds them at all times, and thus, instead of recognizing their ultimate dependence on God, try to be self-reliant. The God-centred individual in Sikhism is a **gurmukh**. Humans can also be *manmukh*, ego-bound or self-centred. This concept is related to another important term, *maya* (illusion). In Sikhism the notion of *maya* refers to worldly attachment or having a materialistic view of the world and thus living in a delusional state. While attachment to one's child, to one's home, to one's job is not necessarily evil, when combined with self-centred attitudes, it may take on evil qualities. Sikhs speak of five main "evils"—lust, covetousness or greed, attachment, wrath, and pride—while acknowledging that many other evils exist as well. *Maya* (illusion) is love turned into possessiveness. *Maya* is God-given attraction to another having turned to lust.

The Spiritual Quest

The Sikh Gurus did not just expound on the human condition: they also offered a hopeful and clear solution to the problem facing humanity. The goal is to move away from ego-bound attitudes and practices and instead become a *gurmukh*, God-centred in everyday living. The path to enlightenment is **nam-simran**, meditation on the Divine Name and essence of the Divine. Through intentional focus on Akal Purakh (Eternal Being), human will and Divine will begin to converge. For the Sikh Gurus, this did not mean that one had to give up one's occupation and house and family; *nam-simran* could and should be practised in the ordinary course of events. While sowing the fields, while mending clothes, while churning butter—all images used by the Gurus—one could practise the discipline of *nam-simran*. Congregational devotional singing (**kirtan**) of praises to Akal Purakh is also essential to the spiritual quest. Women and men are called to be in the company of like-minded people, all striving for union with Akal Purakh, and in this way the personal quest for liberation is enhanced.

The Three Cornerstones of Sikh Practice

Sikhs, when asked about the central beliefs and practices for Sikh women and men, speak of the three cornerstones of Sikhism:

1. remembrance of the Divine at all times, through consistent practice of the Sikh meditative discipline *nam-simran* (meditation on the Divine Name) as well as through *kirtan* (devotional singing) or simply through listening to sacred text;
2. making an honest living without exploitation or fraud; and
3. sharing with others or helping those in need; this may take the form of feeding the hungry, but may also refer to offering **seva** (service) to other Sikhs or to humanity as a whole. Sikhs, both men and women offer manifold forms of *seva* by contributing to the running of gurd-waras, cooking and serving food for the **langar** (communal kitchen) at their local gurdwara, or by contributing to the well-being of the larger community by taking part in activities such as blood drives or the collection of food for shelters or food banks.

History

Sikh History

The Early Sikh Gurus

The study of Sikhism begins with the first Guru of the Sikhs, Guru Nanak, who was born into a relatively peaceful and stable society in what is now Pakistan. His birth was accompanied by auspicious and miraculous signs indicating that his was to be an important life (H. Singh, 1994: 63–71). He grew up in a Khatri Hindu family, that is, in an upper-caste, mercantile family lineage. His mother's name was Tripta, and his father, Kalu, was a village accountant. Nanak had an elder sister named Nanaki, who played an important role in her early recognition of her brother's mission in life. Following the custom of the time, Nanak received an education that would allow him to follow in his father's footsteps, but he showed little interest in the life of business for which he was being prepared. He was often lost in religious musings and was known to be keenly interested in the varied teachings of wandering holy men, both Hindu sadhus and Muslim Sufi masters.

When Nanak was a teenager he was married, according to traditional customs, to a young girl named Sulakhani. The fact that Nanak was upholding family traditions in this way was a great relief to his family, given his earlier tendencies to question or ignore societal norms. His greatest advocate had always been his beloved sister Nanaki. It was upon her urging that her brother Nanak and his new wife, Sulakhani, moved away from his family home to the town of Sultanpur. It was there that his brother-in-law, Nanaki's husband, got him a job with a local official. In Sultanpur, Nanak and Sulakhani had two children, boys named Sri Chand and Lakmi Das. When Nanak was around 30 years old, tradition recounts, he had a life-transforming experience that was to have a far-reaching effect on his understanding of his life's mission. It is told that he had an overwhelming mystical experience of union with God and was charged with teaching others in the practice of love and disciplined devotion to the Divine. From this time forward, Nanak was known as Guru Nanak, and word spread quickly of his great piety and enlightened teachings (H. Singh, 1994: 95–9). Leaving his family behind, Guru Nanak travelled widely, preaching a message of praise and devotion to what he called the Formless One throughout India and neighbouring countries. Eventually, Guru Nanak returned and established a community in the village of Kartarpur for his family and disciples. Daily life revolved around the presence and charisma of the Guru and the practical implications of his message. The Sikhs ("learners" or "disciples") were to rise early in the morning, that mysterious time known as "the ambrosial hour" when the sun's rays are just beginning to light up the world, then to bathe in preparation for the day ahead. Throughout all their daily work activities, the Sikhs were to remember or meditate on the Divine name and essence of God, *nam-simran*. Then as now, this was the central form of meditative practice of the Sikhs.

Along with individual meditation while pursuing daily activities and reciting routine prayers, the Guru's followers, both women and men, were also to come together in the house of the Guru, then known as the *dharmsala*, to praise the Creator through devotional songs (*kirtan*) with other like-minded people. The term *dharmsala* was eventually replaced by **gurdwara**, or "the guru's door," and it is this term that today denotes where Sikhs gather to worship. The community of devotees was, and is still today, called the **sangat** (congregation). The compositions of Guru Nanak were well known to his disciples, and were to be sung. An initiation ritual known as **charan pahul**, or "nectar of the foot," distinguished the early community from other surrounding groups and appears to have been open to all, regardless of caste, original creed, or gender. The Guru—and later, when the community grew, a deputy of the Guru known as a *masand*—would dip his right toe into a bowl of water and the initiate would then drink the water as a token of his or her submission to the Guru. This was significant for a society highly focused on ritual purity and avoiding pollution.

Above all, however, the Sikhs gathered to receive the blessings or *darshan* of their Guru. Central to Hindu devotionalism is the notion of seeing and being seen by the Divine. This notion is extended to being "seen" and "seeing," or simply being in the presence of a spiritual master (Eck, 1998: 5–6). So too for the followers of Guru Nanak. Blessings were to be found in "being seen" by their beloved Guru. Their master had inspired his disciples through his message of liberation for all, through Guru Nanak's life of service to the community and his simple way of life. To be in his presence—at the very least, in the community of those surrounding him—was at the heart of devotees' longing.

Guru Nanak's message was broadly influenced by what religious scholars today call the Sant tradition of North India. The term **sant** is closely related to *sat*, "truth"; the *sants* were "seekers of truth." Combining elements of both Hinduism and Islam, the Sant tradition was closely related to the bhakti devotional movement, which had begun in South India in the sixth century and moved westward and northward through to the fourteenth century. *Bhaktas* (poet-saints) such as the mystic Kabir stressed, above all, devotion and an all-consuming love for the Divine as opposed to the rules, regulations, and social divisions imposed by orthodoxy. Salvation, according to the bhakti world view, "was the birthright of every human being irrespectful of his [*sic*] caste, creed or sex" (Grewal, 1979: 139–40). Other influences on Guru Nanak included the Nath yogis' stress on the possibility of experiencing union with the Divine. Sufism—the mystic dimension of Islam—was also influential, through common themes such as the Oneness of God and the notion of the suffering experienced by devotees as a result of their separation from the Divine. "Remembrance of the name"—being constantly aware of God at all times—was integral to the teachings of the North Indian Sufi orders.

The overall message of Guru Nanak resonated with that of the larger Sant movement. His message was radically different, however, when it came to women's position with respect to the ultimate goal of life, union with the Divine. While Sants such as Kabir were undoubtedly critical of the societal values that supported sectarian divisions and caste structures, the patriarchal value system that aligned women with *maya* (illusion) stayed firmly in place (Grewal, 1996: 144–7). Thus whereas Kabir saw womankind as an obstacle for men on their path to liberation, Guru Nanak invited all, men and women, into a loving relationship with Akal Purakh, the Eternal Being. Women were an integral part of divine creation and as such were not to be viewed as embodiments of pollution, especially with regard to childbirth and menstruation. Nor were they to be regarded as temptresses leading men away from their spiritual quest. Guru Nanak favoured the life of the householder as the ideal in the search for liberation, as opposed to the life of the ascetic. The Divine was to be found in the everyday workings of society, not on the margins of society as represented by ascetic orders of the day.

Similar to other Sants, Guru Nanak and subsequent Gurus used the female voice to describe their devotion to the Divine Lord. Through the female voice, the suffering of humanity, painfully separated and longing for the Divine, was best articulated. The marriage metaphor was favoured above all others in describing the delightful union with Akal Purakh. Sikh scripture is replete with mystical imagery in which the devotee assumes the role of the female lover, whereas the Divine is the ultimate male Beloved (Shankar, 2002: 115). While female imagery for Akal Purakh exists in Sikh scripture, the ramifications of the persistence of this masculine understanding of Akal Purakh are manifold. According to J.S. Grewal, the "bulk of Guru Nanak's verses refer to the conjugal relationship. Metaphorically, God is the only True Husband, and human beings are potentially His wives. The soul-wife seeks, or should seek, union with god-husband. . . . Indeed, she adorns herself only to please her master" (1996: 143).

In the same vein, the woman's place in Guru Nanak's societal milieu, as well as that of subsequent Gurus, was in the home. In this regard, Guru Nanak did not offer women a radical departure from the existing social order. Metaphors for the ideal woman abound in Sikh scripture. She was to be humble, modest, beautiful, utterly devoted, and obedient. Moreover, the procreative role and, above all, the sanctification of motherhood was the ideal for women. While Guru Nanak's message assured both men and women equal access to spiritual liberation, he appeared to be largely content to leave existing social norms as they stood in medieval North Indian society (Grewal, 1996: 157).

While each of the following nine Gurus contributed his own imprint to the early Sikh community, little changed in terms of the original emancipatory message of Guru Nanak. The first two successors, Guru Angad (1504–52) and Guru Amar Das (1479–1574), were carefully chosen to lead the community based not on family lineage but on merit; each Guru was understood to be of the same essence or light (jot) as Guru Nanak. The only wife of a Guru who is mentioned in the Guru Granth Sahib is Mata Khivi, the wife of Guru Angad, who is recalled as caring for pilgrims in her role in the communal kitchen of the Sikhs, known still as langar. The Janam-sakhis help fill the void somewhat by adding details surrounding the wives and children of the Gurus, although they contain inconsistencies as well, especially with regard to the names of Gurus' daughters and even their wives. Bibi Amro, the daughter of the second Guru, Guru Angad, is remembered as the one who initially drew Guru Amar Das into the community through her singing of sacred hymns. With Guru Amar Das and Guru Ram Das, the third and fourth Gurus of the Sikhs, critique of societal norms took the form of breaking with those norms. They encouraged widow remarriage and reinterpreted the practice of *sati* (widow immolation) through a spiritual lens, prohibiting its literal practice—an important rupture in the time-honoured societal practices of upper-caste North India. There are also possible indications that women played important missionary roles in both caring for the needs of established Sikh *sangats* and acting as preachers under the leadership of Guru Amar Das. These positions were known as *manjis* (literally, "string beds"), referring to the additional seats of authority that became necessary to spread the message of the Gurus during the initial development of the community. The *manjis* were replaced by deputies called *masands* ("thrones"), who were responsible for the oversight of specific districts occupied by Sikhs, from the time of the fourth Guru, Guru Ram Das (1534–1606). As the community developed, the *masands* became increasingly powerful; eventually, they were also responsible for initiating new members into the Sikh community. There is no evidence that women occupied these important administrative positions that became necessary as the numbers of Sikhs continued to grow.

Also during the time of Guru Ram Das, succession became restricted to family lineage; from that time all Gurus were of the Sodhi line, a Khatri-caste lineage. This was largely because of the lineage claims to the guruship made by sons of the Gurus who had been bypassed in earlier succession appointments. Devotees' needs began changing with increasing numbers, and the community became increasingly institutionalized, with pilgrimage sites put in place and administrative positions developed that were held by loyal devotees. Perhaps most importantly, beginning with the ascension of the fifth master, Guru Arjan (1563–1606), the hymns composed by his four predecessors as well as his own prolific compositions were collated as sacred scripture. Guru Arjan also completed the construction of the pool (called Amritsar, "pool of nectar"), begun by Guru Ram Das, and built a shrine in the middle of it called the **Harimandir Sahib**—the Golden Temple, as it is known today. He thus provided his followers with a sacred centre for devotional activities. However, with increasing numbers, obvious economic successes, and intimations of political power, the Sikh community and its master, Guru Arjan, came to be perceived as a political threat to the Mughal rulers. Guru Arjan was executed on charges of political interference. Guru Hargobind, his son, became the sixth master, and in response to the actions of the government, significant changes were instituted in the community. Guru Hargobind was fully armed, wearing two swords: *miri*, symbolizing political and temporal power, and *piri*, signifying spiritual authority. He acquired an infantry, set boundaries around his territories, and built a seat of temporal authority—known until today as the **Akal Takht**—across from the Harimandir Sahib; it too was symbolic of the temporal authority of the Guru.

Scholars believe that these significant changes were made in response to the changing political circumstances of the time. However, religious and political transformation does not take place in a vacuum, and it is important to come to a more complex understanding of why these changes may have taken place. The age of the Guru is likely significant in this respect. Guru Hargobind became Guru at the young age of 11 and relied heavily upon trusted leaders and members in the community for advice. While the death of Guru Arjan clearly played a significant role in these developments, other social forces were also at work, especially changes in the composition of the Sikh community. Devotees of the Jat caste had by this time replaced members of the Khatri caste as the majority of Sikhs. Khatris had long held administrative and mercantile positions in the larger community. Jats, on the other hand, were largely peasants who were closely tied to the land, which was to be defended at all cost. They were known for their overt defiance of authority, and it is likely that they had already brought militant ideals into the growing community (H. McLeod, 1997: 34–7). With the increasing institutionalization and militarization of the community, women came to play less central roles, at least with respect to administrative and leadership positions.

The Later Sikh Gurus

Guru Hargobind's successor was his grandson, Guru Har Rai (1630–61), who was followed by the child-Guru, Har Krishan (1656–64), who died of smallpox at the age of eight. He was succeeded by the elderly Guru Tegh Bahadur (1621–75). Guru Tegh Bahadur's writings were the last to be included with those of the first five Gurus, in the final version of the Adi Granth.

The most significant change in the development of the Sikh community stems from the time of the tenth Guru of the Sikhs, Guru Gobind Rai (1666–1708). According to traditional Sikh accounts, in 1699, during the Baisakhi festival, or New Year's celebrations—a time when Sikhs traditionally gathered together in great numbers to celebrate the harvest— Guru Gobind Rai issued a special call to his followers to join him at the centre he had established at Anandpur, in the Shivalik Hills of North India. As the crowd gathered, Guru Gobind Rai called for a Sikh to come forward and offer his head in devotion to his Guru. The assembly was stunned. Finally, one Sikh came forward. The Guru called for four more heads, and again, four devoted Sikhs answered his call. Importantly, each of the five men who stepped forward came from a different caste grouping. According to one tradition, the five followers actually offered their lives to the Guru, and he came out from inside the tent with his sword dripping with the blood of their sacrifice. He then miraculously healed them. Another tradition had the Guru sacrificing five goats instead of his five devotees, as a ruse to test the will of those assembled (McLeod, 1997: 52).

Regardless of the actual events that took place, it is clear that the five men called forward were designated as the *panj piare* ("beloved five") and initiated into a new brotherhood or order. The Guru administered a novel ritual of initiation to these five, called the **khande di pahul**, or sword ritual, whereby water sweetened with sugar (*amrit*) was stirred in an iron bowl with a double-edged sword. This sweetened water was then sprinkled onto each initiate's face, cupped hands, eyes, and hair with the double-edged sword. Guru Gobind Rai then offered the beloved five sanctified food known as **karah prasad** from the same iron bowl. The new initiates were henceforth to be known as part of the order of the Khalsa; the Khalsa brotherhood was to answer to no other authority but its Guru. Each of the five, and the Guru himself, who also underwent the sword ritual, was given the name **Singh**, or "lion," and henceforth the Guru was known as Guru Gobind Singh. The Singhs were also required to adopt elements of what was at that time the uniform of the warrior, including a *kirpan* (dagger), a *kara* (steel bangle) protecting the sword-wielding right wrist, and *kachh* (short breeches), which made it easier for warriors to mount and dismount horses, and thus move quickly in battle, than did the traditional *dhoti* (still worn by males in India today), which consists of a long cloth wrapped around the lower body. However, the injunctions also included an important focus on the body, in the form of *kesh*—uncut hair—and the *kangha*, a small comb to be used and then worn in the hair, emphasized tidiness and cleanliness. These five symbols are known as the **Five Ks** (*panj kakar*), since the words for all of them begin with the letter *k*. The Five Ks, along with the turban that is to keep the uncut hair in place, remain today as the distinctive marks of the Khalsa Sikh.

According to tradition, the Guru also prohibited "four cardinal sins" (*kurahits*) in conjunction with the inauguration of the Khalsa order: Sikhs were never to cut their hair; not to smoke or chew tobacco or consume alcohol; not to eat halal meat (from animals slaughtered according to Muslim law); and not to have sexual relations with Muslim women. This latter injunction was later broadened to prohibit adulterous relationships of any sort. The Guru then called to others assembled to join the Khalsa order; according to tradition, great numbers came forward to show their devotion to their Guru.

With the inauguration of the Khalsa, the Sikhs were clearly identifiable as a religious community, set apart from their Hindu and Muslim counterparts and known henceforth as a community of warrior-saints. Through the distinct name associated with the brotherhood and the ritualized call to arms, the warrior-saint became the new ideal of Sikh identity. However, historical sources also make it clear that many Sikhs continued to follow the practices of the earlier Gurus.

Early prescriptive texts focusing on the Khalsa order are highly gendered and focus for the most part on male identity and ritual life. They are either contradictory or silent about women's inclusion in the military order. Only males were accorded the Khalsa designation "Singh." This is not difficult to understand, given that the tenth Guru's call to arms was clearly intended to create a military order. Female devotees and other Sikhs who may or may not have undergone the rite of *charan pahul* continued their membership in the wider Sikh community, which eventually came to be understood as a lesser order of Sikhs (Hans, 1988: 249).

In the 1740s, for instance, the *Chaupa Singh Rahit-nama* prohibited women's initiation into the Khalsa (McLeod, 1987: 186); women were to be initiated by the rite of *charan pahul*. Chaupa Singh also maintains that a Sikh should never be called by half of his name (MacLeod, 1987: 182), signifying the centrality of "Singh" for the Khalsa order, while referring to women simply as "Sikhnis" or "Gursikhnis." On the other hand, the *Prem Sumarg*, likely also from the eighteenth century, prescribes the sword ritual for both men and women (McLeod, 2006: 3–6). However, gender differentiation remains clearly in place with regard to normative codes. For males, the *Prem Sumarg* calls for weaponry, turban, and breeches (McLeod, 2006: 22); but regulations for females stress, instead of the traditional blue of the Khalsa, a black skirt and bodice. Women are also instructed to study scripture in the company of other Sikhnis and obediently serve their husbands (McLeod, 2006: 27). A formative, gendered, and normative Khalsa identity thus remains firmly in place. Today, the Khalsa male identity continues to have the hegemonizing effect of serving as a "normative model" against which all other Sikh identities are weighed, generally through "negation or deferral", becoming the "authoritative reference" of Sikh identity (Axel, 2004: 26–60).

The Khalsa as a martial order had little relevance for the everyday realities of women. However, exceptions existed. Mai Bhago, a celebrated Sikh female warrior, is known to have taken up arms in the Battle of Muktsar (1705). Varied sources indicate that she did so either disguised as a man or after receiving special permission to wear male-specific garb from Guru Gobind Singh (Macauliffe, 1990: 220). This narrative highlights an important "gendering" process whereby specific images ensure that a masculinized identity retains its position of primacy. The construction of symbols and images that help to explain and reinforce gendered divisions have many and varied sources, including dress codes (Acker, 1991: 167). Through militarized, masculine external markings, a gender-based "theology of difference" contributed to the already established political, cultural and social gender hierarchy of Punjabi society (Jakobsh, 2003: 22–49). Thus the "sphere of social activity predominantly associated with males encompasses the activity predominantly associated with females and is, for that reason, culturally accorded higher value" (Ortner and Whitehead, 1981: 7–8).

A tradition exists that one of the three wives of Guru Gobind Singh was present at the inauguration of the Khalsa and was responsible for the sweetening of the water in the iron bowl (Mann, 2004: 40–1). While this is likely a later tradition designed to give the event a more egalitarian character, many Sikhs firmly believe it to indicate that women played a central role in the creation of the Khalsa, and were initiated into the order through the ritual of the sword (Jakobsh,

2003: 46). Later texts shed light on attempts to conclusively reverse prohibitions on women's initiation, but according to historian W.H. McLeod, they reflect the concerns of a significantly later period (1987: 186). Nonetheless, as noted earlier, it is possible, simply because of the exhortations *not* to initiate women into the Khalsa through the ritual of the sword, that female initiations had indeed taken place. Given the tenuousness of the historical evidence, historians must move beyond the letter of the text to question the reasons behind the regulations put in place by male authority figures and male writers. Clearly, however, women's identity as Sikhs was generally outside the increasingly normative Khalsa ideal.

Guru Gobind Singh's sons had died during his lifetime. Before the Guru died in 1708, he formally ended the institution of human guruship, placing Sikh authority in the Guru Granth Sahib, the repository of revelation, and elevating the community to the level of the Guru Panth. There are differing interpretations as to whether the Guru Panth was to be composed exclusively of Khalsa Sikhs or whether it was to include all Sikhs. Nonetheless, the day-to-day leadership of the Sikhs was to be based in the local congregation, led by an executive called the *panj piare* (modelled on the five beloveds who had offered their heads in devotion to their Guru) and guided by the wisdom and insight of the Guru Granth Sahib. This form of leadership is still followed by Sikhs worldwide today.

Interestingly, Mata Sundri, one of Guru Gobind Singh's wives, appears to have played an important leadership role during one of the most tumultuous times in the community's development. What is surprising, given her lengthy direction of the community, is how little is said of her leadership in Sikh historical accounts. Another wife of the Guru, Mata Sahib Devan, was in later traditions presented as the "Mother of the Khalsa" alongside the Father of the Khalsa, Guru Gobind Singh.

With the formation of the Khalsa, the Sikhs came to be viewed by the ruling Mughals as a political and military force. In their dealings with the Mughals and the local Hindu chieftains, and later with the Afghans who led excursions into Punjab, the motto of the Sikhs was "the Khalsa shall rule" (Mann, 2004: 49).

By the mid-eighteenth century, independent Sikh confederacies (*misls*) had been organized, under the leadership of a commanding chief. A number of Sikh women, rose to positions of power during this time, among them Sada Kaur and Maharani Jindan. According to Purnima Dhavan,

> Women from ruling families did occasionally contest the increasingly circumscribed roles into which the warrior ethos of the Khalsa rulers placed them; however, in each of the cases that have come to light women gained authority only through their status as the sisters, wives, and widows of ruling Sikhs. In other words, similar to the ways in which the social status of men either through a claim to higher caste,

as rulers, or as part of the Khalsa brotherhood was linked to their sense of masculine honour, women in ruling families could use their social status and kinship ties to claim a limited authority in society as "honorary men." This was not an option open to non-elite women. Exceptional circumstances allowed women to assume power, however, as soon as the emergency passed patriarchal control was quickly restored (Dhavan, 2010).

Through his own political astuteness, and guided by his equally ambitious mother-in-law, Maharani Sada Kaur, Ranjit Singh, a young Sikh *misl* leader rose to prominence. Under Maharajah Ranjit Singh, the Sikhs entered four decades (1801–49) of relative peace and prosperity. It is a time remembered as one of Sikh glory, for although the Sikhs were a small minority among Hindus and Muslims, it was a Sikh who ruled a significant portion of northern India.

After Ranjit Singh's death in 1839, one of his widows, Maharani Jindan, ruled briefly as regent for their young son Dalip Singh. However, she was soon displaced, and in 1849 the Sikh kingdom became the final area of the subcontinent to be annexed by the British.

Social Change: The Sikhs, the Raj, and the Singh Sabha Reform Movement

In Punjab, as in other parts of India, reform movements sprang up as a British-educated middle class came to assess and re-evaluate deeply rooted religious belief systems and practices. Among the Sikhs, the **Singh Sabha** (Society of the Singhs), a reform movement, was established in the late nineteenth century. The Singh Sabha included various factions, one of which, the **Tat Khalsa** ("True Khalsa"), believed itself to possess a more purified and exclusively Khalsa-oriented interpretation of the Sikh identity, and ultimately came to dominate the movement. The Tat Khalsa reforms would have far-reaching results, especially their efforts to redefine and explain the essence of Sikhism in a manner that befitted the values and world view of this educated middle class. The movement on the whole was loyal to the British colonists, for it was as a result of the benefits of British or Christian missionary educational initiatives that many Sikhs had acquired middle-class status.

A gendered focus offers a fascinating window into the era of the Singh Sabha. Reformers made great strides in female education during this time. Religious rituals and issues of identity for women also came to the fore. For the most part, overt Sikh identity since the time of Guru Gobind Singh had focused mainly on Sikh males, but the reformers were cognizant of the need for identity markers to distinguish Sikh women from their Hindu counterparts. One marker, at least among the upper classes, involved naming practices. Among the masses, women generally had only one name, but some Hindu and Sikh women were given the second name "Devi"; the equivalent for Muslim women was "Begum." As noted, the appellation "Singh" was central to the Khalsa identity from the late seventeenth century, but it had no female counterpart. The *Prem Sumarg* provides the earliest textual prescription for naming Sikh women. In line with tradition, they were to be identified as "Devi" (McLeod, 2006: 31). Sikh reformers, apparently rejected the *Sumarg*'s directive, given its Hindu connotations. While the process is not at all clear, over time the name **Kaur** came to be associated with Sikh females; while often translated as "princess," it is the Punjabi equivalent of the Rajput word *kanwar*, meaning "prince" (Jakobsh, 2003: 220). According to historian Pashaura Singh, these naming practices were highly politicized, intending to create "a parallel system of aristocratic titles in relation to the Rajput hill chiefs" (P. Singh, 2010: 62).

In any event, Singh Sabha reformers began an ingenious process of standardizing and legitimizing the name Kaur by rewriting Sikh history to suggest that this naming practice had extensive historical, ritual, and religiously sanctioned roots. Sahib Devan, one of Guru Gobind Singh's wives, was increasingly referred to as Sahib Kaur by Singh Sabha writers (Jakobsh, 2003: 210–31). The official *Sikh Reht Maryada* came to stipulate that the name "Kaur" was to be given to all Sikh girls and the name "Singh" to all Sikh boys at the time of their birth. This is the authoritative position taken by Sikhs today with regard to naming practices.

Many of the changes that took place during the Singh Sabha period were the subject of controversy among the various Sikh groups. One contentious issue was Sikh women's initiation into the Khalsa order. For Singh Sabha reformers, by far the majority of whom were male, the redefinition of the status and role of women was a sign of their adherence to the ideals of modernity that their British education had given them. Given what they perceived as the need to return Sikhism to its true egalitarian roots, the lack of a female dimension in the prescribed Khalsa identity was problematic, especially since a highly marginalized group that stood well outside the bounds of Singh Sabha reforms, the Namdhari Sikhs, had been initiating women into their own version of the Khalsa order since the mid-1800s (Jolly, 1988: 89). Singh Sabha reformers, however, viewed themselves as the "true" bearers of Sikh egalitarian principles. Their British education gave them elite status and untrammelled ability to mediate Sikh history. In essence, Sikh history underwent a thorough revisioning process, particularly with regard to women. Female initiation has since this time been presented as stemming directly from the time of Guru Gobind Singh's inauguration of the Khalsa. While women's initiation into the Khalsa order was hotly contested by various Sikh groups, over time the Tat Khalsa vision came to reign. Initially, female initiation was to be distinguished from the male ritual through the use of a single-rather than a double-edged sword (Barstow, 1928: 228). However, the *Sikh Reht Maryada* of 1950 required both women and men to be initiated into the Khalsa order by the double-edged sword, a tradition that continues today. Still, now as then, it is only a minority of men and even fewer women who undergo initiation, although many Sikhs live according to the central tenets put in place by Guru Gobind Singh.

The reform endeavour of the Singh Sabha movement with regard to the reimagining and rewriting of women's history, role, and status in Sikhism was immensely successful. Modifications, interpretations, and in some cases inventions giving women and men equal access to all normative Sikh rites have remained largely unquestioned. Indeed, through the writings of Singh Sabha reformers, many of their reinterpretations have come to hold the status of implicit truth (O'Connell, 1988: 12) among the majority of Sikhs with regard to Sikh women's place in Sikh history and society today. Moreover, the Tat Khalsa world view, though only one of many, has come to be reflected in the majority of textbooks on Sikhism and, perhaps even more importantly, in the ever-expanding number of websites pertaining to the Sikh tradition.

Gender, Roles, and Rituals

The *Sikh Reht Maryada* has attempted to enshrine egalitarian principles with regard to both men and women having access to all forms of Sikh religious observances. The Reht (Code) that is authoritative for Sikhs today stems from 1950 although it incorporates various earlier codes. It establishes definitions for Sikh identity, includes prescriptions for correct Sikh behaviour and avoidances, proper ways of conducting rituals surrounding birth, marriage, and death as well as wider community disciplines and rituals, including processions. For the most part, the *Sikh Reht Maryada* authorizes non-gendered practices and leadership roles. Women and men *may* serve as **ragis** (musicians), *gianis* (learned in matters of Sikhism) and **granthis** (readers of scripture) in gurdwaras. However, deeply engrained patriarchal gender constructions have meant that these attempts at gender equality tend to be disregarded. Women rarely serve as *ragis* or *granthis* in mainstream gurdwaras, except at all-women's gatherings, and are generally absent from gurdwara management committees. In Canada, one exception is the Maritime Sikh Society Gurdwara in Halifax, where an all-woman executive has been put in place by an elected female president numerous times since in the 1990s. Women at this gurdwara serve in all aspects of ritual and religious life.

For the most part, women are also barred from the institution of the *panj piare* (beloved five). This prohibits females from offering a significant

Baisakhi celebrations in Lecce, Italy, 2011.

contribution to Sikh ritual life, because the *panj piare* play a role in all central Sikh rites and ceremonies, including initiation rites, and leads public processions during *gurpurbs* (anniversaries of the Gurus) and Baisakhi celebrations honouring the birth of the Khalsa; however, in some diasporic communities five women may walk directly behind the *panj piare* in public processions (Jacobsen 2011: 27). Marriage and death rituals and praxis are also gender-specific. Females walk behind males when circumambulating the sacred scripture during marriage ceremonies and are prohibited from lighting the funeral pyre of the deceased or even entering cremation grounds, particularly in Punjab where the majority of Sikhs reside (N. Singh, 2000).

Backlash: *Seva* and the Harimandir Sahib

In early 2003, the issue of Sikh women's participation in all ritual activities came to the fore at the Harimandir Sahib—the Golden Temple, the sanctorum of the Sikhs—in Amritsar, (Jakobsh, 2006: 189–94). At the crux of this highly publicized issue were two British **amritdhari** (initiated) Khalsa Sikh women who were refused the right to participate in the important procession that takes place when the Guru Granth Sahib is laid to rest for the night, known as Sukhasan. These two women believed firmly that their tradition offered them full equality to partake in all religious rites and rituals; based on their convictions, and given the blatant discrimination they faced, they lodged a complaint with the highest authorities in Sikhism. These included the Akal Takht, the primary temporal centre where major decisions concerning the Sikh community are made, as well as the **Shiromani Gurdwara Parbandhak Committee**, or SGPC, the institution responsible for overseeing shrines and gurdwaras in Punjab. Pointing to scriptural injunctions as well as to the *Sikh Reht Maryada*, they insisted that it was their right as Sikh women to take part in all aspects of worship and *seva* (service) at the holy shrine. An extensive discourse ensued that also examined other examples of women's exclusion, most especially at the Harimandir Sahib but also in local gurdwaras worldwide. At the Harimandir Sahib, women may not be *ragis*. This is significant, as *kirtan* (devotional singing) is a central activity at the shrine. Moreover, some Sikh women are challenging the male-dominated tradition of the *panj piare*.

Grassroots discussions began taking place, largely sponsored by the 3HO/Sikh Dharma of the Western Hemisphere and the American Gurdwara Parbhandak Committee (AGPC), responsible for the overseeing of many gurdwaras in the United States, and involving numerous Sikh online groups. Protests occurred as well. The mobilization efforts included petitions to the Jathedar of the Akal Takhat, the individual that holds the highest seat of human authority in Sikhism, to allow women's untrammelled access to all forms of *seva* at the Harimandir Sahib. Given the intense public uproar, the SGPC struck a committee to attend to this issue. However, the committee was not able to reach a consensus, and the issue remains unresolved to the present day.

The question of women's full participation at the Golden Temple is complex. In India, and for many Sikhs of the diaspora, the pivotal concern has less to do with egalitarian principles than with the values most central to Punjabi Sikhs namely, modesty and honour. For some, the possibility that a woman in the crowd carrying the Adi Granth might be jostled by men raised the threat of immodesty, which could have a direct bearing on family honour. Some objected that "Western" Sikhs had raised an issue that had never concerned Indian Sikh women. The Sikh women leading the campaign against discrimination increasingly become aware of attitudes associated with ancient Indian prohibitions regarding menstrual impurity or pollution, even though the Sikh Gurus exhorted their followers not to perceive anything in God's creation as having the inherent ability to pollute.

Gender regulation is the process by which a community, in this case that of the Sikhs,

> attempts to define, institute and justify "masculine" and "feminine" behaviour and roles for its members. It is distinct from "sexual regulation" in that the former is concerned with public roles and practices, while the latter is concerned with the "private" encounters between

individuals, usually involving sexual/physical intimacy (Zuckerman, 1997: 354).

In the case of the Sukhasan ritual, the lines between "public" and "private" have become blurred; notions of honour and modesty, normatively associated with sexual regulation, are here brought to the wider stage. What makes this particular incident so important is that Sikh institutions in general have not undertaken the analysis and critique necessary for "enquiring into the religious norms and practices affecting the dynamics of gender construction, the formation of subject and gender identity in order to make clear how religions themselves are oppressive to women" (King, 1998); for the most part, they have limited themselves to general discussions of patriarchy as challenged by Sikh tenets. While the protests did not result in any actual changes at the Harimandir Sahib, these mobilization efforts have been important consciousness-raising initiatives that have continued to reverberate throughout the worldwide Sikh community and have caused Sikhs to re-evaluate women's religious roles and status in their tradition. In this regard, Sikh women are faced with similar hurdles as their counterparts in all other male-dominated religious traditions. Nonetheless, Sikh women take solace in the doctrinal support for full equality provided by selected scriptural references, examples from Sikh history, and injunctions in the *Sikh Reht Maryada* as they continue to challenge deeply ingrained patriarchal values and practices in their tradition.

Seemingly at odds with these examples of discrimination in Sikh gurdwaras is the example of Bibi Jagir Kaur, a female politician who acquired a leadership position in one of the premier seats of Sikh authority. In 1999 and 2004, Bibi Jagir Kaur was elected president of the SGPC, often referred to as the Sikh parliament. The SGPC is responsible for the overseeing of most shrines and gurdwaras in the state of Punjab, including the Golden Temple. While Jagir Kaur's tenures as president were marred by charges of corruption and criminal activity, the fact that a woman rose to prominence in this important male-dominated Sikh institution is highly significant. Her leadership, despite its shortcomings, will potentially lead the way to opening up other public religious roles and devotional activities for Sikh women.

Gender, Symbols, and Identity

The Five Ks

The five external symbols that are worn by *amritdhari* (initiated) and **keshdhari** Sikhs (Khalsa Sikhs who are not initiated) begin with the letter *k* in Punjabi. As already noted, they are *kesh* (uncut hair), *kangha* (a semi-circular comb), *kachh* (short breeches), *kara* (a steel bracelet), and *kirpan* (a dagger). While the turban worn by Sikh males is not officially part of the Five Ks, it is integral to keeping both uncut hair and the comb in place. While Sikh tradition maintains that the Five Ks stem from the time of Guru Gobind Singh's inauguration of the Khalsa, there is in fact a great deal of obscurity surrounding them. The earliest texts name only three of these symbols—*kesh*, *kirpan*, and *kachh*—but do make reference to five weapons that were to be carried by the Khalsa (Grewal and Bal, 1987: 182–9). By the nineteenth century, explicit mention is made of all five of the traditional items beginning with the letter *k*.

There are various meanings attributed to the Five Ks. Uncut hair has been a symbol of holiness and strength in a number of traditions. For Sikhs, hair is a gift from God that must be left in its natural state. Long hair also makes Sikhs highly visible as a religious group, particularly Sikh men. The *kangha*, a small, semi-circular comb is used to keep the uncut hair tidy and in place. It is a symbol that differentiates the Sikhs' uncut hair from the typically matted long hair of Hindu ascetics. A small *kangha* has traditionally been worn by males under the turban, and by women in the hair gathered in a bun. The *kachh* (short breeches) worn by both men and women are today understood as a symbol of chastity. The *kara*, the steel bracelet, is understood to represent the ultimate unity of the Divine in the form of a circle without beginning or end. The *kirpan*, often called a ceremonial sword, varies in length from a few centimetres to a metre. It represents the Sikh struggle against injustice and was used by Guru Gobind Singh as a symbol for the Divine. Sikhs who are not *amritdhari* but who generally follow the injunctions of all the Five Ks are known as *keshdhari* Khalsa Sikhs. While there is some variance in how this term is understood, for the most part *keshdharis* are understood as Khalsa Sikhs even though some may trim their hair or beards; they form the majority of Sikhs in India. In the Sikh diaspora, most Sikhs cut their hair, and thus turbans are often not worn. These Sikhs, known as **sahajdhari** (slow-adopter) or *mona* (shaven) Sikhs (H. McLeod, 1997: 217–25), show their allegiance to Sikhism by wearing at least some of these five symbols, especially the *kara*. A *kirpan* or *kangha* is often worn as a symbol on a bracelet or necklace.

Gender and Hair

Hair must remain uncut not only from the head but from any part of the body. This aspect of Sikh identity has often pitted norms of beauty for women—the shaving of underarms and legs, the plucking of eyebrows or facial hair—against Sikh religious tenets. This issue recently came to the fore when an image of a young bearded and turbaned Sikh woman, Balpreet Kaur, was posted by an editor at Reddit under the topic "Funny" with the comment "I'm not sure what to conclude from this" on 21 September 2012. A friend of Balpreet's sent her the image and she personally responded on Reddit:

> Hey, guys. This is Balpreet Kaur, the girl from the picture. I actually didn't know about this until one of my friends told on facebook. If the OP wanted a picture, they could have just asked and I could have smiled :) However, I'm not embarrassed or even humiliated by the attention [negative and positive] that this picture is getting because, it's who I am. Yes, I'm a baptized Sikh woman with facial hair. Yes, I realize that my gender is often confused and I look different than most women. However, baptized Sikhs believe in the sacredness of this body - it is a gift that has been given to us by the Divine Being [which is genderless, actually] and, must keep it intact as a submission to the divine will (Reddit, 22 Sept. 2012).

The Reddit image and commentary went viral. Within days, the originator of the photo submitted an apology, both for his categorization of the posting as "Funny" and to Balpreet for his offensive comment, noting that making "fun of people is funny to some but incredibly degrading to the people you're making fun of. It was an incredibly rude, judgmental, and ignorant thing to post." He also apologized to Sikhs in general for offending their deeply held tenets and beliefs. Huffington Post subsequently named Balpreet Kaur "Huffington Post's Religious Person of the Year" for her graciousness and "remarkable generosity of spirit" in Kaur's response, in light of her steadfast devotion to the tenets of Sikhism.

While many, perhaps the majority, of Sikh females do remove unwanted body or facial hair, those who interpret the Sikh Reht Maryada's instructions literally must confront both the deeply held notions of beauty and the socially constructed gender identity markers of mainstream society. But these challenges are not limited to non-Sikh society. Young Sikh women must also contest prescribed notions of beauty in their own religio-cultural milieu. "Although men and women are held to the same standard in Sikhism, there is a cultural double standard on kesh. Provided that women maintain long tresses, the community generally looks the other way when it comes to removing facial and body hair" (Abdulrahim, 2011). Another study found similar attitudes in the community: "Why doesn't she just remove it? She looks like a man, how is she going to get married?" (K. Kaur, 2012). Sumita Batra, a Sikh who owns a chain of hair removal studios in the US, stated bluntly: "Let's put religion aside and be real. . . . Who . . . is attracted to a hairy-legged, mustached woman?" (Abdulrahim, 2011).

Regardless of whether they do or do not cut their hair and shave or pluck excess facial hair—in other words, whether they uphold religious tenets that go against the grain of religio-cultural norms, or ignore or reject specific religious tenets—Sikh women are important agents who take part in negotiating, contesting and even resisting particular religious ideals. These contentious issues bring to the fore the reality that there are often significant differences between prescribed religious ideals and the lived realities of devotees. According to David Hall, "we know a great deal about the history of theology and (say) church and state, we know next-to-nothing about religion as practised and precious little about the everyday thinking and doing of lay men and women." Moreover, "we owe a questioning of boundaries . . . and a recognition of the laity as actors in their own right" in understanding the religious lives of individuals (see Hall, 1997: viii–ix).

Unique Characteristics: The Turban as Gendered Identity Marker

The issue of Sikh identity is complex with regard to women, given that with the increased militarization of Sikhs after the creation of the Khalsa in 1699, the symbolism associated with Sikh identity has tended to be heavily gendered in favour of the male ideal of the saint-soldier. For Singh and Tatla, the turban is "synonymous with Sikhs and because of this association the turban has become the premier symbol of communal identity and its honour, whereas an inability to wear it is a sign of collective dishonour" (2006: 127). It is, in many respects, the ultimate male signifier, long associated in Punjab with honour and strength. Historically, for the Khalsa elite of the eighteenth century, the two primary repositories of family honour and prestige were (a) women and (b) the turbans worn by men. When Sikh leaders formed important alliances, they did so through marriage of their womenfolk (daughters) and through turban exchanges (Dhavan, 2010: 72, 74). The centrality of the turban in life-cycle rituals also highlights its gendered aspect. The turban tying ceremony, *Rasam Pagri* or *Rasam Dastaar* takes place when a man has passed away and his oldest son takes over the family responsibilities by tying a turban in front of a gathering. It signifies that he has taken on the responsibilities of his father and is now the head of the family.

Sikh women have not been as easily identifiable as Sikh males of the Khalsa order. As noted earlier, in mainstream Sikhism specific rituals for women's initiation into the Khalsa were officially put in place only in the twentieth century. However, a gendering of Sikh identity symbols has continued to develop over time. I would suggest that the focus on Sikh female identity is highly reminiscent of the Singh Sabha movement's attempts to conclusively carve out "Sikh" ritual space and distinct Sikh identity markers for their womenfolk, with a view to separating Sikh women unambiguously from their Hindu and Muslim counterparts. The tradition of a small group of women wearing turbans had its genesis during the colonial era. The Panch Khalsa Diwan, a radical group on the margins of the Singh Sabha movement, advocated, in the name of the strict egalitarianism they espoused, that *both* women and men were required to wear uncut hair and turbans. Those women who did not agree to wear the traditional male headgear were simply refused initiation (Barrier, 1970: xvi–xxvii; Jakobsh, 2003: 213–14). Teja Singh Bhasaur, leader of the group, was eventually excommunicated, and the group largely disintegrated, marginalized by the increasingly powerful Tat Khalsa element of the Singh Sabha. Remnants of the Panch Khalsa Diwan's teachings can be seen today in a group known as the Akhand Kirtani Jatha, which requires both men and women to wear small turbans. What is fascinating is that Teja Singh Bhasaur's radical mandate requiring initiated women to don turbans, though clearly originating on the margins of Sikh history, has begun to re-emerge from the margins of the Sikh community. This is evidenced by another Sikh group that advocates turbans for women: the 3HO (Healthy, Happy, Holy Organization), also known as Sikh Dharma of the Western Hemisphere. This is a group of people (mostly American) converted to Sikhism in the 1960s and 1970s through the efforts of Harbhajan Singh, later known as **Yogi Bhajan**. Although Bhajan came from a traditional Sikh family, his teachings and practices focused primarily on Kundalini yoga and Tantra. Eventually, Sikh tenets also came to be incorporated into his message, a message that was largely directed toward a white, middle-class, counterculture audience. 3HO Sikhs' insistence on gender equality includes insistence that women as well as men wear turbans (Elsberg, 2003: 95–139). The group also maintains some of the most popular websites on Sikhism, and, despite its extreme minority status in the larger Sikh community, it has in many ways become a "spokesperson" for Sikhism in North America and, through the Internet, for Sikhs worldwide (Jakobsh, 2008).

The Internet has become an important site of contemporary Sikh gender construction (Jakobsh, 2004, 2006). Websites on Sikhism abound, most created by Sikhs with the technological wherewithal to create, manage, and update highly sophisticated, user-friendly websites, generally residing in North America or the United Kingdom. In essence, largely on the basis of their technological skills, these individuals have become the new authorities on Sikhism as it is presented online, much as the Singh Sabha reformers became the authorities in the nineteenth and twentieth centuries. Complex questions of Sikh identities, in the plural, quickly come to the fore: Which Sikh identity is being presented as normative?

If one conducts an image search on the Web for "Sikh women," the results are rather astonishing. Many, if not most, results show Sikh women wearing turbans. Yet "women wearing turbans is almost unheard of in India . . . as a turban is a male symbol par excellence" (Dusenbery, 1990: 346–7).

On one particular site, RealSikhism, the question is asked:

Q: What is the appropriate head covering for Sikh women?

A: The most common head covering for Sikh women is the round turban and a chunni [headscarf] . . . Some Sikh women wear both, while some wear either turban or chunni. . . . The main purpose of the head covering is to cover the head (www.realsikhism.com).

This statement, not atypical in the online milieu, is remarkable in both its definitiveness and its inaccuracy. In fact, the "most common head covering for Sikh women" is *not* the turban, and turbaned women are unequivocally not representative of Sikh female identity. In India, as well as in the diaspora, by far the majority of *amritdhari* (initiated) Sikh females cover their hair with the traditional Indian scarf (*chunni*). Non-Khalsa women generally do not cover their hair except within the bounds of gurdwaras or in the presence of the Guru Granth Sahib. Yet online sources indicate that the turban for women is in fact normative. While there are no statistics available on the numbers of Sikh women who wear turbans, it is highly likely that they are higher in diasporic contexts than in Punjab, the heartland of Sikhism.

Backlash

In an ethnographic study of the perspectives and experiences of 13 Khalsa Sikh women, Cynthia Mahmood and Stacy Brady (2000) focus on, among other issues, the symbolic meanings associated with the turban and the responses— including backlash—that women wearing it have received. In spite of its obvious shortcomings, in particular the small size of the sample of Sikh women's voices, Mahmood and Brady's study is the first to attempt to come to an understanding of these important issues of identity from the perspective of North American Sikh women.

Increasingly, scholars are positing the veil in contemporary Islam as a "metaphor" for Muslim women (see, for example, Yazbeck Haddad and Smith, 2002); I would suggest that the gendering of identity vis-à-vis Sikh females donning the turban can be understood in a similar way. The turban has become part of a symbolic marking system for Sikh women, albeit a small number, in an attempt to distinguish themselves from non-Sikh women, the devoted from the not-so-devoted, the "true" Khalsa from those who might reject the turban as an essential marker of Khalsa membership. Understood in this light, the devotion of Sikh women who choose not to wear the turban may be held suspect. According to one Sikh woman who was asked to preview the Mahmood and Brady volume:

> I am sure that my words will antagonize some of the really religious Sikhs. I don't mean to offend them, and I will stand up firmly for their right to worship as they like. But I can't help getting angry when they deny the label "Sikh" to anybody but themselves. I am a Sikh, too. I am proud of being a Sikh. . . . Nobody should have a monopoly on the Sikh identity. There is room in our religion for everybody. It should be a generous religion, open to people wearing turbans or not. (Mahmood and Brady, 2000: 105–6).

On the other hand, the study also offers glimpses into why some women are adopting the turban. One reason may be the traditional association of the turban with honour. In some cases, women are donning this traditionally male symbol as an expression of agency or, in other words, their demands for gender equality (Mahmood and Brady, 2000: 52, 47). Yet, as some of the stories told by the women informants attest, at times the reactions against wearing a turban may be severe:

> [W]hen I walked in there, I was afraid of how receptive they all would be to [the turban]. . . . My grandmother started crying when she saw me, and I didn't know whether it was out of joy or out of "What the hell have you done to yourself?" I think she said something like "You don't need to do this, why are you wearing the turban, that's not what women Sikhs do, there is no need for this." My mom and my other grandmother were both like that too, like "Why are you doing this?" . . . I have never been stared at like that; I was like an animal in a zoo. . . . Then the guy I liked and wanted to go out with came over, and he was very cool about it, trying to be nonchalant, but I think I knew deep down that I would never get to go out with him if I kept the turban on. (Mahmood and Brady, 2000: 70).

The rise in Punjab of militant leader Jarnail Singh Bhindranwale, closely associated with the call for a separate Sikh state to be known as Khalistan, also played a significant role in Mahmood and Brady's informants' notions of Sikh identity. Initially, Bhindranwale's message had a profound effect on many Sikh males in the diaspora, who followed his call to strengthen their ties to Sikhism by donning turbans. According to Mahmood and Brady's research, a number of women who began to wear turbans were also involved in the Khalistan movement and seeking a more radical understanding of religious Sikh identity (2000: 75–6).

Clearly, a novel process of identity construction for women is beginning to take shape, mainly in the virtual realm. Most of the websites involved are based in North America or the United Kingdom. Through the repeated "visuality and iconicity" of a specific image, the turbaned woman, a "globalized domain of images" has come to be created within the "diasporic imaginary" (Axel, 2004: 35). It must be stressed that these carefully constructed images are also available offline; however, the Internet has a become catalyst for the active construction of a highly particularized, non-normative female Sikh identity, which is invariably *presented* as normative.

Certainly, in light of the travails facing Sikhs in the post-9/11 milieu, the turban is increasingly presented as an *essential* part of Sikh religious identity. "Sikhs are required to wear a turban pursuant to religious mandate and consider the turban to be an outward manifestation of their devotion to God and solemn adherence to the strictures of their belief system" (Gohil and Sidhu, 2008: 1). However, according to the *Sikh Reht Maryada*, the turban is optional for women; only men are required to wear it (Dharam Parchar Committee, 1950: 24). The fact that the turban is presented as a choice for women most likely reflects the time when the current Maryada was framed, during and immediately after the Singh Sabha reform movement, when the marginal, yet highly conspicuous Panch Khalsa Diwan was requiring both male and female Sikhs to don turbans. As noted earlier, there is no evidence that Sikh women wore turbans in the past.

For the most part, the notion of "choice" for females has seemed to satisfy inquirers, but a process of negotiation regarding the legitimacy of the turban for Sikh women is developing, especially in the online realm. One Sikh forum notes: "In Sikh Religion all rules are common between man and woman. Women enjoy as much as spiritual bliss as would a man. Then why should a man wear a turban and woman need not?" (Sweet Sikhi, 2005). Another self-identified feminist Sikh asks, "how can one reconcile the fact that for women it is just a personal decision, but for men it is a must? As a feminist myself it's something I have to contend with" (The Langar Hall, 2008).

The search for personal and collective identity, according to globalization studies, often comes to the fore when individuals in minority religions, especially in diasporic contexts, are experiencing increased levels of insecurity and existential anxiety (Kinnvall, 2004: 742). Narrative texts, written or oral, fictional or fact, verbal or visual, are the primary tools of cultural expressivity (Friedman, 1998: 8–9) in the search for social location in a space of dislocation. Central to this formation is a search for a "narrative about the self" (Hall, 1992: 227), identity not being sui generis or static, but a fluid "process of becoming"

(Kinnvall, 2004: 274). Ties to the past, constructed out of historical (real or imagined) materials (Castells, 2010: 82) are important in the construction of new cultural codes and identities. What is important, from a scholarly perspective, is that the search for a stable identity does not mean that such an identity exists (Kinnvall, 2004:747).

For Sikhs searching for the inherent, egalitarian core of Sikh identity markers, this has meant the reinterpretation, re-visioning or even invention of history (or identity) through foundation myths, symbols, memory, or heroic narratives. One example can be seen in the recent revisiting of the writings of Bhai Vir Singh, an important figure in the Singh Sabha reform movement. Attempting to create the feminine ideal for Sikh women, he wrote a number of novellas featuring female heroines. The fictional Sundri was one such heroine and she continues to inspire today (Bhai Vir Singh, 1988). A recent animated film entitled *Sundri: The Brave Kaur*, based on Vir Singh's book, initially images Surasti (Sundri's original name) in normative Punjabi women's dress, including the traditional *dupatta* (head scarf). But after her transformation into a truly devoted Khalsa Sikh, Sundri (later also called Sundar Kaur) is depicted as a beautiful turbaned Sikh woman (*Sundri*, 2008). The fact that the turban, the ultimate male signifier, is being renegotiated into a female signifier representing "true" devotion to the ideals of Sikhism is a striking example of how Sikh women's identity is being constructed today.

As noted earlier, it is largely in the diasporic milieu that Sikh women are donning turbans. Clearly, it is significant that this process of identity construction is centred in the diaspora rather than in India. One can surmise that the power dynamics associated with Sikh female identity construction are changing. The Internet is playing a major role in this process of change, and most of its key mediators are Western Sikhs, both converts to Sikhism and second-, third-, and even fourth-generation Sikhs whose families originated in India.

Sexuality, Family Structures and Traditions

For Sikhs, following the example of their Gurus, the life of the householder is the ideal and the foundation of Sikh society. Guru Nanak and the majority of subsequent Gurus, with the exception of the child-Guru Har Krishan, were married and had children. The Gurus thus rejected the Hindu ideal of the celibate ascetic; in fact, there is evidence that a number of the Gurus' sons were bypassed because of the choice they made to follow the path of asceticism. Moreover, as noted earlier, the sexual relationship (within the bounds of marriage) was used by the Gurus to convey the highest ideal of the spiritual quest: the fusion of the soul in union with the Divine. Sikhs today are expected to marry and have children to continue the family line. They are also required to marry other Sikhs. The *Sikh Reht Maryada* especially stresses this for Sikh women.

Marriage

Marriage in the South Asian context, irrespective of religion, class, caste, or region, must be understood as the pivotal event of an individual's life, for with it comes a thorough transformation of identity, role, and status. For women, this generally includes a change in residence as well to join her husband's family. While historically marriages often took place without the bride and groom having met each other before their wedding date, today they meet beforehand and increasingly both have a say in the choice of a marriage partner. While some traditional attitudes toward marriage are being challenged, both in India and in the various Sikh diasporas, dating is generally not approved of; however, couples may meet and get to know one another in the company of relatives.

Punjabi Sikh marriages generally follow rules of **hypergamy**: the bride's family, and the bride, are considered to have a lower social status than the groom and his family (Das, 1976: 27; Mooney, 2010). Traditional hierarchies between "wife givers" and "wife receivers" are followed by families throughout the varied religious communities in India, including Sikhs, who largely follow the tradition of *kanyadan*, the "gift of the virgin", in which wife receivers are deferred to because of their acceptance of the female (Mand, 2002: 234). This gift is almost universally accompanied by what is known in Punjabi as *daaj*, a dowry.

Dowry practices were critiqued by a number of Sikh Gurus, yet dowry debt has historically been particularly high in Punjab and continues to constrain many families today as they struggle to pay back debts incurred to ensure that their daughter is well placed and is well received into her new family. While the *Sikh Reht Maryada* unequivocally rejects dowry practices, these injunctions are generally not followed (Dharam Parchar Committee, 1950: 29). In the Sikh diaspora, while dowry may not be demanded outright, it is widely understood to be obligatory. One researcher examining the realities of Sikh women in the United Kingdom recounts that she "did not come across a single woman who had been married without a *daaj*. This is simply because her position would have been vulnerable in her marital home if she had arrived without one, or with one less than that dictated by social conventions. A marriage without a *daaj* would also reflect badly on family status and *izzat* [honour]" (Rait, 2005: 110).

While a woman's dowry was traditionally understood to represent her family inheritance, dowry is increasingly understood today as a necessary gift to her husband and his family. This has, in some cases, resulted in extortion by grooms or their family members. In extreme cases, unsatisfied dowry demands have led to the killing of newly married women—a phenomenon known throughout India as "dowry death."

After her marriage, a woman is quite literally transferred from her father's lineage to her husband's; her husband and his relatives are thereafter responsible for her care. Marriage is thus a family decision, in that two separate family systems are active participants in this transfer. This elaborate institution unites these two families to the extent that they are understood to be almost like blood relations. The central, defining feature of the institution of arranged marriage, particularly for women beyond their natal homes, continues to be the importance of keeping a good family name untarnished. A woman in this system must be flexible and accommodating not only towards her husband, but also towards his family, which has "accepted" her into their family (Mooney 2010). Marrying outside one's caste is traditionally perceived as perhaps the most significant blow to family honour.

A SIKH VALENTINE'S DAY STORY: THE MARRIAGE OF JASJIT KAUR AND S. GURPREET SINGH

Growing up in the capital of Punjab, Chandigarh (often called "The City Beautiful"), like every other girl I grew up with a dream of having a loving life-partner and sharing a blissful journey through the marital bond. My dream did come true, but only after going through times of dark clouds and struggle in my life. I was surrounded with love right from my birth and called the "Miracle Child" in the hospital because I was born after sixteen years of my parents' marriage. My parents' nickname for me was "Nidhi," treasure. But then I lost my mom when I was five years old followed by my dad when I was in grade eleven. I had a difficult time with my step-mother, especially after my dad died. I would often wonder whether I would ever experience true happiness in my life again? Would my dream partner come into my life so my struggles would end? And indeed they did, in true Bollywood style. My local guardian knew of a family who had a son who might be a prospective groom—my father had also known this family. But, they lived in Canada. I was shown a picture of this young man, and he too saw a picture of me. This was the first step. So, our romance started through phone calls and the occasional email, since Internet technology was not yet so common in Punjab. Because I was from a metropolitan city, as was S. Gurpreet Singh, the young man in Canada, we had a lot in common. We decided to get engaged! I visited his family's home in Punjab, surrounded by his mother and father and got engaged on the phone! We had a traditional engagement ceremony with his family members, but, without my prospective groom! Guess what. Life is a gamble. My friends used to argue with me –"how can you choose your life partner without meeting him"? All I could say was that love can flourish under all sorts of circumstances. If I was destined to be loved, I could experience it through a long-distance engagement too.

Sometimes we say that "matches are made in heaven," and this one truly was. We got married in Chandigarh when Gurpreet was thirty years old and I was twenty-four years of age. All I can say is that I was right. I am so blessed to have Gurpreet in my life. Of course, we all have to go through adjustments, especially marriages arranged by our elders. It feels that we are still learning things about one another every day. Our marriage has been blessed by a wonderful son who is now thirteen years old. He is the apple of our eye!

All I have to say this Valentine and many more, is "I love You, Gurpreet. Thanks for being in my life and giving me all the love and support I could hope for." Now I never question my destiny. God gave me a life partner who loves me unconditionally.

Happy Valentine's day to all.

The Love Birds,
Jasjit Kaur and Gurpreet Singh

Jasjit Kaur and Gurpreet Singh live in Ontario, Canada.

Gender, Sexuality, and Honour Codes

Many of the expectations surrounding family values in Punjab are unwritten and follow customary values that appear to be deeply etched into the very fabric of Punjabi Sikh society. They extend, however, far beyond the Sikh community into the majority of the diverse religious communities across India. Central to this value system are kinship rules. Kinship roles, dictated by those rules, are understood as essentially unchanging and as the central organizing principle for social organization in South Asia at large. Women's social identities and status are ultimately linked to their roles as daughters, daughters-in-law, and mothers; these identities in and of themselves are powerful determinants of their relations with the wider society. By ensuring that cultural norms such as women's subservience are followed, power and an honourable position in society at large are gained. Dishonourable conduct, on the other hand, can lead to a perceived and very real ruination of family honour; children, especially daughters, are keenly aware that their actions, if dishonourable in the customary Punjabi Sikh value system, will bring shame not only to their immediate family, but to the extended family, and to the community at large.

As in most regions of India, Punjabi society largely upholds both patriarchal and patrilineal ideals and practices. Gender inequity and women's subordination are firmly embedded in societal structures, kinship, and marriage practices. This has led to a resolute emphasis on the cultural norm of honour or respect (*izzat*) in Punjabi Sikh society. Closely aligned with notions of honour, especially for women, is that of modesty or propriety (**sharam**). Veena Das explains it thus: "Since the sexuality of a woman has to be protected with much greater care than the sexuality of men, great care is made to control expressions of girls' and women's sexuality" (1976: 5–6). For Punjabi males, *izzat* is reflected on an individual level and generally has to do with notions of wealth and status. According to a popular dictum, "A man's *izzat* is his woman's *sharam*." Together, honour and modesty play an important role in maintaining the traditional patriarchal framework of Punjabi society (Mooney, 2010).

Procreation and Sexuality

In Punjab, procreation is understood in terms of "the land," not only in rural areas but in the wider population as well. In this imagery, the female provides the field and the male provides the seed. The man's role in procreation, depositing the seed, is understood as the *gift* of conception. Like family property and family money, the child of this union is understood to belong to the male head of the family (Das, 1976: 3). When that child is male, he is an indivisible part of the patrilineal kinship group; when female, the clear understanding is that although she will receive love and affection from her father, her *true* home will be that of her husband. Given the physical and socio-economic changes that come with a woman's marriage, her allegiances are also expected to be primarily focused on her new family. The Punjabi Sikh daughter is thus traditionally described as "the wealth of others" (Mooney, 2006: 396). These arrangements, alongside the obligatory *daaj*, have led to a general devaluing of the female in some Sikh families. Historically, although unequivocally condemned by the

Gurus as well as by the *Sikh Reht Maryada*, female infanticide was practised, substantially reducing the female-to-male ratio. According to Anshu Malhotra, "Pride, it was felt, did not allow some to marry their daughters beneath their station, while leaving them unmarried was thought to bring disgrace to the girl and her family. This practice of hypergamy, i.e., marrying a daughter into a family of superior status, was seen as an established practice among many castes in Punjab" (2002: 51). Infanticide was the common means of doing away with a surplus of unwanted females. A verse said to have been recited at the burial of a newly born female refers to the practice of placing a bit of *gur* (unrefined sugar) in her mouth and a thread of cotton in her hand. It underscores the desire for males instead of females:

> Eat your *gur* and spin your thread
> But go and send a boy instead (Ibbetson, 1883: 373).

Today, the practice has largely been replaced by ultrasound tests that allow for the screening of unwanted female fetuses, which are then aborted in the numerous abortion clinics in Punjab (as well as in other parts of India). Eleanor Nesbitt reports:

> The juvenile sex ratio in Punjab, the one majority Sikh state, has declined with each successive census, and the fall in the number of female children accelerated sharply between 1991 and 2001, so that there are fewer than eight girls born for every ten boys. In order to check sex-selective foeticide, in 1996 in India the Pre-Natal Diagnostic Techniques (Regulation and Prevention of Misues) Act 1994 came into force. . . . [Nonetheless], the unborn Punjabi female is at greater risk than ever before (2005: 116).

Christine Fair's research among Vancouver Sikhs (1996) indicates that many of the same attitudes and practices may also be found in the diaspora (see also Almond et al., 2009).

Divorce

For Sikhs, marriage is a spiritual union that must be upheld at all costs. The *Sikh Reht Maryada* does not even mention divorce. In India, however, Sikhs (along with Jains and Buddhists) are covered by the Hindu Marriage Act of 1955, and are thus in a legal position to obtain support in the case of divorce. Where Sikhs have migrated to other countries, the marriage and divorce laws of the host country are followed.

Divorce is clearly understood to be dishonorable to both the family and the community at large; yet, as in other communities, divorce is on the increase in Sikh communities (Rait, 2005: 105). The wife and her family of origin carry the weight of dishonour associated with divorce, in keeping with the patriarchal norms of Sikh society. For this reason, many Sikh women stay with their husbands even when their marriages have broken down. In the Punjabi language, divorced women are referred to as "discarded," while the word for "widow" is a term of abuse (Nesbitt, 2005: 115). Although the prevailing notions of honour tend to restrict remarriage possibilities, divorcees are generally understood to be in a similar situation to widows, who are permitted to remarry, according to the *Sikh Reht Maryada*.

Homosexuality

Homosexual behaviour is not condoned in Sikhism, although the *Sikh Reht Maryada* does not address it. In rare instances, gay or lesbian Sikhs have interpreted this omission as allowing for the possibility of same-sex unions. Yet the householder ideal upheld as normative by Sikhs opposes any form of family or sexual relationship that is not procreation-focused and within the bounds of marriage. Most Sikhs would interpret this as pertaining only to heterosexual unions. Moreover, notions of *izzat* and shame tend to prevent deviation from the norm of marriage between a man and a woman, and any attempt to reinterpret scripture is perceived simply as misinterpretation (Jhutti-Johal, 2011: 113).

Conclusion

As with the other traditions discussed in this volume, attitudes toward women from the Sikh perspective are varied—indeed, they are multitude. Clearly, the Sikh Gurus taught that gender was no bar for women with regard to liberation, the ultimate goal of Sikhism. However, patriarchal values and attitudes have historically underscored virtually all forms of religious life for Sikh women and continue to do so today. Reforms and re-evaluations of Sikh women's position have taken place at various stages of Sikhism's development. So too have resounding episodes of backlash, largely under the time-honoured guise of "tradition." What is unique about the present day is that since the late twentieth century, Sikh women themselves have been at the forefront of interpreting, translating, and re-evaluating their tradition. Sikh women are also challenging the dominant systems that have barred them from taking part in all aspects of Sikh ritual life, while at the same time claiming the normative Sikh identity marker as their own.

Glossary

Adi Granth   The Sikh sacred scripture, also known as Guru Granth Sahib.

Akal Purakh   "Eternal Being," an important name for the Divine.

Akal Takht   The principal seat of Sikh temporal authority, adjacent to the Harimandir Sahib (Golden Temple) in Amritsar.

amritdhari **Sikhs**   Khalsa-initiated Sikhs.

charan pahul   "Nectar of the foot"; the original rite of initiation into the Sikh community.

daaj   Dowry.

Five Ks   The five symbolic items worn by all Khalsa Sikhs.

granthi   The custodian or reader at a gurdwara.

gurdwara   The Sikh place of worship; literally, "the guru's door."

gurmukh   A God-centred individual.

Harimandir Sahib   The principal Sikh shrine, in Amritsar, Punjab; also known as the Golden Temple.

hypergamy   A marriage system whereby the bride's family is of lower social status than the groom's.

izzat   Male honour.

janam-sakhis   "Birth stories"; tales of the Gurus and their families.

karah prasad   sanctified food

Kaur   The name now given to all Sikh females at birth, equivalent to "Singh" for males.

keshdhari **Sikh**   A Sikh who is not initiated but follows most if not all of the same regulations as Khalsa Sikhs.

khande di pahul   The Khalsa Sikh double-edged sword initiation ritual.

kirtan   Devotional singing; the core of Sikh worship.

langar   The communal meal offered at every gurdwara.

nam-simran   Sikh devotional discipline; meditation on the Divine Name.

nirguna   God without attributes.

panj piare   "Beloved Five"; originally, the five Sikhs who answered Guru Gobind Singh's call for volunteers willing to sacrifice themselves, who became the first members of the Khalsa.

ragis   Musicians.

saguna   In Sikhism, God with attributes.

sahajdhari   Non-Khalsa Sikh.

sangat   Congregation.

sant   "Seeker of truth."

sati   literally, "good woman"; a woman who immolates herself on the funeral pyre of her husband; the practice of immolation.

seva   Service to others.

sharam   Women's modesty or propriety.

Shiromani Gurdwara Parbandhak Committee (SGPC)   The institution overseeing shrines and gurdwaras in Punjab.

Sikh Reht Maryada   The Sikh Code of Conduct.

Singh   Name now given to all male Sikhs at birth.

Singh Sabha   Reform movement of the late nineteenth century.

Tat Khalsa   "True Khalsa"; a more radical branch of the Singh Sabh movement.

Yogi Bhajan   The founder of the 3HO/Sikh Dharma movement, who converted many Western people to Sikhism.

Further Reading

Bhachu, Parminder. 1988. "*Apni Marzi Kardhi*: Home and Work: Sikh Women in Britain." Pp. 76–102 in Sallie Westwood and Parminder Bhachu, eds, *Enterprising Women: Ethnicity, Economy and Gender Relations*. London: Routledge.

Brah, Avtar. 2004. "Locality, Globality and Gendered Refractions. Sikh Women in 'Western' Diasporas." *Journal of Punjab Studies* 12, 1: 153–65.

Jakobsh, Doris R., ed. 2010. *Sikhism and Women: An Exploration*. Delhi: Oxford University Press.

Mand, Kanwal. 2006. "Social Relations beyond the Family? Exploring Elderly South Asian Women's Friendships in London." *Community, Work and Family* 9, 3: 309–23.

Mooney, Nicola. 2009. *Rural Nostalgias and Transnational Dreams: Identity and Modernity among Jat Sikhs*. Toronto: University of Toronto Press.

Singh, Nikky-Guninder Kaur. 2005. *The Birth of the Khalsa: A Feminist Re-memory of Sikh Identity*. Albany: State University of New York Press.

Film and Online Resources

Amu. 2005. 102 mins. Directed by Shonali Bose. Emerging Pictures. Delhi riots through the eyes of a young Sikh woman.

Arranged Marriages. 2001. 52 mins. Directed by Carol Equer-Hamy. Explores issues of arranged marriages in India. Further information online at www.filmakers.com/index.php?a=filmDetail&filmID=1129.

California Dreaming: Indian Brides Search for Ex-pat Grooms. 2003. Directed by Meera Dewan. A documentary on Punjabi Indian brides duped by non-resident Indians who often harass their families for dowries; largely concentrated on the Doaba region of Punjab.

Crimes of Honour. 1998. 44 min. Directed by Shelley Saywell. Brooklyn, NY: First Run/Icarus Films. A journalist investigates honour killing and its relation to culture and religion.

International Network for the Rights of Female Victims of Violence in Pakistan: http://ecumene.org/INRFVVP/index.htm.

Mistaken Identity: Sikhs in America. 2004. Directed by Vinanti Sarkar, WLWD 2000 Inc.

"Murdered Bride." 2006. *The Fifth Estate*, CBC. 22 May.

Revolutionary Association of the Women of Afghanistan: www.rawa.org.

Sisters in Islam: www.sistersinislam.org.my.

Sikhwomen: www.Sikhwomen.com.

Sundri: The Brave Kaur. 2008. Director, Sukhwinder Singh, Vismad Limited, Sahara Production Singapore. Further information online at www.sundrithemovie.com/index.aspx. An animated film based on Bhai Vir Singh's novel *Sundri.*

See also "Women Make Movies," www.wmm.com, for a growing list of films about women in various religious traditions.

References

Abdulrahim, Raja. 2011. "A Decision on the Razor's Edge." *Los Angeles Times,* 9 October.

Acker, Joan. 1991. "Hierarchies, Jobs, Bodies: A Theory of Gendered Organizations." Pp. 139–58 in Judith Lorber and Susan A. Farrell, eds. *The Social Construction of Gender,* Newbury Park, CA, Sage Publications.

Almond, D., L. Edlund, and K. Milligan. 2009. O Sister, Where Art Thou? The Role of Son Preference and Sex Choice: Evidence from Immigrants to Canada. Cambridge, MA: National Bureau of Economic Research. www.nber.org/papers/w15391.

Axel, Brian Keith. 2004. "The Context of Diaspora." *Cultural Anthropology* 19, 1: 26–60.

Barrier, N. Gerald. 1970. *The Sikhs and Their Literature: A Guide to Tracts, Books and Periodicals, 1849–1919.* Delhi: Manohar.

Barstow, A.E. 1928. *Sikhs: A Handbook for the Indian Army.* Government of India, Publications Branch.

Bhai Vir Singh. 1988. *Sundri,* tr. Gobind Singh Mansukhani. New Delhi: Bhai Vir Singh Sahitya Sadan.

Castells, Manuel. 2010. *The Power of Identity.* West Sussex, UK: John Wiley & Sons Ltd.

Das, Veena. 1976. "Masks and Faces: An Essay on Punjabi Kinship." *Contributions of Indian Sociology* 10, 1: 1–30.

Dharam Parchar Committee. 1950. *Sikh Reht Maryada.* http://sgpc.net/sikhism/punjabi/Sikh%20Reht%20Maryada%28Eng%291.pdf.

Dhavan, Purnima. 2010. "Tracing Gender in the Texts and Practices of the Early Khalsa." Pp. 60–82 in Doris R. Jakobsh, ed. *Women in Sikhism: An Exploration.* Delhi: Oxford University Press.

Dusenbery, V.A. 1990. "Punjabi Sikhs and Gora Sikhs: Conflicting Assertions of Sikh Identity in North America." Pp. 334–55 in Joseph T. O'Connell, Milton Israel, and Willard G. Oxtoby, eds. *Sikh History and Religion in the Twentieth Century.* Toronto: University of Toronto, Centre for South Asian Studies.

Eck, Diana. 1998. *Darcan: Seeing the Divine Image in India.* New York: Columbia University Press.

Elsberg, Constance Waeber. 2003. *Graceful Women: Gender and Identity in an American Sikh Community.* Knoxville: University of Tennessee Press.

Fair, C. Christine. 1996. "Female Foeticide among Vancouver Sikhs: Recontextualizing Sex Selection in the North American Diaspora." *International Journal of Punjab Studies* 3, 1: 1–23.

Friedman, Susan S. 1998. *Mappings: Feminism and the Cultural Geographies of Encounter.* Princeton: Princeton University Press.

Gohil, N.S., and D.S. Sidhu. 2008. "The Sikh Turban: Post-911 Challenges to this Article of Faith." *Rutgers Journal of Law and Religion* 9, 2: 1–60.

Grewal, J.S. 1979. *Guru Nanak in History.* Chandigarh: Publication Bureau Punjab University.

———. 1996. "A Gender Perspective on Guru Nanak." Pp. 141–60 in Kiran Pawar, ed. *Women in Indian History: Social, Economic, Political and Cultural Perspectives.* New Delhi: Vision & Venture.

Grewal, J.S., and S.S. Bal. 1987. *Guru Gobind Singh.* Chandigarh: Panjab University.

Haddad, Yvonne Yazbeck, and Jane I. Smith. 2002. *Muslim Minorities in the West. Visible and Invisible.* Walnut Creek, CA: Altamira Press.

Hall, David D. 1997. "Introduction." Pp. vii-xii in D.D. Hall, ed. *Lived Religion in America. Toward a History of Practice.* Princeton, NJ: Princeton University Press.

Hall, Stuart. 1992. "The Question of Cultural Identity." Pp. 276-323 in S. Hall, ed., *Modernity and Its Futures.* London: Polity.

Hans, Surjit Singh. 1988. *A Reconstruction of Sikh History from Sikh Literature.* Jalandhar: ABS Publications.

Ibbetson, D.C.I. 1883. *Census of the Panjab—1881.* Calcutta: Government of India.

Jacobsen, Knut A. 2011. "Institutionalization of Sikhs in Norway. Community Growth and Generational Transfer." Pp. 19-38 in Jacobsen and Kristina Myrvold, eds. *Sikhs in Europe. Migration, Identities and Representation.* Surrey: Ashgate.

Jakobsh, Doris R. 2003. *Relocating Gender in Sikh History: Transformation, Meaning and Identity.* Delhi: Oxford University Press.

———. 2004. "Constructing Sikh Identities: Authorities, Virtual and Imagined." *International Journal of Punjab Studies* 10, 1 and 2: 127-42.

———. 2006. "Sikhism, Interfaith Dialogue and Women: Transformation and Identity." *Journal of Contemporary Religion* 21, 2: 183-99.

———. 2008. "3HO/Sikh Dharma of the Western Hemisphere: The 'Forgotten' New Religious Movement?" *Religion Compass* 2, 1: 385-408.

Jhutti-Johal, Jagbir. 2011. *Sikhism Today.* London: Continuum.

Jolly, Surjit Kaur. 1988. *Sikh Revivalist Movements: The Nirankari and Namdhari Movements in Punjab in the Nineteenth Century—A Socio-Religious Study.* Delhi: Gitanjali Press.

Kaur, Gurnam.2004. "Guru Granth Sahib and the Gender Equations." Unpublished paper presented at the International Conference on Compilation, Authority, Status & Universal Message of Sri Guru Granth Sahib, Mount San Antonio College, Walnut, CA, May 1-2. www.internationalsikhconference.org/speakers.html.

Kaur, Kirpa. 2012. "Introduction: Hair Speaks: Sikh Women Voicing Spiritual, Sexual and Identity, posted Body Politic." www.scribd.com/doc/83495387/Kirpa-Kaur-v-2.

King, Richard. 1999. "Orientalism and the Modern Myth of Hinduism." *Numen* 46: 146-85.

King, Ursula. 1998. "Feminism: The Missing Dimension in the Dialogue of Religions." Pp. 40-55 in John May, ed. *Pluralism and the Religions: The Theological and Political Dimensions.* London: Cassell Academic.

Kinnvall, Catarina. 2004. "Globalization and Religious Nationalism: Self, Identity, and the Search for Ontological Security." *Political Psychology* 25: 5.

The Langar Hall. 2008. "Recasting Gender for Sikh Women." 26 July. http://thelangarhall.com/general/recasting-gender-for-sikh-women.

Macauliffe, Max Arthur. 1990. (first published 1909). *The Sikh Religion. Its Gurus, Sacred Writings and Authors.* Vol. 5. Delhi: Low Price Publications.

Mahmood, Cynthia, and Stacy Brady. 2000. *The Guru's Gift: An Ethnography Exploring Gender Equality with North American Sikh Women.* Mountain View, CA: Mayfield Publishing.

Malhotra, Anshu. 2002. *Gender, Caste and Religious Identities: Restructuring Class in Colonial Punjab.* Delhi: Oxford University Press.

Mand, Kanwal. 2002. "Place, Gender and Power in Transnational Sikh Marriages." *Global Networks* 2, 3: 233-48.

Mann, Gurinder Singh. 2004. *Sikhism.* Upper Saddle River, NJ ; Prentice Hall.

McLeod, Hew. 1997. *Sikhism.* London: Penguin.

McLeod, W.H. 1987. *The Chaupa Singh Rahit-Nama.* Dunedin, NZ: University of Otago.

——— 2006. *Prem Sumarag. The Testimony of a Sanatan Sikh.* Delhi: Oxford University Press.

Mooney, Nicola. 2006. "Aspiration, Reunification and Gender Transformation in Jat Sikh Marriages from India to Canada." *Global Networks* 6, 4: 389-403.

———. 2010. "Lowly Shoes on Lowly Feet: Some Jat Sikh Women's Views on Gender & Equality." Pp. 156-186 in Doris R. Jakobsh, ed. *Women in Sikhism: An Exploration.* Delhi: Oxford University Press.

Nesbitt, Eleanor. 2005. *Sikhism: A Very Short Introduction.* Oxford: Oxford University Press.

O'Connell, Joseph T., Milton Israel, and Willard G. Oxtoby, eds. 1988. *Sikh History and Religion in the Twentieth Century.* Toronto: University of Toronto.

Ortner, Sherry B., and Harriet Whitehead. 1981. *Sexual Meanings. The Cultural Construction of Gender and Sexuality*. Cambridge: Cambridge University Press.

Rait, Satwant Kaur. 2005. *Sikh Women in England: Their Religious and Cultural Beliefs and Social Practices*. Stoke-on-Trent, UK: Trentham Books.

Rinehart, Robin. 2010. "The Guru, The Goddess: The Dasam Granth and Its Implications for Constructions of Gender in Sikhism." Pp. 40–59 in Doris R. Jakobsh, ed. *Women in Sikhism: An Exploration*. Delhi: Oxford University Press.

Scott, Joan Wallach. 1988. *Gender and the Politics of History*. New York: Columbia University Press.

Shackle, C., and A.S. Mandair. 2005. *Teachings of the Sikh Gurus: Selections from the Sikh Scriptures*. New York: Routledge.

Shankar, Rajkumari. 2002. "Women in Sikhism." Pp. 108–33 in Arvind Sharma, ed. *Women in Indian Religions*. Delhi: Oxford University Press.

Singh, Gurharpal and Darhsan Singh Tatla. 2006. *Sikhs in Britain: The Making of a Community*. London: Zed Books.

Singh, Harbans. 1994. *Guru Nanak and Origins of the Sikh Faith*. Patiala, India: Publication Bureau, Punjabi University.

Singh, Nikky-Guninder Kaur. 1993. *The Feminine Principle in the Sikh Vision of the Transcendent*. Cambridge: Cambridge University Press.

———. 1995. *The Name of My Beloved: Verses of the Sikh Gurus*. San Francisco: HarperSanFrancisco.

———. 2000. "Why Did I Not Light the Fire? The Refeminization of Ritual in Sikhism." *Journal of Feminist Studies in Religion* 16: 64–70.

Singh, Pashaura. 2010. "Revisiting the 'Evolution of the Sikh Community.'" *Journal of Punjab Studies* 17: 1&2: 45–74.

Sundri. *The Brave Kaur*. 2008. Director, Sukhwinder Singh, Vismad Ltd, Sahara Production Singapore.

"Sweet Sikhi." 2005. "Sikhi, Turban and Woman." *DiscoverSikhi.com* 29 Sept. http://forums.waheguroo.com/index.php?/topic/12041-sikhi-turban-and-woman/.

Zuckerman, Phil. 1997. "Gender Regulation as a Source of Religious Schism." *Sociology of Religion* 58, 4: 353–73.

CHAPTER 9

Women in Western
Spirituality Movements

Leona M. Anderson and Pamela Dickey Young

Ceremony at the Goddess Conference Glastonbury, England, 2009.

Kellye Crockett

On 1 May 1999, following a visionary dream I'd had four months earlier, I opened Sacred Source in Kingston, Ontario, as an ecumenical, non-denominational space whose mandate was to provide a haven of peace as well as resources for seekers and followers of all spiritual inclinations. As I was in the middle of completing my doctoral thesis in French linguistics at the time, opening a shop was the furthest thing from my mind on New Year's Day of that year, but that dream on January 4 inspired me to change the course of my life and enter a path of loving service.

Sacred Source was an instant success. I had been practising the art of divination in Kingston for several years already and was well known in the community thanks to frequent and positive media coverage by the local newspaper, magazines, and radio and television stations. I believe the relatively high profile accorded me by these local media, as well as my solid reputation as a Tarot reader, provided an instant clientele and the basis for the shop's success. . . . Neither I nor my staff have encountered any serious opposition to the business, vocal or physical, which does occur in other locations. Again, I believe this is due to the strength of our reputation in the community as well as the very discrete nature of our customer relations and window displays: all items pertaining to the Wiccan tradition are located on the second floor, and never make their way to the front window.

I have also taught the art of bellydance to hundreds of women in the Kingston area and opened Oasis Dance Studio in 2006. I view this art form as a vehicle for personal growth, creativity, sensual expression, and spiritual transformation. Dance is a very spiritual and meditative experience for me; as the Sufi poet Rumi said, "Whosoever knoweth the power of the dance dwelleth in God."

As a child growing up in Prince Edward Island, Canada, I spent a great deal of time alone in nature, mainly because I wanted to pursue studies in biology later on. It was also much more peaceful and enjoyable wandering in the woods, in the swamp, or on the beach, examining the flora and fauna rather than being inside playing Barbie with the other girls. My developing years were greatly influenced by my maternal grandmother. Nana was Irish and Catholic, and even though she attended mass frequently, she held unconventional views of the Church, the pope, and organized religion in general. She also read tea leaves and was known in Charlottetown as a witch.

To this day, I continue to honour the cycles of nature and to prac-tise the esoteric arts of divination and healing. I don't call myself a Wiccan or witch anymore as I feel that labels are confining and a loaded one like "witch" often results in people thinking of you and defining you in only one way, which is diminishing. If I had to choose a description for myself it would be "nature mystic," as this is open to a wide variety of interpretations, or, as I often reply to customers at the shop, "I don't belong to any one particular path—I am simply on a spiritual journey."

Kellye Crockett runs "Sacred Source, Inc." in Kingston, Ontario, where she is an "Intuitive Consultant" providing readings, healing treatments, work-shops, and seminars. She wrote this piece specifically for this book.

Introduction and Overview

Many women have sought out alternatives to traditional hegemonic religions. New Religious Movements are among the fastest growing of all religions, in terms of both numbers of adherents and numbers of distinct groups that can be identified under this rubric. This chapter focuses on several New Religious Movements that are, explicitly or implicitly, feminist in their interests: neopa-ganism, Wicca, and **ecofeminism**, along with a few other practices that can be grouped under the rubric "New Age."

There is a tendency in these movements to prefer the terms "spiritual" and "spirituality" to "religious" and "religion." Behind this preference is a sense that "spirituality" is personal, unique, self-validating, authentic, and authoritative, whereas "religion" is institutional, bureaucratic, social, inflexible, hierarch-ical, and authoritarian. "Spirituality" emphasizes individual experience above all, while "religion" is often assumed to put institutions first. Thus spiritual-ity movements tend to dissociate themselves from mainstream traditions and often situate themselves in opposition to them.

Although some practitioners see Wicca as the revival of an ancient trad-ition, it can also be described as a new religion focused on empowering women to create positive change. And although not all ecofeminists would character-ize their movement as religious, it does have a spiritual dimension insofar as it holds the natural world to be sacred. All the movements and practices discussed here envision women as central; in addition, unlike many more traditional religions, none of them considers women to be evil or stupid.[1] Yet no two of them see women in exactly the same way. Thus they offer a variety of ways of thinking about women. First, then, some general comments on New Age.

There are several factors that make movements of the type we discuss here difficult to come to grips with. For example, there is no one belief or set of beliefs that they share. Although many of them incorporate elements from long-established religious traditions (for example, Buddhism and Judaism), many practitioners do not identify themselves with any "traditional" religion. Nor do they necessarily embrace any particular movement exclusively. In fact, most New Religious Movements position themselves in opposition to "traditional" religions.

A second complicating characteristic is the fact that these movements are not organized in any traditional way: none of them has a single authoritative text, a single person or group of persons who are looked to exclusively for spiritual guidance, or a single set of rituals or practices that all followers subscribe to. In general, the movements we look at here privilege individual experience as the final authority, and this "experience" can be extremely diverse, not only from one movement to another but within individual movements.

Key Characteristics

The feminist spiritualities described here are so diverse that they are almost impossible to categorize. Under the rubric of feminist spirituality, we include neopaganism, Wicca, Goddess religion, transpersonal psychology, and **channelling**; various healing practices, including the use of crystals, astrological charts, herbs, tarot, and group work; and a number of philosophical and psychological movements. Given this multiplicity of practices and concerns, the following sections on channelling and healing are included simply as examples of feminist spiritual practices and concerns; not all feminist spiritualities practise channelling, nor do all focus on healing.

New Age Practices

Channelling

One of the most striking New Age practices is known as channelling: The term is fairly self-explanatory; it refers to the perceived ability of an individual to receive information from a source not accessible through ordinary consciousness. In New Age circles, the information gleaned from the channelling experience is sometimes likened to the more traditional notion of revelation. Generally, the purpose of channelling is learning and guidance: for example, receiving information about the meaning and purpose of life, predictions of future events, and many other types of information that are believed to assist one in living a full and meaningful life. As Michael F. Brown notes, "Channelling . . . exhibits remarkable continuities with the now largely forgotten spiritualism of the nineteenth century" (1997: 11). New Age channellers believe they receive information from a host of sources, including angels, spirit-guides, extraterrestrials, masters, gods, goddesses, and animals. Increasingly, contemporary channellers are drawn to androgynous spirits that have moved beyond gender altogether (11). Sometimes the channelling experience is achieved in a trance state, in which channellers believe that the source transmitting the message takes complete possession of their bodies, at times without warning, completely incapacitating them. This is not always the case, however, and—theoretically—anyone can act as a channel. Although certain individuals are considered to be more gifted than others, channellers claim that the ability can be cultivated, and several do-it-yourself publications are available to that end.

A significant number of channellers are women. One well-known example was Jane Roberts, who claimed to receive revelations from an entity known as Seth from 1963 until her death in 1984. The material dictated by Seth and "scribed" by Jane is known as the Seth material (Roberts, 1970: 11–12) and has been summarized as follows:

> The range of subject matter in Seth's books is broad. From dreams and out of body travel to life after death. Biblical history, space travel, other dimensions, parallel and probable selves, and behavior of subatomic particles are just a few of the topics covered. . . . Throughout Seth's work the main themes return again and again . . . "*You create your own reality,*" and "*You get what you concentrate upon*" (www.secretoflife .com/seth/index.html).

Other New Age channellers include J.Z. Knight, whose famous encounters with her entity, Ramtha, are well documented (Hanegraaff, 1996: 29–30; Knight, 1987), and Eva Pierrakos, who, from 1956 to her death in 1979, received information from "the Guide" and wrote a series of lectures that came to be known as the Guide Lectures or the Pathwork Lectures (Pierrakos, 1990). "The Pathwork" is a registered US trademark and refers to the path of personal transformation and spiritual self-realization set out in the lectures of Pierrakos. Pathwork communities throughout the world, including in the United States and Canada, seek to interpret these teachings, through individual and group work, as a means for spiritual healing and personal growth.

Important to include here as well is *A Course in Miracles*, more generally known as **the Course**. This text, "scribed" by Dr Helen Schucman, is a collection of self-study spiritual materials that, through a process of inner dictation, she identified as coming from Jesus (www.acim.org/AboutACIM/how.html). The Course is said to have travelled by word of mouth and to have been transmitted by photocopy. In 1975 the Foundation for Inner Peace, a non-profit organization, was founded and published the Course (see *A Course in Miracles*, 1985). A workbook consisting of 365 exercises, one for each day of the year, and a brief manual for teachers together form the main text of the Course. Its contents are summarized in the book's introduction as follows:

> This is a course in miracles. It is a required course. Only the time you take it is voluntary. Free will does not mean that you can establish the curriculum. It means only that you can elect what you want to take at a given time. The course does not aim at teaching the meaning of love, for that is beyond what can be taught. It does aim, however, at removing the blocks to the awareness of love's presence, which is your natural inheritance. The opposite of love is fear, but what is all encompassing can have no opposite.
>
> This course can therefore be summed up very simply in this way:
> *Nothing real can be threatened.*
> *Nothing unreal exists.*
> *Herein lies the peace of God* (http://courseinmiracles.com/).

Clearly, women play an important role in the reception of channelled material, often through physical contact with a perceived entity that takes over the channeller's body. Susan Starr Sered, drawing on the work of Hilary Graham and Ross Kraemer, has argued that women are more susceptible to the experience of possession than men because foreign objects commonly invade their bodies and, unlike men, they are socialized to accept these intrusions (1994: 189–90). This is simply to say that it is not a unique situation for a woman to be invaded by an alien organism that occupies a portion of her body. Susan Starr Sered also notes the obvious parallels between pregnancy and spirit possession in her discussion of the gendered dimension of possession rituals (1994: 189). Whatever the explanation, a high percentage of channellers represented in New Age traditions are women.

Jill Galvan, in *The Sympathetic Medium: Feminine Channeling, the Occult, and Communication Technologies*, gives us another explanation for the prominence of women as channellers/mediums. Galvan reads Victorian short stories and novels against the phenomenon of mediumship and the rise of white-collar communications jobs. In a review of Galvan's book, Cathy Gutierrez comments that, like the spirit medium,

> the media girl was successful to the extent that she could erase her own consciousness. Handling sensitive information and often ornery clients, women in communications were the vessels of transmitting information, not for understanding it or acting upon it. Galvan uses the word "automatism" for this nearly trancelike state, where work is done but not intellectually processed: touch typing, writing in short hand, and benignly listening to the sounds but not words of those using the telephone all required this mental absence. . . . Practical matters intrude, of course, and the ability to pay women less than men, their more "sensitive" approach to customers with problems, and the decreased likelihood of corporate spying or takeover all contributed to this new labor pool (Gutierrez 2011: 97).

Whatever the explanation, a high percentage of the channellers represented in New Age traditions are women. It is also worth noting that the last 25 years have seen a rise in this phenomenon in locations outside North America, including South Asia (see, for example, Smith, 2006).

Healing

Health and healing are prominent concerns in many New Age movements. A distinctive feature of many of these movements is that they employ a variety of alternative therapies, including the use of herbs, diet, crystals, shamanic diagnostics and cures, magnetic therapy, massage therapy, and various psychological counselling techniques. The pervasiveness of these therapies is evident in the fact that, as Kemp notes, "since the ascendency of New Age from the 1970s many churches have adopted New Age healing techniques" (2004: 77).

Traditionally, women have often been associated with healing, especially in the context of herbal remedies and midwifery. Women are often assigned, or socialized to accept, the role of household healer or "Dr Mom," responsible for maintaining the physical and mental well-being of the family. It is thus not particularly surprising that women play important roles in the development and administration of many New Age therapies.

A striking feature of New Age healing practices is the mass consumption of products, therapies, and workshops that are widely available online and in specialty shops, many of which are conveniently located in shopping malls. Increasingly, the term "consumer" in this context is synonymous with "woman."

As Karlyn Crowley notes, "by and large white women are the largest consumers of New Age products, as workshop and book sales indicate, and their consumption patterns have spread beyond a particular niche and into the mainstream" (2011: 41). This emphasis on consumption is in many ways the opposite of traditional religions' emphasis on the separation of worldly comfort and spiritual development. In addition, many critics argue that New Age consumers have fallen prey to quack products. In explanation of the large numbers of women who consume these products, some theorists argue that it is because women are excluded from upper-level positions in religious institutions (45). While this may indeed be the case, consumption of spiritual goods is one of the easiest ways to have a spiritual practice, and comparatively affordable. The New Age emphasis on individual empowerment is consistent with the notion that, for many women, the freedom to choose and/or purchase spiritual practices is a source of power and community. Whatever the case, women increasingly use these items to fulfill their own spiritual needs rather than turn to external authorities for answers.

Most New Age healing practices focus on holistic health. "**Holism**" in this context refers to the treatment of the whole person rather a particular ailment. Primary here is the interaction among physical, emotional, mental, and spiritual aspects of the patient's experience, as well as the impact of social factors and the wider environment on his or her well-being (Hanegraaff, 1996: 48–50). The role of the mind is of primary importance in the healing process as described in New Age literature. In this regard, New Age healing practices contain an implicit critique of modern Western medicine. In particular, they reject the mind–body dichotomy, and with it the distinction between physical and mental ailments. It is notable that New Age literature, especially feminist New Age literature, often describes Western medicine as male-dominated and patriarchal.

New Age healing practices commonly concentrate on personal growth and questions of balance and harmony, sometimes employing techniques that diagnose imbalances and cures that address them. Very often, too, these movements draw inspiration from traditional methods of healing, including the use of herbs.

The religious dimension of healing, with its emphasis on meaning and the interpretation of various sorts of suffering, is a common concern in New Age literature. In her study of religions dominated by women, Sered suggests that "illness is significant to female religious specialists not because they are ill more than other people, but because they themselves see their illnesses as meaningful to their religious roles" (1994: 225). She also notes that "women religious leaders tend to attribute greater significance to their illnesses" (222) than other people do. In the context of New Age religions, "holistic healing is concerned with more than simply 'fixing' isolated problems, healing is regarded as promoting harmony in the world and therefore carries at least implicit salvational overtones" (Hanegraaff, 1996: 45).

Neopaganism, Wicca, and Ecofeminism

Two important movements in the women's spirituality tradition, Wicca and ecofeminism, are closely related to the broader movement known as neopaganism. The word "paganism" comes from the Latin *paganus*, "country dweller," but it is used today as a broad term that embraces a variety of religious/spiritual practices and beliefs. "Neopagan" means "new pagan," a reference to looking back from the present day and recovering pre-Christian traditions of nature worship. Neopagan movements are eclectic and malleable but can be grouped together because of a common desire to see human beings regain their proper place within nature rather than over it, against it, or above it. Through ritual and action, neopagans seek to overcome human alienation from the rest of nature.

Magic—or, as many Wiccans spell it, "magick" (to differentiate it from stage magic)—is often viewed as an important part of Wiccan practice. Ecology is also a central concern. The basic idea behind the concern with ecology is that we, in the modern world, have lost pagan wisdom about our relationship to the natural world, and that the recovery of this wisdom is both desirable and crucial to our well-being. Freedom from external religious authorities is an important feature of all these movements, and it gives scope for inventing and reinventing rituals and sacred texts.

Wicca

Probably the most visible of the neopagan movements, especially where women are concerned, is Wicca, also known as "the Craft." Many Wiccans call themselves "witches." While it is safe to say that all Wiccans are neopagans, not all neopagans are Wiccans. The distinctive components of Wiccan traditions include an emphasis on ritual and magic, a common ethical view of the world, and a focus on the Goddess. Magic is understood as evidence of a connection with the Goddess and a source of personal empowerment

Feminist Wicca has been constructed in large part to meet the needs of women who have rejected the patriarchy central to most mainstream religious traditions. The Goddess at the centre stands sometimes alongside a God, sometimes alone. In the former case, she is sometimes thought of as Mother Nature, encompassing both female and male forces. Together, the God and the Goddess create balance. They represent the birth, death, and regeneration of the world: events that are enacted in neopagan rituals. In the latter case, when she stands alone, the Goddess is understood as primary, especially by feminists who are uncomfortable with the idea of a male deity.

Most forms of Wicca today are variations of **Gardnerian Wicca**, which originated in 1939 with Gerald Gardner, a retired British civil servant, who initiated his most important disciple, Doreen Valiente, in 1952. Essentially this is a nature-based movement focusing on two figures: the Goddess of Fertility and the Horned God. Gardner claims to have been initiated by Dorothy Clutterbuck (or simply Old Dorothy), who practised an ancient form of witchcraft that somehow survived the persecutions of the Middle Ages. Despite these claims, it is clear that Gardner did not revive an old religion; he created a new one.

Among other forms of Wicca, there is Alexandrian Wicca, which began with Alex Sanders, the self-proclaimed king of the witches, and his wife, Maxine. Alexandrian Wicca is a modified version of the Gardnerian type. Alex Sanders is thought to have obtained a Gardnerian *Book of Shadows* (http://sacred-texts .com/pag/gbos/index.htm) and started his own **coven** from it. He initiated a large number of people, including Janet and Stewart Farrar.

Dianic Wicca is essentially a women's movement promoting female spirituality. The members of Dianic covens worship the Goddess as the primary deity and the movement constitutes a clear rejection of patriarchal religion. Dianic Wicca emphasizes the Goddess as described by authors including Zsuzsanna Budapest. There are also other varieties of Wicca, including Odinism, which is a modern movement that draws heavily upon Norse and Celtic traditions and essentially seeks to revive pagan traditions of Northern Europe. Members of **eclectic Wicca** do not belong to one tradition or group; more often than not, they practise alone, as "solitaire" Wiccans, and create their own traditions. Eclectic witches have their own beliefs and ideologies, and work with herbs, crystals, and the like for the betterment of their family and community.

Some Wiccan groups are all women and some include men as well. All-women groups tend to be non-hierarchical; mixed groups tend to have three ranks (Berger, 1999: 13). Because in Wicca one is free to function as one's own religious authority, as many as 50 per cent of those who name themselves Wiccans are solo practitioners who might move in and out of covens over periods of time but who typically practise rituals on their own, maybe searching out groups for particular holiday celebrations (Berger, 1999: 50).

Ecofeminism

Many neopagans, including Wiccans, are part of a much larger and more diffuse movement that has been called ecofeminism. Ecofeminists notice that traditionally women have tended to be linked with nature, and therefore have been considered inferior to the men who are credited with creating culture (Ortner, 1974). Some ecofeminists believe that this link exists because women's "nature" is in fact different from men's, and argue that women do have a different understanding of and empathy for the plight of the earth, because they, like the earth, have been oppressed. Others believe that this relationship is more socially constructed than "natural": that is, because women have traditionally been placed on the "nature" side of the nature/culture dichotomy, they are better positioned than men to analyze both their own oppression and the oppression of the earth. At different times in Western society, both nature and women have been seen as passive objects that can be dominated and controlled rather than autonomous entities that are good in their own right.

Ecofeminists have differing views on what should be done about the plight of the earth, but all agree that we need to change both how we think about women and nature and how we behave towards others—human and non-human. Ecofeminists tend to privilege an understanding of the universe as an interconnected whole in which all the parts are intimately related to one another, nothing is unimportant or without value, and the body is not only inseparable from the mind but equally important.

Particularly interesting to students of religion is the way some ecofeminists appeal to "spirituality" both as a means of understanding woman and nature and as a way to change thinking and behaviour:

> Earth-based spirituality influences Ecofeminism by informing its values. This does not mean that every Ecofeminist must worship the Goddess, perform rituals, or adopt any particular belief system. . . . What we are doing, however, is attempting to shift the values of our culture. We could describe that shift as one away from battle as our underlying cultural paradigm and toward the cycle of birth, growth, death, and regeneration, to move away from a view of the world as made up of warring opposites toward a view that sees processes unfolding and continuously changing (Starhawk, 1989: 174).

For spiritual ecofeminists, various spiritual practices can realign our thought processes and in so doing empower us to change our actions:

> If we believe, and experientially *know* through various practices such as meditation and holistic ritual that neither our sisters and brothers nor the rest of nature is "the other," we will not violate their being, nor our own. Ethics of mutual respect would not allow coercion or domination, such as forcing someone to give birth or to kill (Spretnak, 1982: xvii).

The earth is often symbolized as female—as Mother Earth or as Gaia (Ruether, 1992). Earth in this view is a living whole: "When this world is seen as the living body of the Goddess, there is no escape, nowhere else to go, no one to save us. This earth body itself is the terrain of our spiritual growth and development, which comes through our contact with the fullness of life inherent in the earth—with the reality of what's going on here" (Starhawk, 1989: 178). Thus we can see why there have been many interconnections between the ecofeminist movement and various New Age and women's spirituality groups.

History

Neopagans trace their roots to the pagans of pre-Christian Europe, who seem to have based their practice and beliefs on the cycles of the natural world. Pre-Christian pagan traditions are mostly lost to us historically, though some remnants have been extrapolated from various pieces of archaeological evidence, such as Stonehenge. As some neopagans would have it, pagans were persecuted and their traditions went underground and were lost in the process. Margaret Murray contributed to this notion of a long history of persecution by suggesting the historical witch trials were attempts to eliminate adherents of an ancient religion (Murray, 1921; Berger, 1999: 21). "The Burning Times" is a phrase found in Wiccan literature and the subject of a National Film Board of Canada documentary of the same name, produced in 1990. The film argues that the witch hunts that swept Europe from the fifteenth to the seventeenth century contributed significantly to the destruction of pagan religion. Many Wiccans and neopagans believe that these events were motivated by misogyny, religious intolerance, and patriarchy, all of which Wiccans seek to overcome.

The notion of witchcraft as an ancient continuing religion with a long history has been a powerful one for many neopagans, especially feminists, who cherish the idea of a pre-patriarchal religious tradition that could be revived. Within Wicca itself and among religious studies scholars who are interested in Wicca, there are active debates about which parts of the tradition might truly be ancient and which are newly invented. Those who believe Wicca to be the continuation of an ancient religious tradition usually draw on the evidence of prehistoric archaeology to point to times and places where the Great Goddess was central to human worship. The archaeological work of Marija Gimbutas in Central and Eastern Europe led her to use evidence from burial sites to theorize that in the Paleolithic (beginning 40,000 BCE) and Neolithic (8000–3000 BCE) periods, women and men were social equals and that society was peaceful and harmonious. Gimbutas and others propose that the many female figures, especially figures with prominent breasts and genital markings, were goddess figures, pointing to the centrality of goddess worship as connected to social equality for women and men (Gimbutas, 1982, 1989; Stone, 1976). Gimbutas had a profound effect on scholarship concerning the possibility of female deities in ancient civilizations. Though controversial, her groundbreaking work obliged other scholars, whether they agreed with her or not, to grapple with the idea that some ancient civilizations were organized around a female divinity (see Christ and Goldenberg, 1996).

There is also some evidence to support the practice of goddess worship in other locations, including the Indus Valley, where it dates to approximately 2000–3000 BCE. Excavations at the ancient cities of Mohenjo-daro and Harappa have uncovered a large number of female figurines that some have interpreted as fertility goddesses. They have also been understood as confirmation that the worship of a Great Goddess, probably associated with Mother Earth, dominated the religious life of this civilization. The case for the worship of a female figure or figures in this location is complicated, though, by the absence of dominant female figures in the early Vedic tradition in the Indian subcontinent. At the village level in India, there are many goddesses who have probably been worshipped since very ancient times. These goddesses are often associated with agriculture and are worshipped to ensure fertility of crops and the like. Male deities at this level tend to play a secondary role. Worship of goddesses gained significant momentum in the post-Vedic era. The numerous goddesses who figure in mainstream brahmanic Hinduism are sometimes seen as representing a resurgence of a goddess tradition that had been present since the Indus Valley civilization. Whatever the case, goddesses continue to flourish in India in modern times.

Goddesses in all locations tend to be complex and multi-faceted, and there are many ways of understanding them. Sometimes they are interpreted as reflections of family dynamics. Sometimes the goddesses are understood as parts or emanations of one Great Goddess. In his study of the Indian goddess Santoshi Ma, for example, Stanley Kurtz argues that she is simply a variant on the Great Goddess theme, in this case as the goddess with a makeover (1992: 14). There is also a tendency to present the goddesses as if they have (or should have) fixed personalities: thus Kali is consistently depicted as malevolent and Sita as benevolent. While goddesses do have predominant character traits, some tending towards life affirmation and others towards life denial, all possess a range of emotions and character traits. Sorting them into artificial categories is hardly helpful.

All history is interpretation. Those who accept the idea of early societies that valued women and men equally and worshipped the goddess point out that there have been powerful patriarchal academic forces ranged against that idea (Christ, 1997). Other feminist scholars, however, think that the evidence used by Gimbutas and others is not sufficient to make a convincing historical case (Eller, 2000). We cannot know, for example, how all those female figures were used. We do not know for sure if they were goddess figures or what role they played in societal life.

For many Wiccans, the recovery of lost history is less important than the power of goddess traditions in the present. Whether or not there was a religion of the Great Goddess in prehistoric times, there is one today. Whether or not women ever ruled in matriarchies, women are taking power today. Whether or not contemporary witchcraft has its roots in the Stone Age, its branches reach into the future (Starhawk, 1982b: 415–16).

Texts, Rituals, and Interpretations

Wicca is not a text-based religion. Ritual, rather than text, is at its heart, although texts are used in the service of ritual. One of the striking features of Wicca is that it has no official sacred texts or official sacred rituals. Nor are there any universal rules regarding behaviour, primarily because Wicca is not a legalistic or codified tradition. Indeed, the opposite is the case: creativity and invention are highly valued. Individual groups, or practitioners, decide on what is important for their practice. Texts can be drawn from almost anywhere, and the textual material used in rituals often comes from female writers who have nothing to do with Wicca themselves. An example is this passage by the French writer Monique Wittig:

> There was a time when you were not a slave, remember that. You walked alone, full of laughter, you bathed bare-bellied. You say you have lost all recognition of it, remember. . . . You say there are no words to describe it, you say it does not exist. But remember. Make an effort to remember. Or, failing that, invent (1985: 89).

Of course, figures such as Gardner, Budapest, and Starhawk are influential, as are Gimbutas, Stone, and Carol Christ, and excerpts from their works often function as central texts. There is some consistency between groups because material is shared at pagan festivals and through electronic media. One of the most widely quoted texts is from Merlin Stone: "In the beginning, people prayed to the Creatrix of Life, the Mistress of Heaven. At the dawn of religion, God was a woman. Do you remember?" (1976: 1).

Although Wiccan belief and practice vary greatly, there are some ideas that keep recurring. One of these is the Wiccan rede: "eight words the Wiccan rede fulfil—an' it harm none, do what ye will" (see, for example, Budapest, 1989: 214). "Rede" means advice or counsel.[2] This maxim is contrasted to the rules and regulations of organized religions, an important feature of Wicca, as noted above. It is used as a general ethical guideline to indicate that personal freedom is restricted by the need to consider the well-being of everyone. Wiccans are cautious about their relationships with others and especially cognizant of their relationship with the earth. "Harm none" applies equally to people, to animals, and to the earth. The Wiccan rede is easily comparable to the golden rule found in a variety of other traditions.

Another central idea is that what you do, whether for good or for ill, returns to you. Typically, this is expressed in terms of the "Rule of Three":

> *Ever Mind The Rule Of Three*
> *Three Times Your Acts Return To Thee*
> *This Lesson Well, Thou Must Learn*
> *Thou Only Gets What Thee Dost Earn* (http://wiccansage.hubpages
> .com/hub/Ethics-in-Wicca-part-2-The-Threefold-Law)

The Rule of Three basically cautions one to be careful what one wishes for, but it is also about the consequences of actions and the relation of actions and their consequences to the rest of the world. It thus focuses on the interconnectedness of the universe. The Rule of Three is about taking responsibility for one's actions, and it means that whatever you do, it will come back on you. In the end, however, the individual is the final authority, although individuals may have to temper that authority if they choose to belong to groups. Wiccan groups tend to be small (some say no more than 13 members per group), and they formulate and reformulate over time as members enter and leave.

Wiccan rituals have several basic elements. Usually a circle is cast, or marked out, to indicate the sacred space for the ritual. The powers or energies of all four quarters or directions are summoned. After the ritual, there is feasting and celebration, commonly called "cakes and wine." The circle that was marked out is "unwound" at the end (Berger, 1999: 16). In rituals, depending on the group and the purpose of the ritual, various powers and forces are called upon. Goddesses' names, for example, are often invoked to give energy, strength, and assistance to those who need it. Ritual expressions at Wiccan rituals include "hail and welcome," "hail and farewell," and "merry meet and merry part, and merry meet again." Rituals are used both to celebrate the **sabbats** and to "raise energy" for magical workings. Helen Berger explains the last: "According to Gardner, Witches are able to project energy from their bodies, through dance, song, meditation, and directed thought that can be used to perform magical acts" (1999: 11).

Many Wiccan rituals involve a recitation from the "Charge of the Goddess." The "Charge" is a poem attributed to Gardner's disciple Doreen Valiente. It was originally found in Gardner's *Book of Shadows*, a text outlining a sequence of rituals and Craft laws that is revered by Wiccans as a statement of reverence for the Goddess and nature (www.fortunecity.com/greenfield/deercreek/248/101/

charge1.html). More recently, the "Charge" has been reworked by Starhawk (www.reclaiming.org/about/witchfaq/charge.html).

Wiccans use various implements in their rituals. Almost every Wiccan coven has a ritual knife or sword (athame) and a cup (chalice). Some Wiccans have bells, candles, pentacles, brooms, wands, and a number of other tools. Ritual tools connect the practitioner with the elements and are used to direct her personal power. The athame is a ritual knife associated with the element of fire and used to direct energy, as, for example, in casting a ritual circle. The wand is a tool of communication associated with the element of air. The chalice holds the wine that is shared by the celebrants and is associated with the element of water, representing the womb of the Mother. The consumption of the beverage in the chalice symbolizes renewal and revitalization and connection to the Goddess. The pentacle is a disc on which the pentagram (a five-pointed star) is inscribed. It is linked to the element of earth, as it encompasses and protects everything within the circle. It is also a symbol of wisdom and is worn as an amulet of protection. The five points represent the elements: Earth, Air, Water, Fire, and Spirit. In rituals the pentacle symbolizes connection with the earth.

There are eight sabbats throughout the year, which correspond to the ancient agricultural festivals. The celebration of these sabbats is designed to attune the practitioner to nature. The eight sabbats mark important moments in what many Wiccans refer to as the "wheel of the year": the two solstices, the two equinoxes, and four other days.

Ostava, on 21 March, celebrates new beginnings and fertility. It signals the spring. On 1 May (Beltane) fertility and growth are celebrated. The summer solstice is recognized on 21 June, the longest day of the year. Lammas, on 1 August, celebrates first harvest. The autumn equinox, on 21 September, acknowledges death. The recognition of seasonal change from summer to fall culminates in Samhain on 31 October where the interface between the living and the dead is considered strongest. Yule is celebrated on the winter solstice, 21 December. This darkest day also marks the turning of the seasons and heralds the return of the sun. On 2 February, Imbolc (also known as Candlemas) marks the end of winter. Wiccans also celebrate the cycles of the moon in rituals known as esbats.

Rituals are conducted to mark rites of passage: birth and death, menarche, marriage ("handfasting"), menopause, and various stages in relationships. They are also occasions for healing. For the people who perform them, the rituals are about self-empowerment, self-identity, and the capacity to change. They posit an ideal self to which the Wiccan aspires and offer her the power and support to create that ideal self. In feminist Wicca, rituals are usually quite specific about creating strong, powerful women and, if men are part of the group, helping them get in touch with their "feminine" side. Rituals are said to raise "energy"

The May Queen at the Beltane Fire Festival, Edinburgh, Scotland, 2012.

as a power for changing one's life. In any ritual, dancing, singing, or chanting is thought to bring about a group or communal will for change that is allied with the will of the goddesses and gods invoked (see Berger, 1999: 31).

Wiccans embrace and understand the practice of magic in varying degrees. "Magic" usually refers to the ability to affect the outcomes of events through communal or individual thought and ritual action. Some practitioners think that there is a direct causative link between spells and events in the world. Others understand the "magic" to work through the participant's consciousness, which the spell empowers to bring about the desired result. Most Wiccans cast spells, though the practice is not required. Some New Age practitioners also practise magic.

There is an ongoing debate in religious studies over the distinction between magic and religion. In this debate, magic is usually contrasted with religion: magic is seen as a way of manipulating the universe by using specific spells, whereas religion does not see the universe as ultimately manipulable in this way and thus seeks harmony with the universe rather than control over it. The use of magic in Wicca, however, tends to be less about manipulation than about tapping into the power of the Goddess and using that power to effect positive change in the world. The Wiccan world view has been identified as "enchanted." As Wouter J. Hanegraaff, an authority on New Age religion, remarks, "The defence of 'magick' by neopagans is very clearly based on a rejection of the 'cold world of cause and effect' in favour of an 'enchanted' world. . . . Neopagan magic indeed functions as a means of invoking and reaffirming mystery in a world which seems to have lost it" (1996: 84).

Symbols

Wiccans may invoke a variety of gods and goddesses from other mythologies, worship an independent figure known as the Goddess, or worship the Goddess together with a figure known as the God. There are no definite rules. Groups that invoke both the Goddess and the God conceive of them as complementary, not oppositional. For some, the emphasis is on the Goddess, especially the goddess of the earth or the moon. For others, the Goddess/God is a metaphor representing qualities within oneself. For still others, the Goddess/God is a convenient symbol for something that is completely beyond human understanding. In feminist Wicca, although a God is sometimes also invoked, the Goddess is the central divinity. The Goddess of Wicca is understood to be the Creatrix, the Earth Mother, and the Queen of Heaven. Wiccans often refer to their beliefs as thealogy, in reference to the Greek word *thea*, meaning "goddess," emphasizing the Goddess component in their belief system.

Some Wiccans see the Goddess as one goddess having many and varied names from a variety of historical, cultural, and contemporary traditions. Others talk about goddesses in the plural, without reference to one Great Goddess. Some think of the goddess(es) as existing beyond the consciousness of those who invoke them. Others see the goddess(es) only as symbolic of elements within the self. Often, in Wiccan ritual, women name themselves as goddesses. Many would say that all these ways of talking of the goddess(es) are appropriate and valid. Thus polytheism, monotheism, and pantheism often exist side by side, and practitioners reject the need to choose only one way of seeing the world.

The sources of goddess names and images are eclectic and wide-ranging. Some Wiccan covens invoke Greco-Roman goddesses such as Hecate and Isis, or the goddesses of Africa, Northern Europe, or the ancient Near East. Some invoke invented goddesses such as Asphalta, the goddess of parking spaces (Eller, 1993). Sometimes the goddesses are invoked through their historical stories; sometimes only their names are recited.

The symbol of the goddess(es), however one thinks of their existence, is considered crucial for women who are exploring their own religious identities apart from traditional patriarchal religions. In her groundbreaking essay "Why Women Need the Goddess: Phenomenological, Psychological and Political Reflections," Carol Christ argues that the Goddess affirms "female power, the female body, the female will, and women's bonds and heritage" (1979: 276) in ways that are not affirmed when divinity is conceived of as male.

One popular way of speaking of and seeing the Goddess is in the threefold form of maiden, mother, and crone. As maiden, she is associated with the waxing moon. As mother, she is the goddess of fertility and growth and is associated with the full moon. As crone, she is associated with the waning moon and the underworld, including death and decay. This affirmation of the Goddess also serves to affirm women's lives throughout the life cycle.

The Goddess is always associated with nature. She is Mother Earth, alive in all things, closely attuned to the natural cycles of the year. Wiccans often assume that women are more in tune with their bodies, and are more integrated with the rest of the natural world, than men are. However, some critics argue that this dichotomized view of maleness and femaleness reinscribes traditional views of women and valorizes these views, situating women on the "nature" side of the nature/culture split, and men as the culture-creators (see Ortner, 1974). Some feminists argue that this simply replicates a patriarchal gender split with a romanticized view of women as somehow above the baser creations of male culture (such as war). Others worry that this categorization assumes an essentialized view of both women and men that sees female nature and male nature as static, fixed, ahistorical entities.

When the God of Wicca is invoked, he is conceived of as the Horned God, and he functions as the consort of the Goddess. He is often associated with the goat-footed god Pan. Wiccans worship him as the god of fertility and the hunt. He is also the sacrificial victim whose death yields life. He is linked with Dionysius and Adonis as a god of the harvest. His death takes place at harvest and signals the gathering of the grain and his coming resurrection out of the womb of the Goddess. He is also aligned with Osiris as a god of fertility, death, and resurrection. The myth of Osiris describes his death and dismemberment and his resurrection by Isis, who gathers the pieces together and restores him to life again. Cyclical change, death and rebirth, are popular themes in Wiccan ritual. In an ever-repeating cycle, the Goddess gives birth to the Horned God, they fall in love, he dies, and the Goddess descends into the realm of the dead to bring him back.

Sometimes the Goddess is paired with the God in complementary fashion, but in feminist Wicca the Goddess usually takes central place and the God is her consort—necessary for fertility, but not the main force to be reckoned with.

Sexuality

Wiccans see sexuality as essentially positive, and there are several characteristics in Wicca that point towards an open attitude to sexuality. The explicit affirmation of the human body, especially the naked human body, is extended to an affirmation of sexuality as good. Sexuality is part of the sacred, not something separate from it, and is acknowledged as an aspect of Goddess. Motherhood is not separated from sexuality as it tends to be in Christianity, where the most important symbol of motherhood is the Virgin Mother Mary. Nor is sexuality separated from the other aspects of our lives. We are sexual beings, erotic beings, in all we do, not just in genital contact.

The Wiccan festival of Beltane (1 May), when participants dance around the maypole, is an explicit celebration of sexuality. Berger explains the connection: "The dance symbolizes the sex act as men and women holding brightly colored ribbons weave in and out. The maypole is envisaged as a phallic symbol that is placed in a hole in the mother earth" (1999: 17).

In Wicca, there is a desire to negate the rules and regulations imposed on women's sexuality both by Christianity and Judaism and by traditional patriarchal societies in which women are seen as men's possessions, and ownership of them is passed from father to husband. Regulation of female sexuality also serves to guarantee paternity. Wiccans generally reject this sort of thinking and affirm women's sexual autonomy.

The maxim "Do what you will and harm none" leaves quite a bit of latitude for sexual relationships and sexual practice, especially when we recognize that individuals are considered their own final arbiters of authority. Thus, there are no rules governing sexual practice in or outside of marriage except the rule of harming none. This has had interesting ramifications for bringing up a second generation in Wicca, as Berger notes (1999: 92–6). The desire to affirm sexuality and teach children positive lessons about it must be combined with caution, to ensure that children and teenagers are not exploited sexually.

Thus sexual responsibility is important, and the practice of safe sex expected. Although fertility is celebrated, women's control over their own bodies is seen as more important: therefore no ethical questions are posed by the use of birth control. With regard to abortion, it is generally agreed that the decision is the woman's alone.

Gay and lesbian relationships are openly affirmed as good. Some Wiccan groups have only gay or lesbian or bisexual members. A far cry from the rejection or grudging acceptance seen in many mainstream religious traditions, Wicca's affirmation of gay and lesbian sexuality has required some rethinking of the separate gender/sex roles and the emphasis on literal as opposed to symbolic or metaphorical fertility.

Christ provides a compelling description of sexuality in neopaganism:

[S]exuality can be a powerful expression of our connection to others and to all beings in the web of life. Sexual energy can be an almost irresistible force drawing us to connect with ordinary selves, opening up our deepest feelings, connecting us to the soul as well as the body of another, expanding the limited boundaries of the ego. Sexuality can make us intensely aware of our immersion in the rhythms of the universe, our ties to the whole web of life. For us, sexuality can also become a mode of deep communication, a profound expression of intelligent embodied love. All sexual relationships, whether homosexual or heterosexual, monogamous or nonmonogamous, have this potential. But when we use our sexuality [to] dominate or violate, when we take our own pleasure without concern for the other, when we create children we cannot nurture, we rupture the web of life (1997: 147).

Individual and Family Structures and Traditions

Wicca has been primarily a personal pursuit for individuals, and thus until recently has not concerned itself overly with passing the tradition on to the next generation (Berger, 1999: 92–6). Because Wicca is not a proselytizing movement, and because it is so variable from one group to another, there is no promotion of one form of family over another. Like individual sexuality, the family can take many different configurations as long as no one is harmed. Choice is key. This has paved the way for other views of family besides the dominant patriarchal model.

Social Change

Wiccans tend to be optimistic about their ability to connect with the immanent divine and to change their lives and the world. One of the common features of New Age spirituality generally, including the Wiccan tradition, is its emphasis on holism. As Hanegraaff remarks, "the term 'holism,' in a New Age context, does not refer to any particular, clearly circumscribed theory or worldview" (1996: 119). Wicca is particularly critical of traditional systems for their dualistic way of conceiving of the world and of persons in the world, rejecting the idea of duality between body and mind, spirit and matter. It does not, however, usually include a rejection of male/female sexual dimorphism. "The only thing which demonstrably unites the many expressions of 'holism' is their common opposition to what are perceived as non-holistic views, associated with the old culture which the New Age movement seeks to replace or transform" (Hanegraaff, 1996: 119). This statement applies equally to Wicca.

Wicca is concerned with unity, interconnectedness, and interrelatedness. Most Wiccans believe to some degree in the immanence of the deity in the natural world—especially in the cycle of the seasons—and in the individual self. They place great value on the earth, and instead of envisioning a transcendent deity, tend to speak of divinity as immanent in the world. There is a sense of personal connection to the divine life source, which is open to contact through psychic power, mysticism, or natural magic.

A common criticism of Wicca is that, as a fairly homogeneous movement—white, upper-middle-class, mostly well educated—it has often privileged individual fulfillment over social change. Instead of taking part in political activity to achieve change, many of the women studied by Cynthia Eller (1993: 200–4) relied on their spiritual and ritual practices: magic, appealing to the Goddess for intervention, changing themselves.

The women Eller studied were also more likely to look to "art, music, literature, language, mythology, folklore and, most importantly, of course, religion" (1993: 203) than to politics as vehicles for cultural and social change. Wiccans do not expect or even hope for change to be achieved quickly. They recognize that political activists often suffer burnout if there is no community to sustain them over the long haul, and thus they privilege community and support networks. At the same time, many women in this movement have tried to expand the Wiccan agenda along political lines. In *The Politics of Women's Spirituality*, Charlene Spretnak (1982) gathers a collection of articles that seek to show how spiritual power and political power are intimately intertwined.

Starhawk is one of the most famous devotees of the Goddess, but she is also deeply involved in political activism. She is the author of many books, including the early and influential *The Spiral Dance: A Rebirth of the Ancient Religion of the Great Goddess* (1979), and has been a consistent voice for Goddess spirituality for many years. She is a member of the Covenant of the Goddess, a league of covens that has been recognized as a church in the United States since 1975, and she has been active in social movements for more than three decades. She has also been involved in anti-nuclear protests at several US sites; has worked for sustainable development in El Salvador and Nicaragua; and in recent years has been involved in the anti-globalization movement. Her website (www.starhawk.org) includes an "Activism" page, which lists a number of alerts and reports on ongoing economic and ecological actions in which she and other pagans are involved. Along with poetry, spells, and rituals designed to accompany political action, the page explains why she thinks it is important for those who follow the Goddess to be politically involved:

> Because I believe the earth is a living being, because we are all part of that life, because every human being embodies the Goddess, because I have a fierce, passionate love for redwoods and ravens, because clear running water is sacred, I'm an activist. And because the two hundred

richest people in the world own as much wealth as the poorest forty per cent, because every ecosystem, traditional culture, old growth forest and life support system on the planet is under assault, and because the institutions perpetuating this unjust system are global, I'm kept very busy! (www.starhawk.org/activism/activism.html).

Ecological issues and issues involving the status and rights of women and gay/lesbian rights are important political concerns for Wiccans. Referring to a concept borrowed from Anthony Giddens (1991), Berger speaks of the most important type of politics in Wicca as "life politics," by which she means living in a way that is consistent with one's commitments, whether to maintenance of the global ecosystem, to gender equality, or to the rights of others. Wicca is a moral system in the making, one that will never have the rules and regulations that typify the religious and moral systems developed in earlier eras. It does, however, provide a form of political and moral life that helps to unify its adherents (Berger, 1999: 81).

Women's Official and Unofficial Roles

Wicca is popular among feminists because it tends to be woman-friendly and earth-based. Wicca worships the sacred as immanent in nature. Unlike some New Age movements led by charismatic men, Wicca has been self-consciously egalitarian in its leadership patterns. Women have always been leaders in Goddess traditions, which embrace women's leadership rather than coming to it reluctantly, as most other religious traditions have done. Every member of a group may be referred to as a "priestess." Eller emphasizes the importance of women's autonomy in Wicca: "Having struggled to free themselves from traditional religion and from personal relationship in which men were granted automatic authority over them, spiritual feminists are suspicious of anyone telling them what to do" (1993: 90).

Most Wiccans begin their practice by attending festivals or other celebrations. Sometimes they form open groups called *circles*, which anyone can attend. A coven is a more formal group of like-minded Wiccans who meet and sometimes practise magic. New covens are traditionally created through a process called hiving, whereby some members of a group, usually led by a priestess, leave one coven to form their own independent group. Covens celebrate rituals and share both knowledge and companionship. Usually there is a high priestess or priest who leads the rituals and keeps the coven's *Book of Shadows*: a customized reference book that contains liturgy, information on myth, and group members' own writings or records of dreams and magical workings. Many basic versions are available in print and online, for individuals or groups to use, adapt, and add to, as they wish. Not all Wiccans use such a book, however.

Forms and styles of leadership vary from group to group, but new groups often model themselves on existing ones. Leadership responsibilities frequently rotate from person to person (Eller, 1993: 91). This means that each member usually has an opportunity to prepare and lead the group's rituals. Some covens have been organized around a book by a founder figure such as Zsuzsanna Budapest, Starhawk, or Merlin Stone. There are generally three levels of training for a priestess or priest in the Wiccan tradition, though this varies from group to group. Often referred to as "first," "second," and "third degree," these levels are based on both knowledge and experience, and each is acknowledged by a formal initiation ceremony, sometimes involving an oath and the presentation of magical tools. In the first and third degree initiations, the initiate takes on a Craft name. The priestess, who is generally not paid, acts as a guide in rituals, teaches, and gives advice.

Wicca privileges personal experience over any particular belief system and tends to recognize many sorts of personal experience as spiritual. Wiccans have a healthy respect for diversity, and they are fairly tolerant of a wide range of beliefs, but personal experience is almost always the final authority. They generally believe that individuals create their own paths and should be allowed to follow those paths as long as no one is harmed. There is a tendency to speak of "spirituality" and not "religion." Wiccans are suspicious of traditions that require sole allegiance to one way of being or believing: for Wicca, there is no monopoly on truth or revelation. Wicca is not a tradition that seeks converts, and Wiccans tend to be suspicious of any sort of evangelism. The principle of gender equality is sometimes placed side by side with an essentialism that reinscribes women as more connected to the body and nature than men are (Berger, 1999: 45–6). And, like all social and religious movements, Wicca is connected to the wider society's roles and expectations of men and women.

Backlash

In a sense, Wicca itself represents a backlash against institutionalized Christianity, which it holds responsible for the decline of paganism generally and the historic persecution of witches in particular, as well as the negative image of Wiccans today. Typically, Wiccans see Western conceptions of religion as narrow, confining, and given to patriarchy. As Vivianne Crowley remarks, "Wicca does not believe, as do the patriarchal monotheisms, that there is only one correct version of God and that all other God forms are false: the Gods of Wicca are not jealous Gods. We therefore worship the personification of the male and female principle, the God and the Goddess, recognizing that all Gods are different aspects of the one God and all Goddesses are different aspects of the one Goddess, and that ultimately these two are reconciled in the one divine essence. There are many flowers in the garden of the divine and therein lies its beauty (1989: 11–12, quoted in Hanegraaff, 1996: 185).

Another component of the backlash is the fact that many Wiccans understand their legacy as one of persecution. Not until 1951 were laws against the practice of witchcraft repealed in England. Contemporary North Americans are generally content to see religion as an individual choice and so, by and large, there has not been a groundswell of negative reaction to New Age religious choices. We are not claiming that somehow Wicca has become "mainstream" or that its practitioners do not need to be wary of those who might consider their beliefs and practices marginal. Today, however, freedom of religion in both the United States and Canada, coupled with the priority that society gives to individual choice, means that New Age practitioners have basic protections for their religious preferences.

There is an exception to the general tolerance of Wicca, however. Some conservative Christian groups fear all forms of neopaganism as counter to the biblical witness. In particular, polytheism or worship of the Goddess rather than the "one true" God, the embrace of sexuality without "rules," and the use of the term *witch* are seen as antithetical to the Christian scriptures. Wiccans are accused of being Satanists, devil worshippers, and practitioners of black magic. Neopaganism generally and Wicca in particular have thus been "demonized" in some circles and tend to be viewed with suspicion. One source of the demonization is the Wiccan worship of the Horned God, who is sometimes equated, especially among certain Christian groups, with Satan or the Devil. A common citation in this regard is Ephesians 6:12: "for we wrestle not against flesh and blood, but against principalities, against powers, against the rulers of the darkness of this world, against spiritual wickedness in high places." The Christian Broadcasting Network, led by Pat Robertson, uses the terms "Wicca" and "Satanism" interchangeably. The Wiccan position is that they do not worship the devil, nor do they believe in hell. A quick search of the Internet reveals many sites that recount the dangers of Wicca, paganism, witchcraft, and so on. In fact, most of these sites lump together as "occult" many New Age religious views, and thus they often do not differentiate among particular types of neopaganism. Typical of what is found on such sites is the following:

Once I began researching Wicca in order to write and expose it on this web site, within a two-week period several things happened. I had a nightmare so unpleasant that I woke up and immediately knew it was tied to Wicca. I got a flat tire on the freeway, lost my medical insurance at work, was involved in a boating accident where I was injured (and am still recovering from it), have had two individuals attack me personally on the internet and published falsehoods about me, and my e-mail program I use for sending out the CARM newsletter, which has worked for several years, suddenly and unexpectedly crashed. My point is this. When you start tackling the occult, get ready for a ride. The enemy does not like what you're doing so you need to be prayed up. At this point, I recommend CPR. Confess (your sins), Pray (for guidance), and Read (the Bible). It will keep you spiritually alive (www.carm.org/religious-movements/wicca/what-should-christians-do-if-their-child-gets-involved-wicca)

There are also numerous pagan and Wiccan sites that refute these Christian critiques. Thus, interreligious debate between followers of Wicca and followers of other religions is lively on the Internet.

Unique Features

A striking example of a feature that distinguishes goddess religions from the other traditions examined in this book is their elastic concept of the Goddess. She is an inclusive deity, infinitely adaptable. A second distinctive feature has been the loose organization of such movements, and their lack of exclusivity.

Concept of the Divine

The Wiccan conception of the divine is unique in that it generally resists precise formulations about the Goddess. Starhawk describes the Goddess as "the power that comes from within," which she clearly distinguishes from "power-over":

> This book [*Dreaming the Dark: Magic, Sex & Politics*] is about the calling forth of power, a power based on a principle very different from power-over, from domination. For power-over is, ultimately, the power of the gun and the bomb, the power of annihilation that backs up all the institutions of domination. Yet the power we sense in the seed, in the growth of a child, the power we feel writing, weaving, working, creating, making choices, has nothing to do with threats of annihilation. . . . It is the power that comes from within. There are many names for power-from-within, none of them entirely satisfying. It can be called spirit—but that name implies that it is separate from matter, and that

false split . . . is the foundation of institutions of domination. It could be called God—but the God of patriarchal religions has been the ultimate source and repository of power-over. I have called it immanence, a term that is truthful but somewhat cold and intellectual. And I have called it Goddess, because the ancient images, symbols, and myths of the Goddess as birth-giver, weaver, earth and growing plant, wind and ocean, flame, web, moon and milk, all speak to me of the powers of connectedness, sustenance, healing, creating (1982a: 3–4).

Conscious invention is another unique characteristic of neopaganism. In Wicca, for instance, invention is held in high esteem. Hence, whereas many religious traditions change slowly, sometimes imperceptibly, change is a central value in Wicca. If a ritual does not suit the group, it can be changed. If the group needs new customs to accommodate new exigencies, they can be created.

Organization

As we have noted, goddess-based spirituality has no central authority and not a lot of organization, especially bureaucratic organization. Each group makes its own rules regarding leaders, rituals, membership, and so on. Nevertheless, groups that seek tax-exempt status, or the ability to perform legal marriages, are likely to find that gaining mainstream acceptance does require more organization, standardization, and centralized control. This was the case with Wicca, which was accepted as a legal religion in the United States in the mid-1980s, and formed the Wiccan Church of Canada as a non-profit religious organization in 1979 (see its website, www.wcc.on.ca). Additional training for group leaders often results in homogenization of practice as well. Finally, Berger sees child-rearing as also leading to routinization in Wicca. Passing rituals and stories on to children often leads to those rituals and stories becoming more set and less improvisational as children respond to the familiarity of repetition (1999: 86).

The Internet provides a whole new tool for the dissemination of information, and neopagans have been quick to embrace it. A huge variety of material is available, including information about Wiccan groups, rituals, and songs; there are also Wiccan chat rooms. Whereas traditional religions have usually relied on face-to-face contact to attract new people, the Internet allows those who are curious to access the information anonymously. Given the risk of backlash, anonymity may be desirable. At the same time, even though the Internet encourages individuality of expression, it can be a standardizing force when different groups share information and practices.

Notes

1. See Sered, who makes a similar comment with respect to the teachings of female-dominated religions (1994: 210).
2. There are two basic versions of the Wiccan rede. The first is a 26-couplet poem and the second is the last line of that poem. The latter is the most common expression of the rede philosophy found today. See www.waningmoon.com/ethics/rede.shtml for a fuller treatment of the history and use of the rede.

Glossary

channelling   The perceived ability to receive information from a source (spirit, personality, entity) not accessible by ordinary consciousness.

the Course   A collection of New Age self-study spiritual materials.

coven   A formal group of Wiccans.

eclectic Wicca   Practitioners who do not belong to one tradition or group.

ecofeminism   A social, political, and religious movement that explores the connections between the oppression of women and the oppression of nature.

Gardnerian Wicca   A branch of Wicca that is based on the works of Gerald Gardner.

holism   A term used particularly in New Age religions to negate all dualisms (for example, mind/body, spirit/matter, physical/psychological).

sabbat   The eight festivals that mark the passage of the Wiccan year.

Further Reading

Adler, Margot. *Drawing Down the Moon: Witches, Druids, Goddess-Worshippers and other Pagans in America Today.* 2nd edn. Boston: Beacon, 1986.

Center for Studies on New Religions (CESNUR), www.cesnur.org.

Christ, Carol. *Rebirth of the Goddess: Finding Meaning in Feminist Spirituality.* Reading, MA: Addison-Wesley, 1997.

Eller, Cynthia. *Living in the Lap of the Goddess: The Feminist Spirituality Movement in America.* New York: Crossroad, 1993.

Griffin, Wendy, ed. *Daughters of the Goddess: Studies of Healing, Identity and Empowerment.* Walnut Creek, CA: AltaMira, 2000.

Reid, Síân, ed. *Between the Worlds: Readings in Contemporary Neopaganism.* Toronto: Scholars Press, 2006.

Spretnak, Charlene, ed. *The Politics of Women's Spirituality: Essays on the Rise of Spiritual Power within the Feminist Movement.* New York: Anchor, 1982.

Starhawk. *The Spiral Dance: A Rebirth of the Ancient Religion of the Great Goddess.* New York: Harper and Row, 1979.

Films and Online Resources

Association for the Study of Women and Mythology. http://womenandmythology .wordpress.com/

Bearing the Heat: Mother Goddess Worship in South India. 45 mins. Directed by Kristin Oldham. University of Wisconsin–Madison, Center for South Asia, 1994. Various ways of worshipping the Mother Goddess in South India.

See "Women Make Movies," www.wmm.com, for a growing list of films about women in various religious traditions.

References

Berger, Helen A. 1999. *A Community of Witches: Contemporary Neo-Paganism and Witchcraft in the United States.* Columbia: University of South Carolina Press.

Brown, Michael F. 1997. *Channeling Zone: American Spirituality in an Anxious Age.* Cambridge Mass.: Harvard University Press.

Budapest, Zsuzsanna. 1989. *The Holy Book of Women's Mysteries: Feminist Witchcraft, Goddess Rituals, Spellcasting, and Other Womanly Arts.* 1st Wingbow edn. Berkeley, CA: Wingbow Press.

Christ, Carol. 1979. "Why Women Need the Goddess: Phenomenological, Psychological and Political Reflections." Pp. 273–87 in Carol P. Christ and Judith Plaskow, eds. *Womanspirit Rising: A Feminist Reader in Religion.* San Francisco: Harper and Row.

———. 1997. *Rebirth of the Goddess: Finding Meaning in Feminist Spirituality.* Reading, MA: Addison-Wesley.

Christ, Carol, and Naomi Goldenberg, eds. 1996. "The Legacy of the Goddess: The Work of Marian Gimbutas." Special Issue. *Journal of Feminist Studies in Religion* 12 #2: 31-120.

A Course in Miracles. 1985. Tiburon, CA: Foundation for Inner Peace.

Crowley, Karlyn. 2011. *Feminism's New Age: Gender, Appropriation, and the Afterlife of Essentialism.* Albany: SUNY Press.

Crowley, Vivianne. 1989. *Wicca: The Old Religion in the New Age.* Wellingborough, UK: Aquarian Press.

Eller, Cynthia. 1993. *Living in the Lap of the Goddess: The Feminist Spirituality Movement in America.* New York: Crossroad.

———. 2000. *The Myth of Matriarchal Prehistory: Why an Invented Past Won't Give Women a Future.* Boston: Beacon.

Galvan, Jill. 2010. *The Sympathetic Medium: Feminine Channeling, the Occult and Communication Technologies, 1859-1919.* Ithaca, NY: Cornell University Press.

Giddens, Anthony. 1991. *Modernity and Self-identity: Self and Society in the Later Modern Age.* Cambridge, UK: Polity Press.

Gimbutas, Maria. 1982. *The Goddesses and Gods of Old Europe, 6500-3500 BC: Myths and Cult Images.* London: Thames and Hudson.

———. 1989. *The Language of the Goddess: Unearthing the Hidden Symbols of Western Civilization.* San Francisco: Harper & Row.

Gutierrez, Cathy. 2011. Review of Jill Galvan. *The Sympathetic Medium: Feminine Channeling, the Occult, and Communication Technologies.* In *Magic, Ritual, and Witchcraft.* 6:1 pp. 96–99 (http://muse.jhu .edu/login?auth=0&type=summary&url=/ journals/magic_ritual_and_witchcraft/ v006/6.1.gutierrez.html).

Hanegraaff, Wouter J. 1996. *New Age Religion and Western Culture: Esotericism in the Mirror of Secular Thought.* Studies in the History of Religions 72. New York: E.J. Brill.

Kemp, Daren. 2004. *New Age: A Guide.* Edinburgh: Edinburgh University Press Ltd.

Knight, J.Z. 1987. *A State of Mind: My*

Story—Ramtha: The Adventure Begins. New York: Warner Books.

Kurtz, Stanley. 1992. All The Mothers Are One: Hindu India and the Cultural Reshaping of Psychoanalysis. New York: Columbia University Press.

Murray, Margaret Alice. 1921. The Witch-Cult in Western Europe. Oxford, UK: Clarendon.

Ortner, Sherry. 1974. "Is Female to Male as Nature Is to Culture?" Pp. 67–87 in Michelle Zimbalist Rosaldo and Louise Lamphere, eds. Woman, Culture, and Society. Stanford, CA: Stanford University Press.

Pierrakos, Eve. 1990. The Pathwork of Self-Transformation. New York: Bantam Books.

Roberts, Jane. 1970. The Seth Material. Toronto: Bantam Books.

———. 1981. The God of Jane: A Psychic Manifesto. New York: Prentice Hall.

Ruether, Rosemary Radford. 1992. Gaia and God: An Ecofeminist Theology of Earth Healing. San Francisco: HarperSanFrancisco.

Sered, Susan Starr. 1994. Priestess Mother, Sacred Sister: Religions Dominated by Women. New York: Oxford University Press.

Smith, Frederick. M. 2006. The Self Possessed: Deity and Spirit Possession in South Asian Literature and Civilization. New York: Columbia University Press.

Spretnak, Charlene, ed. 1982. The Politics of Women's Spirituality: Essays on the Rise of Spiritual Power within the Feminist Movement. New York: Anchor.

Starhawk. 1979. The Spiral Dance: A Rebirth of the Ancient Religion of the Great Goddess. New York: Harper and Row.

———. 1982a. Dreaming the Dark: Magic, Sex & Politics. Boston: Beacon.

———. 1982b. "Ethics and Justice in Goddess Religion." Pp. 415–22 in Charlene Spretnak, ed. The Politics of Women's Spirituality: Essays on the Rise of Spiritual Power within the Feminist Movement. New York: Anchor.

———. 1989. "Feminist Earth-Based Spirituality and Ecofeminism." Pp. 174–85 in Judith Plant, ed. Healing the Wounds: The Promise of Ecofeminism. Philadelphia: New Society Publishers.

Stone, Merlin. 1976. When God Was a Woman. New York: Harcourt Brace Jovanovich.

Wittig, Monique. 1985. Les Guérillères. Translated by David Le Vay. Boston: Beacon.

Both Guru and Goddess:
Mata Amritanandamayi of Kerala

Michelle L. Folk

*The beautiful fragrant flower of Compassion
blooms in the fullness of divine Love. Compassion
does not see faults and weaknesses, or distinguish
between good people and bad. Compassion does not
recognize boundaries between nations, religions, or
beliefs. Compassion has no ego, thus no fear, lust,
or emotionality. Compassion simply forgives and
forgets—like an open passageway.... Compassion is
the expression of perfect Love.*

—Mata Amritanandamayi (Cited in Canan, 2004: 60)

It is sentiments such as these that have drawn people from all over the world to the Hindu saint Mata Amritanandamayi, the Mother of Immortal Bliss, who is lovingly called Amma (Mother) or Ammachi (Revered Mother) by her devotees. Ammachi is a celibate self-initiated *mahaguru* (great religious teacher) and *sannyasini* (female renouncer) who is believed to be an *avatara* (incarnation) of the divine. The twentieth century saw a number of women gurus attract global followings. In the past, such women would have been known locally, but with the advent of the Internet, women gurus such as Ammachi have been able to establish a global presence with both Hindu and non-Hindu followers (Narayanan, 2004: 168). Ammachi's movement began in 1979 with only three devotees and a makeshift ashram housed in a small thatched hut in a village in Kerala (Raj, 2005: 127). Today it is a transnational organization with a significant institutional structure and substantial wealth that counts hundreds of thousands of people from all over the world among its members.

Although there are a variety of sources that we can turn to for information about Ammachi's life, there is no objective historical account (Raj, 2005: 124).

The accounts we have belong to the hagiographical genre of literature and have contributed to her sainthood and apotheosis. Ammachi's first disciple, a man named Swami Amritaswarupananda, is credited with writing the first official biography. Although his *Ammachi: A Biography of Mata Amritanandamayi* is important (Raj, 2005: 124), I have chosen to focus instead on the account written by the Ammachi devotee Savitri L. Bess, an American transpersonal therapist who offers online counselling and readings in astrology (www.pathofthemother.com and www.spirittapestries.com). Ammachi has been Bess's guru since 1992, when Bess attended one of her appearances in the United States and was overwhelmed by the experience:

> I watched thousands of people come to her one by one. For hours I sat spellbound, witnessing as she held them in her arms, listening to their tales of woe, and wiped tears from their eyes with her delicate brown hands. After minutes in her lap, signs of transformation shone on all their faces. . . . That time I wasn't searching for a spiritual master and was taken entirely by surprise when something slipped into my heart and told me that my meeting with Ammachi had marked the end of my search (Bess 2000: xix).

Bess travelled to India and stayed at her ashram. When she asked Ammachi what she should do as *sadhana* (spiritual practice), Ammachi instructed her to write a book (Bess, 2000: xiii). What follows is a composite account of the saint's life, based on that book, which Bess entitled *The Path of the Mother*.

The framework for Bess's presentation of Ammachi's life and teachings is her own spiritual journey to the Mother, and she offers readers a practical method that they can use for their own spiritual liberation. For Bess, the Mother is manifest in the pantheon of Hindu goddesses that includes Devi, Kali, Lakshmi, Parvati, and Shakti; Bess considers Ammachi to be an incarnation of Kali. The purpose of *The Path of the Mother* is to encourage readers to establish a unique relationship with the divine—to meet the Mother in a personal, intimate way and also in an abstract, universal way (Bess 2000: xx). Inspired by the traditions of many ancient and modern cultures, Bess uses Ammachi as her guide to a personal belief system that embraces the Mother as the absolute creator and sustainer of the universe. In the process of revealing her personal path to liberation, Bess (xxi–xxii) outlines the practices, including meditation, selfless service, and prayer, that readers can follow to discover the Mother within themselves.

Ammachi was born into a low-caste fishing family in the village of Parayakadavu in Kerala on the morning of 27 September 1953. Named

Sudhamani, meaning "Ambrosial Jewel," she was the fourth child of poor but pious parents, Damayanti and Sughunanandan, and her birth was surrounded with signs that suggested that she was special, although her parents did not recognize them at the time. The night before Ammachi was born, Damayanti dreamed that she would give birth to Krishna (an *avatara* of the god Vishnu), and Sughunanandan had a dream about the goddess Devi (Bess, 2000: 16); Damayanti gave birth easily to Ammachi and experienced none of the usual pains associated with childbirth; Ammachi was born without crying and with a smile on her face; and her skin was dark blue in colour. Instead of interpreting this as a sign that their infant daughter was special—both Kali and Krishna are depicted with blue-black skin—her parents were concerned that she was ill, and they asked doctors to cure the condition. Although her skin became lighter as she grew older, it remained darker than her siblings', and continues today to take on a bluish hue when she is in certain devotional states (Bess, 2000: 16–17).

Ammachi also exhibited atypical behaviour for a child. She walked and talked at six months of age, recited prayers at age two, and from the age of three composed devotional songs to Krishna (Bess, 2000, 18). Although an exceptional student, Ammachi was required to withdraw from formal education following the fourth standard after her mother became ill and her parents decided that Ammachi should take over the household duties instead of her older sister, whose chances of finding a husband would be better if she finished school (Bess, 2000: 18–19). Ammachi diligently tended to her household duties, later explaining that she chose to work hard at her chores because they gave her the opportunity to think of Krishna. She carried a picture of the god with her and would imagine herself to be dressing Krishna and his consort Radha as she dressed her siblings for school. Concerned with the poverty in her village, Ammachi stole food and bangles from her family and gave them to the less fortunate (Bess, 2000: 18–21).

In her later teens and early twenties, Ammachi "began to imagine that everything was Krishna, until gradually she noticed that he no longer was outside of her but dwelled inside of her" (Bess 2000: 23). Ammachi's condition remained unknown to the people of Parayakadavu until one day she passed a neighbour's yard where people were gathered during a Krishna holiday listening to tales of the deity. She entered the yard and lay down on a tree branch in the bodily posture assumed by Krishna. People took this to mean that Krishna had possessed the young woman. Wanting to see the god possess Ammachi again, the villagers asked her to perform a miracle. She instructed them to bring her a pot of water, which she turned into buttermilk. She then asked a man to touch the remaining drops of buttermilk and they were transformed into gallons of pudding that were consumed by everyone in the village. They loved Ammachi's manifestation of Krishna, known as Krishna *bhava* (coming into existence), so much that she agreed to repeat it three times a week, and during those times she would take on the playfulness that is associated with Krishna. Once, she teased a Krishna devotee by offering her a banana and then, when the devotee opened her mouth, pulling back and withholding it before eventually dropping it into her mouth (Bess, 2000: 23).

Ammachi's family attempted to arrange a marriage for her, but she refused. Frustrated, Sughunanandan visited an astrologer, who told him that Ammachi was a *mahatma* (great soul) and that any marriage would result in catastrophe for the family (Bess, 2000: 24). Although she had merged with Krishna in consciousness, Ammachi grew disheartened because she missed the joy of longing for him. One day, Ammachi had a beautiful vision of the divine Mother (Devi). Ammachi ached to see Her again and a greater longing arose within her. Ammachi asked Krishna to take her to the Mother, but they could not find her. The longing that she felt for the Mother grew and began to torment her so much so that she was unable to perform her daily chores and would fall into a trance at the sound of chanting (Bess, 2000: 24). Disapproving of her behaviour, Ammachi's brother forced her to leave the family home and she made her home on the beach (Bess 2000: 25). At the age of twenty-two, Ammachi's longing for the divine reached its height. She later described the experience:

> O Mother, my heart is being torn by this pain of separation! . . .
> O Darling Mother! Please open the doors of Your compassionate
> heart to this humble servant of Yours. I am suffocating like one
> who is drowning. If you are not willing to come to me, then please
> put an end to my life. Let that sword with which You behead the
> cruel and unrighteous fall on my head as well! (Bess, 2000: 25)

The Mother answered the saint's pleas for union by appearing to her one day "dazzling like a thousand suns" (Bess, 2000: 26). Ammachi entered a "sublime realm" and avoided human contact from then on, choosing instead to dig holes in the sand on the beach where she lived in joy because she had merged with the Mother (Bess, 2000: 26). In late 1975, Ammachi's contentment in isolation ended when a voice coming from within told her that it was her duty to comfort others who were suffering (Amritaswarupananda, cited in Bess, 2000: 27).

It was at this point that the Mother manifested herself in Ammachi, who after this Devi *bhava* began to be known as Mata Amritanandamayi, the Mother of Immortal Bliss. While some people recognized her divinity, however, others continued to believe that she was possessed (Bess, 2000: 27). Sughunanandan became angry with the Mother and commanded Her to leave his daughter's body. The Mother warned Sughunanandan that Ammachi would die if She left, but he persisted until She complied, leaving Ammachi's body lifeless. Ammachi hovered over the scene, watching people prepare her body for cremation and chant mantras to pacify the goddess. The Mother, encouraged by their prayers, re-entered Ammachi, who then returned to life and said to her father, "Without *Shakti* [the divine feminine] there can be no Krishna" (Amritaswarupananda cited in Bess, 2000: 28; brackets in the original).

In time, Ammachi transformed herself from a low-caste girl enraptured by her devotion to Krishna into one of the most important *mahagurus* of modern times, for Hindus and non-Hindus alike. Her organization, the Mata Amritanandamayi Mission, has its headquarters in Parayakadavu at the Amritapuri Ashram, which was established in 1981 on the location where she was born (www.amritapuri.org/ashram/). Ammachi is both the spiritual and the temporal head of the mission, although temporal leadership has been delegated to her most senior monastics and lay members. Today the mission has *satsang* (religious assembly) groups in countries including Argentina, Australia, Brazil, France, Germany, Israel, Kenya, and the United States. In Canada, there are *satsang* groups in the provinces of British Columbia, Ontario, and Quebec (http://amma.org/groups/north-america).

Along with Amritapuri Ashram and satellite centres around the world, the mission operated 21 *brahmasthanam* ("abode of Brahman") temples in India as of 2012. The *brahmasthanam* temples are unique to the mission, reflecting changes instituted by Ammachi to accommodate the challenges of the modern world. While *pujas* (worship) at temples are traditionally conducted by male priests, Ammachi has both initiated women into the priesthood and advocated that people perform *pujas* themselves rather than pay priests to perform them because, in her words, "If you are hungry, it's not enough that someone else eats" (www.amritapuri.org/activity/cultural/temple/).

Ammachi teaches the importance of both "Education for Life," meaning spirituality, and "Education for Living," which entails living ethically in the world while earning a living, as a way of uplifting humanity. The mission has established a number of educational institutions to facilitate learning as a result. Today it operates some 56 pre-primary to high schools across India that, in addition to teaching languages, science, and technology, seek to develop students' capacity for service, compassion, and humility (www.amritavidyalayam. org). The mission also operates Amrita University, which has campuses in Amritapuri, Bangalore, Coimbatore, Kochi, and Mysore and offers university-level programs in Ayurveda, business, biotechnology, dentistry, engineering, medicine, and nanoscience, among others (www.amrita.edu).

Embracing the Internet, as many modern gurus have, Ammachi is available to devotees on a number of web platforms. Her music can be purchased through iTunes, there is an Amrita Mobile Media App (AMMA), videos are available on YouTube, and she can be followed on Facebook and Twitter. The mission's websites provide news about Ammachi's teachings, the organization's activities, and Ammachi's tour dates around the world. Her online presence also facilitates worship. While followers can sign up for the mission's e-mail newsletter, watch live webcasts, blog about their Ammachi experiences, and write to Ammachi, they can also book *pujas* online and arrange for *prasad* (an offering) to be sent from India to anywhere in the world (www.amritapuja.org/ what_is_puja.htm or www.amritapuri.org/eservices/).

Who are the people who are drawn to Ammachi? And how do they come to know her? Like many contemporary guru organizations, her mission consists of a small core group of disciples who make up the organization's innermost circle and a much larger number of lay devotees who come from diverse cultural, economic, linguistic, national, occupational, and religious backgrounds and do not necessarily see themselves as "members" of a religious organization but rather as "participants" in its activities (Warrier, 2003a: 34). They constitute what Maya Warrier (2003a: 34–5) calls a "floating population" whose loyalties reflect the devotees' personal ties to the guru rather than day-to-day interactions with her or a community of believers.

Selva J. Raj (2005: 128–39) notes differing interpretations of Ammachi and different devotional practices among the various ethnic groups who follow her.[1] The one thing that devotees have in common is the experience of coming to know her as the embodied divine, either through Devi *bhava*—the state in which she reveals her identity as a goddess—or through *darshan*. *Darshan*, defined as "seeing," is a Hindu act of devotion in which the devotee experiences a vision of the divine through an encounter with an icon, a pilgrimage place, or a person such as a saint, *sannyasi* (renouncer), or *sadhu* (holy person) (Eck, 1998: 5).

In traditional Hinduism, physical contact during *darshan* is discouraged for reasons of physical and ritual purity, but Ammachi challenges tradition, warmly embracing Hindus from all castes as well as non-Hindus in her arms as part of *darshan*; it is estimated that Ammachi has hugged more than 32 million people worldwide (www.amma.org). Raj (2004: 212) describes a typical *darshan* session at the Mata Amritanandamayi Center, or M.A. Center, in San Ramon, California, her first ashram in the United States. Before *darshan*, devotees are instructed on *darshan* etiquette (directions on how to hug Ammachi) and are given *darshan* tokens by Ammachi's assistants. They are then taken to Ammachi, who is seated on a throne with a male renouncer on one side, who translates devotees' requests since she speaks only Malayalam, and a female attendant on the other. Ammachi embraces them in her arms, applies sandal paste to their foreheads, hugs, kisses, and strokes them while whispering "Amma, Amma" and "my darling son" or "my darling daughter." She then embraces them again and gives them *prasad* consisting of sacred ash, a rose petal, and a Hershey's kiss (Raj, 2004: 212). It is her warm embrace that people find transformative. Chandra Pillai, an Ammachi devotee living in New Mexico, has said that he attended his first *darshan* not because he was seeking spiritual insight but because Ammachi, like him, came from Kerala; after she had hugged him, he felt compelled to accept her as his guru (Bess, 2000: 104):

> When she put me in her lap suddenly I could feel the difference. I had never felt like that in anyone's presence. Even my own mother or father or anyone. Just being near Amma and touching her made a change in my surroundings. I didn't know what it was. She told us to sit near her, so we did. While I was watching her, I started crying a lot. I couldn't understand why. I wasn't sad. It was a sweet feeling while I was crying (Bess, 2000: 105).

An American woman visiting Amritapuri told Bess (2000: 99) that Ammachi conveyed to her "an experience that she was everywhere and in everything" when she was embraced by the saint during her first *darshan*. It was this encounter that compelled her to accept Ammachi as her spiritual guide.

Ammachi reveals herself as the Mother on Devi *bhava* nights while clad in a colourful silk sari, jewels, and a silver crown. Raj (2004: 212) estimates that between 1,800 and 2,000 people received *darshan* during Devi *bhava* at the M.A. Center in 1999, and he was told that over 10,000 people a night attended Devi *bhava* at the ashram in Parayakadavu. At San Ramon, Ammachi also gave mantras to devotees, performed marriages, and initiated women as well as men into *brahmacharya* (studenthood) and *sannyasa* (renunciation) (Raj, 2004: 213). The latter practice is another challenge to normative Hinduism, which has traditionally restricted these paths to males and taught that females' dharma is limited to marriage and motherhood. When Bess (2000: 93) attended Devi *bhava* at Amritapuri, the doors of the temple would be pulled open to reveal Ammachi, dressed in a colourful sari, jewels, and a crown, sitting on a platform "assuming the attitude of the supreme goddess." A monk clothed in traditional dress would wave a camphor lamp (*arati*) in front of her as she sat immobile with her eyes closed as if in a trance. Ammachi would then throw flower petals to her devotees and onto herself to acknowledge her identity as the divine Mother. Bess (2000: 94) wrote of her experience, "My heart would swoon when I saw her in *Devi Bhava*. I would feel transported to a colourful paradise where only joy prevails." It is through her *darshan* sessions and Devi *bhava* that devotees often have their first personal encounter with Ammachi. For many devotees, it was that first embrace that awakened deep within them the desire to know the Mother.

While Ammachi belongs to the bhakti (devotional) tradition of Hinduism, it is not possible to identify her with any particular branch of bhakti—Shaivism,

Vaishnavism, or Shaktism—because she encourages people to worship whatever form of the divine they like. At the same time, Ammachi herself is the object of devotion for most of her followers, who understand her to be an embodied goddess who helps alleviate human suffering in modern times (Warrier, 2003b: 215). According to Ammachi, one of the ways that suffering is alleviated is through *seva* (service). Generally, bhakti understands *seva* to mean service that is undertaken by an individual and directed toward a deity or guru without the expectation of reward (Warrier, 2003c: 265). Ammachi has said, "Our highest, most important duty in this world is to help our fellow beings" (http://amma. org/teachings/ammas-own-words-service). Of service she has said, "Mother wants the world to know, through her children's example, that a life inspired by love and service to humanity is possible. The beauty and charm of selfless service must never be extinguished from the Earth" (cited in Canan, 2004: 54). The kinds of *seva* open to Ammachi devotees are quite varied and often reflect factors such as the age, culture, economic background, educational level, occupation, religion, and personal commitment of the individual concerned, rather than any expectation or requirement set by Ammachi. However, selfless service of some kind is compulsory.

Individual ascetics who have chosen to reside at the Amritapuri Ashram are required to work as part of their spiritual training. Active service is advocated rather than seclusion or isolation because, according to Ammachi, a true *sannyasi* is someone who is dedicated to serving others (Warrier, 2003c: 267). Ammachi has said that a *sannyasi* should never say, "I have attained a state of actionlessness, therefore I don't have to do any work," and that "If a *sadhak* [spiritual aspirant] does not work, he is cheating the world and cheating God in the name of spirituality" (Warrier, 2003c: 267; brackets in the original). Renunciation "is not renouncing the world and action. [It] is renunciation of the fruits of action. It is the *dharma* of the *sannyasis* to lead the world" (Ammachi, cited in Warrier, 2003b: 267; brackets in the original).

Since the ashram operates on the principle of communal service, either Ammachi or the senior ascetics who oversee ashram operations assign a duty to each person who lives at the centre. Such duties include preparation of food for the ashram's inhabitants; administrative responsibilities such as answering the telephone, sorting mail, or managing the ashram's stores; and work in the accounting office, where records of the organization's income via donations and expenses are kept. Another common assignment is to the mission's press and publications division, where a person may have the responsibility of proofreading, editing, illustrating, binding, art designing, printing, and distributing the mission's many publications (Warrier, 2003c: 268). Younger devotees who come to the ashram for spiritual training are encouraged to complete their education, and the mission often provides funds to help them with this. Many complete undergraduate degrees in English literature, Sanskrit, and philosophy. Others have pursued graduate work in engineering. Students often use their training to help the mission once they graduate (Warrier, 2003c: 265).

Lay people are encouraged to perform *seva* through their local branches of the mission. In India, those wishing to found branches in their local communities approach Amritapuri for permission to establish a satellite site. The mission appoints an ascetic to head each local branch, and activities such as *pujas, bhajans* (devotional songs), performances, and discourses on Ammachi's teachings are set up. A satellite may also establish blood drives, food banks, a *brahmasthanam* temple, a school, or an orphanage. One devotee, a journalist by profession, told Warrier that although distance and the requirements of his job limited the time he could commit to *seva*, he travelled the one-hour distance from his home to his local branch every Sunday to work with the orphanage's children on their homework and teach them sports (Warrier, 2003c: 270). While Ammachi expects service of her followers, they determine the parameters of their service for themselves.

Seva should not be limited to activities that benefit only the mission. They should be extended to all of humanity and to the environment. The mission undertook relief efforts for the 2004 tsunami that struck Asia and Africa, 2005's Hurricane Katrina in the United States, and 2011's earthquake and tsunami in Japan, pledging more than $46 million to victims of the tsunami and $1 million for Katrina (http://amma.org/global-charities/disaster-relief). Its environmental efforts include planting more than one million trees worldwide as part of the United Nations Billion Tree Campaign (http://amma.org/global-charities/green-initiatives). All these activities are interpreted as *seva*.

Clearly, the type and amount of *seva* undertaken is less important than the intentions that inform it. *Seva* should be undertaken selflessly without the expectation of rewards. Selflessness is particularly important today, according to Ammachi, partly to counter the greed, jealousy, selfishness, and egoism of the modern world, and partly because it is the most effective method of progressing towards *moksha* (enlightenment) in modern times. Ammachi blends the traditional Hindu concepts of karma (karma means "to do," "to act") and rebirth with concerns over modernity. Bad thoughts and deeds cause us to accumulate bad karma, and suffering in the individual's present life is a reflection of the bad karma that has been accumulated in previous lives. The goal is to eliminate all karma, either through devotion to a deity or guru or through austerities (Warrier, 2006: 181). Ammachi's Hindu followers believe that their devotion can help to reduce the karma they carry; in fact, some devotees believe that a single hug can wipe out the karmic residue of all their previous lives (Warrier, 2006: 181). They also find the concept of *seva* particularly attractive because, in addition to the spiritual benefit of eliminating the bad karma they accumulate in their daily lives through their materialism, it gives them emotional contentment (Warrier, 2003c: 266).

Ammachi's life and career reflect many of the traits associated with contemporary Hindu female religious leaders. She was born into a low-caste family, lived in poverty as a child, expressed her devotionalism at a young age and was persecuted for it, rejected marriage, and performed miracles (Raj, 2005: 142). Like many contemporary Hindu women saints, Ammachi challenges the traditional pattern of sainthood in Hinduism by hugging her devotees in *darshan*, initiating women into *brahmacharya* and *sannyasa*, allowing *brahmacharinis* to study sacred texts, and permitting women to conduct *pujas* at temples (Raj, 2005: 138). Ammachi is a guru and goddess who, while embracing tradition, also challenges it through her person and her teachings.

Study Questions

1. In what ways does Ammachi's life story inform her religious teachings? How are the events of her life interpreted by her devotees?
2. How does Ammachi interpret *seva*, and what are some of the ways that her devotees practise it?
3. What are some of the innovations that Ammachi has made to traditional Hindu ritual activities such as *darshan*?

Note

1. In the United States, for example, she has followers from a variety of ethnic backgrounds, although a representative of the M.A. Center estimates that the majority are Euro-Americans (Raj, 2005: 128). Western devotees also come from a variety of religious backgrounds. Many of them have been practitioners of Transcendental Meditation or Christian feminists, for example. Although some have no attachment to organized religion, others maintain their ties to Judaism or Christianity. Therefore Ammachi has incorporated Christian ideas into her teachings, and may give her Christian devotees, some of whom call her the female Christ, a Christ mantra (Raj, 2005: 135).

   Raj (2005: 130) describes Ammachi's Western followers as having a dual identity—a personal identity and a spiritual one. They wear Western clothing and use Western names in their daily lives, but observe Indian cultural norms in dress and behaviour at the center, adopting Indian names and wearing Indian dress such as salwar kameez, saris, and rudraksha beads; they wear white in Ammachi's presence because she regularly wears the white cotton sari of an ascetic. By contrast, female devotees in the US who are of Indian origin dress in colourful saris. These differences suggest that Ammachi's Western devotees are drawn to her asceticism and spirituality and have adopted dress and behaviour that reflect this, whereas her Indian followers are attracted to the devotional tradition that she represents and do not feel compelled to change their dress or behaviour (Raj, 2005: 130). What appeals to her Western followers is her role as a charismatic spiritual guide, while her Indian devotees embrace her in the framework of bhakti.

References

Bess, Savitri L. 2000. *The Path of the Mother*. New York: Random House/Ballantine Wellspring.

Canan, Janine, ed. 2004. *Messages from Amma: In the Language of the Heart*. Berkeley, CA: Celestial Arts.

Eck, Diana L. 1996. *Darśan: Seeing the Divine Image in India*. 3rd edn. New York: Columbia University Press.

Narayanan, Vasudha. 2004. "Gurus and Goddesses, Deities and Devotees." Pp. 149–78 in Karen Pechilis, ed. *The Graceful Guru: Hindu Female Gurus in India and the United States*. New York: Oxford University Press.

Raj, Selva J. 2004. "Ammachi, the Mother of Compassion." Pp. 203–18 in Karen Pechilis, ed. *The Graceful Guru: Hindu Female Gurus in India and the United States*. New York: Oxford University Press.

———. 2005. "Passage to America: Ammachi on American Soil." Pp. 123–46 in Thomas A. Forsthoefel and Cynthia Ann Humes, eds. *Gurus in America*. Albany: State University of New York Press.

Warrier, Maya. 2003a. "Guru Choice and Spiritual Seeking in Contemporary India." *International Journal of Hindu Studies* 7, 1/3: 31–54.

———. 2003b. "Processes of Secularization in Contemporary India: Guru Faith in the Mata Armritanandamayi Mission." *Modern Asian Studies* 37, 1: 213–53.

———. 2003c. "The *Seva* Ethic and the Spirit of Institution Building in the Mata Amritanandamayi Mission." Pp. 254–89 in Antony Copley, ed. *Hinduism in Public and Private: Reform, Hindutva, Gender, and Sampraday*. New Delhi: Oxford University Press.

———. 2006. "Modernity and Its Imbalances: Constructing Modern Selfhood in the Mata Amritanandamayi Mission." *Religion* 26: 179–95.

CASE STUDY

Sakyadhita: Daughters of the Buddha Unite

Carmen Webb

Women constitute at least half of the world's Buddhist population. Most of these women are located in Asia, but there are also significantly growing numbers in Europe, Australia, and North America. Yet—because Buddhism has no central structure of authority or governance, and because women in many parts of the world lack the necessary education and access to resources—Buddhist women have often been isolated, unaware of the accomplishments and challenges of Buddhist women in other places, and without opportunities for networking or coalition-building (Tsomo, 2006b: 102). Sakyadhita, "the world's most active international Buddhist women's organization" (Tsomo, 1999a: 56), has developed to meet the needs of these Buddhist women by offering opportunities to facilitate awareness, education, understanding, and support. In order to understand the significance of this organization, its impact on Buddhist women's lives, and the challenges it faces, this case study will examine the conferences that are central to Sakyadhita's character, some of the challenges related to sustaining an international organization made up of members with diverse interests and perspectives, and the accomplishments and future goals of the organization.

Sakyadhita was founded at the conclusion of the First International Conference on Buddhist Nuns held in Bodhgaya, India, in February 1987. While this first conference did not operate under the name Sakyadhita, it has generally come to be regarded as the first Sakyadhita conference, and subsequent international Sakyadhita conferences, held approximately every two years, are numbered accordingly. The conferences are considered instrumental in promoting the principal aims of that first conference, which Karma Lekshe Tsomo,[1] past president of Sakyadhita, describes as a forum "to promote mutual understanding and to encourage Buddhist women in their efforts to practise the Dharma" (1988: 31).

The founding Sakyadhita conference was organized by Karma Lekshe Tsomo, Ayya Khema, and Chatumarn Kabilsingh (also known as Bhikkhuni

Dhammananda) in response to their growing awareness of and distress over the gender-based disparities that nuns were subject to in their communities with respect to the living conditions, access to resources, and support and respect (Tsomo, 2007: 2). The organizers noted that there had been the occasional conference on women and Buddhism, but never one dealing specifically with Buddhist nuns. It was decided that just such a gathering must be established, where nuns could speak and be heard (Tsomo, 1988: 27–8). Tsomo, Khema, and Kabilsingh were in the privileged position of being well educated and somewhat well travelled, and thus were aware that a wide spectrum of expressions of female Buddhist monasticism existed, including fully ordained nuns in the Mahayana tradition, Theravadan and Tibetan nuns who practised in their own tradition but had resorted to a Mahayana ordination, and Theravadan and Tibetan women who lived monastically without ordination or formal recognition of their status. The organizers also knew that others were not so aware. Even inside a single country's borders, misconceptions and ignorance existed. As Ranjani de Silva (2007: 12), president of Sakyadhita Sri Lanka, noted at the first conference:

> It was heartbreaking to realize that, despite this rich heritage, our *dasasilmathas*[2] in Sri Lanka were living in very poor conditions and were not receiving the necessities of life. As Buddhist women, we felt ashamed that we had not taken an interest in them. At the conference, we became awakened.

The Bodhgaya conference and subsequent Sakyadhita conferences have exposed Buddhist women to the range of conditions and practices that exist for women in Buddhism, thus offering opportunities to develop an awareness that could translate, and in many cases has translated, into action (see also Tsedroen, 1988: 50).

Organizers intentionally worked to create a conference environment that would provide opportunities for building awareness, empowerment, knowledge, and coalitions. By bringing together women from East and West, from Mahayana, Theravada, and Tibetan/Vajrayana traditions, from monastic and lay lifestyles, they offered a space for dialogue and understanding to grow. Particular care was taken to avoid the privileging of a particular brand of knowledge, practice, or cultural location. Speakers for the conference were chosen from a variety of knowledge bases, including various Buddhist traditions and, in addition to academically trained women, women who had "real life experience in relation to the topics discussed" (Tsomo, 1988: 32). Session topics ranged from matters of theory and doctrine to community service, moral discipline, and access to education (Tsomo, 1988: 34). Every presentation was followed by small group discussions that offered opportunities to speak and be heard in a respectful atmosphere. Each morning began with a meditation session led by a woman from a different tradition, in order to expose participants to the wide variety of styles that are all part of Buddhism (Tsomo, 1988: 34). Gender distinctions between monastics were also highlighted in non-confrontational ways. At mealtime nuns and monks were seated in the same room at tables of equal height, an arrangement unheard of in many monastic circles (Tsomo, 2007: 3). These efforts at education and diplomacy seemed to pay off. As Tsomo (1988: 27) puts it, "Mahayana Buddhists happily discovered that Theravada practitioners do not spend all day thinking of their own welfare alone, and Theravadan Buddhist[s] were delighted to find that Mahayanists do not have horns and tails." Exposure to these different expressions of Buddhism offered opportunities for understanding and tolerance to develop.

Conference organizers, two of whom were Westerners, also made a significant effort to avoid any privileging of, or domination by, the West at this gathering. Participants from a wide variety of countries, particularly Asian, were sought out and encouraged to attend. The conference location, Bodhgaya, was chosen because of its central location in the Asian Buddhist world as well as its symbolic value as the legendary site of the Buddha's enlightenment. Efforts were made to subsidize Asian nuns' attendance. Presenters were chosen from various geographic locations. One possible exception to this careful planning was the fact that the women chosen to serve as panel presenters tended to be English speakers, "due to time limitations" (Tsomo, 1988: 33).

This first conference attracted 1,500 attendees (Tsomo, 1999b: 1). This was no doubt due in part to the fact that the Dalai Lama gave the opening address. By the end of the conference it was widely agreed that there was a need for an ongoing forum to bring women together in this way. Participants also wanted to broaden the scope beyond the question of ordination in order to encompass a wide variety of issues facing Buddhist women and their ability to participate in the world and have a positive effect on it. On the last day of the Bodhgaya conference, Sakyadhita was officially formed. Some wondered whether the name "Sakyadhita," which means "daughters of the Buddha," might be considered paternalistic. However, it was pointed out that if a men's group chose to call itself "sons of the Buddha," no one would question the name (Tsomo, 2007: 4). A commitment was also made to aim hold an international conference every two years. The list of objectives formulated at the initial conference has been modified over the years as earlier goals have been reached and new objectives have surfaced (Tsomo, 2007: 4–5). Today the objectives are:

- To establish an international alliance of Buddhist women;
- To advance the spiritual and secular welfare of the world's women;

- To work for gender equity in Buddhist education, training, institutional structures, and ordination;
- To promote harmony and dialogue among the Buddhist traditions and other religions;
- To encourage research and publications on topics of interest to Buddhist women;
- To foster compassionate social action for the benefit of humanity; and
- To promote world peace through the teachings of the Buddha.

(*www.sakyadhita.org/home/joinus.html*)

Since that first conference, Sakyadhita has now held 13 international gatherings, all of them in Asia (to facilitate participation by women from that continent). Attendance has never again reached the level achieved at the Bodhgaya event—possibly because inaugural conferences tend to attract particular attention, possibly because of the Dalai Lama's presence, and possibly because people now know that if they are unable to attend one conference, another opportunity will follow. Attendance numbers for subsequent years indicate that the fifth conference, held in Cambodia at the end of 1997 and beginning of 1998, drew the smallest numbers, with just 150 attendees from 24 countries (Tsomo, 1999b: 3), while the eleventh, held in Ho Chi Minh City, Vietnam, in 2009–10 attracted 2600 participants from 37 countries (Wurst 2010: 157). The difference may reflect a variety of factors, including growth in the conference's popularity, location preference, the availability of other conferences in a given year, and global financial conditions.

Regardless of fluctuations in attendance numbers, the conference remains extremely important to the organization and its members. Many women have joined Sakyadhita for the express purpose of attending a conference (Koppedrayer and Fenn, 2006: 151).[3] The conferences offer an opportunity for new and established members to learn about the issues of interest to Sakyadhita, and are really the only times when significant numbers of Buddhist women from around the world are able to meet and dialogue with one another (Fenn and Koppedrayer, 2008: 47).

In the spirit of the first conference, subsequent conferences have included a mixture of "scholarly presentations, sitting meditations, chanting practices, small group discussions, and cultural performances to understand the experiences of Buddhist women around the world" (Tsomo, 2006a: xi). The conferences expose participants from affluent countries to women's issues and living conditions in the developing world—issues and conditions that are often directly related to gender (Tsomo, 1999a: 58–9). Such exposure stimulates an awareness that while "in North America, the prominent issues seem to be sexualities, environment, race, sexual exploitation, and social engagement . . . [i]n Asia, by contrast, the major issues are survival, education, training, and ordination" (Tsomo, 1999b: 3–4). The conferences also offer opportunities for women to talk about how various initiatives, such as those mounted by feminist organizations in the West, have reshaped women's lives and to discuss whether and how the strategies employed in one location might or might not be fruitfully employed in another (Boucher, n.d: 8). In an interesting example of this cross-cultural pollination, Zenju Earthlyn Manuel (2006: 2), an African American Buddhist from California, reported that Tibetan nuns sang "We Shall Overcome" at the Malaysian conference. Cross-cultural exchanges can also take place between women considered equally "Western." Rotraut Wurst (2000: 98–9), the Sakyadhita executive member responsible for Europe from 1995 to 1997, notes that European Buddhist women's exposure to American Buddhist women has suggested to them that a less strict and more pragmatic approach to Buddhism might be worth consideration. At the same time, it has been suggested that Sakyadhita might function as a sort of quality-control mechanism, ensuring that the transmission of Buddhism to the West is sensitive to the necessity for cultural adaptation without wholesale dilution (Tsedroen, 2006: 308–9).

For some of the women attending the conferences from developing nations, where resources for travel and education are generally lacking, the international nature of the Sakyadhita conferences offers exposure to realities that they had been unaware of and might have thought impossible. For example, a number of Sri Lankan *dasasila matas* attending the 1993 conference in Colombo, Sri Lanka, reported that before the conference they had never heard the word *bhikkhuni*,[4] and had no idea that ordained women's orders existed anywhere in the world (Silva, 2007: 12). For many, the conference is their first opportunity to speak at a public event (Tsomo, 1999a: 58), and this may strengthen their sense of their own abilities (Tsomo, 2006b: 106). Jampa Tsedroen (2006: 2) notes that the ways in which women in many parts of the world have been socialized, coupled with their status as women, has often prevented them from voicing their doubts regarding religious authorities. The presentations and discussions facilitated by the Sakyadhita conferences expose women to ways of expressing such doubts and serve as a catalyst for changes that can empower Buddhist women. Practical skill-building is also a part of these conferences. Workshops on "meditation, leadership, reproductive ethics, conflict resolution, environmental health, and peacebuilding skills" help to hone abilities that participants can take home and share with their own communities (Tsomo, 1999a: 58). It has been noted that participation at a Sakyadhita conference often results in more invitations to speak at other venues; the awareness that such a conference creates can also spur the government of the host country to enhance women's health and education programs (Fenn and Koppedrayer, 2008: 55). Further, by demonstrating alternative ways of living as Buddhists, the conferences have created awareness and empowerment to seek alternatives for interested women in countries where women do not have access to ordination (Tsomo, 2006b: 105).

To highlight the positive impacts of the Sakyadhita conferences is not to ignore the tensions that also exist. The emphasis on women's ordination that has always been part of the movement is not embraced by all constituents. For example, some of the Buddhist women who have taken vows and live monastically without ordination, such as the *mae jis* of Taiwan, the *dasasila matas* of Sri Lanka, and the *anis* of Tibet, do not want ordination, for reasons that include the prospect of oversight by ordained monks; see Bartholomeusz, 1994: 136; Fenn and Koppedrayer, 2008: 61). Their reluctance to seek ordination may leave them "in a strange limbo" where, as neither full laywomen nor full nuns, they do not fit into a socially authorized class in a society that is uncomfortable with such outliers (Boucher, n.d.: 10). Related to this issue is the concern expressed by some ordained women that conference organizers have not upheld the Vinaya regulations that require separation of lay and ordained at mealtimes and the provision of preferential seating for the ordained (Koppedrayer and Fenn, 2006: 160). Such criticisms remind us that structures that implement or maintain hierarchy and privileged status are not restricted to one gender. Interestingly, charges that conference presentations too often focus on issues of importance to lay members are met with countercharges that the "nuns' issue" takes up too much attention (Fenn and Koppedrayer, 2008: 54–5, 66–7). Juggling the priorities of diverse social groups and identities is one of Sakyadhita's challenges.

The international composition of the conferences creates conditions for understanding, but it can also cause strain. Related to the tensions between lay and ordained women is the allocation of the financial support available to help nuns attend the conferences. While priority is given almost exclusively to sponsoring Asian nuns, many of them live in countries where religious communities are financially supported by the general community. By contrast, Western nuns live in a culture where they are seen as anomalies, and the general community is under no obligation to support them. Thus they may have very meagre financial resources, and those who receive little or no support to attend the Sakyadhita conferences may, in effect, be barred from attending (Fenn and Koppedrayer, 2008: 68). Although increased sponsorship at the Malaysian conference permitted fuller translation services, there are still those who feel that English predominates, along with Western interests and paradigms (Koppedrayer and Fenn, 2006: 159–60).

Other cross-cultural issues can also reveal tensions. At the seventh conference, in Taiwan, several Taiwanese nuns expressed their uneasiness with Western academic interpretations and representations of their lives, "rais[ing] many important questions concerning the process of cultural exchange, the cultural adaptations of the Buddha's teachings, and the inversion of self image in the eyes of others" (Li, 2002). In a related example, Cherry Cooke (2008), a European attendee at the 2008 Mongolia conference, twice came face to face with her own culture's obsession and dis-ease with the feminine form. In one instance she was dismayed to see primarily Western attendees repeatedly requesting permission to take the photograph of a stereotypically attractive young nun while ignoring "small and squat" older nuns. In another, at a fashion show that was part of the entertainment offered at the conference, "nubile young women . . . modelled dazzling gowns with fur and feathers and very high-heeled shoes" (Cooke, 2008). Many Westerners in the audience were uncertain whether they should clap, as many did, or withhold their applause to avoid encouraging such a display. Competing notions of fairness, womanhood, and cultural sensitivity are all challenges to be faced in such a multicultural organization.

While the importance of the conference event itself cannot be overstated, its value would be far less if its influence did not lead to concrete improvements in women's lives. As one member has pointed out, it is not enough for Sakyadhita to provide the opportunity for women to learn and to network. There is also an obligation to act: "The organizers need to organize. The fundraisers need to raise funds. Those among us skilled in languages need to translate. Those who are prosperous materially need to write checks. All skills are needed and have a place" (Cowie, 2006: 16). Ongoing commitment to action is required in the time between conference events if substantial change is to happen.

In keeping with its original focus, one of Sakyadhita's most high-profile contributions has been its involvement in the reinstatement of the full ordination of women in the Theravadan tradition. Although Sakyadhita was not solely responsible for this development, it was instrumental in drawing attention to the issue, encouraging women's study of the Vinaya and Buddhist history, working with local groups to prepare suitable candidates for ordination, and supporting ordination ceremonies. Sakyadhita has resisted efforts to silence it on this issue. For example, when Sri Lanka was chosen as the site for the 1993 Sakyadhita conference, approval for the conference from the Sri Lankan Ministry of Buddhasasana was required. The Ministry told the organizers that it would give permission only if women's ordination would not be on the agenda. Sakyadhita immediately refused and took its case to the Sri Lankan president, who supported the conference without reservation, forcing the ministry to remove its conditions (Küstermann, 1994). Since that time, and in part because of that conference, full ordination for women in the Theravadan tradition has been re-established, and approximately 500 Sri Lankan women have been fully ordained since 1998. Official resistance remains, however. Sri Lanka Sakyadhita's website (www.sakyadhita-srilanka.org/index.php/Sakyadhita/History) notes that while "the Novice and Higher Ordination of Nuns . . . in Sri Lanka is a fact, the official recognition by the Sangha is still outstanding."

Sakyadhita is now attempting to work alongside other groups to facilitate the establishment of full ordination for women in the Tibetan tradition. In 2007 a conference was held in Hamburg, Germany, specifically to address this issue. Though not officially a Sakyadhita event, it was largely organized by Sakyadhita members (Fenn and Koppedrayer, 2008: 63). Many hoped that the presence and personal support of the Dalai Lama would finally officially open the door to the inauguration of women's ordination in Tibetan Buddhism. This did not happen: although the Dalai Lama affirmed that he had no objections to it, he insisted that a consensus of the "international sangha" was needed before proceeding (Fenn and Koppedrayer, 2008: 64). At the 2011 conference, the panel "Leading Buddhist Women" counselled women in the Tibetan tradition to work on developing their Buddhist scholarship and undertake extended meditation retreats to demonstrate their capabilities (Wurst, 2011: 209).

Sakyadhita's mandate goes beyond creating access to ordination. It also includes developing opportunities and structures for women to acquire the training and education they need to be leaders in their communities. Sakyadhita International and its Sri Lankan chapter established the Sakyadhita Training and Meditation Center in 1999 to provide monastic women with training in "social development, counseling, leadership, health education, . . . first aid . . . monastic training and education, in addition to English and computer classes" (Silva, 2007: 12; see also www.sakyadhita-srilanka.org/index.php/Sakyadhita/Goals). The Center also financially supports these women by giving them "pocket-money" and helping to fund their university education (www.sakyadhita.org). Another Sakyadhita project is the Jamyang Choling Institute (www.jamchoebuddhistdialectics.org) established by Karma Lekshe Tsomo in Dharmasala, India. This institute combines religious and secular education for Himalayan women who would otherwise have access to neither. Additional educational and conference facilities are also in the works. Land has recently been purchased in Bodhgaya, India, by Tsomo through donations received as a result of her speaking and teaching engagements. Noting that in 2,500 years there has not been a single women's monastery in Bodhgaya, Tsomo plans to use the land to build a centre where "women from around the world can dialogue with each other, learn together, and take their rightful place at the Buddhist table" (Tsomo, 2006b: 115). Sakyadhita branches in Europe are hoping to establish something similar on that continent. Noting that Western perceptions of Buddhism are often seriously misinformed, Wurst (2000: 97–9), argues that it is crucial to establish a centralized organization that can provide accurate information about the tradition to those living in places where Buddhism is not widely known, as well as information on retreats, women's groups, counsellors who incorporate Buddhist practice into their work, and so on. To this end she hopes that European Sakyadhita partners will establish an educational centre with a library, conference space, counselling services, and a resource centre (Wurst, 2000: 101). This centre remains a goal rather than a reality, but Wurst's concept does indicate that Sakyadhita is attempting to extend its influence beyond Asia.

Not all Sakyadhita-inspired programs focus explicitly on "religious" training or spiritual development. Sakyadhita members have also played integral roles in the establishment of social programs and services. They have developed shelters for victims of domestic violence and AIDS in Thailand and launched "education projects, healthcare initiatives, monastic training programs, and a handcraft center for women" in India (Tsomo, 1999a: 57). In Nepal a number of education centres have been established, and there are plans to build an orphanage. As well, Sakyadhita members have participated in political and social rallies aimed at challenging social injustices (Tsomo, 1999a: 57–8; see also Tsomo, 2006b). As Sakyadhita becomes better known, association with the organization may give such projects a higher profile and greater legitimacy than they would otherwise have (Fenn and Koppedrayer, 2008: 67). Given the organization's relatively short history and its financial limitations, much has been accomplished so far; there are increasing numbers of conference panels on social justice issues, their relationship to Buddhism, and the importance of incorporating social service as a part of Buddhist practice.

At the same time, many challenges remain. Finances are always an issue. Since individual donations to Sakyadhita remain generally "sporadic and fairly modest" (Fenn and Koppedrayer, 2008: 53), the association must look for larger institutional and corporate sponsorship. Such sponsors have contributed to the availability of technology-based resources and translation services at conferences, although there is concern that their contributions may come with expectations related to conference location, theme, and even focus (Fenn and Koppedrayer, 2008: 51). Further, the risk of burnout and attrition in an organization run by volunteers means that Sakyadhita is in a permanently precarious position (Fenn and Koppedrayer, 2008: 66). Many of its service programs are neither self-sufficient nor likely to be so in the foreseeable future (Fenn and Koppedrayer, 2008: 71), and they will continue to require financial support from governments, institutions, and foundations. Thus they are always at risk when tides turn and budgets must be cut.

Another challenge is that of continuing communication and networking between conferences. While technologies such as fax, email, and the Internet, and social media such as Facebook make communication far easier than it was in the past (Cowie, 2006: 15; Tsomo, 2007: 2; Wurst, 2000: 99), the primary language of Sakyadhita remains English, and the majority of Western women who are Sakyadhita members do not know even one Asian language. This leaves international network-building to a handful of people with the requisite language skills (Fenn and Koppedrayer, 2008: 56).

In terms of history, Sakyadhita remains a relative newcomer. Efforts are under way to encourage the founding of new branches, and an application form and detailed guide to establishing branches have been developed. To date, local branches have been established in Canada, Germany, the United Kingdom, France, the United States, India, Nepal, Taiwan, Thailand, and Sri Lanka. Creating more local affiliates may strengthen the organization as a whole and help with some of the challenges outlined above, but that will depend, in part, on whether more Eastern branches develop to balance the predominance of Western affiliates. The creation and sustenance of Sakyadhita has been an ambitious undertaking, and the organization has been nurtured along with great care and attention to compassion. It will be fascinating to watch as it comes to maturity.

Study Questions

1. In what ways is Sakyadhita a product of its time?
2. If access to women's ordination were to be realized in all Buddhist traditions, how might this change Sakyadhita?
3. How might Sakyadhita meet the challenge of its international membership in terms of understanding the role of social and geographical location in the construction of gender and women's lives?
4. What would be the possible consequences of altering Sakyadhita's conference schedule with regard to the financial resources it relies on? If conferences were held less often, might interest wane, or would this make it easier to put resources into other projects? If they were held more often, might this provide greater visibility or sap resources, with regard to both finances and labour?

Notes

1. Karma Lekshe Tsomo served as president of Sakyadhita from 2000 to 2009. She is an associate professor in the department of religion and theology at the University of San Diego and has published widely on issues relating to women and Buddhism.
2. *Dasasila matas* are Sri Lankan Theravadan women who have taken Ten Precepts and live monastically but have not received full ordination; see Chapter 3.
3. Mavis Fenn and Kay Koppedrayer are the only scholars so far to apply quantitative and qualitative feedback instruments to a study of Sakyadhita.
4. A *bhikkhuni* is a fully ordained Buddhist woman. *Bhikkhus* are fully ordained Buddhist men. The concept of *bhikkhus* is commonplace in Sri Lanka.
5. The code of monastic life in Buddhism.

References

Bartholomeusz, Tessa J. 1994. *Women under the B Tree: Buddhist Nuns in Sri Lanka.* Cambridge: Cambridge University Press.

Boucher, Sandy. n.d. "Daughters of the Buddha, Rising Up: The Sakyadhita Conference 2006." www.sandyboucher.net/documents/sakyadhita.pdf.

Cooke, Cherry. 2008. "Snap-Shots of Mongolia: The Photos I Didn't Take!" *News from Sakyadhita UK*, July. uploads/Activities/Mongolia2008.pdf.

Cowie, Evelyn Diane. 2006. "Seeding the Dharma in the Present Moment." *Sakyadhita: International Association of Buddhist Women* [newsletter] 15, 2: 14–16.

Fenn, Mavis L., and Kay Koppedrayer. 2008. "Sakyadhita: A Transnational Gathering Place for Buddhist Women." *Journal of Global Buddhism* 9: 45–79.

Koppedrayer, Kay, and Mavis L. Fenn. 2006. "Sakyadhita: Buddhist Women in a Transnational Forum." *Canadian Journal of Buddhist Studies* 2: 143–78.

Küstermann, Gabriele. 1994. "Report on the Third International Sakyadhita Conference on Buddhist Women: Colombo, Sri Lanka—October 25–29, 1993." *Sakyadhita: International Association of Buddhist Women* [newsletter] 5, 2. http://sakyadhita.org/docs/resources/newsletters/5.1.1994.pdf

Li, Yuchen. 2002. "Reflections on the 7th International Conference." *Sakyhadita: International Association of Buddhist Women* [newsletter]13,1. http://sakyadhita.org/docs/resources/newsletters/12.3.2002.pdf.

Manuel, Zenju Earthlyn. 2006. "Chanting Japanese in Malaysia." *Sakyadhita: International Association of Buddhist Women* [newsletter] 15, 2: 2–4.

Silva, Ranjani, de. 2007. "Ayya Khemma's Gifts to Sakyadhita." *Sakyadhita: International Association of Buddhist Women* [newsletter] 16, 1: 12–13.

Tsedroen, Jampa. 1988. "The Significance of the Conference." Pp. 47–52 in Karma Lekshe Tsomo, ed. *Sakyadhītā: Daughters of the Buddha.* Delhi: Sri Satguru Publications.

———. 2006. "Bhiksunī Ordination." Pp. 305–9 in Karma Lekshe Tsomo, ed. *Out of the Shadows: Socially Engaged Buddhist Women.* Delhi: Sri Satguru Publications.

Tsomo, Karma Lekshe. 1988. "The First International Conference on Buddhist Nuns." Pp. 17–37 in Karma Lekshe Tsomo, ed. *Sakyadhītā: Daughters of the Buddha.* Delhi: Sri Satguru Publications.

———. 1999a. "Buddhist Women in the Global Community: Women as Peacemakers." Pp. 53–60 in David W. Chappell, ed. *Buddhist Peacework: Creating Cultures of Peace.* Boston: Wisdom Publications.

———. 1999b. "Mahāprajāpatī's Legacy: The Buddhist Women's Movement: An Introduction." Pp. 1–44 in Karma Lekshe Tsomo, ed. *Buddhist Women across Cultures.* Albany: State University of New York Press.

———. 2006a. "Preface." Pp. xi–xii in Karma Lekshe Tsomo, ed. *Out of the Shadows: Socially Engaged Buddhist Women.* Delhi: Sri Satguru Publications.

———. 2006b. "Sakyadhita Pilgrimage in Asia: On the Trail of the Buddhist Women's Network." *Nova Religio* 10, 3: 102–16.

———. 2007. "Auspicious Beginnings: The Inception of Sakyadhita." *Sakyadhita: International Association of Buddhist Women* [newsletter] 16, 1: 2–6.

Wurst, Rotraut. 2000. "Sakyadhita in Western Europe: A Personal Perspective." Pp. 97–101 in Ellison Banks Findly, ed. *Women's Buddhism, Buddhism's Women: Tradition, Revision, Renewal.* Boston: Wisdom Publications.

———. 2010. "11th Sakyadhita International Conference on Buddhist Women." *Internationales Asien Forum. International Quarterly for Asian Studies* 41, 1/2: 157–9.

———. 2011. "12th Sakyadhita International Conference on Buddhist Women." *Internationales Asien Forum. International Quarterly for Asian Studies* 42, 1/2: 208–10.

L'Autre Parole:
A Christian and Feminist
Collective in Quebec

Monique Dumais

One year after International Women's Year (1975), five years after the publication of the Women's *Manifeste* in Quebec and the first issue of *Québécoises deboutte*[1] (1971), seven years after the launch of the Front de Libération des Femmes du Québec (1969), ten years after women's admission to the study of theology in Quebec ecclesiastical schools such as Grand Séminaire (1966), and 63 years after the foundation of the magazine *La bonne parole*[2] ("The good word; 1913), the collective L'autre Parole was founded on 14 August 1976 in the small town of Rimouski (about 43,000 inhabitants), six hours east of Montreal.

The L'autre Parole collective typifies Quebec religious transformation. This case study considers the social and religious context of the group's emergence, and examines its objectives and activities, its approach to theology, and its links with other feminist groups both in Quebec and in other countries.

Social and Religious Context

Quebec society has been deeply marked by the socio-political phenomenon known as the Quiet Revolution, which began around 1960. As Mason Wade ([1964] 1971: 84) summarized it, "Quebec . . . rapidly changed from a rural agricultural society to an urban industrialized one" in which education and social services were controlled by the secular state rather than the Roman Catholic Church. According to Quebec sociologist Guy Rocher, Quebec "shifted very quickly from a mentality where change was perceived as an evil in itself or at least as an attack to order and harmony . . . to an attitude maybe excessively open to change" (1973: 20–1).[3]

All Quebec historians and sociologists recognize the central role that the Roman Catholic Church traditionally played in Quebec society. Under its leadership Quebec was conservative and essentially male-oriented, without visible participation by women in either the Church or the society itself. Women in the province of Quebec obtained the right to vote only in 1940, after more than 20 years of struggle against the opposition of the bishops and priests as well as the Quebec elite and the province's premier, Maurice Duplessis (see Le Collectif Clio, 1992). By the mid-1960s, however, under the influence of Quebec's social transformations and the Second Vatican Council (1962–5), women's movements began to question the status quo and call for new directions in the Church.

An important fact to consider in this context is the very large number of nuns in Quebec at the time. Indeed, the province had the highest proportion of nuns in the Roman Catholic world during the 1940s: one for every 111 women (Denault and Lévesque, 1975: 45). Historian Marta Danylewycz (1987) has explained how attractive the religious life was as an alternative to both the demanding life of a wife and mother and the unvalued life of a spinster. Nuns often had a fair amount of autonomy from the religious hierarchy, and many were innovators in areas such as education, making their own decisions about curriculum and teaching methods, for example. They were, for instance, involved in developing advanced education programs such as *le cours classique*—a humanities program—which was offered to girls by Les Dames de la Congrégation Notre-Dame for the first time in 1910 in Montreal. A nun, Soeur Marie Laurent de Rome (Ghislaine Roquet), was the sole female member of the Royal Commission for Education in Quebec in the early 1960s (Dumais, 1981).

Nevertheless, Roman Catholic religious communities, female as well as male, are always under clerical jurisdiction: they must comply with ecclesiastical or diocesan regulations. In fact, the vow of obedience taken by members of religious orders represents a real challenge for personal growth and social commitment, for it implies submission to a person in authority and acceptance of her or his supervision. But Christians have always identified with the freedom of the resurrected Christ as a model of liberated spontaneity that gives them the freedom to achieve their individual and social missions even when the hierarchy of the Church might appear to desire something different (Radcliffe, 2000; Sölle, 1970). The Second Vatican Council, in its recommendations, invited members to relate to others in a reciprocal fashion rather than hierarchically, and religious communities in Quebec took this invitation seriously, beginning to seek less hierarchical relationships between Church members, religious, and clergy.

Historically, in Quebec, Roman Catholic priests, religious, and laypeople played major roles in three sectors: education, health, and social welfare. During the Quiet Revolution, those functions were taken over by the state. This new social context brought a rapid decline of memberships in active congregations, which were then obliged to find other avenues to express their specific missions (Belzile, [1999] 2001). In terms of education, for example—one of the traditional areas of work for women—religious orders had to choose either to integrate with the public sector or to maintain private schools, most of which came to be located in cities with large population bases.

Over time, the number of nuns in Quebec has declined from 40,000 in 1960 to about 11,500, with an average age of 74 in January 2004 (the most recent data available). Many of them are still committed to social justice (Laurin, 2002). Nicole Laurin, a sociologist who has studied religious community life (in Laurin, Juteau, and Duchesne, 1991), points out that "the vocabulary of [women's religious] communities has changed and resembles in an astonishing way that of the left." Indeed, religious communities reached an important socio-political turning point under the influence of the Canadian Religious Conference (Leclerc, 2002: B5).[4]

The emergence of women's groups marked a significant step for consciousness-raising in the Quebec Roman Catholic Church. Such groups allowed women to establish their own territory: to discover their specific identity, to define their own tasks and mission, to concentrate their energies and creativity. The development of such groups helped women to distance themselves from the patriarchal notion that women's identity was defined by their role as mothers and to explore new ways of asserting their personalities as women. In 1976, four women who were deeply concerned about the study of Christian theology from a gender perspective met and formed a collective that they called L'autre Parole ("The Other Word") to provide a different way for women to experience the Word of God.

Origins

The impetus for L'autre Parole came from Monique Dumais, professor of theology and ethics at the Université du Québec à Rimouski (UQAR). She was just returning from her studies in the United States (at Harvard Divinity School and at Union Theological Seminary in New York), where she had been in contact with such well-known women theologians as Beverly Wildung Harrison, Rosemary Radford Ruether, Elisabeth Schüssler Fiorenza, and Letty M. Russell. In the fall 1975 semester, while teaching a course on Women in Religions and Society, she became aware of the need for a network of communication among women involved in the fields of theology and religious sciences in Quebec. Accordingly, she sent a letter to approximately 20 women, and very quickly received enthusiastic replies from Louise Melançon, professor of theology at the Université de

Sherbrooke; Bibianne Beauregard, studying theology at the same university; and Marie-Andrée Roy, studying theology at the Université de Montréal.

On 15 August 1976, after one day of discussion, the four women decided to form a collective under the name L'autre Parole, inspired by the French feminist Annie Leclerc's book *Parole de femme* (1974). They thought it very important that women express themselves in their own words—words related to their own experiences. Thus they made it their initial overall objective to integrate women's experiences into both theological writing and the Church's activities. The group's principal aims were expressed in the first issue of their newsletter: "at the research level, to rebuild theological discourses in taking into account women's experiences, and at the action level, to undertake steps in order to obtain a complete women's participation in the Church" (*L'autre parole*, September 1976: 2).

Activities

The four founders easily recruited other women from Montreal, Sherbrooke, and Rimouski over the next year, and since then women from Quebec City and, more recently, from Gatineau and Saguenay have joined the collective as well. In 2012, two women priests (one a bishop), ordained according to Roman Catholic rites but not accepted by the official Roman Catholic Church, started to follow our activities (see http://romancatholicwomenpriests.org/). However, the membership of L'autre Parole has never been allowed to grow above 60. In fact, "small is beautiful"—and also very effective. Reflecting, analyzing, writing, responding to official Church documents, and making contact with other feminist groups have been the group's main activities. The celebration of its 35th anniversary was an important event for feminist women involved in religious networks.

Reflection Groups

Solidarity is the basis of any feminist group, and for L'autre Parole it quickly became evident that women should join forces and discover the dynamism of a collective effort to question theological discourses and ecclesiastical practices. A central part of this effort was the formation of reflection groups in which the members of L'autre Parole draw out what is at the heart of their experiences as women.

Eight reflection groups involving three to ten women each—in Gatineau, Saguenay, Montreal (three groups), Québec, Sherbrooke, and Rimouski—allow about 50 women to let new, "other" words emerge in feminist theologies and to undertake collective action (*L'autre parole*, no. 92, Winter 2002). A coordinating committee with representatives from each reflection group meets four or five times a year to facilitate networking. The collective functions on a democratic basis, as its designation suggests, without any elected person as president or director.

A Magazine

L'autre parole is also the name of the group's publication, which appears quarterly. It started in September 1976 as a modest four-page newsletter; then four pages were added to each issue until eventually it became a full-fledged magazine. Regular issues had 44 pages, and special issues, such as no. 72 (for the twentieth anniversary colloquium, *Une EKKLÈSIA manifeste*) and no. 92 (for the twenty-fifth anniversary colloquium) could be much longer. The magazine's appearance improved over time as the group added a coloured rigid cover and drawings, and, as a tribute to its handcrafted origin, began using a different colour of ink for each issue. Since Fall 2011, the magazine has been published only on the web. Full volumes appear twice a year, with six shorter annual Notes called *Brève* presenting news and reviews.

The magazine offers an interesting diversity of themes. One issue each year is devoted to the material produced during the annual colloquium, while another focuses on a specific issue, such as secularity and gender equality (no. 133, September 2012). Other themes have included nuns (no. 14, March 1981); the Spirit (no. 15, June 1981); abortion (no. 17, April 1982; no. 33, March 1987); women and power in the Church (no. 24, May 1984); women's ordination (no. 43, September 1989); thealogy (female language for and images of God; no. 51, September 1991); Quebec women and the future of Quebec (no. 49, March 1991); feminist ecology (no. 74, Summer 1997); Christa (imagining the Christ as female; no. 76, Winter 1998); spiritualities and feminists in dialogue (no. 88, Winter 2001); the arts and women's spirituality (no. 89, Spring 2001); and alternatives to globalization (no. 116, Winter 2008).

It is clear that in *L'autre parole* women are trying to reflect on theological and Church issues as well as social ones. The members of the collective consider their participation in society to be linked to their expressions of faith.

Collective Actions

A major event each year is the colloquium, which is exclusively for members of L'autre Parole. (Other feminist religious groups are invited to special celebrations, such as the twentieth and thirty-fifth anniversaries, or meetings organized for specific purposes, such as the 2000 World March of Women.) The annual colloquium is a time for members to reflect together on a specific topic using feminist readings of the Christian tradition. The theme of the first colloquium, held in August 1978 in Rimouski, was "women's body and the Church". It was an opportunity to explore the main obstacle to women's participation in the Church: the perception of their bodies as impure sexual objects.

Other colloquia have dealt with topics such as L'autre Parole's goals, a rewriting of the Beatitudes (see p. 352), texts from Genesis, feminist spirituality, ecology, women–church (a church movement parallel to the official Church that takes women and their experiences seriously), and Christa. For the 2002 colloquium the topic was a study of women prostitutes, in order to discover and acknowledge solidarity and sisterhood with them. The 2003 colloquium focused on the creation of new feminist rituals; the 2004 colloquium was oriented to women and Quebec politics.

L'autre Parole also uses other means to reach public consciousness. For instance, the collective has organized a number of petitions in response to significant events. In 1979, after Theresa Kane, an American nun who had requested acknowledgment of equality for women and men in the Church, was simply blessed and dismissed by Pope John Paul II, for example, L'autre Parole gathered 500 signatures in support of her request and had the petition published in Le Devoir. And in 1996, the collective published an article denouncing the definitive refusal of women's ordination by Rome (Le Devoir, 7 Jan. 1996: A7). Another way of establishing connection with a larger public has been through rituals, especially in connection with Christmas and Easter. Highlighting music and writing by women, these rituals include new symbols meaningful for women and give participants the opportunity to experiment with innovative prayers, such as a Magnificat (Luke 1:46–55) in which Mary's praise of God is expressed through the five senses (Joubert, 1989: 206–9). These rituals are usually held in churches, to show how women are reclaiming their space. The World March of Women in 2000 offered an excellent opportunity for L'autre Parole to show its openness to other spiritualities, including Baha'i, Buddhism, Judaism, Christianity, Wicca, Voodoo, Hinduism, Indigenous religions, Islam). The colloquium that year was a magnificent celebration that highlighted diverse religious rites. In October 2000 a larger event focusing on women's diverse spiritualities drew some 250 attendees.

Another way of communicating with the public is through the publication of books by members of the collective, such as Souffles de femmes (Dumais and Roy, 1989) and Mémoires d'elles (Roy and Lafortune, 1999). In 2011, the 35 years of the collective's existence were celebrated with the publication of L'autre Parole 1976–2011: 35 ans d'écriture et de réécritures.

Relations with Other Women's Groups

The collective L'autre Parole is also determined to develop relationships and solidarity with other feminist groups, both in Quebec and in other parts of the world. Among those groups is Femmes et Ministères ("Women and ministries"), founded in 1982 as an autonomous network of women involved in Church structures (such as diocesan offices), women members of parish teams, and women theologians teaching pastoral theology. Members of the group share their work and stories in order to promote change and assert their autonomy in relation to the Roman Catholic Church (Cloutier, 1984).

The Femmes et Ministères group is especially well known for commissioning a sociological study of women involved in the Quebec Church that was published under the title *Les soutanes roses* ("The pink cassocks") (Bélanger, 1988). In 1995 the group produced *Voix de femmes, voies de passage* (Baroni, Bergeron, Daviau, and Laguë, 1995), in which they analyzed that research and found the Church to be more diverse than the picture painted by its hierarchy would suggest. They directly questioned some positions of the Roman Catholic hierarchy, particularly with respect to the principle of reception, or passing on of the tradition, which originated with the first Christian churches and was reinstated by the Second Vatican Council. As a process of communion, "reception" requires all the people of God—women as well as men—to receive, interpret, and proclaim the Good News. Femmes et Ministères now has a website offering additional important and meaningful texts on the topic of women and religion (www.femmes-ministeres.org/).

Women in the Church in Quebec have had many options for collaboration, both in the province and in the broader Canadian context. For several years, Le Réseau Oecuménique des Femmes du Québec/Quebec Women's Ecumenical Network gave women of various Christian denominations a forum to work together on the urgent issues facing them. The Association des Religieuses pour la Promotion des Femmes, formed by nuns in 1977 at the incentive of the Canadian Religious Conference, changed its name to Association des Religieuses pour les droits des femmes in 2011.

L'autre Parole is well connected with other groups interested in the status and roles of women in both Church and society. A member of the Fédération des Femmes du Québec (FFQ), it is also involved with two international groups: Femmes et Hommes dans l'Église, now part of Les Réseaux du Parvis en France, and the Groupe Orsay, a group of Protestant women in Paris. These two groups focus on changes in religions, and their goals are close to those of L'autre Parole. Some members of the collective have attended the conferences of these two groups and presented papers.

Innovation: Rewriting through Women's Experience

The most interesting project that L'autre Parole has undertaken is the rewriting of some patriarchal texts, both from the Bible and from the Church. Working in groups of two to four, the women examine a text's original patriarchal context and try to rewrite sections to incorporate women's experiences. Mary Daly describes this radical approach:

> The method of liberation ... involves a *castrating* of language and images that reflect and perpetuate the structures of a sexist world. It castrates precisely in the sense of cutting away the phallocentric value system imposed by patriarchy, in its subtle as well as in its more manifest expressions ([1973] 1985: 9).

The texts produced by these workshops have been very well received, especially their versions of the Beatitudes (Luke 6:20–6) and the first two chapters of Genesis. These texts are used and reproduced by other feminist groups.

Feminist rewriting is grounded in women's experiences. In feminist theology, women's experience serves as a source and norm (Young, 1990: 49–69) that guides the whole enterprise of interpreting the Word of God. Concrete experiences are reflected on in order to perceive their meaning for women's condition and for the Christian tradition. In this way the Word of God receives an interpretation liberated from its patriarchal context and open to all human experiences. In L'autre Parole, the process of collective rewriting allows women to discover a sense of freedom and dynamism. This process of rewriting involves "a shift from an androcentric to a feminist paradigm" (Fiorenza, 1983: xxi). Several American women theologians—Elisabeth Schüssler Fiorenza, Mary Daly, Rosemary Radford Ruether, Letty M. Russell—have been important guides in these feminist critical hermeneutics. Some women theologians writing in French—for example, France Quéré and Elisabeth J. Lacelle, who were not part of the collective—inspired its feminist reflections.

The Beatitudes

Happy are those women whose heart is not hardened because they
    listen to women and to God.
Alas for those men and women who establish and perpetuate
    women's poverty, because they betray God in not acknowledging
    social and economic value for domestic work, in withholding

priesthood in the Roman Catholic Church from women on
the account of their sex, in keeping women out of places where
values that govern their lives are fabricated.

Happy are the soft and aggressive women inhabited by a *will to live*:
you disarm your oppressors in the hope of reconciliation.
Alas for those who sow death; hate and violence you will reap.
Happy are those women who, in becoming aware of their oppressions
are liberating themselves in a word of forgiveness.
Alas for those women for whom to forgive is to give up.

Happy are those women who are working to knead the bread of
autonomy, of equality, of solidarity, together, they will feed
the earth.
Alas for those who are easily satisfied with crumbs falling from the
sacred table.
They paralyze Church growth.
Happy are those women who scream, who shriek and squall to tear
away at the silence of death,
Alas for those men and women who snivel and grumble without
touching the centre of their oppressions.

Happy are these women audaciously taken by the Gospel of Jesus
Christ who have the courage to be faithful more than in thought
and in word, but truly in deeds.
Alas for those women who dissociate thoughts, heart and acts,
because they tarnish the light from the Gospel.
Alas for those women who are staying quiet to be in peace because
they maintain oppression.

Happy are those victims of patriarchal power who find in the violence
they experience strength to build up peace.
Happy are you women scoffed because of your speech; by your
tenacity, you build your liberation.
Alas for you who will have been seduced by a discourse that will
dispossess you from the meaning of your struggle.

   —*Trans. M. Dumais*

Conclusion

The women of L'autre Parole face important challenges: first, reaching the
institutional Church; second, reaching other feminists; finally, grappling with
the ways in which they themselves have been changed by their collective work.

Among the Canadian bishops with whom the collective has tried to connect, Quebec bishops have proven to be the most open-minded. In March 1986 they organized a large conference, involving bishops and representatives of women's groups, to point out and analyze the most difficult issues concerning women and the Church. However, then as always, the bishops' necessary relationship with Rome obliged them to maintain a conservative attitude.

With respect to reaching other feminist groups, the challenge is that to many feminists, any organization with a religious dimension is at first glance suspect because they see Christianity as a major obstacle to women's autonomy and equality. The women of L'autre Parole have to convey the necessity of questioning Christian churches from inside.

Members of the collective continue to struggle to find ways to empower women within a Christian context. Their quest for a better world is not without suffering; the strength of resurrection in Christ (Philippians 3:10) becomes their main dynamic force.

Study Questions

1. What factors influence women's lives in the Roman Catholic Church in Quebec, and how have these changed over the last 50 years?
2. What social circumstances led to the formation of L'autre Parole?
3. What are the objectives of L'autre Parole, and how are they realized?
4. Discuss some of the themes that L'autre Parole has explored.
5. How would you describe the process employed by L'autre Parole in rewriting biblical texts? How does this relate to the discussion of the interpretation of texts in Chapter 6?
6. Which part of the rewriting of the Beatitudes on p. 352 strikes you as the most significant for a woman involved in the Christian Church? Why?
7. How could the themes of social change and backlash discussed in Chapter 6 be applied to the relationship between L'autre Parole and the Roman Catholic Church?

Notes

1. A feminist magazine. The title means "Quebec women standing up!" "*Debouttes*" is an unusual feminized form of the adverb *debout*.
2. *La bonne parole* is a "feminine magazine," according to the first definition given by its women promoters; it was published from 1913 to 1958.
3. Translations into English are the author's.
4. The Canadian Religious Conference is an organization representing all Canadian Roman Catholic men and women in religious orders and congregations.

Further Reading

L'autre Parole. September 1976–present. Free subscription on the web. Transcriptions of all issues are available at www.lautreparole.org/.

L'autre Parole: 1976–2011, 35 ans d'écritures et de réécritures. 2011. Gatineau: Les Éditions ÀTroisBrins.

Dumais, Monique. 1989. "Témoignage d'un groupe de femmes: De l'émergence d'une autre parole chez les femmes chrétiennes et féministes". Pp. 145–52 in Isabelle Lasvergnas, ed. A/encrages féministes. Montréal: Université du Québec à Montréal. Montreal; GIERF, Cahiers de recherche.

——, and Marie-Andrée Roy, eds. 1989. Souffles de femmes: Lectures féministes de la religion. Montreal: Éditions Paulines.

Lacelle, Élisabeth J., ed. 1979. La femme et la religion au Canada français: Un fait socio-culturel. Montréal: Bellarmin.

Roy, Marie-Andrée. 1996. Les ouvrières de Dieu. Montreal: Médiaspaul.

Veillette, Denise, ed. 1995. Femmes et religions. Québec: Les Presses de l'Université Laval; Québec, Corporation Canadienne des Sciences Religieuses/Canadian Corporation for Studies in Religion.

References

L'autre parole. All issues since September 1976: www.lautreparole.org/

Baroni, Lise, Yvonne Bergeron, Pierrette Daviau, and Micheline Laguë. 1995. Voix de femmes, voies de passage: Pratiques pastorales et enjeux ecclésiaux. Montreal: Éditions Paulines.

Bélanger, Sarah. 1988. Les Soutanes roses: Portrait du personnel pastoral féminin au Québec. Montreal: Bellarmin.

Belzile, Louis. [1999] 2001. La Route des ferventes. Audiobook: Radio-Canada. Montréal: Fides.

Cloutier, Linda. "L'Église interpellée par ses filles". La Gazette des femmes, July–August 1984: 14–18.

Collectif Clio, Le. 1992. L'Histoire des femmes au Québec depuis quatre siècles. Montreal: Le Jour.

Daly, Mary. [1973] 1985. Beyond God the Father: Toward a Philosophy of Women's Liberation. Boston: Beacon.

Danylewycz, Marta. 1987. Taking the Veil: An Alternative to Marriage, Motherhood, Spinsterhood in Quebec: 1840–1920. Toronto: McClelland & Stewart.

Daviau, Pierrette, in collaboration with Jacynthe Fortin. 2000. Projets de femmes, Église en projet: Jalons d'analyse sociopastorale. Montreal: Éditions Paulines.

Denault, Bernard, and Benoît Lévesque. 1975. Éléments pour une sociologie des communautés religieuses au Québec. Montreal: Les Presses de l'Université de Montréal et de l'Université de Sherbrooke.

Dumais, Monique. 1981. "Les religieuses, leur contribution à la société québécoise". Canadian Women's Studies/Les cahiers de la femme 3: 18–20.

——, and Marie-Andrée Roy, eds. 1989. Souffles de femmes: Lectures féministes de la religion. Montreal: Éditions Paulines.

Fiorenza, Elisabeth Schüssler. 1983. In Memory of Her: A Feminist Theological Reconstruction of Christian Origins. New York: Crossroad.

Joubert, Denyse. 1989. "Mon âme exalte le Seigneur". Pp. 206–9 in Monique Dumais and Marie-Andrée Roy, eds. Souffles de femmes: Lectures féministes de la religion. Montreal: Éditions Paulines.

Laurin, Nicole. 2002. "Quel avenir pour les religieuses du Québec?" Relations 677: 30–4.

Laurin, Nicole, Danielle Juteau, and Lorraine Duchesne. 1991. *À la recherche d'un monde oublié: Les communautés religieuses de femmes au Québec de 1900 à 1970*. Montreal: Le Jour.

Leclerc, Annie. 1974. *Parole de femme*. Paris: Grasset.

Leclerc, Jean-Claude. 2002. "Les communautés religieuses «passent sur l'autre rive»". *Le Devoir*, 2 July.

Radcliffe, Timothy. 2000. *Je vous appelle amis: Entretiens avec Guillaume Goubert*. Paris: La Croix/Cerf.

Rocher, Guy. 1973. *Le Québec en mutation*. Montreal: HMH/Hurtubise.

Roy, Marie-Andrée, and Agathe Lafortune, eds. 1999. *Mémoires d'elles: Fragments de vies et spiritualités de femmes*. Montreal: Médiaspaul.

Sölle, Dorothee. 1970. *Beyond Mere Obedience*. Minneapolis: Augsburg.

Wade, Mason. 1964. *The French-Canadian Outlook*. 1971. Toronto: McClelland & Stewart.

Young, Pamela Dickey. 1990. *Feminist Theology/Christian Theology: In Search of Method*. Minneapolis: Fortress.

Two Muslim Women in North America

L. Clarke

Aisha al-Adawiya

Muslims made up an unknown percentage of the Africans who were brought to the New World as slaves. African-American Islam was re-created in the early twentieth century by two race-conscious, unorthodox movements: the Moorish Science Temple and the Nation of Islam. In the past few decades, however, most African-American Muslims have been integrated into orthodox Islam. Gender relations have always been a focus of African-American Islam, which has sought to strengthen the family unit as a way of addressing social disruption.

Aisha al-Adawiya is founding director and Chair Emeritus of Women in Islam (www.womeninislam.org), an advocacy and education organization focused on "human rights and social justice." She is also president of Karamah (www .karamah.org), an association of Muslim woman lawyers concerned with Islamic gender issues worldwide, and coordinator of Islamic input for the Black Religious Heritage Documentation Project at the Schomburg Center for Research in Black Culture in Harlem, New York City. Dressed in a brocade jacket with matching head scarf and jewelry, Aisha speaks with the emphasis and confidence of a long-time community activist.

Aisha is a convert who presents her life as the story of her journey to Islam. Like many Black converts of the turbulent 1950s and 1960s, she remembers an early discontent with Christianity and a yearning for something more meaning-ful. Why, she asked herself, were many of those who inflicted "gross injustices" on African-Americans regarded as "upstanding citizens and good Christians in the community"? "I was," she says, "in search of something spiritual, but I didn't know what." In 1961, Aisha left the small Alabama town of her childhood for New York City. Malcolm X was on the scene. "I was fascinated by the social critique of Malcolm X and very much attracted to the teachings on a political level. People were looking for alternative ways to live their lives, and I was part of that." She gravitated toward the emerging health-food movement and began to explore various spiritual paths, including New Age spirituality, Buddhism, and Sufism. And then she found her first Quran, "on the bottom shelf in an occult store in Greenwich Village."

By the time Aisha walked into the Islamic Center of New York one day in 1971 with the intention of uttering the profession of faith (*shahadah*), she says, "I was already Muslim; that was just a formality." One of the things she remembers as having attracted her to Islam was "the position of women." The other was "the right to self-defence."[1] She now took a new, non-slave name, an experience she describes as "empowering and liberating." "Who," she asked herself, "do I want to be like?" She chose "Aisha," after the wife of the Prophet, and "al-Adawiya," the tribal name of Rabi'ah, the famous female mystic of early Islam. "These were examples for me of two powerful women within the Muslim tradition. Aisha was a scholar and stateswoman, and Rabi'ah was a powerful spiritual force in her own right. No one said to them, "'You can't do that, it's not a woman's place.'"

It was nevertheless difficult, Aisha says, to find books about women's contributions to Islam. That situation, she finds, has recently changed with the emergence of "woman scholars grounded in classical Islamic knowledge" able to address the "serious necessity of revisiting the scholarship of past centuries." Muslim women, in her view, are engaged in a struggle to reclaim the rightful place they once owned, for which "the blueprint is the example of the Prophet [Muhammad] and the early community around him." Aisha's treatment of domestic violence, an issue in which she is deeply engaged as president of Karamah, exemplifies her approach. She points to the "model of the Prophet Muhammad," who, she says, "did not engage in any abusive practices, not only against women, but anyone." When asked about the problematic verse of the Quran (4:34) that sanctions discipline of wives, she points to the efforts of female scholars to "re-cast some Quranic verses" and provide better education about "Islamic jurisprudence and women's rights."

Education, in Aisha's view, is the key to restoring women to their rightful place and promoting social justice. "Women have to understand what their rights and responsibilities in marriage are. In fact, both women and men have to be educated. Women raise up nations, both girls and boys, and once they are empowered with knowledge of Islam, they will make different choices for themselves and their families. Boys and girls will understand. We won't have tyrannical husbands and fathers."

Like a good number of Muslims today, Aisha places a great deal of faith in the possibility of thoroughly "adapting" Islamic law, which she usually refers to as "Shariah." Shariah, she insists, is "not static" and can "change according to place and time." This includes laws of marriage and divorce, which need to be "revisited with the input of women." Shariah is also, she explains, "multi-faceted," embracing "food and other very fine nuances of everyday life," whereas "here in America, it has come to mean simply laws related to *hudud* [corporal punishment]." Aisha's concern that the law be correctly understood by "both Muslims and non-Muslims" has been heightened by the anti-Shariah movement in the United States, which has seen more than twenty states pass bills banning the use of Islamic laws in courts.

Aisha refers more to Islamic law now than she did in her interview for the first edition of this book. She cites the marriage contract as one example of the potential benefits of Shariah. Discussion of the contract, she says, should be a "pre-requisite for marriage," since it gives the couple—or, in "a more traditional culture," their parents—the opportunity to negotiate terms. Terms that can be "spelled out" in a marriage contract, Aisha says, are "varied and wide," one example being the right of a wife to continue to work in her profession. The other examples she gives, such as the right of a woman to separate housing and equal support, relate to polygamy. If women were to educate themselves about and "actively utilize" the contract, Aisha says, they would be able to reject polygamy and resist "families who drive its abuse and impose it on their daughters." Aisha nevertheless describes polygamy as "a valid institution, permissible under certain conditions." Islamic "plural marriage," as she sometimes calls it, "has nothing to do with men's sexual desires," and the fact that "most of the wives of the Prophet Muhammad were older women" demonstrates that marrying multiple wives is "solely for the protection of women, as it is a woman's right to have a family, caring, and maintenance." In the final analysis, she sees polygamy as "simply a woman's choice."

In her earlier interview, Aisha had reported that women were being prevented from entering some mosques, including in New York City, and that when they did attend they were treated as "non-people." "Suddenly," she remarked at that time, "you are met with this barrier. It is Islamic to insist that you will enter the *masjid* [mosque]. Don't take no for an answer; just go in!" She is currently involved in an organized effort to conduct workshops in which integration is "not dictated" but brought about "organically" by engaging mosque administrators and women in frank discussion in the hope that they will see the need to "commit to positive change." The organic approach, she says, requires that a clear distinction be made between spatial and social integration and "calling for female-led prayers," two "separate issues" that tend to be "unconsciously or deliberately conflated." Combining "a public stance" with "working from the inside" is, Aisha feels, the best strategy in the face of a trend toward prayer partitions and increased social segregation, seen especially in the more affluent suburban mosques serving recent immigrant populations. Aisha likens the women's space in these elaborate buildings, so different from the storefront mosques she knew as a young convert, to "gilded cages," and she worries that if women are not represented on boards and their "ideas and expertise in building the community" are not taken seriously, the next generation will be lost.

Aisha sees the participation of women as central to the success of Islam, or indeed of any civilization: "Women are really the primary transmitters of ideology and culture in nations, and the power resides in the woman to develop the nation. Abuse and neglect of women lead to the destruction of nations." Islam, in Aisha's view, originally and exceptionally recognized this truth. "Allah gave us the unique experience of childbirth and mothering, and therein lies the power, and Islam creates an environment that can best foster that process of nation building. Although we are presently suffering from the abuse of men and women in Muslim society, we are beginning to understand how women around the Prophet were supported in their special roles." Asked about women and fundamentalism, Aisha retorts, "I do not use the word 'fundamentalist'; I use the term 'fanatic.'" She mentions "gross abuses" against women in the Muslim world, including so-called honour killings. "These are patently against Islam. It is outrageous to say them in the same breath."

Despite her feeling that restoration of the position of women is crucial to the progress of Islam, Aisha prefers to focus on the situation of Muslims in general rather than women's issues alone. When asked what reforms of Shariah are necessary relating specifically to women, she points out that "issues that impact the Muslim community in general also impact women and their families," while practices "oppressive to women" also involve "a cost to the community." Men, she believes, can be "open to the message" of empowering women, and so it is better to "bring them along in that process so that there will be mutual benefit" rather than "alienating" them. This stance seems similar to that of Muslim women's movements elsewhere in the world that reject what they view as the aggressive or conflictual tone of Western feminism.

The original impetus for Aisha's founding of Women in Islam in 1992 was the issue of rape camps in Bosnia. She reports some friction at that time with "feminists," some of whom thought "Islam would have no use for women who were victims of rape and no longer virgins." They did not realize, Aisha says, that from the Islamic perspective, rape victims are unwilling participants and are therefore innocent, and that abortion is allowed by Islam if there is a threat to the woman's life. But Aisha also points out that Black women who were raped during slavery did not abort their children, "so there may be another option—to let them grow up to defend their mothers, families, and nation." On the issue of abortion, as on other issues, Aisha seems to negotiate between liberal and more conservative views—although she herself emphasizes that she is "just a Muslim" and does not "classify" herself as a liberal or conservative.

In the decades since the Bosnian war, Aisha has become more involved than ever with coalition-building around global issues. "So many atrocities have happened in the world," she says, "that my position is that we advocate for the common good, not just the good of Muslims." "Everything," she says, "is interconnected and has international implications; we need to become more educated also about our American laws and Constitution and about women's leadership not just in the mosque but across the board." One of the "new challenges" Aisha is concerned with is female prisoners, some of whom enter the system as Muslims and some of whom "embrace Islam" while incarcerated. She speaks about drawing not only on the resources of Islam, but also "United Nations standards on the treatment of prisoners."

Now a great-grandmother, Aisha finds herself "looking at things we were struggling for years ago and re-thinking how I want to engage many issues." She aspires to be a mentor of young women—as well as young men—so that the community can "build on the success of people who fought similar struggles rather than re-inventing the wheel each time." She is optimistic about young Muslims, whom she describes as "very smart," and the potential of technology to "extend our activity far beyond the local sphere." Though Aisha hints at discrimination when she mentions the failure of immigrants to acknowledge that the first Muslims in America were "Africans who were kidnapped and brought here as slaves," she prefers to think in terms of global rather than African-American or other particular experiences of Islam. She believes that there is a set of "Islamic principles" that is very different from "unjust practices based on culture," and that if these practices are "thrown out," women and Islam will advance together. She is, at the same time, careful to avoid the impression of diverging from the tradition, declaring that she does not want to create a "new Islam" or even reject what she calls a "beautiful culture," but only "attack some of those old conceptions of who we are as Muslims and Muslim women."

Shahnaz

Another influence that has flowed into North American Islam is the experience of the immigrants. Muslims from the Middle East and Europe began to arrive in the United States and Canada as early as the mid-1800s, but most of the immigrant population dates from the last half of the twentieth century. This second wave is much more diverse than the first, hailing from places such as the Indian subcontinent, Malaysia,

Iran, and North Africa. Muslim immigrants—like the convert population, including
African-Americans—must negotiate between their own religious values and those of
the host society. The most sensitive issue by far is that of the position of women. How
does one fit Islamic gender ideals into North American society?

"Shahnaz" (a pseudonym) is a businesswoman in her early sixties and a resident of Montréal, Quebec. She is an active member of the Canadian Council of
Muslim Women, a long-standing national organization dedicated to the articulation of a liberal Islam and the active role of women within it.

Shahnaz immigrated to Canada with her husband in the 1970s from
Pakistan, just as that country was plunged into the civil war that resulted
in the birth of Bangladesh. The family was forced to flee, but Shahnaz still
remembers the life of her upper-class family as somewhat idyllic. She attended
a coeducational, English-language school that included not only Sunnites and
Shiites, but also Ismailis, Christians, and Hindus. There was, she recalls, "no
friction": "only when I came [to Canada] did I notice that this and that person
is Muslim."

Nor was it felt that the position of women was a problem requiring discussion. There was no feeling that women should be segregated or cover their hair,
or indeed any consciousness that this was an issue at all, though cultural norms
did require women to cover their heads with a diaphanous scarf in religious
gatherings. There was, Shahnaz says, "no talk of women and their rights; we
already *had* our rights." The families of the community would gather in the
local sports club, where the women also enjoyed sports of various kinds. The
sports tradition continues in the family; one of Shahnaz's daughters is quarter-
back and owner of the first women's football team in Canada.

Shahnaz remembers her mother as somewhat reserved. Her father was the
stronger figure; he was, she says, "open," a community activist who taught her
that "you don't adapt to Islam, Islam automatically adapts to you." Nevertheless,
he believed it was best to marry at a young age, since this would allow the wife
to "adjust to conjugal duties" and the couple to "grow up together." ("He was,"
Shahnaz remarks half-jokingly, "wrong.") She was married at the age of 17 to a
member of her set, someone she had met in the community sports club. The
proposal was initiated by the man's parents, at his request. Not only she but also
her parents had to approve; this, she says, was partly because of her age but also
a requirement of "the tradition at that time." Parental authority in marriage,
she believes, is "absolutely cultural." Parents "can be involved, but they don't
have to be if the children are of age," and a woman can even propose to a man,
as Khadijah did to the Prophet Muhammad.

Shahnaz was brought up in an observant household, but this appears to
have involved a natural religiosity quite different from the highly conscious,

emphatic style of Islam she would encounter in Canada. Bangladesh and Pakistan, she says, were "Muslim-majority, so everything was Islamic." In Canada, in contrast, she was faced with consciously forming her identity as a Muslim woman. Nevertheless, she emphasizes the ease with which she was able to adapt to the new environment. Adjustment to life in the West, she says, "came naturally"; she describes herself as being "not at all worried" and simply thinking, "I am living in Canada and must live as a Canadian." She declares that, although she used to wear a sari in Bangladesh, adopted the less revealing shalwar-kameez after the flight to Pakistan, and now wears "skirts, trousers and sweaters," her "inside was the same" through it all. Shahnaz is critical of persons whose "lives revolve just around Islam"; she emphasizes that she wants to know about and be involved "in my neighbourhood and the world." She is a member of the Council of Canadians, a progressive, Canadian nationalist organization whose motto is "Acting for Social Justice." She has been active in a variety of causes, from Palestinian affairs to Aboriginal rights, and sometimes attends demonstrations—although, she jokes, "only in the summer" (referring to the severe Canadian winters). Shahnaz places even more emphasis on the importance of integrating into Canadian society than when I first interviewed her nearly ten years ago; although she is also careful to say that integration must be accomplished "within the parameters of Islam."

As for hijab, she remembers that in her vanished life in the former East Pakistan, it "was not even considered a part of faith." Having always dressed "modestly and conservatively," she began to veil after making the pilgrimage to Makkah in 1997. Her hijab consists of modest, rather chic, Western dress— long sleeves and skirts—with matching scarves and pins. Shahnaz emphasizes that the standard of dress demanded by the Quran is simply "modesty"; actual covering of the hair, she says, is "absolutely not required." Muslim women, she says, are able to "choose" and it is up to each believer to interpret the Quranic standard as she wishes, "according to her strength." Her hijab, she explains, is partly a "practical" choice; it fits her busy lifestyle and need to be dressed to pray since she is often at work from morning to night.

Before immigrating to Canada, Shahnaz (like a good number of Muslims in non-Arab countries) used to read the Arabic words of the Quran without understanding, as a kind of incantation. "I did not understand one word; but in Canada, I read the Quran for the first time with meaning." She took it upon herself to read several different translations so that she could understand for herself what the text meant. She studied the interpretations of, among others, Pickthall and Yusuf Ali, but says that she "keeps on coming back" to the liberal-leaning version of the famous Jewish convert Muhammad Asad, as he "touches" her "heart." Her other reading material ranges from the writings of the conservative Indo-Pakistani thinker Mawdudi to the multi-ethnic Muslim

women's magazine *Azizah*, published since 2000 in Atlanta, Georgia (www
.azizahmagazine.com).

Like Aisha, Shahnaz appears to negotiate between liberal views and the
more conservative standards she believes to be dictated by Islam and the
Quran. Man and woman, she says, are equal; "the Quran tells us that they are
created equal, one for the other." But, she adds, males are "given a bit more
responsibility, some extra duties" (an apparent acknowledgment of the statement in Quran 4:34 that men are "set over" women since they are required to
support them). In Shahnaz's view, that extra responsibility takes the form of the
duty to provide for the woman. By contrast, in her first interview she said that
a man would have to provide only if the woman could not provide for herself. A
woman, according to Shahnaz, can be a head of state if she is qualified, but "her
most important duty is to bring up children to be good citizens." After women
are finished with their household responsibilities, they are "free to choose the
profession they want," including political office.

As for polygamy, while Shahnaz used to believe that men are "naturally
polygamous," she now suspects that they rather "pretend to be." She argues that
the Quran limited the number of wives allowed to four in order to improve
on the "the norm" in seventh-century Arabian society of having many more.
The norm today, she says, is one wife, a better standard that is supported by
the Quran when it says that men can have more than one wife only if they can
treat them equally (Q. 4:3) but also notes that it is impossible to do so (4:129).
Polygamy, she concludes, is allowed only in "very restricted" circumstances.

Divorce in Islam has been "misinterpreted," according to Shahnaz. For
example, the man's pronouncing the formula of divorce three times in quick
succession does not, in her view, actually lead to valid dissolution. Shariah,
she insists, requires three declarations, each separated by a "waiting period"
of three menstrual cycles, for divorce to take effect "This," she says, "is what
the Quran says, and then men changed it in later times." Inspired, apparently,
by the hadith statement that "God hates divorce," Shahnaz states that men
do require some grounds for divorce; marriage, after all, "is a responsibility,
and you can't just get up and leave." Women, she thinks, also have the right to
divorce; when pressed on this question, she describes the *khul* divorce, in which
the man agrees to release the woman in return for her giving up some or all of
her dower.

Shahnaz's views on the problematic issue of divorce, like those of many
Muslims, reflect reformist ideas and reformed law more than they do the traditional law. (The idea that triple divorce is not effective, for instance, is a reformist view that has been passed into law by many Muslim states.) She is apparently
unaware of the extent to which male prerogative actually rules the law and of

the continuing struggle in the Muslim world to weaken that prerogative—probably because among the people she knows now in Canada and those she once knew in East Pakistan, social standards did not allow that prerogative free rein.

Shahnaz points to the dower as evidence of Islam's care for women. She recounts that her husband had promised her a large sum when he married her overseas, which grew even larger when they came to Canada because of the rule that dower is payable in local currency. He did well enough in his shipping business (in which Shahnaz is a working partner) that he was finally able to settle the debt by giving her title to the very substantial house in which they now live. "It is her house," jokes her husband. "She could throw me out if she wanted!"

Both Shahnaz and her husband are perplexed by the extremism on the rise in the Muslim world today. They seem hurt by the media's focus on a version of Islam they themselves find strange, and they are anxious to dispel that image. They are especially insistent that Islam gives freedom and respect to women, and angered by extremists they consider to have betrayed Islamic ideals. "One should not," cautions Shahnaz, "judge religion by the acts of its followers."

Study Questions

1. What similarities and differences do you see between Aisha's and Shahnaz's views of Islam? How do their views relate to the descriptions of "conservatives" and "liberals" in Chapter 7 of this book?
2. What did you learn about their views of fundamentalism, and how does this relate to other things you have learned or read on the subject?
3. What issues do Aisha and Shahnaz bring up concerning Shariah, and how do they deal with those issues?
4. How do Aisha's and Shahnaz's views compare with those of other Muslim women you have met, including your classmates?

Note

1. When I interviewed Aishah in 2004 for the first edition of this book, I thought this statement recalled the early, nationalist stage of the African-American Islamic movement, in which it was seen as legitimate to respond to direct assaults on the community. When she saw this in print, however, Aisha objected strongly, writing to me that she had "never been a member of the Nation of Islam or a Black Nationalist" and that her views on "the right to defend one's family and community" derived rather from "basic human rights enshrined in the UN Charter" and her understanding of "the fundamental Islamic principles of self-preservation and non-aggression."

Further Reading

Ebrahimji, Maria M., and Zahra T. Suratwala, eds. 2011. *I Speak for Myself: American Women on Being Muslim*. Ashland, OR: White Cloud Press.

Haddad, Yvonne Yazbeck, Jane I. Smith and Kathleen M. Moore, eds. 2006. *Muslim Women in America: The Challenge of Islamic Identity Today*. New York: Oxford University Press.

Hammer, Juliane. 2012. *American Muslim Women, Religious Authority, and Activism: More than a Prayer*. Austin: University of Texas Press.

Karim, Jamillah. 2009. *American Muslim Women: Negotiating Race, Class, and Gender within the Ummah*. New York: New York University Press.

Roald, Anne Sofie. *Women in Islam: The Western Experience*. 2001. London, New York: Routledge.

Rouse, Carolyn Moxley. 2004. *Engaged Surrender: African-American Women and Islam*. Berkeley: University of California Press.

Tate, Sonsyrea. 2005. *Little X: Growing Up in the Nation of Islam*. Knoxville: University of Tennessee Press.

Van Nieuwkerk, Karin, ed. 2006. *Women Embracing Islam: Gender and Conversion in the West*. Austin: University of Texas Press.

Women's Writing, Women's Religiosity, and Popular Religion in China

Stephanie Balkwill

Geographically the fourth-largest country in the world, and home to the world's largest population, China is vast and varied both physically and with respect to human experience. The landscape of the country changes dramatically from mountain peaks to plains to deserts to river valleys, and this diverse geography has helped to shape the culture and religious beliefs of its people. For example, we know that great cultural divides have existed between the peoples of the North and the South throughout China's more than 5000-year history, and that isolated villages, often tucked away in mountain valleys or foothills, had very different cultural customs than did cities on the wide-open central plains. The Chinese language has also been affected by this diversity, in that although its written form has long been unified by the use of Chinese characters, the local spoken dialects of the language are often mutually unintelligible. Even Mandarin-speakers have trouble understanding the dialects of their fellow speakers from different regions; Beijingers are often at a loss to respond to Shanghainese and vice versa. Indeed, although what we now call China has long been unified by its written language, forms of governance, and shared history, it remains a remarkably diverse country full of geographically disparate yet equally fascinating cultures and languages.

The range of China's geographical specificity is not limited to landscape and language. Religion, too, finds endless variations in local temples, village and city gods, and family shrines. Often referred to as "popular religion," the common practice of religion in China is noted for its wide variety of deities—the god of the stove, the god of test-taking, the god of fertility—and the worship of these gods is often rooted in local history and never mentioned in any religious text. For example, in his study of contemporary popular religion in China, Adam Yuet Chau discusses the localized worship of the Canadian doctor Norman Bethune, who is regarded as a hero in China for his alliance with the Chinese people against the Japanese in the 1930s. Dr Bethune died in China and is still fondly remembered today. In one village he has become a god himself and locals petition him for healing by smoking his favourite brand of cigarettes. Chau uses examples such as this to argue that popular religion in China is so localized that it cannot be represented by any of the mainstream religious traditions—Buddhism, Daoism, and Confucianism—because popular religious beliefs and practices are rooted in local history and not in orthodox religious teaching (Chau, 2008: 1–19, 47). This is not to say that popular religion is not interwoven with the three major religions: only that it has the ability to exist independent of them, in the localized rituals and daily lives of the people who practise it and for whom it has meaning.

Tucked away in the foothills and jaw-droppingly beautiful rice paddies of Southern China's lush, green province of Hunan, famed for its tropical fruits and spicy food, there is a county called Jiangyong, where a form of popular religion is practised that is specifically tied not only to geography, but also to gender. The women of Jiangyong worship a feminized deity known as "The Mother" or Niangniang, who seems to have first appeared in connection with the Han Dynasty (206 BCE–220 CE) goddess known as the Queen Mother of the West, but by the Late Imperial period (1368–1912) became a deity herself in some forms of both Daoist and Buddhist worship. Usually as assistants of more senior deities, these Niangniangs see that the prayers of the faithful are delivered to the deity and further help the deities to administer their grace to the faithful (Pomeranz, 1997: 189). In some places the Niangniangs have acquired such power and prestige that they have developed independent followings. This is the case in Jiangyong where sometimes the Daoist goddess Gu Po is worshipped directly, but more often Niangniang is revered without any reference to the latter. According to the women of Jiangyong, their local Niangniang came into being after two sisters took lunch to their father who was plowing in the field and then died while seated in the lotus position, with their legs crossed in front of them (Liu, 1997: 205). This body position, which is reminiscent of the Buddha and other bodhisattvas, is the standard position for eminent monks on their deathbeds, and thus signaled the transformation of two flesh-and-blood bodies into a singular, ethereal one: Niangniang. This local deity receives the prayers and petitions of the women of Jiangyong, though she cannot be found in any mainstream religious text of the Buddhist, Daoist, or Confucian traditions.

Even more fascinating, during the eighteenth century the local women of Jiangyong began writing their prayers to Niangniang in a non-standard version of Chinese characters used only by them and commonly referred to as *nu shu*, or women's script (Silber, 1995: 49ff; McLaren 2008). These characters, each of which represents a syllable used in the local dialect, were used to write a variety of genres that constitute a unique corpus of writings clearly identified as being "for women only." Though the men of Jiangyong knew about the *nu shu* characters, it was the women who used them to write letters to their sworn sisters within the community, ritualized laments on the unfortunate occasion of marriage and the loss of one's individual freedom, prayers to Niangniang, and folk songs. Traditionally, they embroidered these texts on silk fans and gave them as gifts either to one another or to the deity. Although the origins of the script are highly contested, local women say that *nu shu* was invented by one of their own: a local woman who in the eleventh century became a courtesan to the emperor, a highly coveted position in imperial China. As the story goes, this courtesan invented the script so that she could write letters to her family expressing her discontent with her position without running afoul of the palace censors. Another explanation holds that the characters were developed for use in embroidery, a handicraft long practised by the women of Jiangyong (Liu, 1997: 16–19). Regardless of their origin, these characters form an integral part of Jiangyong women's religious identity.

By and large, most genres of *nu shu* show similar traits: all express personal feelings of pity or resentment at the hard reality of living as a peasant woman, usually in the form of lengthy laments about marriage, motherhood, filial demands, and widowhood. During the time period in which *nu shu* flourished—the latter part of the Late Imperial era—women's lives were strictly regulated under the influence of the patriarchal reinterpretation of traditional learning, paired with Chinese cosmology, that is often referred to in the West as "Neo-Confucianism." As part of this ideological project, women's lives were subject to a doctrine known as the "Three Followings." First promoted in the Han Dynasty by Ban Zhao (see p. 134), it declared that a woman must follow either her father, her husband, or her son, depending on her role as daughter, wife, or widow. Although the Three Followings had existed in Chinese thought for many centuries, government regulation of women's virtue intensified in the Late Imperial period. The same period saw foot-binding flourish at the popular level, although there is no evidence that it was practised in Jiangyong. Many of the *nu shu* writings express bitterness or resentment over the hardship the authors suffer simply because they are women. One of the *nu shu* writers reflects poignantly on the social position of women in her time:

> There is no goodness in daughters; one is limited to producing sons.
> To raise up a beloved son is to complete one's life.
> In these times all life's problems are contained with women.
> Elders and adults have no sympathy for daughters
> (Collected in Zhao, 1992: 5258; trans. S. Balkwill).

A more developed example of the hardships that women faced during this period can be seen in the prayer whose first lines are quoted in Chapter 4 (p. 135). Addressed not to Niangniang but to the Daoist goddess Gu Po, it pleads with the latter to return the woman's husband to her:

> . . . My husband is called Tang Youyi.
> Three years ago he went to Guangxi.
> Since he went to Guangxi he has not returned.
> I do not know into what direction his life has fallen.
>
> He deserted me here to guard over an empty house,
> and also our one son and two daughters.
> The fields and the earth are without workers to plough them.
> Every kind of responsibility is up to me, alone.
>
> When my husband left it was on the pretext of settling our accounts.
> He desired to return here honest and replenished.
> We in the family are extremely destitute. We have not been
>   replenished.
> In looking for a great advantage, our advantage has, instead, been
>   hardship.
>
> On account of "replenishing our accounts" we now have nothing to
>   calculate with.
> I have sold two of our ancestor's traditional lands.
> Although I sold these lands, it was still insufficient.
> So, again, I sold half of our own houses and buildings.
>
> Within the family, I bear the greatest of our hardships.
> For half the year I am starving, full only with profound resentment.
> These days, in the dark of night, I eat only the night.
> Come daylight, I do not know where our rice will come from.
> (Collected in Zhao, 1992: 530–2; trans. S. Balkwill)

When reading this prayer it is important to consider the real-life obligations of the writer. The woman, presumably a Jiangyong resident, has lost her husband to the neighbouring province of Guangxi, where the nearest major metropolis, Nanning, is located. Migration for economic purposes was (and remains) very common. Many husbands travelled to the larger cities in hope of improving their fortunes. However, the fact that this woman's husband has not returned home in over three years suggests that he has either died or abandoned her for the attractions of big-city life. Widowhood and resultant hardship are common tropes in women's writings, particularly of the Late Imperial period. With renewed interest in the Three Followings, it was virtually impossible for a widow to remarry after the death of her husband. Since women depended on men for their livelihood, this made it very difficult for a widow to support herself, let alone her children and perhaps parents as well. The fact that the majority of the extant *nu shu* prayers share these themes of widowhood and suffering suggests that they were common experiences.

Yet the *nu shu* prayers are not only laments about the hardships of marriage and widowhood. When read closely, they also reveal a different voice, one that challenges the status quo. That voice can be heard in their evocations of an afterlife that is free from the confines and responsibilities of marriage and the Three Followings. In the most ancient Chinese writings about the afterlife, it seems that the dead were thought to go to a place called the Yellow Springs, a sort of afterlife in the earth housed under Mount Tai. However, beginning around the fourth century of the Common Era, this vision was displaced by the notion that after death one's earthly body will be transformed into a subtle body that will ascend to the heavens and then roam freely through the cosmos for all eternity. Very likely this shift was related to the domestication of Buddhist ideas of the afterlife—including heavens, hells, and "pure lands." Once Buddhism became the dominant afterlife religion in China, the Yellow Springs were relegated to an inferior position, almost like an earthly hell or a prison. However, the women writers of *nu shu* appear not to have accepted this change. They still looked forward to an afterlife in the Yellow Springs. Why?

The Yellow Springs, and also other subterranean caves and locales that are written about in *nu shu*, are characterized by an overwhelming abundance of female-identified energy. This female energy, *yin*, finds its counterpart in the male-identified energy, or *yang*. Throughout the history of Chinese thought, *yin* and *yang* have endured as the primary explanation for creation; these tandem and complementary energies create the world just as men and women create children. In parallel associations, *yin* is connected to the moon, the earth, female genitalia, concealed treasures, valleys, fertility, weakness, and the ability to be broken or penetrated, whereas *yang* is connected to the sun, the sky or cosmos, male genitalia, wide-open expanses of land, strength, and the ability to fertilize either the land or the female reproductive system through the act of breaking or penetrating. On a cosmic level, *yin* and *yang* also explain the nature of life on the earth as opposed to life in the heavens: *yin* is associated with the earth and represented as hidden valleys and caves teeming with lush foliage that symbolize the pure potentiality of creation, while *yang* is associated with the cosmos and the ability to cast aside one's earthly body and soar gracefully and freely through the celestial realm. Therefore, for the women writers of *nu shu* to choose dwelling in the Yellow Springs over the more orthodox ideal of ascending to heaven is tantamount to choosing *yin* over *yang*.

For example, in the following prayer, the writer is grieving not only the loss of her female cousin, but also the fact that her cousin has gone on to a better world, the *yin* world of the ancient Yellow Springs, whereas she herself must remain in the *yang* world, caring for her male kin. Indeed, this represents a vertical re-orientation of *yin* and *yang* wherein *yin* is not simply *on* the earth but *in* it, and *yang* is not the heavens, but the nature of life on the earth itself. In this re-orientation, *yin* is not simply an afterlife, but a desirable location of secret, hidden happiness, far removed from the present *yang* world characterized by suffering:

> Cousin, if you are a numinous and magnificent spirit
> Then from the *yin* world rely on your dreams to come to my room.
> Ignite the oil lamp in the hall—
> And it will illuminate all four sides of the room where I do
>   embroidery.
>
> I rely on my two successive brothers in law for support.
> But I am tender and cannot accompany you when you leave.
> I can't speak about you having fallen to the *yin* world,
> We rely on you to return to the *yang* world so that we can rely on you
>   as always.
>
> These two feelings are hard to reconcile.
> How many paths remain in this undesirable life?
> Were they not sick, I would begrudge my mother and father in their
>   old age.
> I wait on and serve my elders without contentment.
>
> With my whole heart I desire to go with my cousin to the Yellow
>   Springs,
> But to desert my mother and father is an even greater misery.
> I will wait for my mother and father to return to the *yin* world,
> Then I will be in this world without a concern in my heart.
>
> At that time if your esteemed village has good fortune,
> Then you can invite me to come to your place.
> (Collected in Zhao, 1992 535–7; trans. S. Balkwill).

In order to understand more about these women's lives, their social position, and their religious aspirations, let's turn to an excerpt from another prayer in which the writer laments her situation as a peasant woman. In this case, she has been orphaned by the death of her parents and left to care for herself in a world that does not care for her. Her pain and loneliness are palpable, yet she expresses them eloquently. She closes her prayer with a fascinating petition to Niangniang, asking for deliverance from this cold and lonely world to a kinder, more inspired place—a numinous *yin* cave full of mythological beings. She says:

> When my father died I didn't know how to make it through.
> Then my mother died and went to the *yin* world; doubling my tears.
> Without a mother and without a father, how could I make it through?
> In this extremely pitiful situation who would accompany me?
>
> I only had my father's sister and her grandson to accompany me.
> What could I rely on for all my family's matters?
> I spent the whole night crying for my mother as if I had been cut with
>   a knife.
> Who could care for me with their whole heart?
>
> There was no shady tree before me to rest under,
> and no mountain at my back to support me.
> No one from my uncle's family came to care for me,
> and nobody from my aunt's family came to cherish my young body.
>
> My maternal grandmother had fallen to the *yin* world in her old age.
> All day and all night I cried in melancholy and nobody knew.
> I sat alone upstairs with no way to vent my anger,
> writing a letter to the esteemed spirit.
>
> I am only envious of those Niangniang has cultivated.
> Residing in such coldness as this, Spirit, how many people are there?
> In offering this to you I ask that you take care of me.
> I only want Niangniang to dote on me and cherish my life.
>
> You who are numinous, you who are magnificent, come close to me.
> Collect my true self and bring me to your precious self.
> From what name am I? Dried up and said to be all grayed.
> I am a thousand times worried. Niangniang, receive me.
>
> I only want, numinous spirit, to pass good days.
> It could be that I bear the passing of time from within a hidden cave.

I could frolic about in the hidden winds and waters before me.
And be supported in my easy countenance by the Blue Mountains at
    my back.

On my left side I would have a little sister as my partner,
who would play the flute in these remote immortal caves.
Year after year I would burn incense and complete the cycle of
    pilgrimage.
The myriad populace would pay their deep respect to your spirit.

Having nothing else to do, I would pray to the best of my abilities.
Seeking your appreciation, I will burn pure incense and pure ritual
    paper.
Niangniang, your very nature is true, numinous, and magnificent.
Bless and protect the people, all the thousands of them.
(Collected in Zhao, 1992: 525–8; trans. S. Balkwill).

In this prayer, the writer asks Niangniang to save her by accepting her
into a different reality—a *yin* cave with other women and soothing natural
scenery. In Daoism there is a long tradition of cave grottos that are associated
with celestial beings (Bokenkamp, 1986: 65ff). Fertile and green, often teeming with precious jewels, these grottos are both the playgrounds of fabulous,
mythological beings and the locations where Daoist texts are delivered to the
world, to provide religious inspiration to humanity. They are overwhelmingly
yin. Although these treasure caves are part of a Daoist adept's mystical journey,
they have never been its end point: the final goal of Daoist transformation is
ascension to a heavenly realm. Yet for the woman writers of *nu shu*, these *yin*
grottos themselves appear to be the final goal; there is no hint of an aspiration
to ascend to a *yang* heaven. What the woman writers want instead is a sort of
Buddhist-inspired salvation, the deliverance of their souls from this *yang* world
of suffering to a *yin* world of bliss. In this way, Niangniang functions very much
like the Buddhist Guanyin, the bodhisattva of infinite compassion who saves
sentient beings from all manner of pain and bitterness.

The following excerpt from a prayer illustrates well the bodhisattva-like
salvation that Niangniang offers:

Listen, old phoenix Niangniang, to what I have written down,
I have written a book of my life's pity.
Pay me a visit, Niangniang, and have sympathy for my aches and
    hatred.
Receive my female body so that I can truly arrive at your precious self.

I am a thousand times anxious for Niangniang to accept my female
    body.
With my whole heart I only want the path of the yellow springs.
I don't want to travel along the path of this world.
I want Niangniang to embrace my sufferings and my pains.

I am a thousand times anxious for Niangniang to accept my female
    body.
How is it that I am limited by the production of male children
when I can say that I would be fulfilled by returning to the name of
    my elder sister?
I am a thousand times anxious for Niangniang to accept my female
    body.
(Collected in Zhao, 1992: 529–30; trans. S. Balkwill)

In terms of the traditional categories of "Buddhist" and "Daoist" this prayer makes very little sense; it really begins to make sense only when we consider the gender and social location of the authors. The Daoist afterlife is not associated with any subterranean locale, and in Buddhism the dead can be delivered to a majestic land of tranquillity where they can continue working to eliminate their bad karma without the setbacks associated with suffering, but they need to be reborn as men in order to do so. The prayer makes sense only when we consider the gender and social location of its author. This woman wants to dwell in a *yin* land in her female body, with female friends and a female deity. Her belief system envisions an afterlife that has all the traditional *yin* associations—earthly over heavenly, female-identified over male-identified, concealed over wide-open spaces, symbolically fertile over symbolically fertilizing. In their bravery, strength, and intelligence, the *nu shu* writers developed a quite radical reinterpretation of traditional religious categories, one that allowed them comfort in their struggles while expressing their protest against the injustice they suffered simply because they were *yin* in a *yang* world.

Now that we have discussed in some detail the fascinating and largely unorthodox religious beliefs of the women writers of *nu shu*, it is necessary to recontextualize this type of religion in terms of our original discussion of the common practice of religion in China, for if we can understand the complex interplay of tradition and innovation that the *nu shu* prayers represent, then we are well on our way to understanding the nature of popular religion in China. When studying religion, it is common to approach complex textual material through a clearly delineated tradition that has a defined corpus of books, teachers, and practices, as Buddhism and Christianity do. Yet if we apply this kind of analytical lens to the *nu shu* material, it becomes unintelligible, because the hybrid, women-identified, and localized beliefs reflected in the *nu shu* prayers are specific to the women of Jiangyong and will not be found in any other type of text. Although the woman writers of *nu shu* were clearly aware of many of the doctrines and myths of the three mainstream religions, they certainly did not put them into practice in a way that would have been recognizable to them. This is simply, because the writers' own experiences of living life, with their struggles and triumphs, were much more present to them than any book of doctrine, which some of them might not have been able to read in any case. The woman writers of *nu shu* derived their religious beliefs from their experiences as peasant women living in the far reaches of the Chinese empire. They created a unique form of religion that gave them comfort, hope, and a voice of dissent, and they drew from the three mainstream religions in order to do so.

The *nu shu* material is an eminent example of the range of religious expression possible in a country as diverse as China, where every place has long had its own local religious beliefs and practices. What makes the *nu shu* prayers particularly special is the fact that they were written down. The *nu shu* corpus is crucial for the modern study of Chinese religion because it preserves the voices and otherwise unknowable religious beliefs of people at the margins of Chinese society, in this case of doubly marginalized peasant women. It is also certainly the case that localized religion of this kind, grounded in the daily lives of the vast majority of the Chinese population who do not have access to higher education and do not participate in elite forms of social organization, accounts for the vast majority of religious practice in China, both historically and in the present day. We must therefore be very grateful to the women of Jiangyong; because of their creativity, inspiration, learning, and inability to be silent in the face of adversity, we have a unique set of texts that can help us understand the common practice of religion in China.

We opened this case study with a discussion of Chinese culture in which we noted that although China has long been unified politically and through its written language, local expressions of this unity are extremely diverse. The women of Jiangyong have provided us with an excellent example of this reality. By expressing their unique religious vision in a textual corpus, the women writers of *nu shu* participated in two distinct yet interrelated social worlds—the local and the national. By taking widely held religious concepts such as *yin* and *yang*, rebirth, and the Yellow Springs and making them their own by tying them to their local geography and personal circumstances, the writers of *nu shu* show how local and national identities co-exist, creating a China of tremendous diversity but also of significant solidarity The *nu shu* prayers evoke an image of Chinese religion, and China itself, that is both romantic and realistic—a sometimes beautiful and sometimes strange tapestry, woven of vastly different colors and textures, inspiring in both its harmony and its dissonance.

Study Questions

1. Explain in your own words the relationship between popular religion and the major religions of China. Can you use other examples from China or elsewhere to illuminate your argument?

2. Try to imagine a unique form of religion practised by men in contemporary New York or Beijing. What would it look like?

3. Using *nu shu* as an example, how can we understand the interplay between religious text, religious belief, and religious practice? What roles do texts play for religious adherents?

References

Bokenkamp, Stephen. 1986. "The Peach Flower Font and the Grotto Passage." *Journal of the American Oriental Society.* 106 (1) 65-77.

Chau, Adam Yuet. 2008. *Miraculous Response: Doing Popular Religion in Contemporary China.* Stanford: Stanford University Press.

Liu, Fei-Wen. 1997. "Women Who De-Silence Themselves: Male Illegible Literature (Nu shu) and Female Specific Songs (Nüge) in Jiangyong County, Hunan Province, China." PhD Dissertation. Syracuse University.

McLaren, Anne. 2008. "Nu shu." *Encyclopedia of Women in World History.* Oxford & New York: Oxford University Press.

Pomeranz, Kenneth. 1997. "Power, Gender and Pluralism in the Cult of the Goddess of Taishan." Pp. 182-204 in Theodor Huters, R. Bin Wong, and Pauline Yu, eds. *Culture & State in Chinese History: Conventions, Accommodations, and Critiques.* Stanford: Stanford University Press. 182-204.

Silber, Cathy. 1995. *Nu shu (Chinese Women's Script) Literacy and Literature.* PhD Dissertation. Department of Asian Languages and Cultures: University of Michigan.

Zhao Liming. 1992. *Zhonguo Nu shu ji cheng* 中国女口集成 (A Collection of Chinese Nushu). Beijing: Qinghua University Press.

Index

Credits

The authors gratefully acknowledge the use of the following material:

Excerpt p. 10 from Shastri, H.P., trans. 1952. *The Ramayana of Valmiki.* London: Shanti Sadan, pp. 338-9. Excerpts used by permission. www.shantisadan.org

Excerpts pp. 71 and 72 from *Half the Kingdom.* 1989. Directed by Francine Zuckerman with Roushell Goldstein. Documentary. National Film Board of Canada, Studio D. Used with the permission of Elyse Goldstein and Francine Zuckerman.

Excerpts pp. 82 and 83 from I.B. Horner 1930: 3. *Women under Primitive Buddhism: Laywomen and Almswomen.* Rpt 1990. Delhi: Motilal Banarsidass.

Excerpts pp. 102–103 from Grant, Beata. *Eminent Nuns. Women Chan Masters of Seventeenth-Century China.* Hawai'i: University of Hawai'l Press, 2009, pp. 47, 48 and 74.

Excerpt p. 104 from Grant, Beata. 2003. *Daughters of Emptiness. Poems of Chinese Buddhist Nuns.* Boston: Wisdom Publications.

Excerpt p. 124 from Karlgren, Bernhard. trans. 1950. *The Book of Odes Bulletin of the Museum of Far Eastern Antiquities 22,* p. 264

Excerpt p. 130 from Ebrey, Patricia Buckley. 1984. *Family and Property in Sung China: Yuan Ts'ai's Precepts for Social Life.* Princeton, NJ: Princeton University Press, p. 14.

Excerpts pp. 135, 138 and 139 from Reprinted by permission from *The Annual Review of Women in World Religion,* Volume I edited by Arvind Sharma and Katherine K. Young, the State University of New York Press © 1991, State University of New York. All rights reserved.

Excerpt p. 161 from Elder Judy Swamp, interview in *Mothers of Our Nations.* 48 mins. Directed by Dawn Martin-Hill. Hamilton: Six Nations Confederacy of the Grand River 7 Indigenous Elders and Youth Council and McMaster University, 2004.

Excerpt p. 162 from Clanmother Cathy Smoke, interview in *Mothers of Our Nations.* 48 mins. Directed by Dawn Martin-Hill. Hamilton: Six Nations Confederacy of the Grand River 7 Indigenous Elders and Youth Council and McMaster University, 2004.

Excerpt pp. 162 and 163 from *The Dish with One Spoon.* 75 mins. Directed by Dawn Martin-Hill. Hamilton, ON: Six Nations Confederacy of the Grand River 7 Indigenous Elders and Youth Council and McMaster University, 2007.

Excerpt p. 205 from "The Blood of a Woman" in Dietrich, Gabriele. 1986. *One Day I Shall be Like a Banyan Tree: Poems in Two Languages.* Bel-gaum, India: Dileep S. Kamat.

Excerpt p. 215 from (Ghazali, [1414] 1994: 297–8). al-Ghazali al-Jubayli, Zaynab.